SOCIAL COGNITION
and COMMUNICATION

SOCIAL COGNITION
and
COMMUNICATION

edited by
Michael E. Roloff
Charles R. Berger

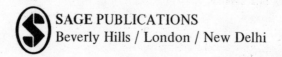

SAGE PUBLICATIONS
Beverly Hills / London / New Delhi

Royalties for this book are being donated to the John Garrison Memorial Fund of Division 2, International Communication Association.

For information address:

SAGE Publications, Inc.
275 South Beverly Drive
Beverly Hills, California 90212

SAGE Publications India Pvt. Ltd.
C-236 Defence Colony
New Delhi 110 024, India

SAGE Publications Ltd
28 Banner Street
London EC1Y 8QE, England

Printed in the United States of America

Library of Congress Cataloging in Publication Data

Main entry under title:

Social cognition and communication.

Includes bibliographies.
1. Social perception—Congresses. 2. Cognition—
Congresses.   3. Interpersonal communication—
Congresses.   I. Roloff, Michael E.   II. Berger,
Charles R.
HM132.S566   1982   302'.12   82-10715
ISBN 0-8039-1898-4
ISBN 0-8039-1899-2 (pbk.)

FIRST PRINTING

Contents

Foreword

This project was designed to meet two goals. First, we tried to clarify the relationship between social cognition and a variety of communication phenomena. While communication scholars have long stressed the importance of thought, few attempts have been made to explore systematically the relationship between thoughts about people and communication. Second, we provided a broad-based approach to communication and social cognition. Social cognition is related to a variety of forms of communication; consequently, we asked individuals from several areas of communication research to share their ideas. We hope that this sharing will stimulate an ongoing dialogue among scholars from different research areas.

In order to meet these objectives, the contributors were invited to Northwestern University in October 1981 to share their ideas. We are deeply indebted to Roy V. Wood, Dean of the School of Speech at Northwestern University, for his financial support. After the symposium, the authors modified their initial thinking, and the results are presented in this volume. The first four chapters examine general approaches to social cognition. Chapter 1 is a review of research and theory conducted in social psychology and provides a general view of social cognition. O'Keefe and Delia (Chapter 2) have reviewed theory and research associated with constructivism and related it to message construction. Sillars (Chapter 3) examines research arising from attribution theory. Finally, Hewes and Planalp focus in Chapter 4 on a model that integrates a number of social cognition processes.

In the second part of the book, one will find chapters that apply theories of social cognition to specific types of communication. Our Chapter 5 focuses on interpersonal communication. Street and Giles (Chapter 6) describe the role of social cognition in interpersonal and intergroup speech patterns. Miller (Chapter 7) is concerned with the role of social cognition in legal communication. Jablin (Chapter 8) explores social cognition in organizational settings. Finally, Reeves, Chaffee, and Tims (Chapter 9) focus on social cognition in mass communication contexts.

We hope the reader finds the book to be as useful as we found putting it together exciting.

Michael E. Roloff
Charles R. Berger

1

Social Cognition and Communication

AN INTRODUCTION

Michael E. Roloff
Charles R. Berger

*A wonderful fact to reflect upon, that every human
creature is constituted to be that profound secret and
mystery to every other.*

Charles Dickens, *A Tale of Two Cities*

*I have learned silence from the talkative, toleration
from the intolerant, and kindness from the unkind; yet
strange, I am ungrateful to those teachers.*

Kahil Gibran, *Sand and Foam*

The preceding quotations make important points about human behavior: Individuals are inherently curious about each other and consequently form impressions of one another that can guide their own behavior. A whole area of social science research has focused on the cognitive processes associated with understanding people and their behavior. While the scholars interested in this area come from a variety of disciplines, each is concerned primarily with the study of social cognition.

A major assumption of this book is that social cognition is a particularly important process involved in all types of communication phenomena. Subsequent chapters will make this point clear. At the outset, however, we must come to understand what is involved in social cognition itself. The purpose of this introduction is twofold. First, we will provide an overview of social cognition and the various processes composing it. This will involve defining the area and examining generalizations arising from it. Second, we will examine social cognition as a communication phenomenon.

Social Cognition: What Is It?

This portion of the introduction will accomplish three things. First, we will define social cognition and describe the processes associated with it. Second, we will examine factors that seem to stimulate or inhibit social cognition. Finally, the mental and behavioral consequences of social cognition will be examined. Since the study of social cognition has been extensive, we will focus only on representative research and theoretical approaches.

Definition of Social Cognition

While the number of books examining social cognition has multiplied in the last few years (see, for example, Weimer and Palermo, 1974; Carroll and Payne, 1976; Wegner and Vallacher, 1977; Hastie et al., 1980; Higgins et al., 1980; Wyer and Carlston, 1980), finding a precise definition of social cognition is difficult. Perhaps because the study of social cognition has emerged from several research areas, definitions of social cognition are typically general rather than specific. For example, Wegner and Vallacher (1977: viii) define social cognition as "how people think about people." This definition is intentionally broad in order to include under social cognition topics such as person perception, attribution, impression formation, cognitive balance, and self-concept. Because the definition is so general, it is necessary that we examine several implications arising from it.

First, social cognition involves thought processes. Because of the internal nature of thought processes, scholars have generally studied social cognition by using self-report questions or by constructing situations that allow the researcher to infer the presence of social cognition. Thought-listing procedures are often used to assess these internal processes (see Tesser, 1978; Perloff and Brock, 1980).

A few researchers have examined the behavioral manifestations of thought (see McGuigan, 1966; McGuigan and Schoonover, 1973). Recently, Cacioppo and Petty (1979) reported changes in oral muscle, cardiac, and respiratory activity accompanying changes in counterarguing in response to anticipation of receiving a counterattitudinal message. In addition, incipient oral muscle activity and nonverbal facial affect were associated with counterarguing during the reception of a counterattitudinal message. Another behavioral indicant of social cognition has been the way an individual breaks an ongoing sequence of behavior into meaningful actions in order to understand it. This has been termed "unitization." Newtson (1973, 1976) has argued that individuals can make behavioral signs, such as pressing a button, when they see a significant action in a sequence, and this sign directly represents their internal cognitive processes. While this procedure has recently been questioned (Ebbesen, 1980; Douglas, 1981), it represents an interesting attempt to find a valid behavioral indicant of mental activity.

Second, social cognition is thought focused on human interaction. While a person's thoughts might dwell on a variety of content areas (such as work or inanimate objects), social cognition represents those thoughts related to people and their behaviors toward each other. Underlying this statement is the assumption that people are motivated to understand their environment. Individuals will attempt to reduce their uncertainty by observing or constructing generalizations about self, others, and the actions in which they engage (Berger and Calabrese, 1975). People may focus thought on specific individuals or behaviors or general classes of individuals and behaviors (see Fishbein, 1980). Communication certainly constitutes a significant behavior represented in these thoughts. In addition, people's social cognitions may be about persons with whom they have or anticipate having face-to-face interactions, as well as about individuals with whom direct communication is not possible. Research indicates that people form expectations about television characters and their behaviors, even though actually meeting characters is impossible, in the case of fiction, and highly unlikely, in the case of public figures (Greenberg and Reeves, 1976; Reeves and Greenberg, 1977; Roloff and Greenberg, 1979).

An important part of this implication concerns what an individual focuses on in the interaction. Duval and Wicklund (1972) have argued that a person's attentional focus is dichotomous. An individual either focuses cognitive activity on self and is in a state called objective self-awareness (also called self-focused attention) or will focus on the environment and will be in a state of subjective self-awareness. Duval and Wicklund acknowledge that attention can shift rapidly between self and environment, but they maintain that a person is either focusing on one or the other at any given instant.

One potential determinant of a person's attentional focus resides within stimuli in the environment. Specifically, any stimulus that is a representation of self will draw attention to the self, and objective self-awareness is created. A stimulus that directs attention toward the environment will create the subjective state. Researchers have created self-focus by having individuals concentrate on their image in a mirror (Buss and Scheier, 1976) or on videotape (Duval and Wicklund, 1972), listen to their own voice on audiotape (Wicklund and Duval, 1971) or a sound attributed to their own heartbeat (Fenigstein and Carver, 1978), and engage in physical activities designed to affect arousal levels

(Wegner and Giuliana, 1980). Although rarely studied, Duval and Wicklund (1972) found that subjective self-awareness can be stimulated by having an individual focus attention on a task.

Research has verified that such mechanisms can focus attention on a variety of self-related processes. Ickes et al. (1977) report that subjects in the objective state listed more self-descriptors and their responses were more individuated than those of subjects not engaged in self-focus. Carver and Scheier (1978) discovered that self-focus tended to increase the use of self-focused sentence completions. More recently, Scheier et al. (1981) found that self-focus heightens phobic reactions.

Thus, a person's attention might be drawn to certain parts of an interaction based on environmental stimuli. However, research has also established that individuals may also manifest stable attentional focus. At least two individual difference variables have been studied that represent different cognitive focus: self-consciousness and self-monitoring.

Fenigstein et al. (1975) argue that people differ in the amount of time they spend reflecting on their internal states and/or the impressions they create in others. A factor analysis of responses to a 23-item questionnaire indicated that self-consciousness consists of three dimensions: private self-consciousness, public self-consciousness, and social anxiety.

Research has indicated that the three dimensions involve different cognitive activity. Private self-consciousness is chronic self-focus. Individuals high in private self-consciousness have been found to describe themselves in greater detail and with longer lists of descriptors than low privates (Turner, 1978b). Recent research by Turner (1980) indicates that high privates remember more self-relevant trait terms in a reaction-time experiment than do low privates. High privates have also been found to be more emotionally and psychologically reactive to situations than low privates (Scheier and Carver, 1977; Carver and Scheier, 1981; Scheier et al., 1981). As might be expected, research indicates that high privates provide more accurate information about their anger (Turner and Peterson, 1977), dominance (Turner, 1978a), and aggression (Scheier et al., 1978) than do low privates. More recently, Underwood and Moore (1981) reported that high privates provide general assessments of their sociability that are more consistent with others' impressions of their sociability than those of low privates.

Public self-consciousness involves focus on self but from the view of others. Public self-conscious individuals are expected to be highly concerned with their image and behavior. Turner et al. (1981) reported that high publics are more aware of their physical appearance than are low publics. High publics also may provide inaccurate self-descriptions when it is to their advantage to do so. Indeed, Turner and Peterson (1977) found that the correlation between self-reported and actual anger was higher for low publics than for high publics. Scheier (1980) has also discovered that high publics are more likely than are low publics to moderate their attitudes in an opinion statement when anticipating interacting with a disagreeing other.

An interesting area of research has concerned the combination of private and public self-consciousness. Turner (1978a) reports that the lowest correlation between self-reported and actual dominance was found among subjects who were low-private and high-public self-conscious. In addition, Scheier (1980) discovered a higher degree of consistency between attitudes and opinions for low-public/high-private self-conscious individuals than with the other combinations of the traits.

Social anxiety is an emotional reaction to a focus on self. Arkin et al. (1980) observed that socially anxious individuals tended to assume more responsibility for failure than for success. Low socially anxious subjects assumed greater responsibility for success than failure. While both high and low socially anxious subjects tended to portray themselves in more flattering ways whenever possible, they did so for different reasons. High socially anxious subjects fear embarrassment and try to avoid further humiliation resulting from admitted shortcomings. Low socially anxious people engage in self-presentation as a means of gaining social acceptance and support rather than as a means of avoiding humiliation.

Self-monitoring is concerned with the control of expressive behavior (Snyder, 1974, 1979). The high self-monitor is an individual who is able to control personal communication so as to adapt to the perceived demands of the current situation. The low self-monitor is in control of personal communications but guides them according to internal standards, such as attitudes and values, rather than the perceived demands of the current situation. Consequently, we might expect that the high self-monitor focuses cognitive activity on the environment in order to determine the appropriate image to be created. The low self-monitor is concerned with expressing accurately own attitudes and values in light of the situation.

The external focus of the high self-monitor has been verified in several areas. Sampson (1978) discovered that high self-monitors define their identities in terms of characteristics that are part of the external rather than the internal environment. High self-monitors can provide more vivid descriptions of prototypic individuals than can low self-monitors (Snyder and Cantor, 1980).

The internal focus of the low self-monitor has also been found. Sampson (1978) reports that low self-monitors define their identities through traits that are part of their internal rather than external environments. Snyder and Cantor (1980) found that low self-monitors gave more vivid descriptions of characteristic selves than did high self-monitors. Interestingly, Tunnell (1980) discovered that low self-monitors gave self-descriptions that coincided to a greater extent with judgments made by acquaintances than did those of high self-monitors. High self-monitors tended to rate themselves higher on personality traits than did acquaintances. Similarly, Lippa and Mash (1981) reported that judges easily reach consensus about a low self-monitor's internal states (such as anxiety) compared with similar judgments about high self-monitors.

While the approaches to social cognition described up to this point have argued that attention is focused on self or environment, they do not spend much time describing what, exactly, in the self and environment the person focuses cognitive activity upon. Certainly, the self and environment can be viewed as complex phenomena composed of many different factors. Taylor and Fiske (1978) have addressed this issue in their discussion of "top of the head" phenomena in the attribution of causality. They suggest that the most salient stimuli in the environment will have a determining influence on the judgments of individuals. They write, "Individuals frequently respond with little thought to the most salient stimuli in their environment. We believe that the causal attributions people make, the opinions people express, and the impressions they form of others in work or social situations are often shaped by seemingly trivial but highly salient information and that, accordingly, such attitudes and impressions show relatively little cross-situational consistency" (1978: 252).

Taylor and Fiske identify three properties that determine the focus of attention. Properties of stimuli such as brightness, contrast, movement, and novelty will produce a higher volume of recall and result in heightened learning and judgments of prominence and causality. Properties of the situation, like environmental cues and instructional sets, will increase the availability of information and create intraindividual consistency. Finally, properties of the perceiver, such as temporary need states and enduring individual differences, may result in multimodal encoding of information that stimulates exaggerated evaluations and perceived representativeness. Consequently, changes in the salience of cues in a situation may lead to differences in cognitive focus resulting in predictable changes in judgments and behaviors.

While the direction of a person's attention seems to be toward the environment or self, recent research in cognitive psychology might indicate that it is not strictly dichotomous. That is, a person might be able to focus on self and the environment simultaneously. Spelke et al. (1976) found that people can be trained to focus attention simultaneously on two different tasks. Through practice, subjects learned to copy dictated words while reading an unrelated short story. Research by Hirst et al. (1980) found that this effect was *not due* to an alternation of attention toward one task or another; nor was it due to task performance becoming automatic or requiring little attention. Thus, they argue that attentional focus may be a skill people may learn to improve so that they may examine a variety of phenomena simultaneously. It should be noted, however, that this research involved two sets of environmental stimuli rather than an environmental and a self-related factor. Therefore, the Hirst et al. findings are suggestive rather than conclusive with regard to a simultaneous self and environmental focus.

The third implication is that social cognition is thought organized in some fashion, focused on human interaction. In order to make sense of the complex information inputs involved in interaction, people are motivated to construct representations of reality. Perceivers organize the environmental stimuli into groups of variables that are to some extent interrelated. Scholars of social cognition have explored the cognitive structure of an individual from a variety of perspectives. We will briefly examine three approaches: attitudinal, implicit theory, and script/ schema models.

Communication scholars are probably more familiar with the attitudinal models used to study social cognition than with the others. Our traditional interest and research in persuasion has compelled us to borrow heavily from a variety of attitude theories. One current attitude theory with important implications for the study of social cognition is expectancy-value theory.

Expectancy-value theory provides a detailed description of the various cognitive units, their interrelationships, and their relationship to behavior (Fishbein and Ajzen, 1975; Ajzen and Fishbein, 1977, 1980; Fishbein, 1980). This theory examines four cognitive units: belief, attitude, subjective norm, and behavior intention. Beliefs are an individual's subjective probabilities about the attributes of objects. When an individual is thinking about an interaction, we might expect to find three general types of beliefs. First, the person perceives certain traits in him- or herself—for example, "I am probably a friendly person." Second, the person has impressions of others—for example, "David is probably an assertive person." Third, the person has expectations about the consequences of behaviors: "If I communicate with David, I will probably find myself submitting to his opinions." It is important to remember that these beliefs are probabilities and may vary.

One person may view self or others as having a .75 probability of being friendly, whereas a different person may assess the probability of own or other friendliness as being only .10. In addition, the subjective probabilities have evaluations attached to them. While being friendly might typically be expected to be a positive trait, characteristics such as assertiveness may be viewed with some ambivalence.

The second cognitive unit is an attitude. An attitude is a person's evaluation of an object of behavior. Attitudes can be predicted by the sum of the products of beliefs and their evaluations. A person's evaluation of self and others can be predicted from the probability that one has certain traits and the evaluation of those traits. The person's attitude toward a behavior should be correlated with the probability that certain outcomes will result from it and the evaluation of the outcomes.

Third, individuals have cognitive units characterized as subjective norms. The subjective norm represents a person's impression of whether his or her significant others would engage in a given behavior. This impression is correlated with the sum of the products of the person's expectations about each significant other (called normative beliefs) and the person's motivation to comply with each significant other.

A behavioral intention is a person's subjective estimate of how likely it is that he or she will engage in a certain behavior. The intention may be stated in a specific manner as to the action, context, target, and time or may be quite general with regard to these criteria. A behavioral intention can be predicted from attitude toward the behavior and subjective norm. The two components may vary in influence when behavioral intention is predicted. Their relative influence depends on factors such as the behavior, situation, and actors.

The theory does not predict that one's attitude toward self or others is necessarily related to a specific behavioral intention. Only in the case in which attitude toward a behavior and attitude toward self and/or others are highly correlated would we find attitudes toward self and others predictive of a given behavioral intention. Attitudes toward self and others may be predictive of sets of intentions rather than any specific one. Fishbein and Ajzen (1975) suggested that an attitude toward an object is related to the sum of the products of a set of intentions to behave toward that object and the evaluation of each intention.

Expectancy-value theory predicts behavior based solely on behavioral intention. If behavior and behavioral intention are stated at the same level of specificity and the behavior is under volitional control, then behavior is equal to behavioral intention. While other attitudinal models differ in the composition of social cognitions (Rokeach, 1980;

Triandis, 1977, 1980), they seek to describe the link between attitudes and behaviors. Of additional importance, the link between social cognition and ultimate action is viewed as occurring in steps. Two or more types of social cognition are related to intention, and intention is finally related to behavior.

Rather than focus on attitudes as a means of organizing social cognitions, other researchers have taken the implicity theory approach. Based on the works of Heider (1958), Kelly (1955), Schutz (1932), Piaget (1932), and, most recently, Wegner and Vallacher (1977), this approach examines the processes by which the social scientist and average human being go about constructing explanations of social phenomena. These explanations are thought to be implicit theories that can be used to test hypotheses about human interaction. The implicit theories are not always operating at a high degree of awareness for the individual and, unlike scientific theory, are assumed to be inherently correct. Wegner and Vallacher (1977: 21) write:

> Human beings, acting as naive psychologists, construct theories about social reality. These theories have all the features of the formal theories constructed by the scientist. They employ concepts and relationships derived from observation; they provide a structure through which social reality is observed; they enable the individual to make predictions. But, as we have pointed out, people are frequently unaware of the theories they employ. For this reason, they immediately assume that the structures they perceive and the predictions they make are correct. Probably the primary difference between formal scientific theory and implicit theory lies in this dimension of assumed correctness.

The implicit theory approach seems, however, to be an organizing principle for a variety of theories rather than a competing theory.

Wegner and Vallacher (1977) have organized a number of theoretical perspectives used to study social cognition according to their notion of implicit theory. The first area is called implicit motivation theory and is concerned with how people try to understand what causes behavior. Perspectives normally considered attribution theories (such as those of Heider, 1958; Jones and Davis, 1965; Kelley, 1967, 1971) are considered descriptions of implicit motivation theory. Second, they describe implicit personality theory, or how people see personal attributes as related to each other. Works by Bruner and Tagiuri (1954), Cattell (1946), Tupes and Christal (1961), Norman (1963), and Wiggins (1973) fall into this area. Third, implicit abnormal psychology theory is concerned with how people decide whether others are good or bad, or how they go about evaluating them. Research concerning interpersonal attraction might reasonably fit into this category (see Byrne, 1971).

Fourth, implicit relations theory examines the expectations people have about relationships. Work by Heider (1958) and Wish et al. (1976) describes these relational expectations. Finally, these researchers describe implicit self-theory, or how individuals perceive themselves. Traditional work on the self-concept describes these theories well (James, 1890: Schutz, 1932; Cooley, 1902; Mead, 1934, Gergen, 1971; Duval and Wicklund, 1972; Wylie, 1973).

Thus, implicit theory provides a general description of the central construct and then examines the research that has explored various types of implicit theories. This approach is quite attractive, given recent research examining implicit theories people have about interpersonal communication (Wish and Kaplan, 1977; Ellis, 1980; Knapp et al., 1980).

A third way to organize social cognition is by means of script/schema theory. Like implicit theories, the script/schema theories assume that social cognitions are organized into some framework so that the individual can make sense of the environment. The difficulty with this area is the large number of terms and the ambiguous nature of their relationships. One finds descriptions of causal schemata (Tesser, 1978; Tversky and Kahneman, 1980), conceptual schemata (Vernon, 1955; Shweder, 1975; Shweder and D'Andrade, 1979), self-schemata (Markus, 1977; Rogers et al. 1977; Kendzierski, 1980; Lord, 1980), person prototypes (Cantor and Mischel, 1977, 1979a, 1979b), and scripts (Abelson, 1976; Schank and Abelson, 1977; Tomkins, 1979).

Causal schemata as described by Tesser (1978) and Tversky and Kahneman (1980) seem to form the broadest concept. Causal schemata represent individuals' models of the causal relationships among variables in the environment. Tesser (1978: 332) defined them as "naive theory about an object which makes salient selected cognitions and provides rules for making inferences." As such, they can be used much like an implicit theory to predict and explain covariation of environmental factors. These schemata may involve the relationships among people and objects and therefore may encompass more than social cognition.

Conceptual schemata, as described by Shweder (1975) and Shweder and D'Andrade (1979), are those causal schemata specifically related to self and others. Shweder and D'Andrade's research has focused on the relationship between self-reports and impressions of others, and conceptual schemata.

Self-schemata are defined by Markus (1977: 64) as "cognitive generalizations about the self, derived from past experience, that organize and guide the processing of self-related information contained in the individual's social experiences." Markus reports that self-schemata facilitate processing and retrieval of self-related information. Kendzierski (1980) found that self-related information was better remembered than situation-oriented information. Lord (1980) reports that self-schemata may be constructed as verbal representations of self rather than as images or visual representations.

Person prototypes (Cantor and Mischel, 1977, 1979a, 1979b) appear to be schemata about others. While self-schemata and person prototypes may be related, Lord (1980) reports that information about others may be organized into visual rather than verbal representations. Kendzierski (1980) has argued that person prototypes summarize information about some attributes across many situations and people.

A script is defined by Abelson (1976: 33) as "a coherent sequence of events expected by the individual, involving him either as a participant or observer." Kendzierski (1980) has argued that scripts focus on a type of situation one has encountered many times. One might have a "theater script" that summarizes the sequence of events that are typically part of going to the theater. Certainly, a script will focus on the role of self and others, just as self-schemata or person prototypes would, but the primary emphasis is on the role of self and others in that particular class of situations.

Thus, a person's social cognitions might be studied as they are related to self, others, or situations. As in the case of attitudes and implicit theories, we should be able to predict certain responses from an individual based on the scripts or schemata he or she possesses.

The fourth implication is that people have social cognitions that vary in the degree to which they are veridical representations of self, others, and behaviors. While the definition of social cognition makes no statement about the accuracy of social cognition, a quick review of research demonstrates an impressive list of errors made by perceivers.

Langer (1975, 1978a) has observed an "illusion of control" operating in social cognition. People tend to overestimate their personal control over outcomes in situations where outcomes occur purely by chance. Our desire to feel as though we have some control over destiny may cause us to overestimate our influence. Research examining logical consistency has discovered that "wishful thinking" may operate in determining the probability of a conclusion based on a major and minor premise (see Dillehay et al., 1966; Watts and Holt, 1970). Subjects tend to overestimate the probability that a desirable conclusion will occur and underestimate the same probability for an undesirable conclusion. Jones and Nisbett (1971) have described "actor-observer differences" in attribution, such that an actor attributes the cause of his or her own behavior to environmental stimuli, whereas an observer attributes personal causes to another's behavior. Others have pointed to a "self-serving bias" to attributing the cause of one's own success or failure (see Bradley, 1978). Actors tend to attribute less self-responsibility for failure than for success. Research also indicates that people may not even be able to report if they have been persuaded or what their recent attitudes have been (Bem and McConnell, 1970). Finally, Tversky and Kahnamen (1980) have reviewed research that indicates that people will ignore base-rate information in making judgments and will be more influenced by factors such as vividness, concreteness, or causal schemata in decision-making.

While other problems have been identified (see Ross, 1977), this short list might prompt a number of pessimistic assessments about social cognition. One might argue that people have little access to higher-order mental processes and consequently must rely on schemata to explain internal processes (see Nisbett and Wilson, 1977; Wilson and Nisbett, 1978) or even external processes (Tversky and Kahneman, 1980). Alternatively, one might explain these problems from an image management (Tedeschi et al., 1971) or demand characteristic view (Adair and Spinner, 1981). Subjects may bias self-reports or judgments of others to provide the questioner with the best possible image of themselves.

While either or both of the positions stated above may be valid, another approach might be that social cognitions may be veridical depending on the situation the person is in. A number of scholars have criticized Nisbett and Wilson (1977) for overgeneralizing (Smith and Miller, 1978; Rich, 1979; White, 1980). These individuals suggest that instead we may find situational cues explaining why deviation between subjective reports and reality occurs. Ericsson and Simon (1980) have developed a detailed model suggesting that under certain circumstances people can verbalize accurate descriptions of internal processes. Unless subjects are prompted to attend to certain cues, they will not and must infer the influence of the cues. Similarly, Shweder (1980: 75) has suggested a "systematic distortion" hypothesis: "*Under difficult memory conditions* judges either (a) infer what 'must' have happened from their general mode of what the world is like, (b) find it easier to retrieve conceptually affiliated memory items, or (c) both." In easy memory conditions, judgments may be veridical. Consequently, social cognition about self, others, or behaviors may indeed be inaccurate in some situations, but when conditions change cognitions may become veridical.

Social cognition represents the organized thoughts people have about human interaction. These thoughts may be focused on self, others, or behaviors. They may be organized into cognitive structures such as attitudes, implicit theories, or scripts/schemata. Finally, they may or may not be veridical, depending on prevailing conditions.

Stimulants of Social Cognition

To suggest that social cognition is a variable is, quite simply, to imply that it varies. Despite this simple conclusion, however, scholars have tended to treat the frequency of social cognition as a constant. Langer (1978b: 35) writes, "Much psychological research relies on a theoretical model that depicts the individual as one who is cognitively aware most of the time, and who consciously, constantly, and systematically applies 'rules' to incoming information about the environment in order to formulate interpretations and courses of action."

Indeed, much of what has been described in this introduction is based on the assumption that social cognition is present most, if not all, of the time. Some theorists are beginning to question this assumption. Langer (1978b) in particular has challenged the assumption by arguing that most people prefer, and consequently are in a state of, "mindlessness." She writes, "A continuum of awareness varies directly with the degree of repeated experience that we have with the activity. The more often we have engaged in the activity the more likely it is that we will rely on scripts for the completion of the activity and the less likely that there will be any correspondence between our actions and those thoughts of ours that occur simultaneously" (1978b: 39). Langer (1978b) has suggested that social cognition is most frequent when one encounters a novel situation or is in some way forced to deviate from a script. Her research has demonstrated behavioral responses to situations that are difficult to explain using models that assume a high degree of social cognition (Langer et al., 1978; Langer and Newman, 1979; Langer and Imber, 1979, 1980; Langer and Weinman, 1981).

While Triandis (1977, 1980) has not specifically focused on the amount of social cognition, he has indirectly dealt with this issue when attempting to predict a person's action. A person's action is hypothesized to be a function of the product of two sets of factors: (1) intention plus habit and (2) physiological arousal and facilitating factors. The habit component is likened to mindlessness. By engaging in a behavior repeatedly, one comes to rely less on intention and its related predictors of affective, social, and consequence factors and more on habit when deciding what to do. Triandis (1977: 205) writes, "Our analysis suggests that, when a behavior is new, untried and unlearned, the behavioral-intention component will be solely responsible for behavior, while, when the behavior is old, well-learned, or overlearned and has occurred many times before in the organism's life span, it is very likely to be under the control of the habit component. In addition, when the person is highly emotionally aroused, habit rather than intention controls behavior."

Thus, social cognition when viewed as a *conscious* thought process should not be considered highly frequent and important in all situations. Important research questions concern when social cognition is stimulated and what influence it might have.

Mental and Behavioral Consequences of Social Cognition

Dostoyevsky (1911) wrote that "Man is a pliable animal, a being who gets accustomed to everything!" If this is true, then people must learn to adapt their social cognitions to situations. In other words, social cognitions are changeable, and these changes are reflected in behavior. Theorists of social cognition support this view.

Social cognition has been viewed as a facilitator or inhibitor of acceptance of persuasive messages. Wicklund and Brehm (1976) have noted that attending to internal inconsistency between attitudes and behaviors may enhance dissonance resulting in change. Roloff (1980) and Berger and Roloff (1980) have reviewed research indicating that when people are self-focused, they seem to be more susceptible to pressures that may ultimately result in attitude change. Recently, Scheier and Carver (1980) observed that self-focus resulting from the presence of a mirror or private self-consciousness inhibited persuasion resulting from counterattitudinal advocacy. Subjects in these situations tended to resolve their dissonance by distorting the extremity of their counterattitudinal behavior. When self-focus was due to camera presence or high public self-consciousness, attitude change was enhanced. Subjects in these conditions resolved their dissonance by changing their attitudes consistent with their discrepant behavior. In addition, Froming and Carver (1981) reported that private self-consciousness is negatively related to compliance with group judgments, while public self-consciousness is positively related.

Other researchers have argued that, rather than simply facilitating attitude change, social cognition may actually stimulate change. The cognitive response approach to persuasion (see Greenwald, 1968; Petty et al., 1980; Perloff and Brock, 1980) has pointed to the importance of a person's thoughts while decoding a persuasive message as a determinant of persuasion. Favorable thoughts generated about the source or message stimulates message acceptance, whereas counterarguments tend to decrease acceptance. The contents of these thoughts are better predictors of message acceptance than is recall of message arguments.

Using a schematic model, Tesser (1978) has reported that thought under the guidance of schemata tends to make a person's beliefs about an object evaluatively consistent. Since attitudes are thought to be a function of beliefs, thought tends to create attitudinal polarization. Tesser argues that if thought produces attitude polarization, then attitudes are probably not as stable as they are typically assumed to be.

Chaiken (1980) has suggested that social cognition may be of two types in persuasive situations: systematic and heuristic. Systematic processes assume an active persuasive target who attempts to evaluate and recall message arguments. Heuristic processes involve minimal cognitive effort, and acceptance is a function of readily available noncontent cues, such as source characteristics. Indeed, Chaiken's research demonstrates that low-involved subjects tend to accept a message on the basis of the source's likability rather than the presence of persuasive arguments, whereas high-involved subjects accept messages on the basis of the presence of arguments rather than source likability.

Most social cognition theorists assume that such changes in mental activities would, under appropriate conditions, result in changes in behavior. The critical question becomes, What are the appropriate conditions?

Fishbein and Ajzen (1975) argue that if a behavior is under volitional control and is at the same level of specificity as an intention, then behavior is a function of behavioral intention. Fishbein (1980: 84) writes, "While I am convinced that there are some behaviors that cannot be predicted from intentions, I can honestly report that I have not yet been able to find them." Thus, behavioral intention seems to be an accurate predictor of behavior.

Tesser's (1978) schema approach takes a slightly different view. Since a person's feelings about a behavior are controlled by schemata operating at a given point in time, it is important that the same schemata be operating at the time one assesses the person's feelings and observes his or her behavior. In other words, schemata guide reports of one's cognitions about a behavior as well as the actual performance of the behavior. Different schemata produce a low correlation between self-reported feelings and behavior.

Roloff (1980) and Berger and Roloff (1980) have reviewed research suggesting that social cognitions are correlated with behavior when the person is self-focused but are not when attention is focused elsewhere. Social cognitions are related to behavior only when they are made salient through environmental or dispositional self-focus.

Therefore, while the relationship between social cognition and change is complex, if viewed under the proper conditions, social cognition may facilitate or stimulate changes in mental activity, which ultimately results in alteration of behavior.

Social Cognition and Communication Processes: Intrapersonal Communication

At this point, we have defined social cognition and examined representative research that describes the processes composing it. It is necessary that we now examine how social cognition is related to a specific type of communication.

A variety of communication scholars have paid tribute to the importance of intrapersonal communication. Wenberg and Wilmot (1973: 21) write, "Ultimately, *all* communication responses take place within a person as he reacts to various communication cues. That is, intrapersonal communication may take place without communication in any of the other arenas, but communication in the other arenas cannot take place without intrapersonal communication. Thus, intrapersonal communication provides the basis for all other communication arenas."

Given such platitudes and the number of scholars who place intrapersonal communication at the center of all communication processes (see Ruesch et al., 1953; Thayer, 1968; Dance and Larson, 1976), it is surprising that it remains such an enigma. There are no major divisions of our professional organizations that focus primarily on intrapersonal communication, and many books devote comparatively little space to its coverage. Despite this limited coverage, a number of scholars have attempted to define it. Two types of definitions are found.

Intrapersonal communication is often conceptualized as communication between a single person and him- or herself. For example, Wenberg and Wilmot (1973: 20) write, "Intrapersonal communication is the communication with oneself. Within this arena, one receives signals that represent one's own feelings or sensations." Brooks (1978: 13) has characterized intrapersonal communication as "the level upon which an individual 'talks to himself' and thus handles events, ideas and experiences."

Intrapersonal communication is also described as processing information about objects in the environment. Applbaum et al. (1975: 19) write:

Intrapersonal communication deals with what goes on inside the individual. It is concerned with how the person perceives things, how information is processed inside the individual, how meaning is attached to the information that has been processed, how this meaning and information [are] added into the already existing patterns and processes that have been established by the individual inside his own head, and how the person behaves and/or communicates as a result of the information perceived and processed. In short, intrapersonal communication is the communicative functions that take place inside the individual, the process an individual goes through to make sense out of the world he lives in.

Thus, intrapersonal communication is an internal process by which the individual communicates with self about stimuli that have influenced his or her perceptual mechanisms. Presumably, this stimulation may come from the environment or from within the individual him- or herself.

A number of similarities can be observed between social cognition and intrapersonal communication. First, both processes are characterized as internal. The individual is thinking, which may mean that he or she is communicating internally with the self. In either case, the process is largely unobservable to others.

Second, both intrapersonal communication and social cognition involve the use of a representational system. Communication scholars have largely described intrapersonal communication as what Mead (1934: 173) referred to as "internalized conversation of gestures." Thought is presumed to take place using language. Berlo (1960: 44) notes, "I am suggesting the *major units of thought are units of language*, that we have difficulty in thinking about an object, a process, any construct for which we have no name, no label, no words." Research on social cognition has also assumed an important role for language (although it should be noted that Lord, 1980, has reported that visual rather than verbal representations may be used for certain social cognitions).

Third, both intrapersonal communication and social cognition may be focused on certain aspects of interaction. We noted earlier that social cognition may be focused on self, others, or behaviors. Mortensen (1972: 123) noted that personal awareness accounts for "the dynamic forces underlying the intrapersonal system of communication." In addition, Applbaum et al. (1975: 19) describe the intrapersonal communicator as having "a number of stimuli in his external world that are available to him at any given moment and he may choose to perceive any single stimuli or any number of these stimuli." Indeed, work by Cegala (1978) suggests that people vary in the extent to which they are involved (that is, aware, responsive, and adaptive) with self and others in an interaction. Thus, both processes are able to focus on similar phenomena.

Fourth, both processes are assumed to have some impact on behavior. Earlier we noted that social cognition allows the individual to adapt his or her mental and behavioral activity to a situation. A similar function is assumed for intrapersonal communication. Berlo (1960: 117) writes, "Every communicator carries around with him an image of his receiver. He takes his receiver (as he pictures him to be) into account when he produces a message. He anticipates the possible responses of his receiver and tries to predict them ahead of time. These images affect his own message behavior." Thus, intrapersonal communication and social cognition overlap in several areas and likely form a base for other forms of communication.

Later chapters in this volume will deal with other areas of communication inquiry. These areas have traditionally been marked off as specialties within the field of communication. Typically, graduate students "major" in one or two of these areas during their graduate careers, and researchers normally research one of these areas. The divisional structure of the International Communication Association reflects this kind of conceptual map. We contend that although such divisions are useful for some purposes, they can also impede the progress of theory development and research by focusing scarce energy on relatively narrow research arenas. We believe that the social cognition focus is a useful one for demonstrating the fundamental unity underlying what *appear* to be diverse communication situations. We are confident that the chapters of this volume will demonstrate this fundamental unity.

References

Abelson, R. Script processing in attitude formation and decision making. Pp. 33-45 in J. Carroll and T. Payne (Eds.), *Cognition and social behavior*. Hillsdale, NJ: Erlbaum, 1976.

Adair, J., and Spinner, B. Subjects' access to cognitive processes: Demand characteristics and verbal report. *Journal for the Theory of Social Behaviour*, 1981, *11*, 31-52.

Ajzen, I., and Fishbein, M. Attitude-behavior relations: A theoretical analysis and review of empirical research. *Psychological Bulletin*, 1977, *84*, 888-918.

Ajzen, I., and Fishbein, M. *Understanding attitudes and predicting social behavior*. Englewood Cliffs, NJ: Prentice-Hall, 1980.

Applbaum, R., Jenson, O., and Carroll, R. *Speech communication*. New York: Macmillan, 1975.

Arkin, R., Appelman, A., and Burger, J. Social anxiety, self-presentation, and the self-serving bias in causal attribution. *Journal of Personality and Social Psychology*, 1980, *38*, 23-35.

Bem, D., and McConnell, H. Testing the self-perception explanation of dissonance phenomena: On the salience of premanipulation attitudes. *Journal of Personality and Social Psychology*, 1970, *14*, 23-31.

Berger, C., and Calabrese, R. Some explorations in initial interaction and beyond: Toward a developmental theory of interpersonal communication. *Human Communication Research*, 1975, *1*, 99-112.

Berger, C, and Roloff, M. Social cognition, self-awareness, and interpersonal communication. Pp. 1-50 in B. Dervin and M. Voigt (Eds.), *Progress in communication sciences* (Vol. II). Norwood, NJ: Ablex, 1980.

Berlo, D. *The process of communication: An introduction to theory and practice.* New York: Holt, Rinehart & Winston, 1960.

Bradley, G. Self-serving bias in the attribution process: A reexamination of the fact or fiction question. *Journal of Personality and Social Psychology*, 1978, *36*, 56-71.

Brooks, W. *Speech communication.* Dubuque, IA: Wm. C. Brown, 1978.

Bruner, J., and Tagiuri, R. The perception of people. Pp. 634-654 in G. Lindzey (ed.), *Handbook of social psychology.* Reading, MA: Addison-Wesley, 1954.

Buss, D., and Scheier, M. Self-consciousness, self-interests, and self-attribution. *Journal of Research in Personality*, 1976, *10*, 463-468.

Byrne, D. *The attraction paradigm.* New York: Academic Press, 1971.

Cacioppo, J., and Petty, R. (1979) Attitudes and cognitive response: An electrophysiological approach. *Journal of Personality and Social Psychology*, 1979, *37*, 2181-2199.

Cantor, N., and Mischel, W. Traits as prototypes: Effects on recognition memory." *Journal of Personality and Social Psychology*, 1977, *35*, 38-48.

Cantor, N., and Mischel, W. Prototypes in person perception. Pp. 4-52 in L. Berkowitz (Ed.), *Advances in experimental social psychology* (Vol. 12). New York: Academic Press, 1979. (a)

Cantor, N., and Mischel, W. Prototypicality and personality: Effects on free recall and personality impression. *Journal of Research in Personality*, 1979, *13*, 187-205. (b)

Carroll, J., and Payne, T. *Cognition and social behavior.* Hillsdale, NJ: Erlbaum, 1976.

Carver, C., and Scheier, M. Self-focusing effects of dispositional self-consciousness, mirror presence, and audience presences. *Journal of Personality, and Social Psychology*, 1978, *36*, 324-332.

Carver, C., and Scheier, M. Self-consciousness and reactance. *Journal of Research in Personality* 1981, *15*, 16-29.

Cattell, R. *The description and measurement of personality.* New York: World Book, 1946.

Cegala, D. Interaction involvement: A necessary dimension of communicative competence. Presented at the annual convention of the Speech Communication Association, Minneapolis, 1978.

Chaiken, S. "Heuristic versus systematic information processing and the use of source versus message cues in persuasion." *Journal of Personality and Social Psychology*, 1980, *39*, 752-766.

Cooley, C. (1902) *Human nature and the social order.* New York: Scribner's.

Dance, E., and Larson, C. *The functions of human communication: A theoretical approach.* New York: Holt, Rinehart & Winston, 1976.

Dillehay, R., Insko, C., and Smith, B. Logical consistency and attitude change. *Journal of Personality and Social Psychology*, 1966, *3*, 646-654.

Dostoyevsky, F. *The house of the dead.* New York: Macmillan, 1911.

Douglas, W. *Unitization, self-monitoring, and the processing of conversational sequences.* Unpublished doctoral dissertation, Department of Communication Studies, Northwestern University, 1981.

Duval, S., and Wicklund, R. *A theory of objective self-awareness.* New York: Academic Press, 1972.

Ebbesen, E. Cognitive processes in understanding ongoing behavior. Pp. 179-225 in R. Hastie et al. (Eds.), *Person memory: The cognitive basis of social perception.* Hillsdale, NJ: Erlbaum, 1980.

Ellis, D. Some effects of task context on implicit communication theory. *Communication Quarterly,* 1980, *28,* 11-19.

Ericsson, K., and Simon, H. Verbal reports as data. *Psychological Review,* 1980, *87,* 215-251.

Fenigstein, A., and Carver, C. Self-focusing effects of heartbeat feedback. *Journal of Personality and Social Psychology,* 1978, *36,* 1241-1250.

Fenigstein, A., Scheier, M., and Buss, A. Public and private self-consciousness: Assessment and theory. *Journal of Consulting and Clinical Psychology,* 1975, *43,* 522-527.

Fishbein, M. A theory of reasoned action: Some applications and implications. Pp. 65-116 in H. Howe (Ed.), *Nebraska Symposium on Motivation* (Vol. 28). Lincoln: University of Nebraska Press, 1980.

Fishbein, M., and Ajzen, I. *Belief, attitude, intention and behavior: An introduction to theory and research.* Reading, MA: Addison-Wesley, 1975.

Froming, W., and Carver, C. Divergent influences of private and public self-consciousness in a compliance paradigm. *Journal of Research in Personality,* 1981, *15,* 159-171.

Gergen, K. *The concept of self.* New York: Holt, Rinehart & Winston, 1971.

Greenberg, B., and Reeves, B. Children and the perceived reality of television. *Journal of Social Issues,* 1976, *32,* 89-97.

Greenwald, A. Cognitive learning, cognitive response to persuasion, and attitude change. Pp. 147-170 in A. Greenwald, T. Brock, and T. Ostrom (Eds.), *Psychological foundations of attitudes.* New York: Academic Press, 1968.

Hastie, R., Ostrom, T., Ebbesen, E., Wyer, R., Hamilton, D., and Carlston, D. *Person memory: The cognitive basis of social perception.* Hillsdale, NJ: Erlbaum, 1980.

Heider, F. *The psychology of interpersonal relations.* New York: John Wiley, 1958.

Higgins, E., Herman, C., and Zanna, M. *Social cognition.* Hillsdale, NJ: Erlbaum, 1980.

Hirst, W., Spelke, E., Reaves, C., Caharack, G., and Neisser, U. Dividing attention without alternation or automaticity. *Journal of Experimental Psychology: General,* 1980, *109,* 98-117.

Ickes, W., Layden, M., and Barnes, R. Objective self-awareness and individuation: An empirical link. *Journal of Personality,* 1977, *45,* 147-161.

James, W. *The principles of psychology.* New York: Dover, 1890.

Jones, E., and Davis, K. From acts to dispositions: The attribution process in person perception. Pp. 220-266 in L. Berkowitz (Ed.), *Advances in experimental social psychology* (Vol. 2). New York: Academic Press, 1965.

Jones, E., and Nisbett, R. *The actor and the observer: Divergent perceptions of the causes of behavior.* Morristown, NJ: General Learning Press, 1971.

Kelley, H. Attribution in social psychology. Pp. 192-238 in D. Levine (Ed.) *Nebraska Symposium on Motivation* (Vol. 15). Lincoln: University of Nebraska Press, 1967.

Kelley, H. *Attribution in social interaction.* Morristown, NJ: General Learning Press, 1971.

Kelly, G. *The psychology of personal constructs.* New York: Norton, 1955.

Kendzierski, D. Self-schemata and scripts: The recall of self-referent and scriptal information. *Personality and Social Psychology Bulletin,* 1980, *6,* 23-29.

Knapp, M., Ellis, D., and Williams, B. Perceptions of communication behavior associated with relationship terms. *Communication Monographs,* 1980, *47,* 262-278.

Langer, E. The illusion of control. *Journal of Personality and Social Psychology,* 1975, *32,* 311-321.

Langer, E. The psychology of chance. *Journal for the Theory of Social Behavior*, 1978, *7*, 185-207. (a)

Langer, E. Rethinking the role of thought in social interaction. Pp. 35-58 in J. H. Harvey, W. J. Ickes, and R. F. Kidd (Eds.), *New directions in attribution research* (Vol. 2). Hillsdale, NJ: Erlbaum, 1978. (b)

Langer, E., Blank, A., and Chanowitz, B. The mindlessness of ostensibly thoughtful action: The role of "placebic" information in interpersonal interaction. *Journal of Personality and Social Psychology*, 1978, *36*, 635-642.

Langer, E., and Imber, L. When practice makes imperfect: Debilitating effects of overlearning. *Journal of Personality and Social Psychology*, 1979, *37*, 2014-2125.

Langer, E., and Imber, L. The role of mindlessness in the perception of deviance. *Journal of Personality and Social Psychology*, 1980, *39*, 360-367.

Langer, E., and Newman, H. The role of mindlessness in a typical social psychological experiment. *Personality and Social Psychology Bulletin*, 1979, *5*, 295-298.

Langer, E., and Weinman, C. When thinking disrupts intellectual performance: Mindfulness on an overlearned task. *Personality and Social Psychology Bulletin*, 1981, *7*, 240-243.

Lippa, R., and Mash, M. The effects of self-monitoring and self-reported consistency on the consistency of personality judgments made by strangers and intimates. *Journal of Research in Personality*, 1981, *15*, 172-181.

Lord, C. Schemas and images as memory aids: Two modes of processing social information. *Journal of Personality and Social Psychology*, 1980, *38*, 257-269.

Markus, H. Self-schemata and processing information about the self. *Journal of Personality and Social Psychology*, 1977, *35*, 63-78.

McGuigan, F. *Thinking: Studies of covert language process*. New York: Appleton-Century-Crofts, 1966.

McGuigan, F., and Schoonover, R. *The psychophysiology of thinking*. New York: Academic Press, 1973.

Mead, G. H. *Mind, self, and society*. Chicago: University of Chicago Press, 1934.

Mortensen, C. *Communication: The study of human interaction*. New York: McGraw-Hill, 1972.

Newtson, D. Attribution and the unit of perception of ongoing behavior. *Journal of Personality and Social Psychology*, 1973, *28*, 28-38.

Newtson, D. Foundations of attribution: The perception of ongoing behavior. Pp. 223-247 in J. H. Harvey, W. J. Ickes, and R. F. Kidd (Eds.), *New directions in attribution research*. Hillsdale, NJ: Erlbaum, 1976.

Nisbett, R., and Wilson, T. Telling more than we can know: Verbal reports on mental processes. *Psychological Review*, 1977, *84*, 231-259.

Norman, W. Toward an adequate taxonomy of personality attributes: Replicated factor structure in peer nomination personality ratings. *Journal of Abnormal and Social Psychology*, 1963, *66*, 574-583.

Piaget, J. *The moral judgment of the child*. London: Routledge & Kegan Paul, 1932.

Perloff, R., and Brock, T. ". . . And thinking makes it so": Cognitive responses to persuasion. Pp. 67-100 in M. Roloff and G. Miller (Eds.), *Persuasion: New directions in theory and research*. Beverly Hills, CA: Sage, 1980.

Petty, R., Ostrom, T., and Brock, T. *Cognitive responses in persuasion*. Hillsdale, NJ: Erlbaum, 1980.

Reeves, B., and Greenberg, B. Children's perceptions of television characters. *Human Communication Research*, 1977, *3*, 113-127.

Rich, M. Verbal reports on mental processes: Issues of accuracy and awareness. *Journal for the Theory of Social Behaviour*, 1979, *9*, 27-29.

Rogers, T., Kuiper, N., and Kirker, W. Self-reference and the encoding of personal information. *Journal of Personality and Social Psychology*, 1977, *35*, 677-688.

Rokeach, M. Some unresolved issues in theories of beliefs, attitudes, and values. Pp. 261-304 in H. Howe (Ed.), *Nebraska Symposium on Motivation* (Vol. 28). Lincoln: University of Nebraska Press, 1980.

Roloff, M. Self-awareness and the persuasion process: Do we really *know* what we're doing? Pp. 29-66 in M. Roloff and G. Miller (Eds.) *Persuasion: New directions in theory and research*. Beverly Hills, CA: Sage, 1980.

Roloff, M., and Greenberg, B. Resolving conflict: Methods used by TV characters and teenage viewers. *Journal of Broadcasting*, 1979, *23*, 285-295.

Ross, L. The intuitive psychologist and his shortcomings: Distortions in the attribution process. Pp. 174-221 in L. Berkowitz (Ed.), *Advances in experimental social psychology* (Vol. 10). New York: Academic Press, 1977.

Ruesch, J., Block, J., and Bennett, L. The assessment of communication: 1. A method for the analysis of social interaction. *Journal of Psychology*, 1953, *35*, 59-80.

Sampson, E. Personality and the location of identity. *Journal of Personality*, 1978, *46*, 552-568.

Schank, R., and Abelson, R. *Scripts, plans, goals and understanding: An inquiry into human knowledge structures*. Hillsdale, NJ: Erlbaum, 1977.

Scheier, M. Effects of public and private self-consciousness on the public expression of personal beliefs. *Journal of Personality and Social Psychology*, 1980, *39*, 514-521.

Scheier, M., Buss, A., and Buss, D. Self-consciousness, self-report of aggressiveness and aggression. *Journal of Research in Personality*, 1978, *12*, 133-140.

Scheier, M., and Carver, C. Self-focused attention and the experience of emotion: Attraction, repulsion, elation, and depression. *Journal of Personality and Social Psychology*, 1977, *35*, 625-636.

Scheier, M., and Carver, C. Private and public self-attention, resistance to change and dissonance reduction. *Journal of Personality and Social Psychology*, 1980, *39*, 390-405.

Scheier, M., Carver, C., and Gibbons, F. Self-focused attention and reactions to fear. *Journal of Research in Personality*, 1981, *15*, 1-15.

Schutz, A. *The phenomenology of the social world*. Evanston, IL: Northwestern University Press, 1932.

Shweder, R. How relevant is an individual differences theory of personality? *Journal of Personality*, 1975, *43*, 455-484.

Shweder, R. Factors and fictions in person perception: A reply to Lamiell, Ross, and Cavanee. *Journal of Personality*, 1980, *48*, 74-81.

Shweder, R., and D'Andrade, R. Accurate reflection or systematic distortion? A reply to Block, Weiss, and Thorne. *Journal of Personality and Social Psychology*, 1979, *37*, 1075-1084.

Smith, E., and Miller, F. Theoretical note: Limits on perception of cognitive processes: A reply to Nisbett and Wilson. *Psychological Review*, 1978, *85*, 355-362.

Snyder, M. Self-monitoring of expressive behavior. *Journal of Personality and Social Psychology*, 1974, *30*, 526-537.

Snyder, M. Self-monitoring processes. Pp. 85-128 in L. Berkowitz (Ed.), *Advances in experimental social psychology* (Vol. 12). New York: Academic Press, 1979.

Snyder, M., and Cantor, N. Thinking about ourselves and others: Self-monitoring and social knowledge. *Journal of Personality and Social Psychology*, 1980, *39*, 222-234.

Spelke, E., Hirst, W., and Neisser, U. Skills of divided attention. *Cognition,* 1976, *4,* 215-230.

Taylor, S., and Fiske, S. Salience, attention, and attribution: Top of the head phenomena. Pp. 249-288 in L. Berkowitz (Ed.), *Advances in experimental social psychology* (Vol. 11). New York: Academic Press, 1978.

Tedeschi, J., Schlenker, B., and Bonoma, T. Cognitive dissonance: Private ratiocination or public spectacle? *American Psychologist,* 1971, *26,* 685-695.

Tesser, A. Self-generated attitude change. Pp. 290-338 in L. Berkowitz (Ed), *Advances in experimental social psychology* (Vol. 11). New York: Academic Press, 1978.

Thayer, L. *Communication and communication systems.* Homewood, IL: Irwin, 1968.

Tompkins, S. Script theory: Differential magnification of affects. Pp. 201-236 in H. Howe (Ed.), *Nebraska Symposium on Motivation* (Vol. 27). Lincoln: University of Nebraska Press, 1979.

Triandis, H. *Interpersonal behavior.* Belmont, CA: Brooks/Cole, 1977.

Triandis, H. Values, attitudes and interpersonal behavior. Pp. 195-260 in H. Howe (Eds.), *Nebraska Symposium on Motivation* (Vol. 28). Lincoln: University of Nebraska Press, 1980.

Tunnell, G. Intraindividual consistency in personality assessment: The effect of self-monitoring. *Journal of Personality,* 1980, *48,* 220-232.

Tupes, E., and Christal, R. Recurrent personality factors based on trait ratings. *USAF Aeronautical Systems Division, Technical Report,* 1961, 61-97.

Turner, R. Consistency, self-consciousness, and the predictive validity of typical and maximal personality measures. *Journal of Research in Personality,* 1978, *12,* 117-132 (a)

Turner, R. Self-consciousness and speed of processing self-relevant information. *Personality and Social Psychology Bulletin,* 1978, *4,* 456-460. (b)

Turner, R. Self-consciousness and memory of trait terms. *Personality and Social Psychology Bulletin,* 1980, *6,* 273-377.

Turner, R., Gilliland, L., and Klein, H. Self-consciousness, evaluation of physical characteristics, and physical attractiveness. *Journal of Research in Personality,* 1981, *15,* 182-190.

Turner, R., and Peterson, M. Public and private self-consciousness and emotional expressibility. *Journal of Consultinga nd Clinical Psychology,* 1977, *45,* 490-491.

Tversky, A., and Kahneman, D. Causal schemas in judgments under uncertainty. Pp. 49-72 in M. Fishbein (Ed.), *Progress in social psychology* (Vol. 1). Hillsdale, NJ: Erlbaum, 1980.

Underwood, B., and Moore, B. Sources of behavioral consistency. *Journal of Personality and Social Psychology,* 1981, *40,* 780-785.

Vernon, M. The functions of schemata in perceiving. *Psychological Review,* 1955, *62,* 180-192.

Watts, W., and Holt, L. Logical relationships among beliefs and timing as factors in persuasion. *Journal of Personality and Social Psychology,* 1970, *16,* 571-582.

Wegner, D., and Guiliano, T. Arousal-induced attention to self. *Journal of Personality and Social Psychology,* 1980, *38,* 719-726.

Wegner, D., and Vallacher, R. *Implicit psychology: An introduction to social cognition.* New York: Oxford University Press, 1977.

Weimer, W., and Palermo, D. *Cognition and the symbolic processes.* Hillsdale, NJ: Erlbaum, 1974.

Wenburg, J., and Wilmot, W. *The personal communication process.* New York: John Wiley, 1973.

White, P. Theoretical note: Limitations on verbal reports of internal events: A refutation of Nisbett and Wilson and of Bem. *Psychological Review,* 1980, *87,* 105-112.

Wicklund, R., and Brehm, J. *Perspectives on cognitive dissonance.* Hillsdale, NJ: Erlbaum, 1976.

Wicklund, R., and Duval, S. Opinion change and performance facilitation as a result of objective self-awareness. *Journal of Experimental Social Psychology,* 1971, *7,* 319-342.

Wiggins, J. *Personality and prediction: Principles of personality assessment.* Reading, MA: Addison-Wesley, 1973.

Wilson, T., and Nisbett, R. The accuracy of verbal reports about the effects of stimuli on evaluations and behavior. *Social Psychology,* 1978, *41,* 118-131.

Wish, M., Deutsch, M., and Kaplan, S. Perceived dimensions of interpersonal relations. *Journal of Personality and Social Psychology,* 1976, *33,* 409-420.

Wish, M., and Kaplan, S. Toward an implicit theory of interpersonal communication. *Sociometry,* 1977, *40,* 234-246.

Wyer, R., and Carlston, D. *Social cognition, inference, and attribution.* Hillsdale, NJ: Erlbaum, 1980.

Wylie, R. *The self concept.* Lincoln: University of Nebraska Press, 1973.

2

Impression Formation and Message Production

Barbara J. O'Keefe
Jesse G. Delia

This chapter concerns the role of social cognition in message production and communication. The social cognition-communication relationship has been thought to be of critical importance by those working within a wide range of cognitive, developmental, and interactionist theoretical frameworks (such as Mead, 1934; Asch, 1952; Kelly, 1955; Piaget, 1926/1959; Werner and Kaplan, 1963; Blumer, 1969; Feffer, 1970; Rommetveit, 1974). All these theoretical analyses, in one way or another, take communication and social interaction to be processes dependent on speakers' and hearers' abilities, in Kelly's (1955) terms, to construe one another's construction processes and, thus, to formulate and interpret messages in terms of understandings of the other's perspective. Within their quite different analyses of social and communicative development, for example, both Piaget (1926/1959) and Mead (1934) argued that a primary determinant of the child's developing ability to manage communication is an increasing capacity for understanding another's frame of reference (role taking or social perspective taking).

The most important work advancing this general idea has been tied to cognitive-developmental theory. Piaget's initial analysis of communicative development posited a shift from "autistic speech," rooted in a self-embedded language-thought fusion, through "egocentric speech," in which there is an effort toward communication but only a partial and ineffective differentiation of one's own perspective from that of one's own communicative partner, to effective "social speech" scaffolded off the conceptual differentiation and coordination of perspectives. Thus, in Piaget's analysis communicative development is seen as rooted in, and reflective of, general processes of conceptual development, particularly those social cognitive achievements underlying the decline of egocentrism and the emergence of the capacity to take divergent social perspectives.

The Piagetian analysis gave rise to a research tradition examining the general quality of children's communication across childhood and, in particular, investigating the relationship among various indices of perspective-taking and communicative quality. (For a summary of early communication research following Piaget, see Alvy, 1973.) Most recent research has focused on "referential communication," emphasizing the accomplishment of intelligibility and communicative efficiency. Since this research has been reviewed elsewhere (see Glucksberg et al., 1975; Asher, 1979; Shantz, 1981), we need not deal with its particulars here. Suffice it to say that research on perspective taking and communicative development has not yielded a consistent pattern of support for the Piagetian analysis. The general egocentrism explanation, in particular, has come in for hard knocks (see Shatz, 1978; Asher, 1979).

There have been several changes in direction in the study of social cognition and communicative development following the decline in interest in the general cognitive egocentrism hypothesis, but in most permutations, the essential outlines of the listener-adaptation model of communicative development have been maintained. This model, given detailed expression in our own work (see Delia and O'Keefe, 1979), holds that the speaker's knowledge of the listener constitutes a basis for selecting among alternative messages or message elements so as to produce a message tailored to the listener's perspective or needs.

In moving away from the general egocentrism account for an expected social cognition-communication link, various investigators have preserved the general listener-adaptation model by such maneuvers as (1) pursuing the hypothesis that it is not general perspective-taking abilities but specifically *social* perspective-taking skills that underlie effective message adaptation (see Shantz, 1981); (2) showing that the production of listener-adapted communications in particular tasks may be too difficult to complete successfully because of inadequate attention and memory capacities rather than because of general egocentrism (Shatz, 1978); (3) positing factors other than social perception processes that are also necessary to the production of listener-adapted messages, including, for example, vocabulary, message strategies, and linguistic comparison processes (see Higgins, 1976; Delia and Clark, 1977); and (4) arguing for the importance to listener-adapted communication of skills and knowledge permitting the effective application of perspective-taking and message adaptation skills in a particular content domain (Atlas, 1980; Ammon, 1981).

Our concern in this chapter is with a line of research in this vein that we and our colleagues have conducted within a general constructivist framework built on aspects of Kelly's personal construct theory, Werner's organismic-developmental theory, and Mead's symbolic interactionism (see the general discussions by Delia et al., 1982; Delia and O'Keefe, 1979; B. O'Keefe and Delia, forthcoming). Our analysis of the social cognition-communication relationship has involved three major shifts in direction from previous research in the area. First, rather than focusing on perspective taking as the basic social cognitive process underpinning communicative adaptation, we have concentrated on the processes involved in forming interpersonal impressions within a framework stressing the use of interpretive structures, or interpersonal constructs, for construing and understanding other persons' actions. Within this framework, we have treated the number and quality of an individual's interpersonal constructs as establishing stable features of the discrimination among listeners and, hence, of providing the foundation for listener-sensitive communication. Second, we have adopted a hierarchical coding approach to the analysis of messages that takes the message strategy as the basic unit of analysis (see Clark and Delia, 1979). The hierarchical systems within which we have coded message strategies have ordered the strategies along various dimensions reflecting the extent to which the strategies themselves imply sensitivity to the perspectives of message recipients. Third, we have also employed a parallel hierarchical coding approach to the analysis of message producers' rationales for their message choices (see B. O'Keefe and Delia, 1979; Burke and Clark, forthcoming). In addition to these three major shifts in conceptualization and research strategy, like several other researchers in the area we have conceived construals of listener characteristics to be a necessary, but not sufficient, basis for the production of listener-sensitive communications (see Delia and Clark, 1977; Delia and O'Keefe, 1979). In particular, we have emphasized the importance of the strategic repertoire that must be developed for translating perceptions and intentions into adapted communications.

Our shift away from the standard approach to investigating the social cognition-communication relationship has been fruitful in permitting us to employ a common framework and methods to study a variety of communicative objectives and contexts, to study populations of varying ages from early childhood into adulthood, and to establish a clear correlational relationship between communicative strategy quality and the development of differentiated and abstract sets of interpersonal constructs employed in person perception. We have found consistent relationships between our construct system indices and the person-centeredness of message strategies (and rationales for them) in the range of .40 to .80.

In the context of other research on the social cognition-communication relationship, our findings are striking, especially given the consistency of results across ages and contexts. It is not necessary to summarize this work in detail here, but consider the following.

(1) The relationship of construct differentiation and abstractness to the quality of message strategies and the listener-centeredness of rationales for message choices has been demonstrated in cross-sectional designs to hold across the span of development from early childhood to adulthood for persuasion communication situations (see Clark and Delia, 1977; Delia, Kline, and Burleson, 1979; Burke and Clark, forthcoming) and for situations requiring comforting another (see Burleson, 1981a; Burleson, forthcoming). These relationships have also been shown in a childhood developmental study using a longitudinal design (Delia, Burleson, and Kline 1979). Across the span of development, the correlation of construct differentiation and message quality declines somewhat, and construct abstractness becomes a stronger predictor of the message strategy and rationale codings (Delia, Kline, and Burleson, 1979; Burleson, 1981a).

(2) The same pattern of correlations between construct system characteristics and the quality of message strategies and message rationales obtains within age-homogeneous groups of children and adults (Burke, 1979; Kline, 1981b; B. O'Keefe and Delia, 1979; Applegate, 1980a; Applegate and Delia, 1980; Burleson, 1981b).

(3) A similar pattern of correlations holds across a wide range of communicative functions. Our research has relied heavily on a common paradigm: Subjects are presented with a hypothetical situation that specifies a communicative goal the subject is asked to adopt and execute by formulating a message. This methodology permits us to establish generality by having subjects respond to several situations of the type being studied in a given investigation. Moreover, this methodology permits the investigation of a diverse set of communicative objectives (such as situations requiring persuasion, comforting, gaining compliance with a behavioral directive, or protecting another's face). This methodology also has the advantage of permitting the elicitation of rationales for message choices. The relationship between construct system characteristics and the person-centeredness of message strategies and rationales has been of a similar magnitude across all these contexts

and communicative objectives (typically at least .45 and seldom exceeding .75).

(4) A similar relationship of construct system features and communication strategies has been demonstrated in a study involving the systematic coding of persuasive strategies in a face-to-face bargaining situation (Applegate and Wheeler, 1981) and in participant observation studies of naturally occurring comforting, compliance-gaining, and managerial situations (Applegate, 1980b; Husband, 1981). Thus, results obtained by having subjects produce messages in response to hypothetical situations are consistent with those obtained in studies of situated interaction. (See Applegate, 1980b, for a general discussion of methodological triangulation in investigating the social cognition-message relationship.)

(5) The relationship of interpersonal construct system characteristics to message features also has been shown to hold for the implicit subsidiary objective of face protection in situations organized around a dominant compliance-gaining objective (Kline, 1981a, 1981b; Applegate, 1982). Thus, even if message strategies relevant to the accomplishment of an objective that is only implicit within the situation are coded, the person-centeredness of strategies used by those with differentiated and abstract constructs is evident.

The task of this chapter is to begin to unravel exactly how the interpersonal construct system organizes "person-centered" message production. In general, we have interpreted the relationship in terms of the listener-adaptation model of communication. Delia, Kline, and Burleson (1979: 244) state, for instance, that "within our constructivist perspective, social perception is conceived to occur through a system of bi-polar dimensions or constructs. Constructs are the schemes within which others' behaviors are interpreted, evaluated, and anticipated. . . . Since it is the impression one forms of another that serves as the basis for message formulation and adaptation, individuals who form more differentiated, stable, and psychologically-centered impressions tend to produce more listener-adapted messages. Thus the development of a complex system of interpersonal constructs is a necessary prerequisite for the formulation of sensitively adapted messages." If nothing else, the body of research just referred to points to the utility of our measures of construct system characteristics for predicting person-centered message strategies and choices. However, the results are problematic in supporting the listener-adaptation interpretation we have advanced. Indeed, we now believe that this interpretation requires revision.

To address this issue requires that we return to our analysis both of interpersonal construct system properties and of message strategies.

There is reason to believe, we now think, that our understanding of person perception has been too much influenced by the prevailing general model of impression formation and that our analysis of message strategies has been too influenced by the legacy of the Piagetian emphasis on egocentrism-perspectivism. To understand better how it is that interpersonal constructs organize message production, we therefore must consider anew how it is that impressions are formed and the role of interpersonal constructs in that process, and we must address more exactly what it is our message and rationale coding systems index. Accordingly, in the next section our previously presented analysis of impression formation processes is extended. In a subsequent section, the general problem of message analysis is addressed. In a final section, these two lines of analysis are brought to bear in interpreting the research establishing the relationship between interpersonal construct system properties and the production of person-centered messages. Our goal is not to untangle this problem completely, for that surely will require considerable further research. Rather, our aim is to provide a fresh orientation to the problem, one that we believe could have general importance for understandings of the cognitive organization of interpersonal behavior.

Interpersonal Constructs, Interpersonal Schemas, and the Formation of Impressions

The "Assimilatory" Tradition in the Study of Impression Formation

Research on social cognition was dominated in its infancy by the notion of "social intelligence," that is, the supposition that individual perceivers differ in their sensitivity and adaptation to information concerning others. The "social intelligence" concept gave rise to a major line of research in social cognition that is of continuing importance: the investigation of the determinants of differential accuracy in person perception. For the most part, early research on the accuracy of impressions focused on the judgment of personality traits and employed a research paradigm based on the simple matching of perceiver and target responses to questionnaires and personality inventories. In the mid-1950s this research paradigm came under serious criticism (see Cronbach, 1955; Gage and Cronbach, 1955), and there eventuated both a significant change in the character of research on the accuracy of interpersonal perception and a shift in research emphasis away from the problem of accuracy to the question of how inferences are made and organized in forming overall evaluations and impressions of others.

Perhaps the most important feature of this latter tradition has been its reliance on variants of the research design employed by Asch (1946) in his classic study of central attributes in impression organization. In this basic paradigm, subjects are presented with trait lists, behavioral anecdotes, filmed action scenes, or the like and asked to form an overall impression of a target figure from the array of provided information. The impression is then reported variously on an overall evaluative scale, by means of an adjective checklist, or, in some cases, by reporting the content of the impression orally or in writing.

A second important general characteristic of this research tradition has been its emphasis on impression formation as a constructive process in which available information is translated into the categories of, and elaborated within, the implicit personality theory of the perceiver. The grounding of social perception research within a metaphor depicting the perceiver as a naive personality theorist was initially advanced by Bruner and Tagiuri (1954) in the first edition of the *Handbook of Social Psychology*. Within our own research program, this notion has been elaborated through viewing the impression formation process as involving "(1) the ordering of stimulus information to the perceiver's conceptual dimensions, (2) the attribution by inference of other qualities based on related conceptual dimensions, (3) the establishment of unity and coherence in the impression through organization around central, often motivational, constructs, (4) an implicit evaluation of the total impression, and finally (5) a recoding of the impression attributes into the subject's own verbal code if and when he is called upon to do so" (Delia, 1976: 153).

There are several features of the foregoing model and research paradigm that are of note. First, primary emphasis is placed on the reconstruction of information about another within the unique dimensions of the individual perceiver's cognitive system. Second, the elaboration of impressions is represented as based on a chain of inferences in consequence of the relationships of elicited constructs to other dimensions in the perceiver's interpersonal cognitive system. Third, a central process is taken to be the integration of elicited and inferred constructs into a unified, general impression reflecting the organizing links among the constructs in the perceiver's cognitive system. Finally, by implication, the processes crucial to understanding impression formation are assumed to be subject to effective investigation through studying the interpretation, inferential extension, and integration of an array of provided information describing a target person. What this all means is that, in the terms of Piaget's cognitive-developmental theory, impression formation has been viewed as largely an assimilatory process (external structures are assimilated to the cognitive system) rather than as an accommodative process (cognitive structures fail to provide an adequate organization of external structures and so undergo accommodative change).

Within the assimilatory tradition only minimal attention has been given to such questions as: Do patterns of behavior evoke particular constructs in individuals who have similar social backgrounds? How and to what extent are impressions organized to provide understanding and to guide action within behavioral contexts? What processes are involved in the elaboration and organization of an impression over time as new information becomes available in varying behavioral contexts? and How and what kinds of interpretive and information-seeking strategies permit accommodation to new information across time and contexts? There are, of course, some significant exceptions to the claim that such questions have not been addressed. Most significantly, attribution researchers have given considerable attention to the patterns of action that lead to particular attributions and to the effect of such attributions on specific intentions and behaviors (see, for example, Shaver, 1975). In addition, quite early in the general tradition of person perception research, Jones and Thibaut (1958) called attention to the use of particular interpretive orientations that mobilize fundamentally different sets of dimensions for understanding others in certain judgment and action contexts. However, such analyses have not been seen as significant for a general understanding of impression formation. In the few cases in which a framework such as that of Jones and Thibaut has been pursued, it has tended to be in combination with the mainstream model of impression formation (see, for example, Press et al., 1975). Moreover, how intentions and goals within contexts of action mobilize the use of particular interpretive schemes that yield a context- or action-relevant, as opposed to a general, impression has received almost no research attention at all. The result has been a divorce of the study of impression formation from the study of behavior, even though it is always assumed or asserted that impressions provide the anticipations that channelize and guide action. One of the greatest needs in the study of impression formation is the elaboration of frameworks reconciling and integrating the traditional models and paradigms in the study of impression formation and attribution processes.

Constructs, Schemata, and the Organization of Construals

Within a constructivist research tradition, Crockett (1977, forthcoming) has recently presented the beginning points for such an approach through elaborating implications of Neisser's (1976) analysis of schemata for understanding impression formation. The following discussion draws heavily on Crockett's analysis and details some of the continuities of this approach with research on construct differentiation and impression organization. Since our aim here is not to present a complete and detailed analysis of impression formation processes, we will merely outline a series of propositions presenting our analysis.

Behavior, which is represented as patterns of action, is given meaning within patterns of dispositional constructs. With this proposition we wish to point to the deep connection between processes of construal and interpretation and the segmentation and representation of behavior. Behavior is not seen within everyday life as a continuous stream, but as punctuated. Basic construal processes that are little understood and studied segment behavior and serve its representation in terms of patterns of actions (probably the best-known line of work on this problem is that following Newtson, 1973, 1976). The representation of events in terms of concrete patterns of actions constitutes one's "episodic" knowledge of another. A number of impression formation theorists and researchers have noted that our knowledge of others involves both such episodic experiences and dispositional judgments that interpret and give meaning to those experiences (see Warr and Knapper, 1968; From, 1971; Lingle and Ostrom, 1979; Crockett, forthcoming). Frequently, episodic perceptions themselves have been seen as constructed through the direct application of highly abstract dispositional constructs (for instance, such a view is implied in the analysis of Delia et al., 1974). While research on this question will be necessary before very systematic statements can be made, it is evident from our remembering and reinterpreting actions that episodic knowledge is, to some degree, remembered independent of dispositional attributions (thus making evident the importance of incorporating Tulving's [1972] distinction between episodic and semantic memory in the study of impression formation; see Crockett, forthcoming).

Adoption of the distinction between episodic and dispositional knowledge of others provides the beginning point, as Crockett (forthcoming) implies, for a shift in impression formation research toward an "accommodation" orientation considering such questions as: What patterns of behavior invoke particular dispositional constructs? How and under what conditions does reinterpretation of the dispositional construct explaining given episodic events occur? Are there systematic individual differences in the extent to which the episodic knowledge giving rise to dispositional inferences is remembered and, thus, available for reinterpretation?

Episodic and dispositional construals of persons are organized by interpersonal schemata. Crockett (1977: 11) defines an interpersonal schema as "an expected pattern of qualities in another person or of

relations among people and objects in a perceiver's conceptual world."
He invokes this concept to remedy what he takes to be a basic weakness
in the traditional model of impression formation, namely, its failure "to
capture the organized, hyothesis-testing aspect of impression formation. The constructs in most impressions are organized around some
central pattern, or schema, which enables the perceiver to make sense of
the information, to search for new information that will eliminate
ambiguities, and to arrive at a subjectively satisfying understanding of
what the other person is like" (1977: 8).

Our interest in the present discussion is not to detail the characteristics and forms interpersonal schemata can take. It is important to note,
however, that Crockett's conception of interpersonal schema is not
equivalent to "interpersonal construct" (see Crockett, forthcoming).
Constructs provide discriminations and specific beliefs; schemata
organize constructs and thus provide for the patterns among beliefs.
Hence, Crockett (1977: 11) claims, "once a schema is invoked to account
for the behavior of a particular person, or for the relations between the
person and others, it promotes the attribution to that person of a variety
of related sentiments, abilities, motives, aspirations, character traits,
and other qualities." Moreover, some schemata "prescribe the actions
that must be observed, and the constructs by which those actions must
be interpreted, in order for other constructs to be inferred" (Crockett,
forthcoming).

Under the direction of interpersonal schemata, impression formation
thus is taken to involve not only interpretation and inference, but also
the progressive elaboration of an organized set of beliefs in accommodation to new information. Crockett (1977) notes that since schemata
organize patterns of expectation, new information about a person will
tend to be interpreted and organized to confirm an invoked schema.
However, his use of the concept of interpersonal schema implies a much
closer connection between context and construal than the traditional
assimilatory model. In that model, as we saw, the emphasis has been on
the construction of an interpersonal impression in terms of the
perceiver's judgmental dimensions and implicative links among them.
The concept of interpersonal schema similarly suggest an active
interpretive and inferential process, but one in which the impression is
not so much "constructed" as elaborated to account for the other's
temporally unfolding behavior. Thus, our adoption of the concept of
interpersonal schema is meant to mark a shift in emphasis in our
constructivist understanding of social cognition toward an "accommodative" model of impression formation.

The organization of interpersonal impressions provides context- and action-relevant understandings and anticipations of others. The traditional conception of impression formation has emphasized the overall integration of beliefs about another into a "general impression." Such an approach divorces the study of impressions both from the behavior on which beliefs are based and from the process of social interaction. As we have seen, howevever, the concept of interpersonal schema serves to link the study of impressions to a consideration of their experiential bases in behavioral contexts. Unfortunately, we know very little about how impressions are elaborated, changed, and integrated as part of a temporal process of interaction within concrete behavioral contexts. But what little we do know suggests that the general impression integration model may not serve us very well. There is a tendency even among theorists who invoke the schema concept to see schemata merely as higher-order constructs that provide the cognitive links among a bundle of constructs. Such a viewpoint serves to maintain the notion that perceivers are implicit personality theorists who seek to form organized overall impressions of others' personalities. We believe a more fruitful line is to abandon the search for the *general* organization of personality impressions and to adopt as an alternative working hypothesis the idea that interpersonal schemata are mobilized by contexts and interactional goals. Such a working hypothesis suggests that the organization of impressions often may not involve an extended understanding of the other's psychodynamic characteristics; indeed, we would argue that many impressions, although highly organized and providing useful guides to action, involve only limited attributions concerning the other's personality. Often an interpersonal impression is elaborated to account for and predict another's behavior only within quite limited behavioral contexts. An impression is elaborated in such a form because the contexts of interaction to which it is tied are circumscribed and the perceiver finds little need to invoke schemata that would channelize inferences about other behavioral contexts in which the likelihood of interaction is slim. Given such a view, the metaphor of the perceiver as personality theorist appears off the mark; the perceiver acts more as a social psychologist attempting to elaborate a pattern of concepts for explaining, understanding, and predicting the other's behavior within a range of contexts.

This viewpoint is given limited statement in Delia's (1980) comments on the role of context in shaping the development of interpersonal relationships. The point expressed there, which is generalized here, is that contexts and goals mobilize particular patterns of expectations;

these contextually focused interpersonal schemata do much of the work in organizing interpersonal impressions and relationship-relevant behavior. Delia et al. (1975) provide some support for this viewpoint in their demonstration that impressions tend to be elaborated to subserve the needs of specific contexts of anticipated interaction (see also Press et al., 1975). Rubin (1977) also demonstrated the close connection between the schematization of constructs within impressions in anticipation of the interactional context, and in a related study (Rubin, 1979) she showed that information seeking in the service of impression elaboration is similarly channelized by the expectation of interaction within particular contexts.

Systemic variations in interpersonal constructs and schemata that develop as a function of social experience provide differential capacities to form stable, organized impressions across time and contexts. Just as the individual's impressions are elaborated to accommodate to new information about another, so, over time and with social experience, the individual's system of interpersonal constructs and schemata can be expected to undergo elaboration and differentiation. With increasing age, children develop more differentiated sets of interpersonal constructs, form constructs for representing and explaining a wider range of human conduct and psychological experience, and acquire progressively more complex schemata for organizing and integrating their attributions (see research cited in Delia et al., forthcoming). Moreover, as we have remarked elsewhere (Delia and O'Keefe, 1979: 165), "as a result of differential ranges of social experience, of the variety of individual reactions to interpersonal conflicts, and of a host of other factors that are, at best, poorly understood, any group of adults will contain some individual with highly differentiated, abstract, hierarchically integrated, developmentally advanced sets of interpersonal constructs and others with sparse, globally organized, developmentally primitive sets of constructs" (see Crockett, 1965). Such developmental and individual differences in the availability of differentiated, complex sets of interpersonal constructs and schemata have important implications for social cognition and interpersonal behavior. Indeed much of the work with which we have been associated has been directed toward investigating some of these implications. One theme of this research is particularly pertinent to the present discussion of general impression formation processes, namely, the relationship of construct differentiation to the formation of organized and temporally stable interpersonal impressions.

In our research on impression formation and interpersonal communication, we have tended to focus on a particular aspect of the perceiver's interpersonal construct system: construct differentiation, or the relative number of constructs available to the perceiver for making discriminations (see D. O'Keefe and Sypher, 1981, and Crockett, forthcoming, for discussions of the reliability and validity of our approach to assessing construct differentiation or, as it has historically been labeled, "cognitive complexity"). To assess construct differentiation we have employed a simple and direct procedure. Study participants are asked to complete a Role Category Questionnaire in which they list and describe a set of personally known others, typically peers; then, the number of attributions contained in these impressions is counted (see Crockett, 1965). In some research, we also have coded such qualities as the relative personality-centeredness or abstractness of the constructs (from specific behavior, to role and general behaviors, to interests and attitudes, to personality and motivational attributions).

There is a good deal of research suggesting that observed developmental and individual differences in construct differentiation and abstractness reflect characteristics of the perceiver's interpersonal cognitive system and not merely characteristics of the particular impressions from which they are derived: (1) Similar changes with age in the differentiation and abstractness of interpersonal constructs have been identified in cross-sectional designs by several researchers (Scarlett et al., 1971; Livesley and Bromely, 1973; Peevers and Secord, 1973; Delia et al., forthcoming). (2) Stable individual differences in these changes across childhood have been observed in a longitudinal study (Delia, Burleson, and Kline, 1979). (3) Intercorrelations among construct system properties in individual impressions written by the same perceiver tend to be quite high (.40 to .80). (4) There are significant relationships between the differentiation and abstractness of impressions of known others and the same or other theoretically related characteristics coded from impressions based on provided information (see D. O'Keefe and Sypher, 1981). (5) Construct differentiation and abstractness consistently have been correlated with several social cognitive and communicative skills on tasks not involving as targets the same individuals described in the Role Category Questionnaire (see the general validity discussions of D. O'Keefe and Sypher, 1981, and Crockett, forthcoming). (6) Construct differentiation is significantly related to social perception and behavioral processes not involving verbal response methodologies for assessment (see Delia and Crockett, 1973; D. O'Keefe and Delia, 1981).

We find it particularly important that individuals with differentiated, abstract sets of interpersonal constructs, be they young or old, appear better able to form organized impressions of others. This is true both for naturally formed impressions (which are more likely to represent and account for variability in another's behavior; see Delia et al., forthcoming) and for impressions based on provided inconsistent information (which are more likely to provide contextual and motivational explanations reconciling the inconsistency; see Nidorf and Crockett, 1965; Rosenbach et al., 1973; Press et al., 1975; Biskin and Crano, 1977). Moreover, individuals with more differentiated sets of interpersonal constructs are able to integrate blocks of sequentially presented information describing another and to form an impression that provides the basis for more stable interpersonal attitudes (Mayo and Crockett, 1964; Klyver et al., 1972; Delia et al., 1975; D. O'Keefe, 1980).

All of this suggests that the perceiver with a highly differentiated set of abstract interpersonal constructs is better able to accommodate to diverse or newly available information in forming an organized and coherent impression of another. It seems likely that such impression organization reflects not merely processes of construct differentiation, but also operations involving variations in the number, complexity, and organization of the perceiver's interpersonal schemata. Indeed, it could be that our assessment of construct differentiation itself reflects not so much the number of constructs available for making discriminations as the extent to which the perceiver has available schemata that permit elaboration (and retrieval) of impressions in accommodation to diverse information about others. Research on this possibility is certainly called for. However, whatever the specific mechanisms involved, it is clear that individuals who attribute extensive sets of interpersonal constructs to others organize their social understandings and actions in distinctive ways.

The task of the following sections is to explore systematically what our message-coding systems tap and how it is that construct differentiation and construct abstractness relate to message production. While treating only the social cognition-message production relationship, our discussion can be taken as one approach to the more general question of how cognitive processes organize the production of interpersonal behavior.

Messages, Message Analysis, and Message Production

The research summarized in the introductory section indicates that there is some important relationship between impression formation processes and message production. As we noted, this research has commonly been interpreted as support for the general hypothesis that developments in social cognition are prerequisite to the production of listener-adapted messages. Social cognition is thought to play an important role in the process of listener-adaptation, since adapting messages to particular listeners requires representing the communication-relevant attributes of the listener and of the listener's perspective on the situation and potential messages. Thus, as perceivers develop their abilities to classify listeners and construct and coordinate perspectives, they should differ in their ability to produce appropriate messages.

Though this line of reasoning is plausible, it does not present a specific explanation of the role of social cognition in message production. This hypothesis simply creates an expectation that social cognition (and impression formation in particular) are related in some way to the process of message production. Obviously, knowing *that* an activity or skill is important to accomplishing a task is different from knowing exactly *how* an activity or skill contributes to task accomplishment. Thus, not surprisingly, the argument that messages are produced through a process of listener-adaptation based on perspective taking has served principally to produce expectations about the role of social cognition in communication rather than an explicit model of message production. However, that social cognition is seen as related to message production through a process of listener-adaptation creates an unfortunate focus that influences the analysis of messages and limits conceptions of the role of social cognition in message production.

In this section we criticize methods of message analysis and views of message production based on the concept of listener-adaptation and outline an alternative view of the message production process based on analysis of the message producer's communicative intentions. Our position is developed through (1) an analysis of the concept *message* from the standpoint of the message producer, (2) examination of two alternative views of *message analysis*, and (3) discussion of two alternative views of *message production*.

Messages

Because in this chapter we are interested simply in the process of message production (and not communication generally), we are concerned here only with those aspects of behavior that are designed to communicate. Consistent with this interest, we define "message" from the message producer's viewpoint. Messages are those configurations of elements or features in behavior or human manufactures that are designed to communicate.

By "designed to communicate" we mean intended to make publicly available some mental state (such as wants, beliefs, or ideas) of the message producer, or intended to accomplish some other purpose through making mental states publicly available. This is, of course, only an abstract characterization of the class of behavioral intentions that lie behind messages; any actual message will be motivated by some more specific intention or set of intentions.

Of course, in describing messages as designed to accomplish intentions, we in no way mean to imply that either intentions or the process of message design is necessarily conscious. A person may become conscious of intentions or of some aspects of the process of message design, and the fact of consciousness may produce some significant alterations in the way message production works. But our aim here is to describe the ways in which, in general, both conscious and unconscious intentions shape message production. While some theorists are uncomfortable with the notion of unconscious or implicit intention, we are not; and we take solace in the fact that many contemporary theories of language and communication (see Searle, 1969; Grice, 1976) are built on analyses of implicit or unconscious intentions.

Message Analysis

It is not at all unusual to conceptualize "message" as we have, seeing messages as ways of carrying out communicative intentions. It is less common, however, to find theorists and researchers who analyze messages in term of the way behavior is organized to accomplish intentions. Instead of functionally analyzing messages, most research on communication development classifies or analyzes messages in terms of some ad hoc set of categories or within categories reflecting some generalized dimension of development like "listener-adaptedness" (see the discussion by Clark and Delia, 1979).

The analysis of messages in terms of such analytic systems has generally proved not very profitable. Using a global conception of listener-adaptedness or perspectivism, for example, some researchers have simply assessed the ability of speakers to produce different messages for different listeners, with no attention to whether alterations in messages for different hearers are functionally related to the task at hand. For instance, Shatz and Gelman (1973) asked 4-year-old children to explain a toy to listeners of two different ages, 4 and 2 years old. Explanations offered to the older listeners differed significantly from those offered to younger listeners in a number of ways, including length of explanation, length of sentences, vocabulary, and so on. However, though it is clear that the 4-year-old explainers were producing different messages for different hearers, it is not at all clear that these alterations were functionally related to the communication task. Clark and Delia (1976) note the absence of any clear tie to communicative functions in several other message analytic schemes employed in communication development research.

The importance of basing message analysis in conceptions of communicative function can be seen in work by Alvy (1973) and Delia and Clark (1977) on the development of persuasive message production. These studies presented children with pairs of potential persuadees; children were asked how they would make the same request to each of the two hearers. As in Shatz and Gelman's study, the pairs of messages produced were analyzed for evidence of adaptation: the construction of different messages for different listeners. However, Alvy and Delia and Clark went beyond this simple indication to analyze the various strategies children employed in carrying out their task. Even among children who adapted their messages, methods of adaptation differed. The possibility of conducting such a qualitative analysis of messages is obviously based on an understanding of the communicative function of message features, the way specific features of messages are related to accomplishing the task at hand.

Although an understanding of what the message producer is attempting to accomplish through communication is central to the effective analysis of a message, researchers have continued to focus on listener-adaptation or perspectivism as the central feature of messages. Consider, for example, the message classification system used by Clark and Delia (1976), which defines general types of messages that might be produced when a child is asked to make a request of a listener. Each message type reflects one possible response to an influence situation in which the persuadee is presumed to be reluctant to grant the request. Clark and Delia identified four basic message strategies: simple request, elaborated request (in which the needs of the persuader are stressed), counterarguing (in which the objections of the persuadee are anticipated and refuted), and advantage to other (in which the advantages of compliance to the persuadee are stressed). In research on the development of persuasive message production, Clark and Delia (Clark and Delia, 1976; Delia, Kline, and Burleson, 1979) have shown that these four message types appear to be developmentally ordered: As children develop, they first produce simple requests, then elaborated requests, then counterarguments, and finally messages emphasizing advantages to the persuadee.

Clark and Delia interpret this ordering as evidence that listener sensitivity, or perspectivism, increases with age, but we no longer find this interpretation fully adequate. It is quite easy to imagine circumstances in which a simple or elaborated request would be the most "listener-adapted" strategy, given an accurate understanding of the listener's perspective. For example, consider a situation in which a parent has no substantial objection to a child having a toy but does not want to buy the toy unless the child really wants it. In this case, a child's message that focuses on his or her own wants is in fact more "listener-adapted" than a message that includes counterarguments or advantages to the parent. Clark and Delia (1976: 1010) recognized this possibility and noted that "the . . . hierarchical interpretation is not unequivocal, of course. A child capable of using a high-level strategy might purposefully revert to a lower-level one. . . . While reversion to a lower-level strategies [in the service of listener-adaptation] is a possibility, the converse is not. It is difficult to imagine that a child with limited perspective-taking abilities could construct a message based on refutation of counterarguments or advantage to the other. The usage of higher-order persuasive strategies would seem to indicate advanced levels of perspective-taking ability, although the failure to invoke higher-order persuasive strategies cannot unequivocally be interpreted as reflecting a lower level of perspective taking."

We think there is an additional consideration necessary to an interpretation of this empirical ordering: the structural character of the persuasion situation. Persuasion occurs when one person wants something from another person who is presumably unwilling to satisfy the want. Thus, the essential structure of a persuasion situation implies two people, persuader and persuadee, with competing agendas. Approached in this way, the ordering of Clark and Delia's four message strategies can be explained as a function of increasing success in reconciling the needs of persuader and persuadee in the message—from emphasizing one's own agenda to denying the validity of the persuadee's agenda to manufacturing a common agenda. Clark and Delia's message strategies represent four alternative actions that form a set of generalized options for dealing with the competing wants of persuader and persuadee. The strategies are not ways of adapting messages to listeners, nor are the strategies ordered by increasing listener-adaptedness, although variations in social perceptions are implicated in the strategic ordering.

Thus, in some research a listener-adaptation view of message production has led to message analysis that is unrelated to communicative function. In our own research and the research of others, this predominant listener-adaptation view of message production has encouraged hasty interpretation of natural developmental orderings of message strategies in terms of simple perspectivism and has discouraged other interpretations.

Message Production

The focus on listener-adaptation and perspective taking leads all too easily to an overly simplified conception of the process of message production—namely, a model in which message design is seen as the shaping of some preexisting message content or the selection among alternative strategies to fit the requirements of a specific communication situation. Much of the existing research and theorizing on the development of listener-adapted communication can be seen as quite consistent with this simple model, exploring different aspects of the "adaptation process": the ability to assess communication-relevant characteristics of the listener (Delia and Clark, 1977), the ability to edit or select appropriate message contents (Flavell et al., 1968), the ability to appraise the adequacy of one's own message choices (Flavell, 1981), the ability to adjust the expression of message contents to fit listener needs and attributes (Shatz and Gelman, 1973; Delia and O'Keefe, 1979), and the ability to apply general knowledge concerning message formulation in a specific case (Atlas, 1979; Ammon, 1981).

This way of thinking of message production is clearly oversimplified. It is simply not plausible that messages begin as packages of potential arguments or contents; obviously, messages begin as purposes (or, in our terms, communicative intentions). Message contents are generated in relation to purposes, both the specific purposes or intentions that grow out of the task at hand and the generalized tacit purposes that might accompany any act of communication (such as intelligibility, efficiency, and face protection). One essential step in the process of message production must involve shaping a message to satisfy simultaneously the various constraints placed on the message by its multiple purposes or functions. Moreover, a person may have a general idea about what kind of message ought to be produced in a given situation but be unable to general a message of that type, which suggests that at some point in the message production process a general message strategy is created prior to the actual construction of a message to be expressed. It makes no sense to suppose that messages are adapted to listeners only *after* these processes have produced a potential message or that all these different processes are aspects of a process of listener-adaptation based on perspective taking.

The conception of message production as involving only a set of processes for adapting messages to particular recipients is not just oversimplified, but also limits the role social cognition might be seen to play in the production of messages. When attention is focused on the process of selecting among potential strategies and adjusting preexisting messages, researchers are led to think of social cognition only as supplying bases for selection and adjustment. In fact, social cognitive processes might be involved at many different stages in the process of producing a message; in particular, representations of listeners and social situations might generate the communicative intentions out of which messages originate or the semantic contents to be given expression.

There are alternatives to a view of message production as listener-adaptation, as indirectly suggested by the work of Brown and Levinson (1978) on politeness. Brown and Levinson argue that many acts of communication are intrinsically face-threatening (that is, impose on or imply disagreement with another person). At the same time, one general goal of message design is efficiency: the desire to be clear or intelligible. Brown and Levinson argue that the various techniques a culture generates for dealing with face-threatening situations politely are all methods for reconciling the inconsistent goals of communicating efficiently and preserving face.

This analysis of politeness can be taken as a model of the general analysis of message design. Messages can be seen as the product of multiple communicative intentions and message design as the product of reconciling multiple objectives in performance. Thus, message production can be seen as a multistage process in which (1) the objectives (or intentions) behind a message are generated; (2) if necessary, competing or inconsistent objectives are edited or reconciled through the selection of a message strategy; (3) message contents are selected to actualize the strategy, creating a potential message (which may, at this point, be monitored and edited); and (4) the message is produced as verbal and nonverbal behavior. This model suggests that the primary processes in message design are the generation and reconciliation of message objectives, not taking the listener's perspective on potential messages and adjusting them.

Rejecting a view of message production as primarily a process of listener-adaptation does not involve rejecting the claim that at least some potential messages are monitored and censored, edited, or adjusted prior to actual production. Everyone's experience includes many instances in which recognition of how a potential message would be heard by a listener leads to second thoughts and adjustments of the message. It is our claim that such adjustments or adaptations play a secondary role in message production, altering potential messages that are already structured by communicative intentions and organized by integrative plans. Moreover, we would argue that most communications are produced without extensive monitoring and editing. We find considerable merit in Langer's (1978) argument that interactants can produce and interpret behavior with minimal mindfulness.

If message "adaptation" is seen as less important in message production than traditionally has been supposed, does this imply that social cognition also plays a secondary role? Theorists have typically argued that impression formation and perspective-taking are important in message production because these processes supply bases for adaptation. But the view of message production *as* listener-adaptation conflates two very different ways knowledge of the listener may play a role in the design of a message: (1) in supplying bases for monitoring and altering a potential message, and (2) in generating some or all of the intentions that motivate and shape potential messages. In the next section we argue that impression formation processes play a central role in shaping the sets of communicative intentions that, in turn, result in messages.

Impression Formation Processes and Message Production

The body of research summarized in the introductory section now can be seen as requiring further interpretation. Each of the studies summarized testifies to the utility of measures of construct system properties for predicting the use of message strategies. Message strategies purportedly reflect variations in person-centeredness or listener-adaptation. But we have argued, on the one hand, that the interpretation of construct system measures has been based on too structural a conception of impression formation processes and, on the other hand, that a view of message features as reflecting listener-adaptedness is based on too limited a view of message production.

The task of interpreting these results is complicated by the fact that most of the results take the form of correlations among measures of construct system properties and measures of message features. Such results are intrinsically ambiguous; they can be produced by a variety of spurious and genuine relationships between variables. However, it is possible at this point to rule out two general classes of explanations: (1) those asserting that the measures used in this research are invalid, so the correlations do not in fact reflect any relationship between social cognition and communication, and (2) those granting the validity of the measures used but arguing that the correlation is spurious.

Some critics have suggested, in effect, that the measures used in this research might not be valid measures of construct system characteristics or the quality of message strategies (see Becker and Hewes, 1978; Powers et al., 1979; Leitner et al., 1975). The commonest version of this criticism begins with the observation that construct differentiation scores are generally produced by counting the number of constructs used in describing people. "Describing" is, of course, a verbal communication task, so the putative correlation between construct differentiation and message characteristics might, in fact, reflect nothing more than the effects of general verbal ability or fluency, motivation, or some such factor on two similar verbal communication tasks.

As an explanation of correlations between construct differentiation and the *number* of message units produced, this argument has some superficial plausibility, but it cannot account for results involving alternative construct elicitation procedures (see Kline, 1981a, 1981b; Church and Applegate, 1981), qualitative analyses of constructs produced (Burleson, 1979, Applegate and Delia, 1980; Borden, 1981), or qualitative analyses of message strategies and rationales (Clark and Delia, 1977; Delia et al., 1979; B. O'Keefe and Delia, 1979; Applegate and Delia 1980; Church and Applegate, 1981; Borden, 1981; Burleson, 1981a, 1981b; Kline, 1981a, 1981b; Applegate and Wheeler, 1981). Beyond this, however, the truth of this claim depends on assuming that measures based on the Role Category Questionnaire are not really measures of interpersonal construct system properties, but rather measure something else. As we noted earlier, there is substantial evidence that the Role Category Questionnaire produces reliable and valid measures of interpersonal construct system properties that are related to a range of theoretically coherent cognitive characteristics and behavioral choices. (For a summary of relevant material, see D. O'Keefe and Sypher, 1981.)

A second way of "explaining" these results grants the validity of the measures involved but suggests that the observed correlations are spurious, resulting from the simultaneous influence of some third process on both the construct and message variables. For example, Delia (1980) has discussed the possibility that a generalized tendency toward psychological elaboration or a value orientation that puts a high priority on interpersonal relationships might lead to the development of a differentiated and abstract system of constructs and to the production of messages displaying sensitivity to listener needs.

There are several reasons for rejecting this sort of account, at least provisionally. First, the relationship between interpersonal construct system properties and message production is developmental: As the construct system develops toward differentiation and abstractness, message strategies change. (This claim is supported by results from both cross-sectional and longitudinal developmental studies, as we have noted earlier; see Delia, Kline, and Burleson, 1979; Delia, Burleson, and

Kline, 1979; Burleson, 1981a.) Thus, if some third factor produces both construct system developments and message developments, it must also alter systematically with age. This criterion rules out many potential underlying causes, such as environmental factors (for example, social class, home life), personality traits (such as introversion-extroversion), and value priorities (such as valuing interpersonal relationships above material gains). At the same time, construct system and message variables are significantly correlated within age groups and across age groups with age partialled out, so age or maturation alone is unlikely to account for the observed relationship (see Delia, Kline, and Burleson, 1979; Burleson, 1981a). Second, some research suggests that interpersonal constructs are directly implicated in message production. For instance, Delia and Clark (1977) found that identification of communication-relevant listener characteristics was a necessary condition for listener-adaptation. Finally, many plausible underlying causal factors (such as rhetorical sensitivity, interpersonal value orientation, empathic motivation, and Machiavellianism) have been found to show very little common variance with our measures of construct system and message properties (see Borden, 1979, 1981; Burleson, 1981b; Kline, 1981a).

Now if the various measures employed in this research are valid and the correlations are not spurious, what remains are two general hypotheses:

> *Hypothesis 1:* Variations in messages cause or generate variations in construct system characteristics.

> *Hypothesis 2:* Variations in construct system characteristics generate or cause variations in messages.

At this point, we suspect both these hypotheses may be true. Construct system development could lead to the production of more complex social behavior, which in turn elicits more complex responses from others. This would produce a more complex social world that, finally, requires an even more elaborated interpersonal construct system to interpret and predict behavior and psychological experience. However, research in this area has proceeded on the simple assumption that construct system properties must influence message production, and not vice versa. Thus, the only studies that bear directly on this issue are investigations employing Alvy's multiple situation communication task (Delia and Clark, 1977; Delia, Burleson, and Kline, 1979). Although these studies directly support the claim that learning to identify listener characteristics precedes and is a requirement for production of certain message characteristics, they (1) reflect performance in only one kind of communication task, and (2) directly demonstrate the role of specific impressions of listeners, but not general properties of construct systems, in message production.

Hence, the last task we take up in this chapter is constructing a more specific conception of the relationship between impression formation processes and message production. Because what evidence we have suggests that (whether or not message production also influences construct development) interpersonal constructs play some role in generating messages, we propose a specific mechanism through which construct system characteristics express themselves in behavior. Our view of the relationship between interpersonal construct system characteristics and message characteristics is developed through (1) addressing the question of what, specifically, our message analysis systems are detecting, and (2) discussing the role of construct system characteristics in producing those specific message features. Our essential claim is this: Increasing differentiation and abstractness in the interpersonal construct system lead to more complex configurations of interpersonal objectives, which in turn lead to the production of messages that address multiple tasks simultaneously.

What message features are being detected in constructivist coding systems? Before answering this question, we want to bring two general facts about messages into focus. First, people produce messages in the course of situated activities. Plainly, messages are produced in the service of the specific aims people have in the context of these activities. A message is a means to accomplish a person's aims in some particular situation; message design reflects the fact that messages are ways to accomplish specific aims in specific situations. In discussing the situated character of messages, most theorists are led to focus on the contextual character of *meanings*; but we want to emphasize the situation-specific character of the *jobs* messages are meant to do.

Second, the jobs messages are meant to do differ in complexity. There are two ways in which the task a message addresses can be made more complex. Task complexity increases when people recognize obstacles to achieving their aims. For example, making a request is a more complex task when the target person is likely to refuse the request than when the target is likely to comply. Task complexity also increases when the same message must serve multiple aims and especially when the message must serve competing aims. For example, the task of correcting a child's bad behavior is complicated by a desire simultaneously to preserve face or protect feelings.

Seen in this context, several features of the methods we have used to elicit and analyze messages come into focus: (1) Subjects are asked to respond to potentially complex communication situations; (2) the qualitative message analysis systems reflect the degree to which particular kinds of task complexity are recognized and reconciled; and (3) the quantitative message scores subjects are assigned also reflect the perception of task complexity. Each of these features deserves further elaboration.

In these studies, subjects are put in potentially complex communication situations. Subjects have been asked to make unusual requests, requests to strangers (who presumably would be under little obligation to comply), or large requests (see Clark and Delia, 1976; Delia and Clark, 1977; Delia, Kline, and Burleson, 1979; B. O'Keefe and Delia, 1979; Applegate and Wheeler, 1981). Parents have been asked how they would deal with a child who behaved badly (Applegate and Delia, 1980); college students and managers have been asked what they would say to a group member who fails to do his or her share of the group's work or who is reporting late to work (Kline, 1981a, 1981b; Husband, 1981); mothers, children, and college students have been asked what they would say in situations involving hurt feelings and interpersonal conflict (Applegate and Delia, 1980; Burleson, 1981a, 1981b; Husband, 1981). As a general rule, the hypothetical situations we have used encourage subjects to have multiple aims and to recognize obstacles to aims.

Our coding systems reflect the degree to which subjects recognize and reconcile the demands of complex communication situations. When people face complex message tasks, they have three basic techniques available for dealing with the conflicts between aims and obstacles or conflicts between competing aims. These are selection, temporal or behavioral separation of expression, and integration.

Selection. If two aims come into conflict, the conflict can be resolved by selecting (giving priority and expression to) one and ignoring the other. Consider the case of a person who wants something that would involve some degree of imposition on someone else. Simply to make the request of the target person despite the imposition is a result of giving priority to one's own wants; a decision not to make the request results from giving priority to the desire not to impose. Similarly, if an aim comes into conflict with a perceived obstacle, the conflict can be resolved by giving priority to the aim or to the problem. Consider the case of a child who wants something from a strange adult. The child might make the request (although anticipating rejection), thus giving priority to expressing the aim. Alternatively, the child might decide not to make the request, thus giving priority to the obstacle.

Temporal or Behavioral Separation. When multiple aims compete or when aims encounter obstacles, the conflict can be resolved through addressing elements in temporally or behaviorally separated aspects of a message display. Making a request but apologizing for the imposition separates expression of competing aims in temporally sequenced components of a message. Both making the request and dealing with the imposition are addressed—first one and then the other. Giving direct, unambiguously, negative criticism verbally while maintaining a friendly demeanor addresses multiple objectives simultaneously but separates their expression into different components of a message display (verbal and nonverbal).

Integration. Messages can be designed to accomplish multiple aims simultaneously or simultaneously to advance aims and remove obstacles. One method of integration is compromise, reflected in a tradeoff between two message aims or between aim and obstacle. The various ways requests can be done "off record" (Brown and Levinson, 1978; see also the set of conversational influence strategies analyzed by Jacobs and Jackson, forthcoming) represent a set of possible compromises between the aims of clear communication and avoidance of face threat. A second method of integration is synthesis, the creation of a message strategy that accomplishes both aims or that deals with aims and obstacles equally and simultaneously in the same message. A good example of such a synthetic strategy is a persuader's supporting some request by emphasizing advantages to the other person, a strategy that simultaneously advances one's own needs and attempts to remove obstacles to consent.

Examination of various constructivist message analysis systems shows that the essential features of messages that these coding systems detect are (1) the recognition of obstacles and possession of multiple aims and (2) the reconciliation of primary aims with perceived obstacles and with subsidiary aims.

Consider, as an example, Applegate's investigations of the use of "person-centered" message strategies among mothers and their children, day-care teachers, college students, and teacher trainees (Applegate, 1978; see also Applegate and Delia, 1980; Applegate, 1980a, 1980b). In one study, he asked mothers to respond to seven hypothetical communication tasks. The seven tasks included four "regulative" situations, in which mothers were asked to modify the behavior of their child in some way, and three "interpersonal" situations, in which conflicts in feelings figured prominently. The message analysis system used to categorize responses to the regulative situations was a set of nine hierarchically ordered categories. Both the categories in this system and their hierarchic order can be seen as reflecting variations in attempts to accomplish multiple aims in messages. The first three categories (physical punishment, commands, and rule giving) all involved messages produced with a single aim, the primary aim of the subject's assigned task: to modify the child's behavior. The next three categories involved messages that addressed the obstacle of gaining the child's compliance (offering reasons for rules, discussing consequences of noncompliance, and discussing general principles behind appropriate behavior). The final three categories involved messages in which the mother simultaneously corrected the behavior, offered reasons for compliance, and encouraged the child to be empathic in his or her social conduct (describing feelings, helping the child to make an empathic response through analogy, leading the child to reason through the situation, and so on). Mothers were also asked to provide justifications for their strategies; though Applegate describes his coding categories for strategy justification in terms of adaptation to the child's perspective, it is plain from the category description that what adaptation *means* is recognition and reconciliation of obstacles and subsidiary intentions with primary aims (see Applegate and Delia, 1980; Applegate, 1980b).

Messages produced in response to the three interpersonal situations in Applegate's study of mothers' communicative strategies were classified using a second coding system that essentially reflected the degree to which a mother increasingly dealt with multiple dimensions of interpersonal conflicts, including hurt feelings, the reasons for and consequences of hurt feelings, and the child's ability to understand and empathize in conflict situations (see Applegate and Delia, 1980). Thus, the lowest-level strategies deal with the immediate situation without regard to the child's need for affirmation or psychological support; categories in the intermediate range index strategies dealing with the immediate situation in ways that address the child's need for support; strategies coded at the highest levels deal with the immediate situation, provide psychological support, and help the child to reason through the situation and to learn from it.

Most constructivist coding systems are based on a hierarchic ordering of message structures in terms of the degree to which multiple dimensions (obstacles and aims) of complex communication situations are recognized and reconciled in messages. We have discussed coding systems used by Clark and Delia (1976) and Applegate (1978, 1980a, 1980b; Applegate and Delia, 1980). Most of the coding schemes used in our research have been built off these systems. Many investigations employ one or more of these systems with little or no modification (see, for example, Clark and Delia, 1977; Borden, 1979; Church and Applegate, 1981). Husband's (1981) research on managerial communication developed a straightforward elaboration of Applegate's systems for regulative and interpersonal communication adapted to the context of organizational leadership. Burleson's (1981a, 1981b, forthcoming) research on comforting communication employs a modification of Applegate's system for analyzing interpersonal communication situations that reflects the same increasing complexity of jobs the message accomplishes. Delia, Kline, and Burleson (1979) elaborated Clark and Delia's (1976) system for ordering persuasive strategies while preserving the basic structural distinctions it makes; other studies have employed the Delia et al. version of Clark and Delia's system for coding persuasive strategies (for example, Burke, 1979; Applegate and Wheeler, 1981).

The only coding systems employed in the research we have discussed that are not directly derivative from Applegate's and Clark and Delia's systems are Kline's (1981b, 1982) two systems for the analysis of face support in persuasive situations, although even her systems incorporate some of the distinctions made in Applegate's system for coding regulative communication. What is striking about Kline's systems, given the present analysis, is the extent to which they directly order strategies to reflect accomplishment of multiple aims.

Kline begins with the assumption that, because of the preference for face support, individual differences in the provision of face support will be most evident when the communication task is difficult. Hence, she selected situations in which the speaker had some legitimate basis for reprimanding the message recipient for improper or inadequate performance. In such a situation, our culture sanctions the use of direct face threat. If face support is to be provided, it will enter as a subsidiary objective introduced by the speaker, for the dominant intention built into the structure of the situation concerns the need to gain compliance. Working off Brown and Levinson's (1978) analysis of the two basic face needs (the needs for a positive identity and to be free of imposition), Kline constructed two systems for coding the degree of support provided the face of the message recipient. One system, which indexed evaluative face support, is ordered from threats, commands, and directives (which seek compliance directly, without regard to the recipient's face needs), through the identification of the consequences of the inappropriate action or of possible ways of alleviating its causes as ways of gaining compliance while implicitly affirming the identity of the message recipient as a person who would not willfully act to create problems (addressing obstacles and subsidiary aims), to seeking compliance by reasoning through the situation and providing overt and direct support to the other's potentially threatened identity (integrating the accomplishment of multiple tasks in the message). A second system, which we need not detail here, orders strategies similarly as they are relevant to the multiple aims of gaining compliance while recognizing the message recipient's need for behavioral freedom or autonomy of action. Kline's systems thus directly recognize the relationship between dominant intentions and tacit subsidiary intentions in the organization of messages.

So far we have focused on the qualitative coding systems employed in constructivist research. Many of these studies also report a quantitative message analysis based on the number of message units (arguments or appeals) a subject produces. Multiple aims and perceived obstacles can be addressed in a message either through separate accomplishment of each aim or through simultaneous accomplishment of multiple aims. Similarly, obstacles can be addressed in separate message units or in the course of doing something else. Thus, both quantitative and qualitative analysis of messages can be seen to reflect the complexity of the job a person wants a message to do (that is, the number of subsidiary aims and perceived obstacles to be addressed). Quantitative analysis of the number of strategies produced are primarily sensitive to the number of objectives addressed in separate message units; qualitative message analyses are primarily sensitive to the use of integrated strategies for addressing multiple objectives simultaneously. This observation leads us to our final question.

What role do construct system differentiation and abstractness play in message production? Obviously, we believe that construct differentiation and abstractness influence the number of subsidiary aims and obstacles a person will address in a message. However, it is not clear whether this is because (1) increases in differentiation and abstractness increase the number of aims a person has and the number of obstacles recognized, (2) increases in differentiation and abstractness influence the priority people give to obstacles and subsidiary aims, or (3) increases in differentiation and abstractness influence the availability of strategies for addressing obstacles and subsidiary aims.

In some circumstances, failures to address obstacles or subsidiary aims appear to be due to a lack of available strategies. For example, Delia and Clark (1977) report that many children recognized obstacles in a complex persuasion task but were nonetheless unable to produce messages addressing the perceived obstacles. This result led Delia and Clark to argue that recognition of situational demands is insufficient for producing a message to deal with those demands. Children must also acquire a repertoire of strategies for, in our terms, addressing and integrating competing situational demands.

In other circumstances, failures to address obstacles or subsidiary aims appear to be due to not having relevant subsidiary aims or not giving them priority. In one of her studies, Kline (1982) made the subsidiary aim of face protection explicit for half her subjects by telling them to protect the feelings and face of the message recipient while reprimanding him and seeking behavioral change. The other half of the subjects were only told to address the erring individual's inappropriate behavior. Differences in construct differentiation and abstractness led to differences in the use of face-saving strategies only when face saving was not mentioned as an explicit aim in the instructions. When subjects were told to accomplish their objective while preserving face, differences in messages produced by those high and low in construct differentiation were sharply attenuated.

Thus, there is evidence suggesting that the differences in message production we have observed are due both to the kinds of intentions people have and the availability of strategies for addressing multiple intentions and obstacles. Given this observation, the simplest plausible models of the relation of construct system characteristic to message production suggest that construct system differentiation and abstractness lead to a person consistently having multiple intentions toward others and recognizing obstacles posed by the wants, abilities, and beliefs of the other; as a result, the person consistently faces complex communication tasks, which in turn leads the person to develop a repertoire of strategies (or leads to increased availability of strategies). So the question becomes, why do construct system characteristics lead people to address more complex communication tasks (that is, to have multiple objectives and recognize obstacles)?

We can imagine two different specific mechanisms that might connect construct system characteristics to the kinds of configurations of intentions and perceived obstacles that motivate complex message design. These two mechanisms are suggested by two different analyses of the process that produces construct differentiation scores on the Role Category Questionnaire (our primary measure of construct system characteristics).

Our reanalysis of the process of impression formation suggests that scores on the Role Category Questionnaire (RCQ) ought not to be interpreted as straightforwardly reflecting the number of constructs a person has. Seeing the RCQ as "sampling" construct systems is consistent with a view of impression formation as an essentially assimilatory process in which a general impression is created by an implicit personality theory. But a "sampling" interpretation of the RCQ is inconsistent with a view of impression formation as a process of accommodation in which knowledge of others need not exist as an organized general impression and in which knowledge of others is organized and reorganized by schemas as information is integrated and as the perceiver's aims and plans shift. Available research suggests that construct differentiation on the RCQ might be interpreted within this alternative view of impression formation in two rather different ways.

RCQ construct differentiation might be a measure of abstract differentiation. The RCQ asks subjects to describe another person in abstract terms: in terms of personality traits, habits, beliefs, values, and so on. Subjects are generally asked to avoid physical description. In general, physical descriptions are not scored even when the subject produces them. Thus, the instructions encourage abstract, dispositional description, and the scoring rules prevent many types of concrete descriptions from contributing to differentiation scores. The RCQ can therefore be seen as measuring abstract differentiation, reflecting primarily the number of *dispositional* constructs available for interpreting people's behavior.

There is some evidence for this interpretation. Several assessments of construct abstractness have used a modified version of the Role Repertory Test (Kelly, 1955) to elicit constructs (for example, Applegate, 1978; Borden, 1979; Kline, 1982). In some instances, probe questions have been used to determine clearly the character of the discrimination the subject is making. These elicited constructs are then coded within a system ordering them from concrete, highly behavioral, and context-bound to abstract, psychological, and dispositional. The scores given to the individual constructs are then summed. Such scorings that conflate abstractness and differentiation are positively correlated with construct differentiation scored from the RCQ, although the magnitude of the correlation is not consistent across studies. This and the similar predictive range of the two construct system properties suggest that the RCQ may tap primarily abstract dispositional differentiation.

Hence, one potential explanation of the relationship between construct system characteristics and message production focuses on the role dispositional constructs might play in generating intentions and recognizing obstacles. Construing dispositions is different from construing physical characteristics or social roles. As Jones and Davis (1965) have observed, the inference of dispositions from behavior rests on and is related to judgments of intention and ability. Dispositional constructs might well be lower-order schemas that organize inferences about intentions and abilities and direct attention toward motivational and related psychological states of other people.

On this account, behavioral information is processed by, among other things, the various dispositional schemata a person has available. This would automatically entail detailed inferences about the configuration of intentions, needs, abilities, and other immediate psychological states of the other and would, in turn, make the internal states of the other a real and important element of the perceiver's phenomenal field. These aspects of the phenomenal field (or perceived situation) would figure in a person's plans just like any other aspect of the situation.

Differences in the number of dispositional constructs people have would lead to differences in the extensiveness or elaboration of inferences about immediate psychological states of targets and thus to differences in the prominence or salience of states of the target in the phenomenal field. As a result, the greater the number of dispositional constructs a person has, the more likely the person will address obstacles posed by the internal states of the target and the more likely the person will have intentions directed toward internal states of the other.

The preceding view of the relation of RCQ construct differentiation to message production rests on an interpretation of RCQ scores as measuring abstract (dispositional) differentiation. But there is a second, very different, interpretation available. For the sake of simplicity, let us suppose that all perceivers have the same numbers and types of constructs, but perceivers differ in the degree to which their beliefs about others are organized into stable general impressions by higher-order schemas. Asking subjects to produce general impressions would lead to just the kind of differences in impressions we have observed in the RCQ. Differences in the degree of organization among beliefs would lead to differences in retrieval of beliefs about the target. Subjects with more extensively organized impressions would produce greater numbers of specific beliefs about others and would receive higher differentiation scores; subjects with disorganized impressions (sets of beliefs) would find retrieving beliefs more difficult and would produce sparser impressions and receive lower differentiation scores. Even assuming (as we usually do) that perceivers differ in the number and quality of their constructs, performance on the RCQ might be primarily a function of the degree of organization among a person's beliefs and unrelated to actual numbers of constructs.

There is evidence for this interpretation too. The more extensively knowledge of the other is schematized as a general impression, the more stable and context-independent evaluations and impressions should be, since thinking about the person would automatically retrieve cross-contextual information as well as information generated in or relevant to the immediate context. In fact, research summarized earlier does indicate that construct differentiation is related to stability of impressions and evaluations.

Moreover, persons who lack (to some extent) target-specific schemas for organizing their beliefs should be led to rely more on simple general principles, like evaluative consistency principles, to direct their search for beliefs and to organize their behavior toward others. D. O'Keefe (1980) summarizes research showing that construct differentiation is negatively related to reliance on evaluative consistency in selecting behavioral intentions toward others and to the evaluative consistency of beliefs reported about others.

Differences in the ability to retrieve beliefs about others (due to differences in impression organization) would obviously lead fairly directly to (1) differences in the elaboration of situated concepts of the target and (2) differences in the ability to retrieve information about the target which is relevant to the communicator's purpose. This would lead, in turn, to differences in the degree to which the needs, wants, beliefs, and characteristics of the target become objects of dominant or subsidiary intentions and are perceived as obstacles to a perceiver's intentions.

At present, interpretations of RCQ differentiation scores either as measuring abstract differentiation or impression organization seem equally plausible. Both interpretations are supported by some (but not extensive or unambiguous) evidence. Both interpretations suggest that RCQ differentiation scores are produced by the operational features of schemas, rather than sheer numbers of constructs a person has. And both interpretations suggest that the relation of construct system characteristics and message production is attributable to the way differences in the elaboration of situated perceptions of the internal states of others, which in turn leads to differences in the number of intentions and obstacles communicators design their messages to address.

Conclusion

Our primary aim in this chapter has been to understand the observed relationship between "interpersonal construct system" characteristics and message characteristics. In pursuit of this aim, we have developed an analysis of the relationship between impression formation processes and message production that has wider implications for the analysis of interpersonal behavior and the role of cognitive processes in organizing behavior.

We have argued that constructivist message analysis systems do not assess listener-adaptation or perspectivism, but instead order messages in terms of the complexity of the job a message is designed to do (the number of subsidiary intentions and obstacles addressed). This argument implies that multifunctionality is a real and important quality of messages; messages are multifunctional because they are designed to be multifunctional.

The idea that messages are multifunctional is not foreign to communication theory. For example, Watzlawick et al. (1967) made the distinction between content and relationship levels of communication a central element in their analysis of interpersonal behavior. However, communication researchers have generally chosen to focus on single dimensions of behavior and have tended to view multifunctionality (complexity of the message task) as an obstacle to their analysis rather than an important property of behavior. For example, most coding systems used to classify interpersonal behavior are built on the assumption that a message serves (or can be classified in terms of) a single dominant function—in other words, that a message can be assigned to one and only one functional category.

However, our analysis suggests that complexity (organization of behavior to accomplish multiple aims and address obstacles) is itself an important dimension of behavior. Differences in message complexity display themselves across a wide range of situations in which the dominant intention of the communicator may be persuasion, regulation, or dealing with interpersonal conflict. Initial research suggests that differences in message complexity can be found in conversational interaction as well as responses to hypothetical communication tasks (Applegate, 1980b; Husband, 1981; Applegate and Wheeler, 1981). Moreover, our analysis suggests that the method (or strategy) by which behavior is organized to accomplish complex tasks is as important as the fact that a complex task is addressed.

Such a conception allows one to begin to see how individual differences in impression formation processes function as one underlying cause of message complexity. In contrast to previous efforts to explain the role of social cognition in interpersonal behavior, we have offered a specific analysis focusing on the exploitation of knowledge of the other in the construction of interpersonal plans and the consequences of interpersonal plans for produced messages. While advances have been made in efforts to explain the role of cognition in organizing behavior generally (see, for example, Schank and Abelson, 1977), theorists have been frustrated in their efforts to explain the role played by knowledge of persons in message production. We believe the source of their frustration has been an inadequate conception of the process through which person knowledge is exploited in the production of interpersonal behavior (including message production) and an inadequate conception of the features of behavior that person knowledge influences or generates.

We thus believe that the orientation outlined in this chapter can provide the beginning point for a general understanding of the role of social cognition in behavioral production with its break from the traditional treatment of behavior as simple, atomistic units (whether those units are defined as learned reactions to particular stimulus patterns or as acts generated by single intentions). Our analysis has led us to a framework in which *behavioral complexity* can be made a central object of investigation through attention to the configurations of multiple and competing intentions and perceived obstacles the behavior addresses. We believe that some behavior does more work than other behavior, and that this difference should be seen as a central theoretical problem for general theories of interpersonal behavior. We hope through our empirical work to make a contribution to advancing understanding of two critical aspects of this problem: (1) how social cognitive schemas produce the intentions and the recognition of obstacles that generate behavior of varying degrees of complexity and (2) the nature and role of behavioral strategies that organize the multiple and competing plans and perceived obstacles into a coherent behavioral configuration.

References

Alvy, K. T. The development of listener adapted communication in grade-school children from different social-class backgrounds. *Genetic Psychology Monographs*, 1973, *87*, 33-104.

Ammon, P. Communication skills and communicative competence: A neo-Piagetian process-structural view. In W. P. Dickson (Ed.), *Children's oral communication skills*. New York: Academic Press, 1981.

Applegate, J. L. *Four investigations of the relationship between social cognitive development and person-centered regulative and interpersonal communication.* Unpublished doctoral dissertation, University of Illinois at Urbana-Champaign, 1978.

Applegate, J. L. Adaptive communication in educational contexts: A study of teachers' communicative strategies. *Communication Education*, 1980, *29*, 158-170. (a)

Applegate, J. L. Person- and position-centered teacher communication in a day care center. In N. K. Denzin (Ed.), *Studies in symbolic interaction* (Vol. 3). Greenwich, CT: JAI Press, 1980. (b)

Applegate, J. L. *Construct system development and identity-management skills in persuasive contexts.* Presented at the annual meeting of the Western Speech Communication Association, Denver, 1982.

Applegate, J. L., and Delia, J. G. Person-centered speech, psychological development, and the contexts of language usage. In R. St. Clair and H. Giles (eds.), *The social and psychological contexts of language*. Hillsdale, NJ: Erlbaum, 1980.

Applegate, J. L., and Wheeler, J. *The impact of construct system development and persuasive strategy development on face-to-face persuasive interaction.* Presented at the annual meeting of the Central States Speech Association, Chicago, 1981.

Asch, S. E. Forming impressions of personality. *Journal of Abnormal and Social Psychology,* 1946, *41,* 258-290.

Asch, S. E. *Social psychology.* Englewood Cliffs, NJ: Prentice-Hall, 1952.

Asher, S. R. Referential communication. In G. J. Whitehurst and B. Z. Zimmerman (Eds.), *The functions of language and cognition.* New York: Academic Press, 1979.

Atlas, M. A. *Addressing an audience: a study of expert-novice differences in writing.* Technical Report No. 3. Pittsburgh: Carnegie-Mellon University, 1979.

Becker, S. L., and Hewes, D. E. *The potentials and limitations of constructivism for the study of communication.* Presented at the annual meeting of the Speech Communication Association, Minneapolis, 1978.

Biskin, D. S., and Crano, W. Structural organization of impressions derived from inconsistent information: A developmental study. *Genetic Psychology,* 1977, *95,* 331-348.

Blumer, H. *Symbolic interactionism: Perspective and method.* Englewood Cliffs, NJ: Prentice-Hall, 1969.

Borden, A. W. *An investigation of the relationships among indices of social cognition, motivation, and communicative performance.* Unpublished doctoral disertation, University of Illinois at Urbana – Champaign, 1979.

Borden, A. W. *An investigation of the relationships among social-cognitive indices, interpersonal values, and interpersonal communicative accuracy.* Presented at the annual meeting of the International Communication Association, Minneapolis, 1981.

Brown, P., and Levinson, S. Universals in language usage: Politeness phenomena. In E. N. Goody (Ed.), *Questions and politeness.* Cambridge: Cambridge University Press, 1978.

Bruner, J. S., and Tagiuri, R. The perception of people. In G. Lindzey (Ed.), *Handbook of social psychology* (Vol. 2). Reading, MA: Addison-Wesley, 1954.

Burke, J. A. *The relationship of interpersonal cognitive development to the adaptation of persuasive strategies in adults.* Presented at the annual meeting of the Central States Speech Association, St. Louis, 1979.

Burke, J. A., and Clark, R. A. An assessment of methodological options for investigating the development of persuasive skills across childhood. *Central States Speech Journal,* forthcoming.

Burleson, B. R. The development of comfort-intending communication skills in childhood and adolescence. *Child Development,* forthcoming.

Burleson, B. R. *The influence of age, construct system developments, and affective perspective-taking on the development of comforting message strategies: A hierarchical regression analysis.* Presented at the annual meeting of the International Communication Association, Minneapolis, 1981. (a)

Burleson, B. R. *The influence of social cognition and empathic motivation on adults' comfort-intended message strategies.* Presented at the annual meeting of the Speech Communication Association, Anaheim, California, 1981. (b)

Church, S. M., and Applegate, J. G. *Construct system development and person-centered communication in a police bureaucracy.* Presented at the annual meeting of the International Communication Association, Minneapolis, 1981.

Clark, R. A., and Delia, J. G. The development of functional persuasive skills in childhood and early adolescence. *Child Development,* 1976, *47,* 1008-1014.

Clark, R. A., and Delia, J. G. Cognitive complexity, social perspective-taking, and functional persuasive skills in second- to ninth-grade children. *Human Communication Research,* 1977, *3,* 128-134.

Clark, R. A., and Delia, J. G. Topoi and rhetorical competence. *Quarterly Journal of Speech,* 1979, *65,* 187-206.

Crockett, W. H. Cognitive complexity and impression formation. In B. A. Maher (Ed.), *Progress in experimental personality research* (Vol.2). New York: Academic Press, 1965.

Crockett, W. H. *Impressions and attributions: Nature, organization, and implications for action.* Presented at the annual meeting of the American Psychological Association, Washington, D. C., 1977.

Crockett, W. H. The organization corollary. In J. C. Mancuso and J. R. Adams-Webber (Eds.), *Systems of personal constructs.* New York: Praeger, forthcoming.

Crockett, W. H., Press, A. N. Delia, J. G., and Kenny, C. T. *Structural analysis of the organization of written impression.* Unpublished manuscript, University of Kansas, 1974.

Cronbach, L. J. Processes affecting scores on "understanding of others" and "assumed similarity." *Psychological Bulletin,* 1955, *52,* 177-193.

Delia, J. G. Change of meaning processes in impression formation. *Communication Monographs,* 1976, *43,* 142-157.

Delia, J. G. *Cognitive structure and message structure: Recent constructivist research.* Presented at the annual meeting of the Speech Communication Association, New York, 1980.

Delia, J. G., Burleson, B. R., and Kline, S. L. *The development of interpersonal cognition and communicative abilities: A longitudinal analysis.* Presented at the annual meeting of the Central States Speech Association, St. Louis, 1979.

Delia, J. G., Burleson, B. R., and Kline, S. L. The organization of naturally formed impressions in childhood and adolescence. *Journal of Genetic Psychology,* forthcoming.

Delia, J. G., and Clark, R. A. Cognitive complexity, social perception, and the development of listener-adapted communication in six-, eight-, ten-, and twelve-year-old boys. *Communication Monographs,* 1977, *44,* 326-345.

Delia, J. G., Clark, R. A., and Switzer, D. E. Cognitive complexity and impression formation in informal social interaction. *Speech Monographs,* 1974, *41,* 299-308.

Delia, J. G., Crockett, W. H., Press, A. N., and O'Keefe, D. J. The dependency of interpersonal evaluations on context-relevant beliefs about the other. *Speech Monographs,* 1975, *42,* 10-19.

Delia, J. G., Kline, S. L., and Burleson, B. R. The development of persuasive communication strategies in kindergartners through twelfth-graders. *Communication Monographs,* 1979, *46,* 241-256.

Delia, J. G., and O'Keefe, B. J. Constructivism: The development of communication in children. In E. Wartella (Ed.), *Children communicating.* Beverly Hills, CA: Sage, 1979.

Delia, J. G., O'Keefe, B. J., and O'Keefe, D. J. The constructivist approach to communication. In F. E. X. Dance (Ed.), *Human communication theory: Comparative essays.* New York: Harper & Row, 1982.

Feffer, M. H. A developmental analysis of interpersonal behavior. *Psychological Review,* 1970, *77,* 197-214.

Flavell, J. H., in collaboration with Botkin, P. T., Fry, C. L., Wright, J. W., and Jarvis, P. E. *Role-taking and communication skills in children.* New York: John Wiley, 1968.

Flavell, J. H. Cognitive monitoring. In W. P. Dickson (Ed.), *Children's oral communication skills.* New York: Academic Press, 1981.

From, F. *Perception of other people.* New York: Columbia University Press, 1971.

Gage, N. L., and Cronbach, L. J. Conceptual and methodological problems in interpersonal perception. *Psychological Review,* 1955, *62,* 411-422.

Glucksberg, S., Krauss, R., and Higgins, E. T. The development of referential communication skills. In F. Horowitz (Ed.), *Review of child development research* (Vol. 4). Chicago: University of Chicago Press, 1975.

Grice, P. Logic and conversation. In P. Cole and J. L. Morgan (Eds.), *Syntax and semantics, Volume 3: Speech acts*. New York: Academic Press, 1976.

Higgins, E. T. Social class differences in verbal communicative accuracy: A question of "which question?" *Psychological Bulletin*, 1976, *83*, 695-714.

Husband, R. L. *Leadership phenomenology: A case study and social cognitive correlates.* Unpublished doctoral dissertation, University of Illinois at Urbana-Champaign, 1981.

Jacobs, S., and Jackson, S. Structure and strategy in conversational influences. *Communication Monographs*, forthcoming.

Jones, E. E. and Davis, K. E. From acts to dispositions: The attribution process in person perception. In L. Berkowitz (Ed.), *Advances in experimental social psychology* (Vol. 2). New York: Academic Press, 1965.

Jones, E. E., and Thibaut, J. W. Interaction goals as bases of inference in interpersonal perception. In R. Taguiri and L. Petrullo (Eds.), *Person perception and interpersonal behavior*. Stanford, CA: Stanford University Press, 1958.

Kelly, G. A. *A theory of personality* (2 vols.). New York: Norton, 1955.

Kline, S. L. *Construct system development, empathic motivation, and the accomplishment of face support in persuasive messages.* Presented at the annual meeting of the Speech Communication Association, Anaheim, California, 1981. (a)

Kline, S. L. *Construct system development and face support in persuasive messages: Two empirical investigations.* Presented at the annual meeting of the International Communication Association, Minneapolis, 1981. (b)

Kline, S. L. *Individual differences in the accomplishment of face support in persuasive communication.* Unpublished doctoral dissertation, University of Illinois at Urbana-Champaign, 1982.

Klyver, N., Press, A. N., and Crockett, W. H. *Cognitive complexity and the sequential integration of inconsistent information.* Presented at the annual meeting of the Eastern Psychological Association, 1972.

Krauss, R. M., and Glucksberg, S. Socialization of communication skills. In R. A. Hoppe, G. A. Milton, and E. C. Simmel (Eds.), *Early experience and the processes of socialization*. New York: Academic Press, 1970.

Langer, E. J. Rethinking the role of thought in social interaction. In J. H. Harvey, W. Ickes, and R. F. Kidd (Eds.), *New directions in attribution research* (Vol. 2). Hillsdale, NJ: Erlbaum, 1978.

Leitner, L. M., Landfield, A. W., and Barr, M. A. *Cognitive complexity: A review and elaboration within personal construct theory.* Unpublished manuscript, University of Nebraska at Lincoln, 1975.

Lingle, J. H., and Ostrom, T. M. Retrieval selectivity in memory-based impression judgements. *Journal of Personality and Social Psychology*, 1979, *37*, 180-194.

Livesley, W. J., and Bromley, D. B. *Person perception in childhood and adolescence.* London: John Wiley, 1973.

Mayo, C. W., and Crockett, W. H. Cognitive complexity and primacy-recency effects in impression formation. *Journal of Abnormal and Social Psychology*, 1964, *68*, 335-338.

Mead, G. H. *Mind, self, and society.* Chicago: University of Chicago Press, 1934.

Neisser, U. *Cognition and reality.* San Francisco: Freeman, 1976.

Newtson, D. Attribution and the unit of perception in ongoing behavior. *Journal of Personality and Social Psychology*, 1973, *28*, 28-38.

Newtson, D. Foundations of attribution: The unit of perception of ongoing behavior. In J. H. Harvey, W. J. Ickes, and R. F. Kidd (Eds.), *New directions in attribution research* (Vol. 1). Hillsdale, NJ: Erlbaum, 1976.

Nidorf, L. J., and Crockett, W. H. Cognitive complexity and the integration of conflicting information in written impressions. *Journal of Social Psychology*, 1965, *79*, 165-169.

O'Keefe, B. J., and Delia, J. G. Construct comprehensiveness and cognitive complexity as predictors of the number and strategic adaptation of arguments and appeals in a persuasive message. *Communication Monographs*, 1979, *46*, 321-340.

O'Keefe, B. J., and Delia, J. G. Psychological and interactional dimensions of communicative development. In H. Giles, R. St. Clair, and M. Hewstone (Eds.), *Advances in language, communication, and social psychology*. Hillsdale, NJ: Erlbaum, forthcoming.

O'Keefe, D. J. The relationship of attitudes and behavior: A constructivist analysis. In D. P. Cushman and R. D. McPhee (Eds.), *Message-attitude-behavior relationship*. New York: Academic Press, 1980.

O'Keefe, D. J., and Delia, J. G. Construct differentiation and the relationship of attitudes and behavioral intentions. *Communication Monographs*, 1981, *48*, 146-157.

O'Keefe, D. J., and Sypher, H. E. Cognitive complexity measures and the relationship of cognitive complexity to communication: A critical review. *Human Communication Research*, 1981, *8*, 72-92.

Peevers, B. H., and Secord, P. F. Developmental changes in attribution of descriptive concepts to persons. *Journal of Personality and Social Psychology*, 1973, *27*, 120-128.

Piaget, J. *Language and thought of the child*. New York: Humanities Press, 1959. (Originally published in 1926)

Powers, W. G., Jordan, W. J., and Street, R. L. Language indices in the measurement of cognitive complexity: Is complexity loquacity? *Human Communication Research*, 1979, *6*, 69-73.

Press, A. N., Crockett, W. H., and Delia, J. G. Effects of cognitive complexity and of perceiver's set upon the organization of impressions. *Journal of Personality and Social Psychology*, 1975, *32*, 865-872.

Rommetveit, R. *On message structure*. New York: John Wiley, 1974.

Rosenbach, D., Crockett, W. H., & Wapner, S. Developmental level, emotional involvement, and the resolution of inconsistency in impression formation. *Developmental Psychology*, 1973, *8*, 120-130.

Rubin, R. B. The role of context in information seeking and impression formation. *Communication Monographs*, 1977, *44*, 81-90.

Rubin, R. B. The effect of context on information seeking across the span of initial interactions. *Communication Quarterly*, 1979, *27*, 13-20.

Scarlett, H. H., Press, A. N., and Crockett, W. H. Children's descriptions of peers: A Wernerian developmental analysis. *Child Development*, 1971, *44*, 439-453.

Schank, R., and Abelson, R. *Scripts, plans, goals, and understanding*. Hillsdale, NJ: Erlbaum, 1977.

Searle, J. *Speech acts*. Cambridge: Cambridge University Press, 1969.

Shantz, C. U. The role of role-taking in children's referential communication. In W. P. Dickson (Ed.), *Children's oral communication skills*. New York: Academic Press, 1981.

Shatz, M. The relationship between cognitive processes and the development of communication skills. In B. Keasey (Ed.), *Nebraska Symposium on Motivation (Vol. XX)*. Lincoln: University of Nebraska Press, 1978.

Shatz, M., and Gelman, R. The development of communication skills: Modifications in the speech of young children as a function of listener. *Monographs of the Society for Research in Child Development*, 1973, *38* (No. 152).

Shaver, K. An introduction to attribution processes. Cambridge, MA: Winthrop, 1975.

Tagiuri, R., and Petrullo, L. (Eds.). *Person perception and interpersonal behavior.* Stanford, CA: Stanford University Press, 1958.

Tulving, E. Episodic and semantic memory. In E. Tulving and W. Donaldson (Eds.), *Organization of memory.* New York: Academic Press, 1972.

Warr, P. B., and Knapper, C. *The perception of people and events.* New York: John Wiley, 1968.

Watzlawick, P., Beavin, J. M., and Jackson, D. D. *Pragmatics of human communication: A study of interactional patterns, pathologies, and paradoxes.* New York: Norton, 1967.

Werner, H., and Kaplan, B. *Symbol formation.* New York: John Wiley, 1963.

3

Attribution and Communication

ARE PEOPLE "NAIVE SCIENTISTS" OR JUST NAIVE?

Alan L. Sillars

We are often faced with the problem of looking beyond the surface of events and trying to discern something about the dispositions of people. Why is your spouse being unreasonable? Is it a personality problem or too much caffeine? Do your teacher ratings indicate that you are a lousy teacher or do the students simply fail to appreciate someone who demands their best effort? (The brightest students probably like you the most.) Is the baby crying at 3:00 a.m. because she's spoiled and wants attention, or is it because she's teething and needs to be comforted? (My pediatrician friend informs me that we teethe until at least age 25.) The answers we give to many similar questions frame the context in which we respond to social situations and often determine the practical consequences of interaction. Communication thus rests on attributional premises. It is in this general sense that we consult attribution theory in this chapter for its implications toward a social cognitive view of human communication.

It is a challenging task indeed to write a "new" review of the literature on attribution theory. There are a number of excellent reviews already published (for example, Ross, 1977; Kelley and Michela, 1980; Nisbett and Ross, 1980; Harvey et al., 1976, 1978, 1981; Frieze et al., 1979), including a comprehensive review of attributional research in areas allied with the communication sciences (Seibold and Spitzberg, 1981a). Therefore, this chaper does not so much introduce a new or unfamiliar area as it provides a perspective on a relatively familiar set of ideas. My purpose is to contrast several views of attribution with an eye toward the overall metaphor for social actors projected by different views. A number of implications for our understanding of human communication are suggested, particularly in the areas of interpersonal and small group communication.

Defining the Scope of Attribution Theory

The literature surrounding attribution theory is massive and its boundaries are not clearly drawn. However, the field is largely focused on a question phrased by Heider (1944, 1958) that originally stimulated interest in attribution: given an observation of behavior, how do we reason backward from observed behavior to the unobserved causes of the behavior? We are not content simply to record observations but must instead equate behaviors with explanatory psychological concepts. If we were stripped of our extensive psycho-vocabulary of motives, personality traits, intentions, and so forth, the social world would be chaotic, unpredictable, and impossible to describe in a parsimonious way. Therefore, the idea came to fruition that lay people are "naive psychologists" whose activities are largely governed by the need to understand and to create cognitive and perceptual order.

The purview of attribution theory is further defined by three related tasks of the naive psychologist: *description, explanation,* and *prediction* (Ross, 1977). Description is involved, for example, in labeling the personal traits or intentions of an actor. Explanation is involved in the attribution of causality for an action. Typically, researchers have partitioned causal attributions into four categories: stable-personal factors (such as "ability"), unstable-personal factors (such as "effort"), stable-situational factors (such as "task difficulty"), and unstable-situational factors (such as "luck"; see Heider, 1958; Weiner et al., 1972). The final attributional task, prediction, is closely related to description and explanation, because predictability is achieved by coordinating behaviors to invariant dispositions or processes (Heider, 1958). For example, character or ability attributions lend themselves easily to prediction because of the inherent stability of these dispositions.

In the remainder of this chapter, perspectives on the attribution process are considered and their implications for communication are noted. Essentially, the present portrait of social actors within attribution theory resembles a mosaic. A plurality of competing concepts have received some support, including logical, nonlogical-inferential, motivational, and perceptual processes. However, the literature provides little indication about how different subsystems interact. We begin our review by considering normative principles of attribution, which suggest a rational and reflective metaphor for social actors (see also Hewes and Planalp, this volume) and then proceed to consider inferential bias (see also Roloff and Berger, this volume), motivational bias, and fundamental attribution biases, which occur through a combination of basic processes. The final section suggests several possible implications for our view of human communication.

Normative Theories

By far, the dominant force in attribution theory has been a related set of works by Heider (1944, 1958; Heider and Simmel, 1944), Jones and his colleagues (Jones and Davis, 1965; Jones and McGillis, 1976), and Kelley (1967, 1972a, 1972b, 1973). Although these authors emphasize different aspects of the attribution process, the basic picture of attribution they depict is similar. At the heart of each theory is a "commonsense" description of how people make attributions. That is, each theory describes an inferential sequence that we intuitively expect a reasonable person to follow. This sequence is generally logical, systematic, and cognitively mediated. Kelley (1972a) even describes people as "intuitive scientists" who employ attribution rules analogous to formal scientific inquiry. One gets the feeling from the theories of Heider, Jones, and Kelley that the steps people go through in making attributions generally reflect the steps one *should* follow to make the most accurate attribution from the available data. Thus, these theories may be referred to as "normative," because they provide a normative baseline for judging the adequacy or rationality of attributions.

It should be emphasized that the normative status of these theories does not preclude recognition of attribution biases. Attributions may be biased by inadequate information, false assumptions, motivations, or various principles of cognitive and perceptual organization. As we see throughout this chapter, Heider presented a broad view of attribution based on a combination of logical and nonlogical processes. Jones and McGillis (1976) noted that attributions often exceed the rational prescriptions of correspondent inference theory. In fact, they suggest that some of the most interesting research findings based on correspondent inferences have been those that identified departures from the theory.

Thus, the "normative" label is indeed a loose fit. What distinguishes normative theories is that they characterize attribution in terms of a logical baseline that people approximate to varying degrees. People are comparable to scientists who sometimes employ shoddy methodology and who may occasionally fudge the data.

Heider's Naive Analysis of Action

Many, if not most, of the ideas that have dominated attribution theory were introduced to the field by Heider. One such idea, which apparently colored normative theories of attribution, is the belief that intuitive knowledge of interpersonal relations may contribute heavily to psychological theories. Heider (1958) stressed that the ordinary person has a profound understanding of him or herself and that we may shed light on the attribution process by making this intuitive knowledge explicit. Thus, Heider's "naive analysis of action" and other normative theories have a highly intuitive flavor, even to the point that some critics have viewed the theories as too obvious (Heider, 1976).

Heider regarded the attribution process as an "intuitive factor analysis" in which the causal structure of events is assigned to personal or environmental factors. The attribution of an event to personal or environmental factors determines the extent to which an individual is held responsible for that event. Since Heider's (1958) system for determining personal causality has been summarized by many sources (see Shaver, 1975), the details are not reiterated here. At the risk of oversimplifying, there are two assumptions of Heider's naive analysis of action that have been particularly influential in terms of subsequent developments of attribution theory (for example, Jones and Davis, 1965): (1) Personal causality is judged within the context of situational factors contributing to or impeding an action, such that an act is believed to imply more about the qualities of an actor when the situation could not have caused the act and when the act is difficult to produce. (2) Less personal responsibility is attributed to the unintended consequences of an action than to intentional outcomes.

The Theory of Correspondent Inferences

The theory of correspondent inferences, first stated by Jones and Davis (1965) and then modified by Jones and McGillis (1976), is largely an elaboration and formalization of Heider's naive analysis of action. However, Jones and Davis go further than Heider in predicting which particular dispositions are likely to be inferred from an action. Jones and Davis propose that a series of criteria are applied to determine if the effects of an action are correspondent with an actor's dispositions. First, the observer considers whether the effects of an action were intentional. Only intended effects are used to infer the actor's dispositions.

Upon determining intentionality, the perceiver distinguishes *common* and *noncommon* effects of an action. Common effects are effects shared by alternative actions, whereas noncommon effects are not shared. Only noncommon effects are used to infer attitudes and traits. For example, if a person chooses the University of Illinois over Ohio State, we assume that he or she likes something about the program or people at Illinois (noncommon effects). The fact that Illinois is a Big Ten institution located near cornfields does not tell us anything about the attitudes of the actor, because these qualities are also shared by Ohio State. Furthermore, when there are few noncommon effects, judgments of correspondence tend to be more extreme and confident because the basis of the action is less ambiguous than if there are many noncommon effects (Newtson, 1974). Thus, if a person decides to raise chickens rather than attend Ohio State, it is unclear what motivated the decision because the alternatives are dissimilar on many grounds.

Finally, correspondence is increased to the extent that the assumed *valence* of an effect is low (Jones and McGillis, 1976). Valence refers to the desirability of an effect according to a person's reference group ("category-based" expectancy) or according to the judge's prior conception of the actor ("target-based" expectancy). Behavior that confirms expectancies can generally be accounted for by situational causes, such as social conformity, so the tendency to attribute dispositional causes is greater when behavior violates expectancies (see, for example, Jones and Harris, 1967; Jones et al., 1971).

To summarize, correspondent inferences and Heider's naive analysis of action are attempts to formalize our commonsense understanding of causality and personal responsibility. Their general thrust is that personal attributions are made when actions are intentionally chosen in a context relatively free of restrictive social roles, norms, and other situational causes of behavior. The theories have provided an interesting heuristic for aquaintance formation (see Berger et al., 1976), persuasion (Seibold and Spitzberg, 1981a, 1981b), and many other areas. However, it is important to emphasize that the theorists viewed normative principles as idealized criteria. An equally important part of the theoretical statement of Heider (1958) and Jones and Davis (1965) was that people often make personal attributions when normative criteria suggest that they should not (see Ross, 1977; Jones, 1979). These points are discussed at greater length when we consider fundamental attribution biases later in this chapter.

The ANOVA Cube

We have considered to this point primarily the conditions under which personal causality is attributed. Kelley's theory (1967, 1972a, 1972b, 1973) has a broader focus that encompasses how we make attributions to situations and things as well as to the personal dispositions of actors. In this system, causality is attributed to the conditions that are perceived to covary with an effect, including the person, entity, situation, or some combination thereof (hence, the attribution process is compared to the statistical procedure, ANOVA). For example, given the observation that Tara, the infant, spits her food, is this because Tara is a "fussy baby" (person attribution), her food tastes lousy (entity), eating time is a time when all babies spit (situation), or all three factors are at work? The decision rules provided by

Kelley to resolve such issues have been extensively reported and require only a quick summary.

Two types of attributional logic are proposed by Kelley, one applying to multiple observation contexts and the other to single observation contexts. When the attributor has the opportunity to observe another person on multiple occasions, attributions are determined by the observed covariation of the behavior on three dimensions: *(1) distinctiveness*—the extent to which different entities evoke similar behavior; *(2) consensus*—the extent to which different actors behave in a similar way; and *(3) consistency over time and modality*—the extent to which the behavior is similar in different contexts. According to the covariance principle, an effect is attributed to the conditions that are present when the behavior is present and absent when the behavior is absent. For example, the pattern of low distinctiveness, low consensus, and high consistency leads us to infer that a stable personal trait is causing a behavior.

In single observation contexts the observer does not have the ability to directly observe covariation, so alternative rules are used. Two such rules are the *discounting* and *augmentation* principles. The discounting principle is that "the role of a given cause in producing a given effect is discounted if other plausible causes are also present (Kelley, 1972a: 8)." Discounting can be construed as a generalization of the principle of noncommon effects (Jones and McGillis, 1976). The augmentation principle is that "if for a given effect, both a plausible inhibitory and a plausible facilitative cause are present, the role of the facilitative cause will be judged greater than if it were alone presented as a plausible cause of the effect" (Kelley, 1972a: 12). A very similar idea is again expressed in correspondent inferences by the concept of expected valence (Jones and McGillis, 1976). Some research has supported the discounting and augmentation principles (see Kelley, 1972a; Himmelfarb and Anderson, 1975), although there are, again, many cases in which the effects of the situation are underestimated in personal attributions (see later section on "fundamental attribution biases").

Finally, in single observation contexts the attributor may also intuit an assumed pattern of data or "causal schema" based on a covariance pattern that is expected to accompany certain effects (Kelley, 1972b). For example, we assume that multiple necessary causes are required to produce extreme effects, whereas multiple sufficient causes may account for moderate effects (Cunningham and Kelley, 1975; Kun and Weiner, 1973).

Kelley's theory, more than any other attributional logic, directly embodies the intuitive scientist metaphor. Consequently, the status of the theory has been the stage for a general debate concerning the adequacy of normative principles of attribution. This makes the empirical status of Kelley's theory especially important. However, the status of Kelley's theory is clouded by issues concerning the adequacy of the covariance rule in general and the effects of consensus information in particular.

Empirical Status of Covariance. Do people use covariation information in the manner suggested by Kelley's model? In one respect they probably do not. Specifically, people have demonstrated a notably weak ability to accurately *estimate* the degree of covariation between two events. Covariation estimates in many instances appear to be based more on prior intuitive theories than on actual observed covariation. A number of studies on illusory correlation (see Hamilton, 1979) have indicated that prior expectations cause people to imagine relationships among things when no correlation exists and to overlook relationships that do exist. For example, clinical psychologists report correlations between personality and projective tests that have intuitive appeal but no empirical validity (Chapman and Chapman, 1967, 1969), and occupational stereotypes cause individuals to imagine illusory correlations between personality and occupation (Hamilton and Rose, 1978). Research on the dynamics of illusory correlation indicates that preconceptions dramatically affect encoding and memory of actors' behaviors (Zadny and Gerard, 1974; Cohen, 1977). Consequently, Nisbett and Ross (1980) argue that accurate assessment of covariation tends to occur only in restrictive circumstances—when stimuli are almost perfectly correlated, the stimuli are distinctive, salient, and motivationally relevant, and there are opportunities for decisively testing covariation hypotheses.

Does the aforementioned research empirically invalidate the covariance principle? To the extent that covariance is viewed as a rule governing the use of objective information, the answer is probably yes. However, people may still use some covariance-like logic in making attributions, based on their (often inaccurate) perceptions of covariation. This possibility is tenable, since studies that did not require subjects to engage in difficult covariation estimation tasks have generally found that attributions are responsive to covariation considerations (for example, McArthur, 1972, 1976). Thus, Kelley and Michela (1980: 462) concluded from their review that "the covariation principle should probably be qualified as applying to perceived covariation."

Empirical Status of Consensus. Even the conclusion that people are responsive to perceived covariation must be qualified because several studies have found that people make little use of consensus information in estimating the causal role of a particular actor or in predicting a particular outcome (McArthus, 1972, 1976; Kahneman and Tversky, 1973; Nisbett and Borgida, 1975; Feldman et al., 1976; Orvis et al., 1975; Nisbett et al., 1976). Kahneman and Tversky (1973) and Nisbett et al. (1976) explain the underutilization of consensus information by arguing that we make little use of abstract consensus information (for example, a *Consumer Reports* survey on the reliability of Volvos) in comparison with more concrete and emotionally interesting information (for instance, that a friend had to junk his Volvo after three years; see Nisbett and Ross, 1980).

Recent arguments and data about consensus have partly resurrected the concept but with several contingencies attached. Briefly, consensus information may be utilized to the extent that (1) the credibility of the information is assured—for example, by indicating that the consensus information was drawn from a random sample of individuals (Wells and Harvey, 1977); (2) attributions are directed toward self rather than another person (Hansen and Donoghue, 1977; Hansen and Stonner, 1978); (3) the attributes being judged are socially defined rather than physically defined (Hansen and Lowe, 1976; Gottlieb and Ickes, 1978); and (4) well-rehearsed schemata are available for explaining how consensus information and individual traits are causally related (Ajzen, 1977; Nisbett and Borgida, 1975).

As we have now seen, Kelley's "intuitive scientist" metaphor breaks down in certain respects. Although people are responsive to perceived covariation, they are weak in evaluating objective covariation. Consensus information (objective or perceived) tends to be used only under restrictive circumstances. What, then, are the probable consequences of these tendencies? First, as suggested in the next section on inferential bias, vivid, strongly held impressions are slow to change because subsequent observations of covariance are biased by prior theories. Second, as a further consequence of biased covariation estimation, people will tend to overestimate the consistency of behavior that fits strongly held impressions. For example, the family literature is ripe with examples of family members describing one another in terms that are overgeneralized and inadequately differentiated according to the situation (see Weiss et al., 1973; Thomas, 1977; Kelley, 1979). Third, the confidence people place in attributions may be inflated by the fact that they can draw from memory evidence—albeit exaggerated or illusory— of covariation. Fourth, the attribution of a behavior to "something about the person" is especially likely to depart from normative criteria, since dispositional attributions are governed by consensus information in Kelley's model, and consensus information is frequently under-utilized. As we see in subsequent sections of this chapter, conclusions similar to these four are supported elsewhere in the attribution literature.

To conclude this section, we have seen moderate support for normative principles, but this support is tempered by an equal recognition that people do not approximate normative criteria in many circumstances. Lack of support for normative principles does not invalidate the use of these theories as a "rational baseline" for identifying attributional bias. Nonetheless, one might still question whether a rational baseline model misrepresents the basic processes involved in attribution (see Fischoff, 1976). Given the intuitive status of normative theories, it is possible that they represent implicit theories about how we reason (see Nisbett and Wilson, 1977) more than the way we actually reason. To consider this possibility further, we now turn to inferential processes that are basically nonnormative.

Inferential Bias

In contrast to the rather complementary image of social actors suggested by normative theories, a more humble portrait is offered by a loosely affiliated set of nonnormative inferential concepts. While it is difficult to coin an appropriate umbrella term for these concepts, they suggest a picture of the attribution process in which people are relatively unsystematic, nonreflective, and nonexhaustive in weighing attributional data. Instead of searching for the "best" explanation, people may settle on the first sufficient explanation that comes to mind (Kanouse, 1972; Taylor and Fiske, 1978; Wyer, 1980). Furthermore, attributions must satisfy phenomenological rather than logical criteria.

This view of attribution is heavily indebted to concepts from decision theory (see, for example, Slovic and Lichtenstein, 1971; Kahneman and Tversky, 1973) and cognitive psychology (Shank and Abelson, 1977; Carroll and Payne, 1976; Cantor and Mischel, 1977). These disciplines have run a different course from much of attribution theory. Fischoff (1976: 421) points out that normative attribution theories find people to be relatively systematic and unbiased in social inference, whereas

judgment researchers reveal people to be quite inept at all but the simplest inferential tasks—and sometimes even at them—muddling through a world that seems to let them get through life by gratuitously allowing for a lot of error.

My discussion of inferential bias is intended to be brief and illustrative, because it overlaps with the chapter by Roloff and Berger later in this volume. Two areas are covered: the role of salience in attribution and the effects of prior theories and schemas.

Salience

Several lines of research converge to indicate that the perceptual or emotional salience of a stimulus determines the extent to which it is used as a cue in making attributions. Nisbett and Ross (1980) propose that information exerts a disproportionate influence on social inference to the extent that it is vivid in any respect, that is, emotionally interesting, concrete and imagery-provoking, and proximate in a sensory, temporal, or spatial way. However, salience or vividness often bears little or no relationship to the actual diagnostic value of a cue. For example, focusing one's attention on an individual increases the tendency to see the individual as responsible for surrounding events (see Heider, 1958; Duval and Hensley, 1976; Taylor and Fiske, 1978). Simple manipulations that increase the salience of an actor through the seating patterns of observers, the actor's clothes, or a beam of light increase the extent to which the actor is seen as setting the tone and topic of conversations (Taylor and Fiske, 1978: McArthur and Post, 1977). Other effects that may be attributable to the relative salience of information include the disproportionate influence of negative versus positive information on overall impressions (see Kanouse and Hanson, 1972), the tendency to overlook the informational value of effects foregone (that is, costs) in correspondent inferences (Newtson, 1974), and the tendency to underutilize abstract consensus information in dispositional attributions (see, for example, Nisbett et al., 1976).

Two approaches have been taken in explaining salience effects. The first approach is to suggest that salience effects are related to memory processes. Specifically, salient information is more "available" in memory; that is, it is more easily retrieved (see Tversky and Kahneman, 1973), perhaps because it is encoded in both iconic (image) and verbal forms (see Taylor and Fiske, 1978; Nisbett and Ross, 1980). Taylor and Fiske (1978) suggest that memory availability is important because attributions are usually made "off the top of one's head," or with little thought. Consequently, images that are easily recalled have disproportionate influence. Furthermore, Nisbett and Ross (1980) note that, along with increasing memory availability, vivid information is more likely to recruit additional supportive information from memory and is subject to greater rehearsal because it remains in thought longer.

The effects of one's focus of attention on causal attributions may also be explained by the direct perception of causal relationships, without the mediation of memory or other inferential processes. McArthur (1980) suggests that the visual salience of an actor may affect an observer's attributions because the observer focuses on the effects that the salient actor has on another actor, rather than vice versa. Since causality occurs in both directions, the sequence may be perceptually organized to reflect the causal influence of either actor. McArthur cites the research of Newtson and his collegues (Newtson et al., 1978; Massad et al., 1979) and Heider and Simmel (1944) to show that perceivers segment behaviors when there are salient changes in the stimulus field and the segmentation of an event affects causal attributions. This analysis owes much to Heider (1958; Heider and Simmel, 1944). Although Heider stressed perceptual determinants of attribution along with explicit inference, the former emphasis in Heider's writing has not received much attention until recently (see McArthur, 1980; Newtson, 1980; Weary Swanson, Harvey, and Yarkin, 1980; Weary, Rich, Harvey, and Ickes, 1980).

Effects of Prior Theories and Schemas

We have already seen that prior beliefs affect judgments about the covariation between events, because expectancies guide the coding and retrieval of information. To this let us add two other effects of existing knowledge structures on subsequent attributions. First, prior attributions are not adequately reevaluated in light of new data (see Ross, 1977; Nisbett and Ross, 1980; Kelley and Michela, 1980). Initial attributions act as cognitive "anchors" for the integration of further information, and subsequent adjustment of these anchors tends to be gradual, even when the initial inference is without foundation and subsequent data are drastically disconfirming (Tversky and Kahneman, 1974; Ross et al., 1975). Moreover, new information that contradicts prior attributions is viewed critically, whereas the reliability and validity of congruent observations tends to be assumed (Ross, 1977; for additional explanations of perseverance in attributions, see Nisbett and Ross, 1980).

Second, attributions may be biased by the activation of inappropriate "schemas," which are abstract structures for integrating information based on spatial, temporal, or associative relationships (Cohen and Ebbesen, 1979), such as the "script" for appropriate restaurant behavior (see Schank and Abelson, 1977) or the traits associated with a particular persona or stereotype. Activation of a particular schema directs coding and recall of information in such a way that information is either integrated within the schema or it tends to be ignored or forgotten (Cohen, 1977; Zadney and Gerard, 1974; see Hamilton, 1979). Therefore, attributions may be determined by the activation of a particular schema. However, the activation of schemas may be based on criteria that are not strongly related to the schema's diagnostic value, such as its availability in memory or superficial resemblances to the data at hand (Nisbett and Ross, 1980).

The Question of Dual Processing

Thus far, two views of social actors have been presented. In contrast to the logical or scientific-like impression conveyed by normative models, the literature just reviewed on inferential bias suggests that we tend to make attributions with little thought, using criteria that are, at best, loosely related to the appropriateness of the attribution, and then view subsequent data in a self-confirming manner. Intuitively, an extreme statement of either view is unrealistic. In an effort to suggest a middle ground, several authors have alluded to the idea that the "intuitive scientist" and "top of the head" metaphors may correctly describe different modes of processing (Taylor and Fiske, 1978; Jones, 1978; Kelley and Michela, 1980). Taylor and Fiske (1978) suggest that Kelley's ANOVA model may apply to instances of controlled processing, which is relatively self-conscious and is likely to be used in difficult, unpracticed, and involving situations. The effects of salience and social schemas may be greatest during automatic processing, which is nonreflective and is most likely in situations that are frequent, redundant, and boring. Unfortunately, the issue is not resolved this easily. Although Taylor (1975) found that high involvement decreased salience effects, Nisbett and Borgida (1975) found that the effects of concrete versus statistical summary information on decisions were *increased* when the decision was more involving. While the matter is thus poorly understood at present, it is nonetheless appealing to assume that there are different modes of attributional processing and that certain conditions determine the extent to which each mode is prominent.

Motivational Bias

The black sheep of attribution theory has been the view that attributions are affected by motivational states, such as needs, wishes, and cognitive consistency pressures. Although Heider (1958) gave equal status to motivational and logical determinants of attribution, the trend thereafter has been to give cognitive interpretations to supposed signs of motivational bias (for example, Miller and Ross, 1975; Brewer, 1977; Nisbett and Ross, 1980). What seemed to attract many individuals to attribution theory was the argument that one could explain behavior with respect to affectively neutral information-processing concepts, as opposed to elusive motivational phenomena (see Bem, 1965, 1972). But despite the general feeling that cognition is king, motivational proponents have persisted, and there is now a fair amount of data to bolster the view that motivations have significant effects on attributions. Two types of motivational bias have received the bulk of attention: self-serving bias, or "egotism," and enhancement of personal control.

Self-Serving Attributional Bias

Self-serving attributional bias, or egotism, is the tendency to take credit for good outcomes and to deny blame for bad ones (Snyder et al., 1978). Numerous studies have found signs of self-serving bias (see Miller and Ross, 1975; Bradley, 1978; Zuckerman, 1979). A prominently referenced example is a study by Beckman (1970). Beckman found that teachers accepted greater causal responsibility for children who increased their learning performance than for children who declined in performance. Although this finding did not emerge from later research (Beckman, 1973), the teachers in this study accepted more responsibility for improved performance than was granted by neutral observers. However, the interpretation of this and similar studies is clouded by two issues. First, the evidence is not consistent. People do not appear to make self-serving attributions in many circumstances. Second, most studies do not directly show that self-serving bias is caused by the arousal of ego defensiveness, as the concept assumes.

Miller and Ross's (1975) critical review reveals little solid evidence of self-serving bias. Although the authors acknowledge that actors may make self-enhancing attributions during conditions of success, they do not find evidence that actors deny blame for failure, in comparison with a neutral baseline (that is, attributions for intermediate performance or attributions by observers). The tendency to make self-enhancing attributions for success can be explained by nonmotivational factors (Miller and M. Ross, 1975; L. Ross, 1977). For example, success is more intentional than failure and is usually more consistent with self-expectancies.

The critical arguments of Miller, M. Ross, L. Ross, and others have since stimulated more solid documentation of self-serving bias (see Bradley, 1978; Snyder et al., 1978; Zuckerman, 1979), including a few studies, by the critics themselves, that supported self-serving bias (Miller, 1976; Sicoly and M. Ross, 1977; M. Ross and Sicoly, 1979).

However, Bradley (1978) and Snyder et al. (1978) caution that self-serving biases are likely to occur only under certain conditions. Specifically, the situation must present a threat to self-esteem and provide an opportunity to protect self-esteem through self-serving attributions. The authors reason that self-serving attributions are less likely if they are implausible, if the actor wishes to appear modest for the sake of self-presentation, or if the attributions are apt to be disconfirmed by observers or one's subsequent performances (Bradley, 1978; Snyder et al., 1978; see also Wells et al., 1977). In these situations, self-esteem needs are best met by nondefensive or counterdefensive attributions.

Perceived Control Bias

Prediction and control have been regarded as the main goals of attribution by many theorists (see Kelley, 1972a; Jones et al., 1972). In some cases the need to feel in control conflicts with reality—for example, when events are products of chance or other uncontrollable factors. Some theorists propose that we are motivated to restore a sense of predictability and control following accidents or disasters by overattributing personal responsiblity for these events and under-estimating the role of chance.

One such theorist is Walster, who suggests that personal blame for human misfortune increases with the severity of the consequences. According to Walster, we restore a sense of predictability by blaming people for disastrous occurrences and therefore feel better able to avoid victimization ourselves. In a study supporting the theory, Walster (1966) found that a car owner was judged to be more responsible for causing an accident when the consequences of the accident were more severe, even though other conditions of the accident were identical. Several studies have failed to replicate this finding, but these studies have been criticized for not creating an involving simulation of a disaster (Wortman, 1976). Wortman (1976) cites support for Walster's hypothesis from Chaiken and Darley (1973) and several sociological sources.

Lerner's (1970) just-world hypothesis is similar in implication to Walster's theory. The just-world hypothesis states that we are motivated to believe in a just world, where everyone gets what he or she deserves. The belief in a just world leads to derogation of the victim of misfortune if no other means of restoring justice are available. Several studies have found that subjects' evaluations of a victim of suffering are increasingly negative to the extent that the victim's fate is unjustified (see Lerner et al., 1976).

However, the issue again arises concerning whether evidence of perceived control bias can be accounted for by nonmotivational factors.

Specifically, the representativeness heuristic (causes are perceived to resemble effects; see Kahneman and Tversky, 1973) easily accounts for the finding that badness is attributed to people who suffer bad things. Brewer (1977) accounts for the finding that outcome severity increases attribution of responsibility by noting that severe consequences are unusual and therefore are perceived to be less likely to occur without personal intervention.

The argument that cognitive processes can account for perceived control biases does not disprove motivational interpretations, but it leaves the issue in doubt. To my knowledge, there are no data that clearly test the motivational interpretation of this phenomenon. However, we can address a more general question that lies behind the particulars of this issue.

The General Status of Motivations in Attribution Theory

The argument has repeatedly come up that nonmotivational inferential processes can account for the same phenomena that motivational biases are used to explain. However, the question still remains, what do we gain from a nonmotivational model of social cognition? On the one hand, one can see the argument that motivational explanations of attribution have been overextended. It is too easy to accuse other people of rationalization, and this may inhibit understanding of their inferential underpinnings. On the other hand, an exclusively cognitive model seems ill suited to emotionally laden phenomena, such as conflict and self-evaluation (Rogers, 1980; Weary, Swanson, Harvey, and Yarkin, 1980). Rogers (1980) argues that a more appropriate approach is to view cognition and affect as distinct processing systems that interact in complex ways.

Thus, we again see authors arguing for a view of attribution that recognizes distinct modes of attributional processing. The view remains controversial, because the interaction of affect and cognition is poorly understood (Rogers, 1980). Still, the argument supports a growing sense that the attribution process should be seen as pluralistic.

Fundamental Attribution Biases

Two related biases have received enormous attention because of their robustness and strong implications: the "fundamental attribution error" and the actor-observer difference. Each represents a bias in the extent to which we attribute causality to the person or situation. They are discussed in a separate section because they apparently accrue from a combination of basic processes rather than a single cause or set of related causes.

Overattribution of Personal Causality

Although Heider's naive analysis of action suggests that people weigh personal responsibility against mitigating environmental factors, Heider (1944: 361) also states that although "changes in the environment are almost always caused by acts of persons in combination with other factors, the tendency exists to ascribe the changes entirely to persons." This tendency has been termed the "fundamental attribution error" by Ross (1977). Ross (1977) and Jones (1979) review evidence that has accumulated in support of the fundamental attribution error. The fundamental attribution error is significant from a theoretical standpoint because it incorporates several distinct attribution processes discussed by Heider and subsequently expanded upon by many others. From a practical standpoint, the concept has attracted attention because it explains inaccuracies that inhere in judgments about the personality, ability, attitudes, and motives of other people.

The fundamental attribution error has several alleged manifestations. For example, observers tend to infer that an actor's statements reflect the actor's true attitudes, even when the observer is aware of unusually strong mitigating circumstances, such as the fact that the actor was *assigned* to argue a certain position by a debate coach (Jones and Harris, 1967; Jones et al., 1971; A. Miller, 1974, 1976; Snyder and Jones, 1974). Furthermore, observers are notably insensitive to the effects of social or conversational roles on behavior. In a study in which one person was allowed to ask another person questions from his or her own store of esoteric knowledge (as in doctoral prelims), participants and observers tended to downgrade the respondent for not being able to answer all of the questions (Ross, Amabile, and Steinmetz, 1977). However, the respondent was at an obvious strategic disadvantage.

Not only do people overlook situational causes in making attributions for a particular behavior; they tend also to describe behavior in overly general terms, with too little recognition of situational variation in behavior. For example, Kelley (1979) notes that intimate couples are virtually unable to describe relationship problems in specific, behavioral terms, even when coaxed to do so. Instead, they tend to substitute phrases that refer to general traits and attitudes of their partners.

Some scholars have argued that trait psychologists as well as lay psychologists have been victimized by the fundamental attribution error in overestimating the degree of personal consistency that typically occurs in behavior (see Mischel, 1973; Endler, 1975; Ross, 1977; Nisbett and Ross, 1980; see also Endler and Magnusson, 1976; Magnusson and Endler, 1977; Hewes and Haight, 1979). The contemporary critique of trait psychology was initiated by Mischel (1968, 1973), who pointed to the poor performance of many pencil-and-paper measures of personality when correlated with behaviors. Mischel argued that the poor construct validity of these measures was not due to methodological defects but to the fact that people are not as consistent in their behavior as trait measures generally assume.

Several reasons have been suggested for why people tend to overattribute personal as opposed to situational causality. First, behavior has highly salient properties that tend to "engulf the field," meaning that behavior stands out perceptually over contextual factors (Heider, 1958: 54; see also the previous discussion of salience effects on attributions). Second, personal attributions are more parsimonious than situational descriptions of behavior (Heider, 1958: 51). Personality attributions, in particular, imply a strong degree of coherence and predictability. Third, we may prefer to blame personal causes for unfortunate events because it allows us to restore cognitive balance (Heider, 1958: 235; see also the previous discussion of perceived control bias). Finally, an observer may lack the opportunity to observe inconsistency in the actor's behavior and consequently may overgeneralize the actor's dispositions. Even when the observer views the actor on many occasions, the degree of apparent consistency in the actor's behavior may be misleading, because the observer is a constant element in the actor's environment. Argyle and Little (1972) point out that people may behave consistently in the presence of a particular observer because of a jointly negotiated identity or because the actor deliberately avoids creating the impression of inconsistency.

The Actor-Observer Difference

Jones and Nisbett's (1972: 80) widely noted actor-observer hypothesis states that "there is a pervasive tendency for actors to attribute their actions to situational requirements, whereas observers tend to attribute the same actions to stable personal dispositions." In effect, this qualifies the fundamental attribution error as applying only to the observer of a behavior, whereas the actor or person performing a behavior has an opposite tendency to focus on situational causes. The actor-observer difference has been demonstrated in many contexts (see Jones and Nisbett, 1972; Ross, 1977; Kelley and Michela, 1980). For example, studies have consistently found that human conflicts tend to be attributed to the negative characteristics of one's partner or adversary. One's own role is typically regarded as a response to situational demands, including instigations by the other party (Orvis et al., 1976; Thomas and Pondy, 1977; Rosenberg and Wolfsfeld, 1977; Sillars, 1981). The actor-partner difference may be moderated or even reversed by factors such as attributional style and self-esteem (Ickes and Layden, 1978), "empathy instructions" (Regan and Totten, 1975), anticipated discussion of attributions (Wells et al., 1977), and interpersonal relationship satisfaction (Sillars, 1981). Yet, overall support for Jones and Nisbett's hypothesis has been quite robust.

Explanations for the actor-observer difference again draw on a varied set of processes. First, the actor's behavior "engulfs the field" for the observer, but the situation is salient for the actor (Jones and Nisbett, 1972; Duval and Hensley, 1976). Second, there is a "false consensus" bias—a tendency for people to assume that others are like themselves and would typically act the same way in the same situation (Ross, Greene, and House, 1977). A person's own attitudes and behavior are therefore seen as situational. Another person's behavior, to the extent that it departs from the observer's self-perceptions, is seen as unusual and is attributed to stable personal dispositions (see Ross, 1977). Third, the actor may be motivated to attribute negative events, such as conflict or failure, to the situation in order to protect self-esteem. Fourth, the actor is more cognizant than the observer of situational factors affecting his or her choice of behavior and of past situational variation in the actor's behavior (Jones and Nisbett, 1972). The latter point has been used to suggest that the actor's attributions are usually more accurate (Jones and Nisbett, 1972; Monson and Snyder, 1977). However, other authors deny that actors have privileged access to the true causes of their behavior (Nisbett and Wilson, 1977; Nisbett and Bellows, 1977).

The upshot of the fundamental attribution error and the actor-observer difference is that people do not offer equally complex explanations for complex social phenomena. Rather, causal explanations tend to center on the salient attributes of other people. We have again seen that many of basic concepts have been used to account for attribution. Some of these factors are quite normative, such as the lack of information. The remaining factors involved in the fundamental attribution biases derive from each of the nonlogical processes previously discussed. Further implications of the basic attribution processes and fundamental attribution biases are noted in the final section, to which we now turn.

Implications for a Social Cognitive View of Communication

At this point let us consider how attributional concepts may contribute to thinking in several areas of communication research.

Implication 1: Subjective Uncertainty in Communication

Normative attribution theories suggest that we hedge our claims to understanding another person when there are competing explanations for their behavior, such as external motives or restrictive social norms. This principle has been an interesting heuristic for communication research. Berger and his colleagues, in particular, provide an extensive framework for interpreting interpersonal communication as a process of uncertainty reduction (see Berger et al., 1976). These authors suggest that, in an effort to reduce attributional uncertainty, observers may enact interaction strategies and select observational contexts that minimize confounding explanations of the actor's behavior (Berger et al., 1976; Berger and Perkins, 1978). Another example of research on communication from the premise of normative attribution theories is Jones and Wortman's (1973) analysis of ingratiation. Jones and Wortman suggest, for example, that the effective techniques of flattery are those that minimize the appearance that flattery is being used to manipulate, such as flattering people behind their backs.

The view that people are relatively aware of the biased and ambiguous nature of some observations is to be contrasted with the picture we get from several other sources. These sources suggest that the more striking tendency may be the extent to which people are overly trusting of their attributions, rather than their sensitivity to bias. Several factors suggest a tendency for people to be overconfident in their attributions. People attribute traits and attitudes on the basis of behaviors that are virtually dictated by situational demands, despite the obvious problems of doing so (Jones and Harris, 1967; Ross, Amabile, and Steinmetz, 1977). Predictions tend to be extreme, with too little allowance for error (Fischoff, 1976). Reevaluation of prior predictions and explanations tends to be inadequate, because existing theories govern the selection, coding, evaluation, and recall of new data (Ross, 1977; Hamilton, 1979; Wyer and Carlston, 1979). Subjective evidence for one's attributions may be generated from covariance estimates that are illusory (see previous discussion of covariation). Thus, the level of confidence placed in attributions may far exceed the level of accuracy.

Whereas Berger and his colleagues have addressed a series of questions about communication derived from the intuitive scientist metaphor, we may also derive a set of questions about communication based on non-logical attribution processes. For example, under what circumstances do people make overly rich interpretations of verbal and nonverbal messages or assign disproportionate weight to salient message characteristics? An example of research in this vein is a study by Daly and Korinek (1981). These authors demonstrated that one's expectations of how conversations will proceed are governed by one's own recent and concrete experiences, which make a particular sequence available in memory. The finding is used to explain an observation of family clinicians that even the most deviant interaction patterns are often considered by family members to be typical of other families.

Implication 2: The Nature of Metacommunication

Some of the points within attribution theory have implications for how we view "metacommunication," which refers to the set of cues that contextualize a message and indicate how it is to be taken (Bateson, 1951, 1972). Although the term is not always used consistently (see Bochner and Krueger, 1979; Wilmot, 1980), it is generally held that relationships are defined on such dimensions as power and affect through metacommunication and that metacommunication consists largely (though not exclusively) of nonverbal communication. Quantitative research on metacommunication (see Ellis, 1978, 1979; Rogers and Farace, 1975; Rogers-Millar and Millar, 1979) has predominantly employed a researcher-imposed definition of what metacommunicative cues mean (Wilmot, 1980). Yet, several authors have suggested that the participants' view of metacommunication is equally important, if not primary (Wilmot, 1980; Folger and Poole, 1981; Folger and Sillars, 1980; Planalp and Hewes, 1981), particularly when the researcher wants to extrapolate from interaction patterns to phenomenological variables, such as satisfaction and personality perceptions (Cappella, 1977). Attribution theory offers some insights concerning what a view of metacommunication as "socially constituted" entails.

The primary inplication is that impressions of metacommunication will be based on cues that are perceptually and motivationally salient and on implicit theories and schemas that link salient cues to inferences concerning message intent. Hence, establishing a common interpretation of metacommunication may be problematic, because, as we have seen, the salience of cues differs according to the actor's perspective. This problem is compounded by the fact that a large number of nonverbal cues may be construed as metacommunicative, since nonverbal communication lacks the sort of explicit digital coding rules that characterize verbal communication (Watzlawick et al., 1967). Hence, the actor will form impressions of metacommunication based on cues that dominate his or her focus of attention, namely, the visual and paralinguistic cues of the partner (as opposed to the actor's own cues). This further suggests that the actor will frequently attribute personalistic intent to the partner's cues when the same cues are seen by the partner as nonsignificant and noncommunicative. Finally, cues will be filtered, coded, and retrieved according to the actor's prior impressions of the relationship, or what Wilmot (1980) calls "relationship-level metacommunication." Hence, the actor's impressions of metacommunication may become quite idiosyncratic. This further suggests that any effort to develop interaction coding schemes based on culturally shared interpretations of metacommunication (see Folger and Poole, 1981) faces difficult obstacles. The interpretation of metacommunication may depend too heavily on the individual's perspective for us to document a consensually shared vocabulary of dominance, affect, and so forth.

Implication 3: Punctuation of
Communicational Sequences

Although communication is characterized by circular causality, the actor-observer difference suggests that actors will tend to attribute a linear cause-effect sequence for their interactions. As we have seen, the tendency is to overattribute interaction to other people and to underestimate one's own causal role. This is essentially a rephrasing of the punctuation concept in communication theory (Watzlawick et al., 1967). However, the concept has added explanatory power if approached from an attributional perspective, because the attribution literature reveals causes of punctuation differences (such as information imbalances and focus of attention) and conditions under which punctuation differences are likely to be moderated (for example, in the presence of a neutral third party, instructions that induce empathy).

We should expect difference in the punctuation of communicational sequences to be quite pervasive given the special difficulty of causal inference in an interactive setting. Causality may be exceedingly complex during interaction, because several causes of behavior are confounded, including personality, relationship history, negotiated expectancies, reciprocal attributions, and reciprocal effects of behavior. Since causality is highly complex and ambiguous, we can expect, further, that non-normative criteria have a greater effect on inference in interactive situations than in noninteractive situations. An additional complication is that attributions in interactive situations may be tested in a self-confirming fashion (see Snyder and Bangestad, 1981). For example, given the expectation that another person is an extrovert, people tend to ask questions and behave in a way that preferentially elicits evidence of extroverted behavior (Snyder and Swann, 1978a, 1978b). Thus, there are strong reasons to expect actor-observer differences to be a pervasive factor in interpersonal communication.

Implication 4: Communication and Conflict

Several authors point out that communication is often ineffective in resolving tense, emotional conflicts (Newcomb, 1947; Etzioni, 1967; see also Rubin and Brown, 1975). This problem may be cast partly in attributional terms. Actor-observer biases are likely to be exaggerated in emotional conflicts, thereby making it difficult for the parties to develop a common definition of the issues.

The most obvious way that attributions might be affected by the intensity of conflict is by an increasing presence of self-serving bias, due to the level of emotional involvement. In addition, discrepancies in the information each party has about the other are likely to increase, because communication tends to be distorted or cut off in hostile conflicts (Newcomb, 1947; Deutsch and Krauss, 1962). Perhaps most notable is the fact that emotional behavior is exceedingly salient. As we have seen, salient information tends to dominate causal attributions. Therefore, the parties will tend to blame one another for their conflicts, because the most salient information to each party consists of the negative and more dramatic actions of the other party. Further, this effect should increase to the extent that there is overt expression of emotions. Finally, high levels of stress reduce conceptual complexity, which includes the ability to differentiate and simultaneously consider multiple points of view (see Schroder et al., 1967). These abilities are apparently instrumental in reducing actor-observer bias, since several studies show that actor-observer differences are diminished by encouraging subjects to take the perspective of the other (Wegner and Finsuen, 1977; Regan and Totten, 1975; Taylor and Achitoff, 1978). Overall, these points indicate that there tends to be an increasing schism between actor-observer perspectives as conflicts escalate.

Tentative support for this reasoning exists. Bernal (1978), in a study of marital couples, and Sillars (1980a, 1980b), in two studies of college roommates, found increasing actor-observer attributional differences as a function of decreasing relationship adjustment and increasing severity of conflict. Less direct evidence is provided by Kahn (1970), who found that marital satisfaction was negatively related to shared perceptions of nonverbal communication. Further, Suedfeld and Tetlock (1977) and Sillars and Parry (1982), in studies of political and interpersonal conflicts respectively, found that increasing levels of stress were associated with communication that tended to depict a one-sided, black-white view of conflict.

These points suggest that some moderation in attributional bias and stress levels may often be necessary before communication is effective in further reducing conflict. Indeed, some accounts suggest that one of the primary functions of third-party mediation may be to reduce attributional discrepancies, since attribution biases tend to subside in the presence of a neutral third party (see Bradley, 1978; Wells et al., 1977).

Implication 5: Familiarity and the Accuracy of Social Inference

One implication of Kelley's covariance principle is that attributions are principally biased by lack of information. Extrapolating further, this implies that people who increase their familiarity with one another tend to develop more accurate and congruent attributions. From this standpoint we might expect the most interesting biases in social inference to occur when we are unfamiliar with a person, since the problems should tend to resolve themselves in long-term relationships. However, a broader view of the literature on attribution and interpersonal relationships indicates that this simple trajectory of familiarity increasing accuracy is misleading.

While it is true that informatioin about another person increases our ability to predict his or her attitudes and behavior in certain respects (Cline, 1964; Kraupl, 1956; Obitz and Oziel, 1972; Honeycutt et al., 1981), there are several characteristic ways that the accuracy and congruence of attributions may be problematic in close relationships (see Sillars and Scott, 1981). For example, several studies note instances in which parents and spouse tend to perceive their own behavior as less controlling, less rejecting, and more affectionate than it is perceived by other family members (Fichten, 1978; Hawkins, et al., 1980; Dalusio, 1972; Zucker and Barron, 1971). Moreover, intimate partners tend to overestimate the extent to which they share the same attitudes and perceptions of relationship issues (Byrne and Blaylock, 1963; Levinger and Breedlove, 1966; Williamson, 1975; Harvey et al., 1978). Although Kelley's covariance model implies that familiarity increases accuracy and consensus about attributions, more recent work by Kelley and his colleagues (Kelley, 1977, 1979; Orvis et al., 1976) emphasizes the prevalence of attributional conflicts among intimates, that is, disagreements centering on one partner's explanations of the other's behavior.

Sillars and Scott (1981) suggest that communicative accuracy and congruence of attributions within close relationships should be seen as the function of several interacting factors. On one hand, accuracy on some dimensions should tend to be increassed, relative to nonintimate relationships, because there tends to be greater depth and breadth of self-disclosure (Altman and Taylor, 1973), greater opportunity to establish shared communicative rules (Cushman and Whiting, 1972), and generally more information about the partner's present and past

(Davis, 1973) than in nonintimate relationships. On the other hand, one's vantage may be obscured by the high degree of interdependence between one's own and the partner's style of behavior and the corresponding difficulties of causal attribution, by a tendency for the longevity of a relationship to accentuate perseverance and confidence in attributions, and by the biasing effects of negative, stressful, and emotional interaction, which tends to occur with greater frequency and proportion in intimate than in nonintimate relationships (Simmel, 1904; Straus, 1974; Winter et al., 1973; Ryder, 1969; Birchler et al., 1965; Fitzpatrick and Winke, 1979). Therefore, the development of more accurate and congruent attributions does not depend simply on the sheer bulk of information present but on characteristics of the relationship that govern the way information is processed, such as the amount of conflict and stress present and the ideology and interaction style of relationship partners (Sillars and Scott, 1981; Fitzpatrick and Indvik, 1978; Fitzpatrick and Best, 1979).

Conclusion

Attributions frame the context in which messages are initiated and received. Therefore, one's view of human communication may be informed by the way attribution processes operate. The portrait of social actors depicted by attribution theory is pluralistic. People are both reflective and spontaneous, rational and rationalizing, logical and illogical. The current problem is how to integrate different processes. In an attempt to reconcile different interpretations of attribution, several authors have suggested that there are multiple processing systems that obey different processing rules (see Taylor and Fiske, 1978; Duval and Wicklund, 1972; Rogers, 1980). However, there is still little indication of how these processes might interact. The implication of the present standoff is that researchers concerned with social cognition and interaction should attempt to specify when different processes are likely to dominate.

References

Ajzen, I. Intuitive theories of events and the effects of base-rate information on prediction. *Journal of Personality and Social Psychology,* 1977, *35,* 303-314.

Altman, I., and Taylor, D. A. *Social penetration: The development of interpersonal relationships.* New York: Holt, Rinehart & Winston, 1973.

Argyle, M., and Little, B. R. Do personality traits apply to social behavior? *Journal for the Theory of Social Behaviour,* 1973, *2,* 1-35.

Bateson, C. Information and codification: A philosophical approach. Pp. 168-211 in J. Reusch and G. Bateson (Eds.), *Communication: The social matrix of psychiatry.* New York: Norton, 1951.

Bateson, G. *Steps to an ecology of mind.* New York: Ballantine, 1972.

Beckman, L. Effects of students' performance on teachers' and observers' attributions of causality. *Journal of Educational Psychology,* 1970, *61,* 76-82.

Beckman, L. Teachers' and observers' perceptions of causality for a child's performance. *Journal of Educational Psychology,* 1973, *65,* 198-204.

Bem, D. J. An experimental analysis of self-persuasion. *Journal of Experimental Social Psychology,* 1965, *1,* 199-218.

Bem, D. J. Self-perception theory. Pp. 2-62 in L. Berkowitz (Ed.). *Advances in Experimental social psychology* (Vol. 6). New York: Academic Press, 1972.

Berger, C. R. *The acquaintance process revisited: Explorations in initial interaction.* Presented at the Speech Communication Association Convention, New York, 1973.

Berger, C. R., and Calabrese, R. J. Some explorations in initial interactions and beyond: Toward a development theory of interpersonal communication. *Human Communication Research,* 1975, *1,* 99-112.

Berger, C. R., Gardner, R. R., Clatterbuck, G. W., and Schulman, L. S. *Perceptions of information sequencing in relationship development.* Presented at the Speech Communication Association Convention, Houston, 1975.

Berger, C. R., Gardner, R. R., Parks, M. R., Schulman, L., and Miller, G. R. Interpersonal epistemology and interpersonal communication. Pp. 149-172 in G. R. Miller (Ed.), *Explorations in interpersonal communication.* Beverly Hills, CA: Sage, 1976.

Berger, C. R., and Perkins, J. W. Studies in interpersonal epistemology I: Situational attributes in observational context selection. Pp. 171-184 in B. D. Ruben (Ed.), *Communication Yearbook 2.* New Brunswick, NJ: Transaction, 1978.

Berkowitz, L., and Rawlings, E. Effects of film violence on inhibitions against subsequent aggression. *Journal of Abnormal and Social Psychology,* 1963, *66,* 405-419.

Bernal, G. *Couple interactions: A study of the punctuation process.* Unpublished doctoral dissertation, University of Massachusetts, 1978.

Birchler, G. R., Weiss, R. L., and Vincent, J. P. Multimethod analysis of reinforcement exchange between maritally distressed and nondistressed spouse and stranger dyads. *Journal of Personality and Social Psychology,* 1978, *31,* 349-360.

Bochner, A. P., and Krueger, D. L. Interpersonal communication theory and research: An overview. Pp. 197-212 in D. Nimmo (Ed.), *Communication Yearbook 3.* New Brunswick, NJ: Transaction, 1979.

Bradley, G. Self-serving biases in the attribution process: A reexamination of the fact or fiction question. *Journal of Personality and Social Psychology,* 1978, *36,* 56-71.

Brewer, M. B. An information-processing approach to attributions of responsibility. *Journal of Experimental Social Psychology,* 1977, *13,* 58-69.

Byrne, D., and Blaylock, B. Similarity and assumed similarity between husbands and wives. *Journal of Abnormal and Social Psychology,* 1967, *67,* 636-640.

Cantor, N., and Mischel, W. Traits as prototypes: Effects on recognition memory. *Journal of Personality and Social Psychology,* 1977, *35,* 38-49.

Cappella, J. N. Research methodology in communication research: Overview and commentary. Pp. 37-54 in B. Ruben (Ed.), *Communication Yearbook 1.* New Brunswick, NJ: Transaction, 1977.

Carroll, J. S., and Payne, J. W. The psychology of the parole decision process: A joint application of attribution theory and information processing psychology. Pp. 13-32 in J. S. Carroll and J. W. Payne (Eds.), *Cognition and social behavior.* Hillsdale, NJ: Erlbaum, 1976.

Chaikin, A. L., and Darley, J. M. Victim or perpetrator? Defensive attribution of responsibility and the need for order and justice. *Journal of Personality and Social Psychology,* 1973, *25,* 268-275.

Chapman, L. J., and Chapman, J. D. Genesis of popular but erroneous diagnostic observations. Journal of Abnormal Psychology, 1967, *72*, 193-204.

Chapman, L. J., and Chapman, J. D. Illusory correlation as an obstacle to the use of valid psychodiagnostic signs. *Journal of Abnormal Psychology,* 1969, *74*, 271-280.

Cline, V. B. Interpersonal perceptions. Pp. 221-284 in B. A. Mahr (Ed.), *Progress in experimental personality research.* New York: Academic Press, 1964.

Cohen, C. *Cognitive basis of stereotyping.* Presented at the American Psychological Association Convention, San Francisco, 1964.

Cohen, C. E., and Ebbesen, E. B. Observational goals and schema activation: A theoretical framework for behavior perception. *Journal of Experimental Social Psychology,* 1979, *15*, 305-329.

Collins, W. A. Effects of temporal separation between motivation, aggression, and consequences: A developmental study. *Developmental Psychology,* 1973, *8*, 215-221.

Collins, W. A. Children's comprehension of television content. Pp. 21-52 in E. Wartella (Ed.), *Children communicating: Media and development of thought, speech, understanding.* Beverly Hills, CA: Sage, 1979.

Cronen, V. E., Pearce, W. B., and Snavely, L. M. A theory of rule-structure and types of episodes and a study of perceived enmeshment in undesired repetitive patterns ("URPs") Pp. 225-240 in D. Nimmon (Ed.), *Communication Yearbook 3.* New Brunswick, NJ: Transaction, 1979.

Cunningham, J. D., and Kelley, H. H. Causal attributions for interpersonal events of varying magnitude. *Journal of Personality,* 1975, *43*, 74-93.

Cushman, D. P., and Craig, R. T. Communication systems: Interpersonal implications. Pp. 39-59 in G. R. Miller (Ed.), *Explorations in interpersonal communication.* Beverly Hills, CA: Sage, 1976.

Cushman, D., and Whiting, G. An approach to communication theory: Toward consensus on rules. *Journal of Communication,* 1972, *22*, 217-238.

Dalusio, V. E. *Self-disclosure and perceptions of that self-disclosure between parents and their teenage children.* Unpublished doctoral dissertation, American International University, 1972.

Daly, J. A., and Korinek, J. T. *Availability in conversational decision-making.* Unpublished manuscript, University of Texas, 1981.

Davis, M. S. *Intimate relations.* New York: Free Press, 1973.

Deutsch, M., and Krauss, R. M. Studies of interpersonal bargaining. *Journal of Conflict Resolution,* 1962, *6*, 52-76.

Duval, S., and Hensley, V. Extensions of objective self-awareness theory: The focus of attention-causal attribution hypothesis. Pp. 165-198 in J. H. Harvey, W. J. Ickes, and R. F. Kidd (Eds.), *New directions in attribution research* (Vol. 1). Hillsdale, NJ: Erlbaum, 1976.

Duval, S., and Wicklund, R. A. *A theory of objective self awareness.* New York: Academic Press, 1972.

Ellis, D. G. Trait predictors of relational control. Pp. 185-192 in B. D. Ruben (Ed.), *Communication Yearbook 2.* New Brunswick, NJ: Transaction, 1978.

Ellis, D. G. Relational control in two group systems. *Communication Monographs,* 1979, *46*, 153-166.

Endler, N. S. The case for person-situation interactions. *Canadian Psychological Review,* 1975, *16*, 12-21.

Endler, N. S., and Magnusson, D. *Interactional psychology and personality.* New York: John Wiley, 1976.

Etzioni, A. The Kennedy experiment. *Western Political Quarterly,* 1967, *20*, 361-380.

Feldman, N. S., Higgins, E. J., Karlovac, M., and Ruble, D. M. Use of consensus information in causal attributions as a function of temporal presentation and availability of direct information. *Journal of Personality and Social Psychology*, 1976, *34*, 694-698.

Fichten, C. M. *Videotape and verbal feedback: Effects on behavior and attributions in distressed couples.* Unpublished doctoral dissertation, McGill University, 1978.

Fischoff, B. Attribution theory and judgment under uncertainty. Pp. 421-452 in J. H. Harvey, W. J. Ickes, and R. F. Kidd (Eds.), *New directions in attribution research* (Vol. 1). Hillsdale, NJ: Erlbaum, 1976.

Fitzpatrick, M. A., and Best, P. Dyadic adjustment in relational types: Consensus, cohesion, affectional expression and satisfaction in enduring relationships. *Communication Monographs*, 1979, *46*, 167-178.

Fitzpatrick, M. A., and Indvik, J. *What you see may not be what you have: Communicative accuracy in marital types.* Presented to the Speech Communication Association Convention, Minneapolis, 1978.

Fitzpatrick, M. A., and Winke, J. J. You always hurt the one you love: Strategies and tactics in interpersonal conflict. *Communication Quarterly*, 1979, *27*, 3-11.

Folger, J. P., and Poole, M. S. Relational coding schemes: The question of validity. In M. Burgoon (Ed.), *Communication Yearbook 5.* New Brunswick, NJ: Transaction, 1981.

Folger, J. P., and Sillars, A. L. Relational coding and perceptions of dominance. In B. W. Morse and L. A. Phelps (Eds.), *Interpersonal communication: A relational perspective.* Minneapolis: Burgess, 1980.

Frieze, I. H., Bar-Tal, D., and Carroll, J. S. *New approaches to social problems: Applications of attribution theory.* San Francisco: Jossey-Bass, 1979.

Gottlieb, A., and Ickes, W. Attributional strategies of social influence, pp. 261-298 in J. H. Harvey, W. J. Ickes, and R. F. Kidd (Eds.), *New directions in attribution research* (Vol. 3). Hillsdale, NJ: Erlbaum, 1978.

Hamilton, D. L., and Rose, T. *The role of associatively-based illusory correlation in the maintenance of stereotypic concepts.* Unpublished manuscript, University of California at Santa Barbara, 1978.

Hamilton, D. L. A cognitive attributional analysis of stereotypic. Pp. 53-131 in L. Berkowitz (Ed.), *Advances in experimental social psychology* (Vol. 12). New York: Academic Press, 1979.

Hansen, R. D., and Donoghue, J. M. The power of consensus: Information derived from one's own and others' behavior. *Journal of Personality and Social Psychology*, 1977, *35*, 294-302.

Hansen, R. D., and Lowe, C. A. Distinctiveness and consensus: The influence of behavior information on actors' and observers' attributions. *Journal of Personality and Social Psychology*, 1976, *34*, 425-433.

Hansen, R. D., and Stonner, D. M. Attributes and attributions: Inferring stimulus properties, actors' dispositions, and causes. *Journal of Personality and Social Psychology*, 1978, *36*, 657-667.

Harvey, J. H., Ickes, W. J., and Kidd, R. F. *New directions in attribution research* (Vol. 1). Hillsdale, NJ: Erlbaum, 1976.

Harvey, J. H., Ickes, W. J., and Kidd, R. F. *New directions in attribution research* (Vol. 2). Hillsdale, NJ: Erlbaum, 1978.

Harvey, J. H., Ickes, W. J., and Kidd, R. F. *New directions in attribution research* (Vol. 3). Hillsdale, NJ: Erlbaum, 1981.

Harvey, J. H., Wells, G. L., and Alvarez, M. D. Attributions in the context of conflict and separation in close relationships. Pp. 235-260 in J. H. Harvey, W. J. Ickes, and

R. F. Kidd (Eds.), *New directions in attribution research* (Vol. 2). Hillsdale, NJ: Erlbaum, 1978.

Hawkins, J. L., Weisberg, C., and Ray, D. W. Spouse differences in communication style: Preference, perception, and behavior. *Journal of Marriage and the Family,* 1980, *42,* 585-593.

Heider, F. Social perception and phenomenal causality. *Psychological Review,* 1944, *51,* 358-374.

Heider, F. *The psychology of interpersonal relations.* New York: John Wiley, 1958.

Heider, F. A conversation with Fritz Heider. Pp. 3-18 in J. H. Harvey, W. J. Ickes, and R. F. Kidd (Eds.), *New directions in attribution research* (Vol. 1). Hillsdale, NJ: Erlbaum, 1976.

Heider, F., and Simmel, M. An experimental study of apparent behavior. *American Journal of Psychology,* 1944, *57,* 243-259.

Hewes, D. E., and Haight, L. The cross-situational consistency of communicative behaviors: A preliminary investigation. *Communication Research,* 1979, *6,* 243-270.

Himmelfarb, S., and Anderson, N. H. Integration theory applied to opinion attribution. *Journal of Personality and Social Psychology,* 1975, *31,* 1064-1071.

Honeycutt, J. M., Knapp, M. L., and Powers, W. G. *On knowing others and predicting what they say.* Unpublished manuscript, University of Illinois, 1981.

Ickes, W., and Layden, M. A. (1978) Attributional styles. Pp. 119-156 in J. H. Harvey, W. J. Ickes, and R. F. Kidd (Eds.), *New directions in attribution research* (Vol. 2). Hillsdale, NJ: Erlbaum, 1978.

Ickes, W., Patterson, M. L., Rajecki, D. W., and Tanford, S. Cognitive consequences of reciprocal versus complementary responses to pre-interaction expectancies. *Social Cognition,* forthcoming.

Jones, E. E. A conversation with Edward E. Jones and Harold H. Kelley. Pp. 371-387 in J. H. Harvey, W. J. Ickes, and R. F. Kidd (Eds.), *New directions in attribution research* (Vol. 2). Hillsdale, NJ: Erlbaum, 1978.

Jones, E. E. The rocky road from acts to dispositions. *American Psychologist,* 1979, *34,* 107-117.

Jones, E. E., and Archer, R. L. Are there spcial effects of personalistic self-disclosure? *Journal of Experimental Social Psychology,* 1976, *12,* 180-193.

Jones, E. E., and Davis, K. E. From acts to dispositions: The attribution process in person perception. Pp. 219-266 in L. Berkowitz (Ed.), *Advances in experimental social psychology* (Vol. 2). New York: Academic Press, 1965.

Jones, E. E., and Gordon, E. M. Timing of self-disclosure and its effects on personal attraction. *Journal of Personality and Social Psychology,* 1972, *42,* 358-365.

Jones, E. E., and Harris, V. A. The attribution of attitudes. *Journal of Experimental Social Psychology,* 1967, *3,* 1-24.

Jones, E. E., Kanouse, D. E., Kelley, H. H., Nisbett, R. E., Valins, S., and Weiner, B. *Attribution: Perceiving the causes of behavior.* Morristown, NJ: General Learning, 1972.

Jones, E. E., and McGillis, D. Correspondent inferences and the attribution cube: A comparative reappraisal. Pp. 389-420 in J. H. Harvey, W. J. Ickes, and R. F. Kidd (Eds.), *New directions in attribution research* (Vol. 1). Hillsdale, NJ: Erlbaum, 1976.

Jones, E. E., and Nisbett, R. E. The actor and the observer: Divergent perceptions of the causes of behavior. Pp. 78-94 in E. E. Jones et al. (Eds.), *Attribution: Perceiving the causes of behavior.* Morristown, NJ: General Learning, 1972.

Jones, E. E., Worchel, S., Goethals, G. R., and Grumet, J. F. Prior expectancy and behavioral extremity as determinants of attitude attribution. *Journal of Experimental Social Psychology,* 1971, *7,* 59-80.

Jones, E. E., and Wortman, C. *Ingratiation: An attributional approach.* Morristown, NJ: General Learning, 1973.

Kahn, M. (1970) Nonverbal communication and marital satisfaction. *Family Process,* 1970, *9,* 449-456.

Kahneman, D., and Tversky, A. On the psychology of prediction. *Psychological Review,* 1973, *80,* 237-251.

Kanouse, D. E. Lauguage, labelling, and attribution. Pp. 121-136 in E. E. Jones et al. (Eds.), *Attribution: Perceiving the causes of behavior.* Morristown, NJ: General Learning, 1972.

Kanouse, D. E., and Hanson, L. R. Negativity in evaluation. Pp. 47-62 in E. E. Jones et al. (Eds.), *Attribution: Perceiving the causes of behavior.* Morristown, NJ: General Learning, 1972.

Kelley, H. H. Attribution theory in social psychology. Pp. 192-240 in D. Levine (Ed.), *Nebraska Symposium on Motivation* (Vol. 14). Lincoln: University of Nebraska Press, 1967.

Kelley, H. H. Attribution in social interaction. Pp. 1-26 in E. E. Jones et al. (Eds.), *Attribution: Perceiving the causes of behavior.* Morristown, NJ: General Learning, 1972. (a)

Kelley, H. H. Causal schemata and the attribution process. Pp. 151-174 in E. E. Jones et al. (Eds.), *Attribution: Perceiving the causes of behavior.* Morristown, NJ: General Learning, 1972. (b)

Kelley, H. H. The processes of causal attribution. *American Psychologist,* 1973, *28,* 107-128.

Kelley, H. H. An application of attribution theory to research methodology for close relationships. Pp. 87-114 in G. Levinger and H. L. Rausch (Eds.), *Close relationships: Perspectives on the meaning of intimacy.* Amherst, MA: University of Massachusetts Press, 1977.

Kelley, H. H. *Personal relationships: Their structures and processes.* Hillsdale, NJ: Erlbaum, 1979.

Kelley, H. H., and Michela, J. L. Attribution theory and research. *Annual Review of Psychology,* 1980, *31,* 457-501.

Kelley, H. H., and Stahelski, A. J. Errors in perceptions of intentions in a mixed-motive game. *Journal of Experimental Social Psychology,* 1970, *6,* 379-400.

Krauple, T. F. Awareness of one's social appeal. *Human Relations,* 1956, *9,* 47-56.

Kulik, J. A., and Brown, R. Frustration, attribution of blame, and aggression. *Journal of Experimental Social Psychology,* 1979, *15,* 183-194.

Kun, A., and Weiner, B. Necessary versus sufficient causal schemata for success and failure. *Journal of Research on Personality,* 1973, *7,* 197-207.

Lerner, M. J. The desire for justice and reaction to victims. Pp. 209-229 in J. R. Macaulay and L. Berkowitz (Eds.), *Altruism and helping behavior.* New York: Academic Press, 1970.

Lerner, M. J., Miller, D. T., and Holmes, J. G. Deserving and the emergence of forms of justice. Pp. 134-162 in L. Berkowitz and E. Walster (Eds.), *Advances in experimental social psychology* (Vol. 9). New York: Academic Press, 1976.

Levinger, C., and Breedlove, J. Interpersonal attraction and agreement. *Journal of Personality and Social Psychology,* 1966, *3,* 367-372.

Magnusson, D., and Endler, N. S. *Personality at the crossroads.* New York: John Wiley, 1977.

Massad, C. M., Hubbard, M., and Newtson, D. Selective perception of evens. *Journal of Experimental Social Psychology,* 1979, *15,* 513-532.

McArthur, L. Z. The how and what of why: Some determinants and consequences of causal attribution. *Journal of Personality and Social Psychology,* 1972, *22,* 171-192.

McArthur, L. Z. The lesser influence of consensus than distinctiveness information on causal attributions: A test of the person-thing hypothesis. *Journal of Personality and Social Psychology,* 1976, *33,* 733-742.

McArthur, L. Z. Illusory correlation and illusory causation: Two epistemological accounts. *Personality and Social Psychology Bulletin,* 1980, *6,* 507-519.

McArthur, L. Z., and Post, D. Figural emphasis and person perception. *Journal of Experimental Social Psychology,* 1977, *13,* 520-535.

McLeod, J. M. and Chaffee, S. H. The construction of social reality. Pp. 50-99 in J. T. Tedeschi (Ed.), *The social influence processes.* Chicago: Aldine-Atherton, 1972.

Mead, G. H. *Mind, self, and society.* Chicago: University of Chicago Press, 1934.

Millar, F. E., Rogers-Millar, L. E., and Courtright, J. A. Relational control and dyadic understanding: An exploratory predictive regression model. Pp. 213-224 in D. Nimmo (Ed.), *Communication Yearbook 3.* New Brunswick, NJ: Transaction, 1979.

Miller, A. G. Perceived freedom and the attribution of attitudes. *Representative Research in Social Psychology,* 1974, *5,* 61-80.

Miller, A. G. Constraint and target effects in the attribution of attitudes. *Journal of Experimental Social Psychology,* 1976, *12,* 325-339.

Miller, D. T. Ego-involvement and attributions for success and failure. *Journal of Personality and Social Psychology,* 1976, *34,* 901-906.

Miller, D. T., and Ross, M. Self serving biases in the attribution of causality: Fact or fiction? *Psychological Bulletin,* 1975, *82,* 213-225.

Miller, G. R., and Steinberg, M. *Between people: A new analysis of interpersonal communication.* Palo Alto, CA: Science Research Associates, 1975.

Mischel, W. *Personality and assessment.* New York: John Wiley, 1968.

Mischel, W. Towards a cognitive social learning reconceptualization of personality. *Psychology Review,* 1973, *80,* 252-283.

Mizerski, R. W., Golden, L. L., and Kernan, J. B. The attribution process in consumer decision making. *Journal of Consumer Research,* 1979, *6,* 123-140.

Monson, T. C., and Snyder, M. Actors, observers, and the attribution process. *Journal of Experimental Social Psychology,* 1977, *13,* 89-111.

Newcomb, T. M. Autistic hostility and social reality. *Human Relations,* 1947, *1,*69-86.

Newtson, D. Dispositional inference from effects of actions: Effects chosen and effects foregone. *Journal of Experimental Social Psychology,* 1974, *10,* 489-496.

Newtson, D. An interactionist perspective on social knowing. *Personality and Social Psychology Bulletin,* 1980, *6,* 520-531.

Newtson, D., Rindner, R., Miller, R., and LaCross, K. Effects of availability of feature changes in behavior segmentation. *Journal of Experimental Social Psychology,* 1978, *14,* 379-388.

Nisbett, R., and Bellows, N. Verbal reports about causal influences on social judgments: Private access versus public theories. *Journal of Personality and Social Psychology,* 1977, *35,* 613-624.

Nisbett, R., and Borgida, E. Attribution and the psychology of prediction. *Journal of Personality and Social Psychology,* 1975, *32,* 932-943.

Nisbett, R., Bordiga, E., Crandall, R., and Reed, H. Popular induction: Information is not necessarily informative. Pp. 113-134 in J. S. Carroll and J. W. Payne (Eds.), *Cognition and social behavior.* Hillsdale, NJ: Erlbaum, 1976.

Nisbett, R., and Ross, L. *Human inference: Strategies and shortcomings of social judgment.* Englewood Cliffs, NJ: Prentice-Hall, 1980.

Nisbett, R., and Wilson, T. D. Telling more than we can know: Verbal reports on mental processes. *Psychological Review,* 1977, *84,* 231-259.

Obitz, F. W., and Oziel, J. L. Varied information levels and accuracy of person perception. *Psychological Reports*, 1972, *31*, 571-576.

Orvis, B. R., Cunningham, J. D., and Kelley, H. H. A closer examination of causal inference: The roles of consensus, distinctiveness and consistency information. *Journal of Personality and Social Psychology*, 1975, *32*, 605-616.

Orvis, B. R., Kelley, H. H., and Butler, D. Attributional conflict in young couples. Pp. 353-380 in H. H. Harvey, W. J. Ickes, and R. F. Kidd (Eds.), *New directions in attribution research* (Vol. 1). Hillsdale, NJ: Erlbaum, 1976.

Parks, M. R. Relational communication: Theory and research. *Human Communication Research*, 1977, *3*, 372-381.

Planalp, S., and Hewes, D. E. A cognitive approach to communication theory: *Cogito ergo dico?* In M. Burgoon (Ed.), *Communication Yearbook 5*. New Brunswick, NJ: Transaction, 1981.

Prus, R. Resisting designation: An extension of attribution theory into a negotiated context. *Sociological Inquiry*, 1975, *45*, 3-14.

Regan, D., and Totten, J. Empathy and attribution: Turning observers into actors. *Jouural of Personality and Social Psychology*, 1975, *32*, 850-856.

Reusch, J., and Bateson, G. *Communication: The social matrix of psychiatry*. New York: Norton, 1951.

Rogers, E. L., and Farace, R. V. Analysis of relational communication in dyads: New measurement procedures. *Human Communication Research*, 1975, *1*, 229-239.

Rogers, T. B. Models of man: The beauty and/or the beast? *Personality and Social Psychology Bulletin*, 1980, *6*, 582-589.

Rogers-Millar, L. E., and Millar, F. E. Domineeringness and dominance: A transactional view. *Human Communication Research*, 1979, *5*, 238-246.

Roloff, M. E. *Interpersonal communication: A social exchange approach*. Beverly Hills, CA: Sage, 1981.

Rosenberg, S. W., and Wolfsfeld, G. International conflict and the problem of attibution. *Journal of Conflict Resolution* 1977, *21*, 75-103.

Ross, L. The intuitive psychologist and his shortcomings: Distortions in the attribution process. Pp. 173-220 in L. Berkowitz (Ed.), *Advances in experimental social psychlogy* (Vol. 10). New York: Academic Press, 1977.

Ross, L., Amabile, T. M., and Steinmetz, J. L. Social roles, social control, and biases in social-perception processes. *Journal of Personality and Social Psychology*, 1977, *35*, 485-494.

Ross, L., Greene, D., and House, P. The false consensus phenomenon: An attributional bias in self perception and social perception processes. *Journal of Experimental Social Psychology*, 1977, *13*, 279-301.

Ross, L., Lepper, M. R., and Hubbard, M. Perseverence in self perception and social perception: Biased attributional processing in the debriefing paradigm. *Journal of Personality and Social Psychology*, 1975, *32*, 880-892.

Ross, M., and Sicoly, F. Egocentric biases in availability and attribution. *Journal of Personality and Social Psychology*, 1979, *37*, 322-336.

Rubin, J. Z., and Brown, B. R. *The social psychology of bargaining and negotiation*. New York: Academic Press, 1975.

Ryder, R. Husband-wife dyads versus married strangers. *Family Process*, 1969, *7*, 233-238.

Schank, R., and Abelson, R. P. *Scripts, plans, goals, and understanding: An inquiry into human knowledge structures*. Hillsdale, NJ: Erlbaum, 1977.

Scheff, T. J. A theory of coordination applicable to mixed motive-games. *Sociometry*, 1967, *30*, 215-234.

Schroder, H. M., Driver, M. J., and Streufert, S. *Human information processing: Individuals and groups functioning in complex social situations*. New York: Holt, Rinehart & Winston, 1967.

Seibold, D. R., and Spitzberg, B. H. Attribution theory and research: Formalization, review, and implications for communication. In B. Derbin and M. J. Voight (Eds.), *Progress in communication sciences* (Vol. 3). Norwood, NJ: Ablex, 1981. (a)

Seibold, D. R., and Spitzberg, B. H. *Adding "inference" interaction-influence link: Attributional approaches to persuasion*. Presented at the International Communication Association Convention, Minneapolis, 1981. (b)

Shaver, K. G. *An introduction to attribution processes*. Cambridge, MA: Winthrop, 1975.

Sicoly, F., and Ross, M. Facilitation of ego-biased attributions by means of self-serving observer feedback. *Journal of Personality and Social Psychology*, 1977, *35*, 734-741.

Sillars, A. L. Attributions and communication in roommate conflicts. *Communication Monographs*, 1980, *47*, 180-200. (a)

Sillars, A. L. The sequential and distributional structure of conflict interactions as a function of attributions concerning the locus of responsibility and stability of conflicts. Pp. 217-235 in D. Nimmo (Ed.), *Communication Yearbook 4*. New Brunswick, NJ: Transaction, 1980. (b)

Sillars, A. L. Attributions and interpersonal conflict resolution. Pp. 279-305 in J. H. Harvey, H. J. Ickes, and R. F. Kidd (Eds.), *New directions in attribution research* (Vol. 3). Hillsdale, NJ: Erlbaum, 1981.

Sillars, A. L., and Parry, D. Stress, cognition, and communication in interpersonal conflicts. *Communication Research*, 1982, *9*, 201-226.

Sillars, A. L., and Scott, M. D. *Communicative accuracy and person perception in close relationships: An integrative review*. Presented at the Speech Communication Association Convention, Anaheim, California, 1981.

Simmel, G. The sociology of conflict. *American Journal of Sociology*, 1904, *9*, 490-525, 675-689, 798-811.

Slovic, P., and Lichtenstein, S. Comparison of Bayesian and regression approaches to the study of information processing in judgment. *Organizational Behavior and Human Performance*, 1971, *6*, 649-744.

Snyder, M., and Bangestad, S. Hypothesis-testing processes. Pp. 171-196 in J. H. Harvey, W. J. Ickes, and R. F. Kidd (Eds.), *New directions in attribution research* (Vol. 3). Hillsdale, NJ: Erlbaum, 1981.

Snyder, M., and Jones, E. E. Attitude attribution when behavior is constrained. *Journal of Experimental Social Psychology*, 1974, 10, 585-600.

Snyder, M., Stephan, W. G., and Rosenfield, D. Attributional egotism. In J. H. Harvey, W. J. Ickes, and R. F. Kidd (Eds.), *New directions in attribution research* (Vol. 2). Hillsdale, NJ: Erlbaum, 1978.

Snyder, M., and Swann, W. B. Hypothesis-testing processes in social interaction. *Journal of Personality and Social Psychology*, 1978, *36*, 1202-1212. (a)

Snyder, M., and Swann, W. B. Behavioral confirmation in social interaction: From social perception to social reality. *Journal of Experimental Social Psychology*, 1978, *14*, 148-162. (b)

Snyder, M., Tanke, E. D., and Berscheid, E. Social perception and interpersonal behavior: On the self-fulfilling nature of social stereotypes. *Journal of Personality and Social Psychology*, 1977, *35*, 656-666.

Steiner, I., and Field, W. Role assignment and interpersonal influence. *Journal of Abnormal and Social Psychology,* 1960, *61,* 239-246.

Straus, M. (1974) Leveling, civility and violence in the family. *Journal of Marriage and the Family,* 1974, *36,* 13-29.

Suedfeld, P., and Tetlock, P. Integrative complexity of communication in international crises. *Journal of Conflict Resolution,* 1977, *21,* 169-184.

Taylor, S. E., and Achitoff, P. *To see ourselves as others see us: Empathy, role-taking, and actor-observer effects.* Unpublished manuscript, Harvard University, 1978.

Taylor, S. E., and Fiske, S. T. Point of view and perceptions of causality. *Journal of Personality and Social Psychology,* 1978, *32,* 439-445.

Thomas, E. J. *Marital communication and decision making: Analysis, assessment, and change.* New York: Free Press, 1977.

Thomas, K. W., and Pondy, L. R. Toward an "intent" model of conflict management among principle parties. *Human Relations,* 1977, *30,* 1089-1102.

Tversky, A., and Kahneman, D. Availability: A heuristic for judging frequency and probability. *Cognitive Psychology,* 1973, *5,* 207-232.

Tversky, A., and Kahneman, D. Judgment under uncertainty: Heuristics and biases. *Science,* 1974, *185,* 1124-1131.

Walster, E. Assignment of responsibility for an accident. *Journal of Personality and Social Psychology,* 1966, *3,* 73-79.

Watzlawick, P., Beavin, J. H., and Jackson, D. D. *Pragmatics of human communication: A study of interactional patterns, pathologies, and paradoxes.* New York: Norton, 1967.

Weary, G., Rich, M. C., Harvey, J. H., and Ickes, W. J. Heider's formulation of social perception and attributional processes: Toward further clarification. *Personality and Social Psychology Bulletin,* 1980, *6,* 37-43.

Weary, G., Swanson, H., Harvey, J. H., and Yarkin, K. L. A molar approach to social knowing. *Personality and Social Psychology Bulletin,* 1980, *6,* 574-581.

Wegner, B. M., and Finsuen, K. Observers' focus of attention in the simulation of self perception. *Journal of Personality and Social Psychology,* 1977, *35,* 56-62.

Wegner, B. M., Frieze, I., Kukla, A., Reed, L., Rest, S., and Rosenbaum, M. Perceiving the causes of success and failure. In E. E. Jones et al. (Eds.), *Attribution: Perceiving the causes of behavior.* Morristown, NJ: General Learning Press, 1972.

Weiss, R. L., Hops, H., and Patterson, G. R. A framework for conceptualizing marital conflict: A technology for altering it, some data for evaluating it. Pp. 309-342 in L. A. Hamelynck, L. C. Hundy, and E. J. Mash (Eds.), *Behavior change: Methodology, concepts, and practice.* Champaign, IL: Research Press, 1973.

Wells, G. L., and Harvey, J. H. Do people use consensus informaton in making causal attributions? *Journal of Personality and Social Psychology,* 1977, *35,* 279-293.

Wells, G. L., Petty, R. E., Harkins, S. G., Kagehiro, D., and Harvey, J. H. Anticipated discussion of interpretation eliminates actor-observer differences in the attribution of causality. *Sociometry,* 1977, *40,* 247-253.

Williamson, L. K. *Self and other: An empirical study of perception in diadic marital communication system.* Unpublished doctoral dissertation, Temple University, 1975.

Wilmot, W. Metacommunication: A re-examination and extension. Pp. 61-72 in D. Nimmo (Ed.), *Communication Yearbook 4.* New Brunswick, NJ: Transaction, 1980.

Winter, W. D., Ferreira, A. J., and Bowers, N. Decision making in married and unrelated couples. *Family Process,* 1973, *12,* 83-94.

Wortman, C. B. Causal attributions and personal control. Pp. 23-52 in J. H. Harvey, W. J. Ickes, and R. F. Kidd (Eds.), *New directions in attribution research* (Vol. 1). Hillsdale, NJ: Erlbaum, 1976.

Wortman, C. B., Adesman, P., Herman, E., and Greenberg, R. Self-disclosure: An attributional perspective. *Journal of Personality and Social Psychology,* 1976, *33,* 184-191.

Wyer, R. S. The acquisition and use of social knowledge: Basic postulates and representative research. *Personality and Social Psychology Bulletin,* 1980, *6,* 558-573.

Wyer, R. S., and Carlston, D. E. *Social cognition, inference and attribution.* Hillsdale, NJ: Erlbaum, 1974.

Zadney, J., and Gerard, H. B. Attributed intentions and information selectivity. *Journal of Experimental Social Psychology,* 1974, *10,* 34-52.

Zucker, R. A., and Barron, F. H. *Toward a systematic family mythology: The relationship of parents' and adolescents' reports of parental behavior during childhood.* Presented at the Eastern Psychological Association Convention, New York, 1971.

Zuckerman, M. Attribution of success and failure revisited, or: The motivational bias is alive and well in attribution theory. *Journal of Personality,* 1979, *47,* 245-287.

4

There Is Nothing as Useful as a Good Theory . . .

THE INFLUENCE OF SOCIAL KNOWLEDGE ON INTERPERSONAL COMMUNICATION

Dean E. Hewes
Sally Planalp

It is so reasonable to insert between the stimulus and the response a little wisdom. And there is no need to apologize for putting it there, because it was there before psychology arrived.

Miller, Galanter, and Pribram (1960)

Interpersonal communication, like other forms of information gathering, is guided by the twin motivators of simple curiosity and a need for self-efficacy. A sense of understanding, whether of the social world or the physical, seems as much a goal of human action as food, shelter, love, or power—and for good reason. The knowledge that understanding implies provides the basis for all goal-directed human action. Whether we seek affection, control, or simple enlightenment, our understanding of the social world makes our goals more obtainable.

Given this commonsensical sketch of human motivation, it is no wonder that communication researchers have been drawn toward the study of the communication strategies used to acquire social knowledge (see, for instance, Berger, 1979; Berger et al., 1976). This research has been guided, quite rightly, by an image of human beings as "intuitive scientists" (Heider, 1958; Kelley, 1967; Kelly, 1955) who are as vitally interested in the pursuit of knowledge as any professional. Of course, on many occasions we intuitive scientists may not be permitted the luxury of indulging our curiosities, we may be too taxed to seek more than minimally useful understanding (see Berger et al., 1976: 150-151) or we may not want more (Langer, 1978). Nevertheless, we are all scientists in our pursuits, whatever our job descriptions say. Moreover, as we shall see, "intuitive theories" share many informative structural similarities with formal scientific theories, since both arise from a common aim—the practical representation of useful knowledge.

If the image of the "intuitive scientist" has any merit for the study of interpersonal communication, it must suggest research questions. In general terms those who adopt it must identify what aspects of the scientific enterprise correspond to the task of communicators engaged in interpersonal exchanges. There are, of course, a number of aspects of scientific inquiry amenable to this kind of metaphorical extension. For example, the hypothesis-testing duties of both professional and lay scientists give rise to useful comparison in Kelley's (1972) normative ANOVA of the attributional process—a comparison that has proved highly productive in both social psychology (Kelley and Michela, 1980) and communication research (Seibold and Spitzberg, 1981; Sillars, this volume).

An alternative derivation from the image of the "intuitive scientist," arising from within the field of communication, is embodied in the efforts of Berger and his colleagues (for instance, 1979; Berger and Calabrese, 1975; Berger et al., 1976, 1977). These researchers have treated communication strategies as tools employed in the pursuit of social knowledge in much the same way as scientific instruments are tools for physical scientists. This tool orientation places primary emphasis on enumeration of these tools (Berger, 1979), elaboration of the motives that guide their use (that is, "uncertainty reduction"; see Berger and Calabrese, 1975; Berger et al., 1977), and identification of the limitations on their effectiveness in gathering accurate information (Berger et al., 1976). In effect, Berger and his colleagues are attempting to answer these three questions: What motivates the lay scientist? What communication tools are available to the inquiring lay scientist? How useful are these tools in gaining needed knowledge of others?

But if we are to take the notion of the "intuitive scientist" seriously, we must go beyond the answers to these highly informative questions. Although in general terms both lay and professional scientists are motivated to reduce uncertainty, a more detailed consideration of the process of uncertainty reduction is needed. Uncertainty reduction probably is not accomplished by the application of raw induction to the data acquired by means of communication strategies. If it is not, what principles beyond raw induction permit us to reduce uncertainty? Do these principles affect the veridicality of newly acquired social knowledge positively, negatively, or, perhaps, both?

In order to answer these questions, we obviously need to know something more about the process of uncertainty reduction. We have drawn on two sources of such information that manifest striking parallels—parallels that seemingly arise from the common use of the scientific metaphor. On one hand, we derive useful insights from philosopher Norwood Hanson's (1958) work on the "logic" of scientific discovery. On the other, we explore the complex literatures of cognitive and social psychology on attention, interpretation, memory, decision making, and mental representation of knowledge. Our organizing premise is that the professional scientific enterprise is a particularly intensive, self-reflexive, rigorous, and public version of the information acquisition and interpretation tasks faced by all social actors. Science is, after all, formalized common sense (Heider, 1958; Whitehead, 1929). It is precisely because science is both formalized and public that it is useful for the study of interpersonal uncertainty reduction. And it is precisely because science is grounded in common sense that something more than a metaphor links the formal and intuitive scientific enterprises. This is not to ignore differences between the two enterprises. In fact, these differences prove to be central later in our discussion. Nevertheless, the similarities give us a platform from which to launch a discussion of the nature and veridicality of interpersonal uncertainty reduction.

Some Preliminaries on "Uncertainty Reduction"

Before plunging into a detailed discussion of the acquisition of interpersonal information, we need to establish some framework to guide our inquiry. Our framework flows from the points of overlap we see between professional and lay scientists, coupled with a strong commitment to a cognitive approach to communication theorizing (see Planalp and Hewes, 1982). We begin outlining our framework by returning to our first question: What principles beyond raw induction permit us to reduce uncertainty?

Let us begin to answer this question with a trivially true statement: To reduce uncertainty we must discover knowledge about the social world. Unfortunately, although the statement is trivial, its implications are not. How do we "discover knowledge"? Norwood Hanson (1958) provides the beginnings of an answer in his discussion of the logic of professional scientific discovery. This logic of discovery is grounded in one element of Aristotle's typology of inference: ἀπαγωγή. Hanson translates this element as "retroduction," an inferential strategy to be constrasted with and distinct from both induction and deduction. Retroduction amounts to observing a fact and then positing a plausible explanation for it, subject to revision. Unlike deduction, it is synthetic. It yields insights not implied by the original premises. Unlike induction, retroduction is not a strategy for testing the empirical truth of an inference, only the plausibility of that inference (Hanson, 1958: 85-86; see also Peirce, 1931-1935: Vol. V, para. 146, on a similar point concerning the analogous "abduction"). Thus retroduction seems to bear a useful resemblance to the logic of discovery employed by intuitive scientists (Cicourel, 1978, on abduction).

Hanson (1961: 33; 1958: 86) sketches a schematic of retroductive reasoning as follows:

(1) Some [salient] surprising, astonishing [or at least unexplained] phenomena p_1, p_2, p_3, . . . are encountered.

(2) But p_1, p_2, p_3 . . . would not be surprising [or at least unexplained] were a hypothesis of H's type to obtain. They would follow as a matter of course from something like H and would be explained by it.

(3) Therefore there is good reason for elaborating a hypothesis of the type H; for proposing it as a possible hypothesis from whose assumption p_1, p_2, p_3, . . . might be explained.

Of course not all Hs are equally plausible. Thus, whatever the source of an H, it does not make construal of the world arbitrary, although it may have some influence on that construal (Suppe, 1974). Reality is not *completely* governed by the whims of retroducers or their world views.

Hanson's analysis of the "logic" of scientific discovery relies heavily on the existence of sources of plausible explanations of social events. Without some Hs, the world really is incomprehensible. For Hanson, some form of prior knowledge serves as the wellspring for plausible Hs. That knowledge may range from partial analogies drawn from adjudged similar phenomena to fullblown theories, may be accurate, partially so, or pure fiction, and may be held with greater or lesser degrees of confidence. Nevertheless, the tools of uncertainty reduction, whether professional or lay, cannot be applied without the guidance of theories, hypotheses, or metaphors (Kelly, 1955; Leatherdale, 1974; Miller and Steinberg, 1975: Ch. 1; Turner, 1967). *Uncertainty is defined in relationship to prior knowledge; uncertainty reduction is guided by that knowledge.* Clearly, an understanding of the structure and content of social actors' prior interpersonal knowledge is crucial to a complete understanding of uncertainty reduction.

Of course, it is one thing to indicate that such knowledge is necessary for the acquisition of interpersonal information and quite another to describe how it serves that function. Unfortunately, Hanson is not clear on this issue (Suppe, 1974: 66). Neither he nor other like-minded philosophers (Feyerabend, 1975; Kuhn, 1970) have described in detail how prior knowledge influences the labeling of objects or events or of the relationships among objects and/or events, although they have documented the existence of biases apparently created by prior knowledge. What factors might affect the relationship between social knowledge and uncertainty reduction? If we adopt a cognitive approach to communication theorizing (see Planalp and Hewes, 1982), four broad classes of factors come to mind: *goals* (both interpersonal and cognitive), *communication tools* (Berger et al., 1976; Berger, 1979), *cognitive functions* (focusing, integration, inference, storage, retrieval, and so on), and *cognitive capacities* (that is, inherent or practical limitations on cognitive functions). Uncertainty reduction is targeted by the goals of the observer on particular aspects of the interpersonal setting. But even if we could specify a typology of generalized interpersonal goals and the goal-path linkages inherent in the associated communicative and observational tools (see, for example, Goffman, 1969, on uncovering strategies; Lyman and Scott, 1970, on relationship games; and Berger, 1979, on tools for uncertainty reduction)—a task beyond the scope of this essay—we would still need to identify the inferential tasks mandated by the goal and the context in which it is to be satisfied. For instance, in an initial interaction with a peer, an actor might want to reduce uncertainty about the other only enough to pass an evening pleasantly. The actor needs to utilize social knowledge to retroduce plausible interpretations of the other's behavior limited to this context; however, should the other be a potential employer, the actor might well be involved not only in generating plausible interpretations, but in deducing their consequences and testing them as well ("induction," as used by both Hanson, 1958: 85, and Peirce, 1931: Vol. V, para. 171 and Vol. VII, n. 115). Finally, our social actor might compare generalizations made about this prospective employer and others he or she has known to see if these impressions are internally consistent (deduction): Is the prospective employer relatively insightful? Would he or she be easy to work for? In short, each of the interrelated inferential tasks of retroduction, induction, and deduction implies different relationships between social knowledge and the process of uncertainty reduction. Thus, *uncertainty is reduced in the context of specifiable, although often implicit, goals.* These goals confer differing levels of importance on the inferential tasks to be performed in any given interpersonal encounter. It is through these tasks that an actor's cognitive functions and communication tools are brought to bear in attaining those goals.

Of course, most forms of inquiry, both formally scientific and interpersonal, are guided by multiple objectives and limited resources. In professional scientific activity, budgetary, technological, and/or ethical considerations may require compromise and increased efficiency in data gathering. Similarly, in interpersonal inquiry, too, each interaction may have numerous goals (relational maintenance, exploitation of the other, impression management, and so forth; see Clark and Delia, 1979; Sillars, 1980)—each requiring different types of information for its realization and careful balancing with other goals in the creation of a message (see O'Keefe and Delia, this volume), and all demanding satisfaction in the midst of ongoing interaction. All these goals may call for considerable investment of energy, and none may be pursued individually and vigorously without sacrificing other goals. In other words, since we intuitive scientists have limited capacities to attend to and process incoming information, *the process of uncertainty reduction can only be understood in terms of the constraints imposed by the diversity of goals coupled with cognitive capacity limitations.*

This conclusion and the two italicized conclusions preceding it offer a preliminary answer to the first question we posed in the introduction to this chapter: Uncertainty reduction does not seem to be accomplished primarily through raw induction. Plausible hypotheses, derived from prior social knowledge, are generated to explain surprising or interesting aspects of social events. Interactants' goals determine what social knowledge will be brought to bear, what inferential tasks are needed to reduce uncertainty about the social events, and what cognitive functions and communication tools are needed to accomplish the goals. Limitations on cognitive capacities provide practical constraints within which uncertainty can be reduced.

In order to identify more fully the processes by which uncertainty is reduced, we need to address both the nature of social knowledge (its structure and content) and the ways in which social knowledge interacts with goals, cognitive functions, capacity limitations, and communication tools. In the second section of this chapter, we focus on the nature of social knowledge, its structure and content. In a portion of the third section, we tie social knowledge to cognitive functions, capacity limitations, and to a lesser extent, goals and communication tools. Also, in the third and fourth sections, we attempt to answer the second question we posed in the introduction: Do the principles governing uncertainty reduction affect the veridicality of newly acquired interpersonal information? As we noted earlier, *Weltanschauungen* philosophers of science such as Hanson (1958), Kuhn (1970), and Feyerabend (1975) strongly suspect that the sources of uncertainty reduction in

formal scientific inquiry—the Hs in Hanson's description of retroduction—serve to guide the perception and interpretation of scientific data.
In the interpersonal realm, theorists such as Hamilton (1979), Hastie
(1981), Taylor and Crocker (1981), and Nisbett and Ross (1980) have all
documented similar influences of prior social knowledge. In the third
section we link social knowledge, through cognitive functions and
capacity limitations, to various sources of interpersonal misunderstanding, demonstrating that many of these apparently nonrational biases
represent pragmatically rational efforts to cope with the complexity of
interpersonal communication. Finally, in the fourth section, the
potentially positive contributions of social knowledge are discussed.

The Nature of Social Knowledge

In the preceding section, we drew on Hanson's account of retroductive reasoning as a model of the process by which intuitive scientists
reduce uncertainty about their social worlds. According to Hanson,
when people encounter novel phenomena, they generate plausible
hypotheses to account for them and make them understandable.
"Intuitive theories" are, perhaps, the major source of plausible hypotheses and so play a critical role in reducing uncertainty. Without theories,
novel events would have to be understood through raw induction, an
impossible task, given the richness of the social world. Because we take
the image of the intuitive scientist seriously, we must look for theories
that are used by intuitive scientists in the same way that scientific
theories are used by the professional.

Indeed, references to "intuitive" or "implicit" theories abound in the
literature. "Implicit" is used to describe structured knowledge about
personality, "implicit personality theories" (Schneider, 1973), and about
relationships, "implicit theories of relationships" (Rands and Levinger,
1979). It is also used to make arcane terms like "schema" more
understandable (Fiske and Kinder, 1981; Hastie, 1981; Rumelhart,
1980a). But are implicit theories truly comparable to scientific theories?
To answer this question, we must first determine the basic properties of
scientific theories and then judge whether implicit theories have the
same properties.

Philosophers of science have struggled for decades to refine definitions of a scientific theory, but always on the bedrock of two
fundamental properties. A scientific theory (1) must be a connected set
of propositions and (2) must bear some specifiable relation to observ-
able events (Campbell, 1920; Turner, 1967). Without the first property
there is no theory; without the second the "theory" is not scientific.

Hempel (1952: 36) provides a compelling image of how a scientific theory is structured based on these two properties.

> A scientific theory might therefore be likened to a complex spatial network: Its terms are represented by the knots, while the threads connecting the latter correspond, in part, to the definitions and, in part, to the fundamental and derivative hypotheses included in the theory. The whole system floats, as it were, above the plane of observations and is anchored to it by rules of interpretation.

Hempel's analogy is striking because it is precisely the one used to describe how knowledge is represented in memory. Knowledge of the world (including the social world) is likened to a network of abstract propositions that are anchored in experience—a semantic network (see Anderson, 1976, for a review). Moreover, within the complete network of world knowledge are found sets of propositions that function as semiautonomous units for particular content domains (Anderson, 1981), much like specific scientific theories. Even though these semi-autonomous units are referred to by a variety of names, such as "schemas" (Fiske and Linville, 1980; Rumelhart and Ortony, 1977), "scripts" (Bower et al., 1979; Schank and Abelson, 1977), "prototypes" (Cantor and Mischel, 1979; Ebbesen and Allen, 1979), "frames" (Goffman, 1974; Minsky, 1975) and "story grammars" (Mandler and Johnson, 1977; Thorndyke, 1977), they all consist of sets of interrelated propositions that are anchored to various aspects of the social world, including people, events, messages, and relationships. Thus, in the most basic sense they are "implicit social theories."

The differences between scientific and intuitive knowledge arise, not in the definition of the term "theory," but in the distinction between "scientific" and "intuitive." Wegner and Vallacher (1977) have noted that scientific theories are formalized and available for public scrutiny, whereas implicit theories are developed, retained, and used below the level of awareness. They are implicit in the sense that the intuitive scientist ordinarily uses them without being aware of it, or even aware that they exist. Therefore, implicit theories are usually studied by indirect means (Ericsson and Simon, 1980; Nisbett and Wilson, 1977a). In addition, scientific theories must be subjected to falsification before confidence is placed in them, but intuitive theories are often presumed to be true. After all, intuitive scientists do not have the luxury of with-holding conclusions and action until the theory has been adequately tested, as professional scientists do. They must act as if their implicit theories were true or be paralyzed by uncertainty.

What, then, might be learned by viewing implicit theories as counterparts of scientific theories? First, because implicit theories are used less self-consciously than scientific theories, they are less well understood. In particular, structural issues common to all scientific theories have been considered extensively, whereas structural issues have been addressed on an instance-by-instance basis for implicit theories. As a consequence, each researcher must address the same structural issues anew, a situation that is exacerbated by the lack of a standardized vocabulary for referring to implicit theories. The analogy between scientific and implicit theories, therefore, helps to draw attention to structural properties common to all scientific theories and all implicit theories.

Second, common structural properties may serve as a skeleton upon which representations of implicit theories can be built. One of the most prevalent criticisms of implicit theories is that they are vague, serving only as placeholders for some unobservable entity that influences information acquisition and interpretation (Fiske and Linville, 1980). Even though this criticism may be accurate in many cases, it need not be if the content and structure of implicit theories can be specified. As Fiske and Linville point out, just as the concept "theory" explains nothing, the concept "implicit theory" (including schemas, prototypes, scripts, and story grammars) explains nothing. Both must be instantiated as some specific, content-laden theory and used to acquire and interpret data in order to have any explanatory value. Furthermore, to the extent that both types of theories can be specified clearly and in detail, their explanatory powers can be improved. Structural properties common to all theories may provide guidelines for elaborating implicit theories, making predictions less equivocal and explanations more satisfying.

In the sections that follow we explicate three structural components of theories: (1) theoretical terms that are tied to observables via rules of correspondence, (2) linkages between theoretical terms, and (3) calculi used to make derivations from theories (Campbell, 1920; Turner, 1967). In addition, the position of theories within broader frameworks of knowledge is considered. In each case, similarities between scientific and implicit theories are briefly noted; then the importance of each component for the study of communication is discussed and illustrated with a research example. Finally, after implicit theories have been analyzed as a class, differences among types of implicit theories— scripts, story grammars, schemas, and prototypes—are considered.

Theoretical-Observational Ties. To return to Hempel's description, a scientific theory consists of theoretical terms tied to observables through rules of interpretation. Theoretical terms give the theory generality, observables give the theory empirical impact, and rules of interpretation join the two, thus permitting retroduction (explaining observed events by their relationship to theoretical terms) and induction (testing theories by operationalizing them). These same structural features are found in implicit theories. Theoretical terms in implicit theories provide general guidelines for dealing with the social world, observational terms make those guidelines applicable to specific situations, and rules of interpretation permit retroduction and induction.

Without ties between observations and implicit theories, messages would be isolated phenomena, without meaning and unrelated to what we know. When observed events are linked to some theory that can account for them (retroduction), they have been understood or comprehended (Keenan, 1978; Ortony, 1978). Indeed, research indicates that messages are incomprehensible if they cannot be related to some appropriate knowledge structure (Bransford and McCarrell, 1974), that they are comprehended differently depending on the knowledge used to account for them (Anderson, Reynolds, Schallert, and Goetz, reported in Anderson, 1977; Bransford and McCarrell, 1974), that they are comprehended more richly by persons with expert knowledge (Chiesi et al., 1979; Spilich et al., 1979), and that they are comprehended more easily if appropriate knowledge structures are readily available (Planalp and Tracy, 1980).[1]

In two parallel studies, Spiro (1977) and Cohen and Ebbesen (1979) carried the research a step further by using experimental instructions to vary the implicit theories used to comprehend messages and assessing the interpretive biases that resulted. Spiro (1977) found that when subjects were told the experiment involved interpersonal relations, they distorted information in memory to make it consistent with Heider's balance principles (1958), but when they were told that it was a memory experiment, no such distortions were found. Similarly, when Cohen and Ebbesen (1979) told their subjects that their task was to form an impression of the actor in a videotape, their judgments were more strongly influenced by implicit personality theories than those of other subjects, who were told their task was simply to remember the events on the tape. These studies are noteworthy because they go beyond the claim that different implicit theories yield different interpretations to take particular implicit theories (balance and implicit personality theory) and predict how they will influence the interpretation of messages. Together they provide a clear demonstration that communication can be better predicted and understood if the structure and content of implicit theories can be specified.

Theoretical Linkages. In the preceding section we were concerned with the nature of linkages between theoretical terms and observables.

In addition, theoretical terms themselves must be linked to form hypotheses. In terms of Hanson's account of retroduction, phenomena p_1 and p_2 are explained not just by being tied to theoretical terms, but also by linkages *between* theoretical terms. Because of theoretical linkages, phenomena p_1 and p_2 are seen as associated in some way. As would be expected, theoretical linkages are as integral a part of implicit theories as they are of scientific theories. In both, they permit the co-occurrence of phenomena to be explained and one phenomenon to be predicted if the other is observed.

Several types of theoretical linkages are found in implicit theories. The first type, *correlation*, is found in implicit personality theories (Rosenberg and Sedlak, 1972; Schneider, 1973) and a number of implicit theories guiding communication (Rands and Levinger, 1979; Wish and Kaplan, 1977). Correlational linkages indicate what theoretical entities (traits, behaviors, or communicative acts) "go together" or are associated. The second type of linkage, which we call *generative*, is found only in story grammars, or implicit theories of how stories are structured (Mandler and Johnson, 1977; Thorndyke, 1977). These grammars are used to generate any and all possible structures of culturally accepted story structures by rewriting theoretical terms such as "setting" and "event structure" as a series of components. The third type of linkage, *temporal*, stipulates in what temporal order instances of theoretical terms will be observed. They are found in the "script," "a predetermined, stereotyped sequence of actions that defines a well-known social situation" (Schank and Abelson, 1977: 41), as well as in story grammars. The final type of theoretical linkage is *causal*. Since implicit social theories are most often concerned with human agents making choices that bring about effects, causal elements need not provide necessary and sufficient conditions for an effect to occur, but only reasons for it occurring (Mandler and Johnson, 1977). Causal linkages are found in story grammars and scripts where characters' actions cause some later outcome.

All these types of theoretical linkages (correlational, generative, temporal, and causal) serve as the basis of expectations about what attributes co-occur, how parts of an episode will be interrelated, what events follow others, or what events will be produced by others. But do they have any effect on our perceptions of others or our interpretations of messages? Perhaps the most striking effects are found with correlational linkages. When people are led to believe that a theoretical relationship exists between events (such as test responses and neurotic symptoms) and then are asked to estimate the relationship based on observations, they consistently overestimate the degree of observed relationship. They perceive an "illusory correlation" in the data (Chapman and Chapman, 1969; Jennings et al., forthcoming). Analogs in interpersonal communication have not yet been investigated, but possibilities are numerous. Implicit theories may produce illusory correlations between requests and refusals, between certain opinions and supportive responses, between dominant statements and submissive responses—in fact, between any two communicative acts that might be associated. Thus, in a variety of domains, theoretical linkages not only produce hypotheses about relationships between observations but may also incline the observer to confirm them.

Deductive Calculi. Once theoretical terms have been linked to form propositions, propositions in turn are linked to form an interconnected network—a theory. The formal theory is then used to move from a set of observables through a series of theoretical linkages to a new set of conclusions. This requires rules for traversing a series of theoretical linkages, a deductive calculus (Turner, 1967). Implicit theories must have calculi as well. Just as the calculi of formal scientific theories provide the basis for logical deductions from the theory, implicit calculi provide the basis for making psycho-logical deductions. Psychological deductions based on a series of propositions may go beyond simple expectations based on single propositions and may not correspond to formal logical deductions. For instance, a defense attorney might convince a jury that social environments cause sociopathology and that sociopathology causes crime, but *not* that social environments cause crime. More may enter into the reasoning than would be expected from the separate propositions or from formal logic (see Luria, 1976). Logical or not, implicit calculi must reflect how people use implicit theories to reason.

Since chains of reasoning depend on the type of link in the chain, different approaches have been used to build calculi for correlational, generative, temporal, and causal deductions. One approach is to avoid considering calculi altogether by representing multiple links of correlation as multidimensional arrays in which all terms are completely intercorrelated (Rosenberg and Sedlak, 1972; Wish and Kaplan, 1977). Because the degree of correlation between any two items can be determined directly by the distance between them in space, no calculus is needed. A second approach to implicit calculi is to use a logical system as a stand-in for psychological processes. The most notable example is the use of phrase structure grammars as calculi in story grammars (Mandler and Johnson, 1977; Thorndyke, 1977). By applying phrase structure rules, the theorist can deduce relationships among events in the story and determine whether a given story is "grammatical" or comprehensible. The implicit calculi underlying a series of temporal or causal linkages have received little attention compared to correlational and generative links. Whereas temporal chains are straightforward and require little elaboration (if A precedes B and B precedes C, A precedes C), causal chains are much more complex, particularly in human affairs, where multiple causes and effects operate simultaneously and people are held accountable for the effects of their behavior (Miller, this volume). Although an enormous amount of research has been devoted to implicit theories of causation (Heider, 1958; Kelley, 1972; Sillars, this volume), the work has not been extended to the study of deductions made from causal chains.

Building calculi that accurately represent implicit deductive systems is, undoubtedly, the most serious challenge in building implicit theories. There is no well-established starting point, and the criterion of psychological reality is a formidable one. In fact, one gets the impression that the more sophisticated the attempt to formalize a calculus, the more seriously the criterion of psychological reality is taken and the more heated the debates become (Black and Wilensky, 1979; Mandler and Johnson, 1980; Rumelhart, 1980b). Difficult though it may be, the challenge of building psychologically real calculi could reap great benefits for all areas of communication research. For example, scholars of interpersonal communication, small group communication, and rhetoric are united by a concern for the psycho-logic of everyday argument (Jackson and Jacobs, 1980; Leff and Hewes, 1981). Systems of formal logic clearly fail to capture logic-in-use (Henle, 1962; Wason and Johnson-Laird, 1972), at least in part because everyday argument is never content-free but rather dependent on constraints imposed by implicit theories of their subject matter. Regardless of how formally "logical" arguments are, they will be less convincing if they contradict deductions derived from implicit theories. Counterintuitive conclusions (that is, conclusions that contradict intuitive knowledge and reasoning) may not convince, but rather may lead to questioning of the logical premises of the argument, its logical force, or its relevance to the situation at hand (Henle, 1962). The person who argues effectively and the effective scholar and teacher of argument must know how to adapt arguments to intuitive knowledge and deductions from it.

In the preceding section, we identified the structural similarities between formalized scientific theories and implicit theories. We now turn to a consideration of how implicit theories are embedded within broader frameworks of knowledge and what this implies for information acquisition and interpretation.

Embedding. Scientific theories seldom stand alone as explanations for events. Rather, they are embedded within philosophical frameworks, approaches to studying an area of content, and metatheories (Delia, 1977; Kuhn, 1970; Planalp and Hewes, 1982). Larger frameworks of knowledge establish continuity between theories and give theories their fundamental, untested assumptions. Approaches and metatheories help scientists (and students) understand events at a high level of abstraction and guide us to the deeper levels provided by the theories they encompass. When no theory addresses an issue, we can appeal to more abstract knowledge for interpretations; we are never at a complete loss for information.

The same is true for implicit theories. They too are embedded within broader frameworks of knowledge, in this case superordinate structures of semantic memory. Embedding provides continuity among implicit theories and enables individual theories to "inherit" fundamental characteristics from superordinate structures (Brachman, 1979). If no implicit theory is available or well enough developed to inform events, implicit theorists can always resort to more abstract structures of knowledge and hence more abstract understanding. For example, a person who has never read a story could achieve some level of understanding of one by appealing to knowledge about other literary forms or human affairs in general. A country cousin who has never been to a restaurant would nonetheless recognize "eating behavior," and people who know something about games but nothing about baseball could achieve some ballpark understanding of the game (Chiesi et al., 1979; Spilich et al., 1979).

One important implication of embedding in interpersonal settings is that social actors are never completely uncertain about their interlocutors (Berger, 1979) because they know about people in general, people in the same social role, people who dress like that, and so on. That knowledge, in turn, can be used to guide the search for more specific information about the person as an individual. For example, out-of-role behavior provides information beyond what is presumed and so is more closely attended to and better remembered (Jones and Davis, 1965). Knowledge about future interactions or relationships with another (such as professional colleagues or dating partners) may also influence what people or what behaviors will be monitored (Berscheid and Graziano, 1979). Implicit theories, then, provide general guidelines for acting in the social world and for acquiring more detailed knowledge to guide future action.

Types of Implicit Theories. By using a common phrase—implicit theories—to refer to a variety of knowledge structures, including schemas, prototypes, scripts, and story grammars, we have chosen first to emphasize their similarities. Because they all appear in the literature under different labels, it is easy to neglect common properties and view work on different types of knowledge structures as separate lines of research that overlap only in vague and inconsequential respects. Although they share substantial common characteristics that can be clearly articulated by analogy with scientific theories, differences between the types are real. The labels "schema," "prototype," "script," and "story grammar" designate certain research emphases or commitments to particular types of social knowledge and thus can be thought of as special interest topics within the broader area of implicit theories.[2]

The term "schema" is used to refer to implicit theories in the broadest sense (Bobrow and Norman, 1975; Hastie, 1981; Rumelhart and Ortony, 1977; Rumelhart, 1980a). They are generic knowledge structures, suitable for everyday use in a wide range of domains such as self-schemata (Markus, 1977), political schemata (Fiske and Kinder, 1981), person schemata (Taylor et al., 1978), and interpersonal and relational schemata (Housel and Acker, 1979; Planalp, forthcoming). Indeed, many researchers view the schema as a pivotal construct capable of unifying the subdisciplines of social, learning, cognitive developmental, information-processing, and clinical psychologies (Abelson, 1981; Fiske and Linville, 1980; Simon, 1976; Wyer, 1980). As the "building blocks of cognition" (Rumelhart, 1980a), schemata influence a wide range of cognitive processes. Early theorists uncovered schematic influence on attention and perception (Neisser, 1968), integration and inference (Bartlett, 1932; Kant, 1902), memory (Bartlett, 1932), action, and motion (Head, 1920; Piaget, 1963). The modern schema is a synthesis of these roots and "serves to emphasize the necessary interrelations among perception, attention, comprehension, memory and action" (Craik, 1979: 65).

Scripts and story grammars are special cases of schemas used to represent conventionalized knowledge of social action and story structure, respectively. Like other types of schemas, evidence for their existence is gleaned both by asking subjects about structure directly or indirectly (Bower et al., 1979; Pollard-Gott et al., 1979) and by observing their effects on comprehension (Schank and Abelson, 1977; Thorndyke, 1977), memory (Bower et al., 1979), and production of actions and messages (Abelson, 1981). Unlike other types of schemas, they represent sequentially occurring events and so must contain temporal or causal linkages between events in the series. Evidence for the linkages can also be found by querying subjects about the expected ordering and measuring reordering in memory (Bower et al., 1979;

Mandler, 1978). Because scripts and story grammars pertain to well-defined areas of content (so that theoretical terms and linkages can be identified), they are the most clearly developed and well-researched members of the schema family.

A prototype (Rosch and Mervis, 1975), on the other hand, is not a type of schema but rather an idealized formulation of *any* type of schema. Since any particular instance conforms to the prototype by degrees, there can be more or less prototypic instances of scripts, stories, persons, relationships, and so forth. Thus, using the term "prototype" merely draws attention to the problematic linkages between theoretical and observed events faced in any implicit theory. Any research directed toward understanding the relationships between idealized schemas and highly variable events is research on prototypes, regardless of the label used (see Hastie, 1981, for a comprehensive review). Similarly, research on object prototypes (Rosch and Mervis, 1975) or person prototypes (Cantor and Mischel, 1979) is schema research, even though it is labeled differently. The names may change, but the issues are the same.

Our reasons for categorizing all types of social knowledge—schemas, scripts, story grammars, and prototypes—as implicit theories should now be apparent. First, we use the category "implicit theory" to unify a relatively diverse literature by outlining a basic structure shared by all types of knowledge and placing each separate type within that common framework. Second, we make explicit the basic components any implicit theory must have so that researchers can more rigorously describe and test any particular theory. Finally, the analogy with scientific theories carries the assumption that implicit theories are used by the intuitive scientist to explain existing data and to guide the search for new data that may support or falsify the implicit theory. In the section that follows, we describe how implicit theories influence the gathering and interpretation of information.

A Functional Analysis of Social Knowledge: The Issues of Bias and Irrationality

Most popularized accounts of formal science emphasize the positive attributes of theories (as in Kaplan, 1964, or Shaw and Costanzo, 1970)—after all, we hardly acquire knowledge through raw induction alone. *Something* must guide the generation of plausible explanations. On the other hand, both philosophers of science and psychologists warn us that our theories, formal or intuitive, strongly filter our perceptions and interpretations (Feyerabend, 1975; Hanson, 1958; Kuhn, 1970; in cognitive psychology, Kelly, 1955; Nisbett and Ross, 1980; Taylor and

Crocker, 1981). Theories are godsends or tools of the devil, depending on whom you ask. Clearly, there must be some middle ground.

We have adopted a position akin to that espoused by Nisbett and Ross (1980) in assessing the advantages and disadvantages of theories for the intuitive scientist. Although Nisbett and Ross sometimes overemphasize the negative aspects of intuitive theories, they do not fall err to the common confusion of "bias" with "irrationality." Frequently the rational and, therefore, bias-free inquirer is compared to the perfect scientist using ideal procedures to analyze an unrestricted supply of data. Bias is defined against this ideal, normative standard (Nisbett and Ross, 1980: Ch. 1), as in Kelley's (1972) cubal ANOVA model. Thus, for example, the fact that a simple manipulation of visual focus alters subjects' attributions of causality (Storms, 1973) makes the "fundamental attribution error" irrational by ideal standards (Ross, 1977).

While this is a heuristic method for defining rationality, there is another. Rationality may be defined in terms of an actor's goals, resources, and capacities (Garfinkel, 1974). This sense of pragmatic rationality is consistent with our premises concerning uncertainty reduction voiced at the outset. In effect, the "intuitive scientist" can be more accurately compared to the scientist in the trenches rather than the ideal scientist. As a consequence, bias is separated from irrationality. Bias may result when expedient, useful, and generally legitimate simplifying assumptions are applied in the complex world of human action (Leff and Hewes, 1981; Nisbett and Ross, 1980), but it is understandable bias, even rational bias, because no professional or lay scientist lives in an ideal world. Coping successfully with the real world, given limited access to data and limited cognitive capacities for utilizing it, can be a rational activity, even if some biases result.

Thus, our tactic for analyzing the interrelationships between implicit theories and cognitive functions is this: We engage in the reconstruction of the antecedents of known biases under the assumption that they result from the rational adaptation of human beings to physiological and social constraints in the fulfillment of their goals (see Popper, 1962: Vol. 2). We make this assumption of pragmatic rationality since the alternative is to encourage the proliferation of types of biases with minimal regard to their explanations, as, for example, in Taylor and Crocker's compendium (1981; see especially the discussion of "Type I errors"). If biases are simply the result of flaws in our physiological or social development, then they are simply *there*. No explanations are necessary; an exhaustive list is all that is needed. If biases result from some rational compromises among goals and a few basic, identifiable physiological constraints, such as limitations on memory or processing capacity, then we can begin to answer "why questions" about biases and do so parsimoniously.

We have also adopted this functional orientation to bias since it allows us to fill in some gaps in Hanson's analysis of the logic of discovery as applied to interpersonal uncertainty reduction. With it we can determine why intuitive scientists are not crippled by these supposedly irrational biases. In addition, we can begin to identify the underlying cognitive mechanisms that produce such biases by tying our discussion of the advantages and disadvantages of theories to specific cognitive functions. This we do by drawing on a set of interrelated cognitive functions (focusing, storage, integration/inference, retrieval, selection, and implementation) that are central to a complete understanding of interpersonal communication (Planalp and Hewes, 1982). The positive and negative influences of prior social knowledge on uncertainty reduction are illustrated for each cognitive function.

Making Forgivable Mistakes

Functional treatments of formal theories usually emphasize their utility in focusing attention on intriguing phenomena, summarizing observations, explaining diverse phenomena, inspiring hypotheses, guiding research, and the like. Because theories are instrumental in carrying out all these activities, they are highly economical tools for scientific inquiry. In fact, theories are often so efficient that only violations of their predictions are really striking (Toulmin, 1953: Ch. 3). As a result, unexpected errors (biases), the deviations from ideal normative rationality, cause more furor than the mundane uses of a successful theory (see, for example, Kuhn, 1970). As we explore the advantages and disadvantages of prior social knowledge (intuitive theories) for each of six cognitive functions, bear in mind that the research tends to focus on the unexpected errors. A balanced view must also include the mundane consequences of prior knowledge on uncertainty reduction.

Focusing. Interpersonal exchanges are unusually rich sources of information about ourselves, others, and the rules of social behavior. Data can be drawn from the physical and social context and from paralinguistic, verbal, and nonverbal channels. Human beings do not have an unlimited capacity to cope with this influx of information (Kahneman, 1973; Planalp and Hewes, 1982). To avoid being swamped by this wealth of data and yet gain goal-related information efficiently, we must be able to focus our attention on relevant stimuli and ignore the irrelevant (Neisser, 1976: 79-107; Norman, 1976: 6-32). Stimuli become relevant or irrelevant depending on our goals, the knowledge we already have to facilitate meeting those goals, that which we need to acquire, and the consistency of the observed information with prior knowledge. Thus, the cognitive function of focusing permits us to utilize our implicit theories to obtain needed information efficaciously—an important advantage of prior knowledge, since our ability to focus is inherently limited.

Probably we have all suffered from a failure of the focusing function in complex social settings involving two or more nearly simultaneous tasks. For example, trying to carry on a coherent conversation (goal) while following a baseball game (goal) is taxing at best. No matter what we do, we are likely to miss something. Should the topic of the conversation be familiar and our partner cogent, our burden in extracting the topic of the conversation and responding competently is eased (Tracy, 1981); should we be knowledgeable fans who know how plays unfold, we can, again, successfully respond to competing demands (see Chiesi et al., 1979; Spilich et al., 1979). In either case, prior social knowledge permits us to meet our competing goals efficiently. Thus, focusing is as rational in the social world as it is in the scientific; focusing permits us to learn from unusual events, to avoid dangers, to exploit fortuitous accidents, and to pursue our goals single-mindedly in data-rich environments. Focusing is a rational adaptation of any capacity-limited system to a changing environment, made more success-ful by the availability of prior social knowledge.

Unfortunately, focusing has its dark side as well. When we concen-trate on one aspect of the perceptual field, we are not concentrating on other aspects. Thus, we run the risk of obtaining incomplete or nonrepresentative data (Nisbett and Ross, 1980). Consider the conse-quences of this in an example drawn from Taylor's (1981) work on stereotyping. Taylor and her colleagues have found that solo members of work groups—one woman in an otherwise all male group, one man in an otherwise all female group, and so on—draw disproportionately more attention than either the other members of the group or themselves in identical interactions in which they are not solo members. This increased attention leads to biased assessments of the influence, positive or negative, these solo members have on the group discussion (Taylor and Fiske, 1975, 1978), a result consistent with the "focus-of-attention" explanation of the fundamental attribution error (Ross, 1977; Taylor and Fiske, 1975). In other words, the more we attend to the behavior of an individual to the exclusion of that person's environment, the more the individual appears to be the principle initiator (cause) of his or her own action. Unlike more artificial tests of this hypothesis (Storms, 1973), Taylor's depends on the implicit theories of observers to define the group's composition as either aberrant or informative and thus worthy of increased attention. The very reasonable, even necessary, strategy of using prior social knowledge to reduce uncertainty leads to a source of bias. The bias is excusable because there simply are no other ways for capacity-limited systems to gather data.[3] Nevertheless, the social consequences to solo group members are no less significant.

Storage/Retrieval.[4] Storage and retrieval processes are intimately involved in the acquisition of social knowledge. Without storage, new information could not be integrated with old; without retrieval, new information could not be accumulated to change prior expectations. The problem is that new information may not be stored so as to make it easily accessible for later use (Chanowitz and Langer, 1978), or it may not be retrievable due to lack of effort, accident, inappropriate cuing, and so on. Unlike the professional scientist, the lay scientist relies almost exclusively on fallible human memory to store data. Like the professional scientist, the lay scientist does need to examine stored data to draw inferences about interpersonal exchanges, other people, or relationships with those people.

How, then, can a rational being cope with the vagaries of memory? The legal profession provides one answer. When faced with needed missing data, the least risky option is to rely on "presumptions of fact" (Thayer, 1898), that is, facts which, though not directly observed, can be inferred from observed facts (1898: 547). This inferential process cannot bridge the gap between facts observed and facts supposed without relevant prior knowledge. If that knowledge is even partially valid and if the inferential process is executed correctly, presumed facts are likely to be better than missing data.

This constructive aspect of human memory also has negative implications, as illustrated by the now classic research of Cantor and Mischel (1977). Their research represents a direct reaction to two facets of the study of personality/behavior relationships: (1) Mischel (1968) and others (Hewes and Haight, 1979) demonstrated empirically that direct relationships between personality and individual behaviors were far weaker than anticipated by our implicit theories of personality or than we would want for predictive purposes, yet (2) "the stubborn assumption that there are pervasive cross-situational consistencies in an individual's behavior . . . is, quite literally, one of our most ancient convictions. . . . [Few beliefs] are as compellingly self-evident" (Bem and Allen, 1974: 506). The apparent paradox created by these two facets was to be resolved, in part, by identifying the cognitive, rather than behavioral, functions of traits (Mischel, 1973). Cantor and Mischel (1977) argued that personality traits serve as organizing principles (implicit theories) for remembering the behavior of others. They hypothesized that "if trait concepts are analogous to visual-pattern prototypes or scripts for standard episodes, then one would expect to find some bias in a recognition memory test toward recognizing nonpresented but highly related examples of trait concepts" (1977: 40), and they obtained support for this hypothesis. In other words, the presumed correlation between a trait and its varied instantiations makes viable the summary of the behaviors performed by a trait-consistent individual. Cantor and Mischel's results (see also Cantor and Mischel, 1979) and the work of others (Hastie, 1981; Taylor and Crocker, 1981; Wyer and Srull, 1980) clearly demonstrate a consistent "false-positive" bias produced when prior social knowledge about others or social events fills in missing data. Our implicit theories of traits contain multiple propositions linking the trait to its behavioral manifestations. By filling in missing data with theory-consistent information, we increase artifactually the apparent cross-situations consistency of the trait. The effect of this bias is to create a greater impression of consistency in others' behavior than is in fact the case (Ross, 1977). This bias is forgivable if we presume that the subjects in this research felt compelled to perform knowingly beyond the limits of their own memories *or* if people in general cannot easily differentiate veridical recall from inference (see Spiro, 1980). In either case, presumptions of fact are better than no facts at all; in this case, Type II error is apparently perceived as more costly than Type I.

Integration and Inference. Uncertainty is reduced about others and social contexts so that they become more meaningful to us (retroduction). We may then use that interpretation to support existing theories, alter them (induction), or make inferences to unobserved or unrecalled events (deduction). Central to all these activities are the interrelated cognitive functions of integration and inference, where the former concerns the combining of new data with prior knowledge (retroduction, induction) and the latter, deductions from existing theories. Without integration we could not construct, support, or falsify our theories about the social world; without inference we could not anticipate and adapt to new situations and people.

These two functions would be unalloyed boons were it not for the inherent ambiguity of the social world (Hewes, 1980a: 47-48; 1980b: 397-398). Any set of data are open to multiple interpretations (Turner, 1967). Facts do not necessarily contain their own interpretations. The effects of this intrinsic ambiguity are exacerbated for lay scientists because they cannot always obtain information necessary to reduce it (see Berger, 1979; Berger et al., 1976). How, then, can this ambiguity be reduced rationally?

Hanson's logic of discovery provides the answer. The key step is to retroduce an explanation, that is, to posit an explanation of interesting, ambiguous facts, which, if true, would explain them (Hanson, 1958: 85-86; Peirce, 1931: Vol. V, para. 146). This leads to bias insofar as the attributed interpretation is demonstrably incorrect. For example, Duncan (1976) had college students view one of four videotapes of "similar" heated arguments between two people in which one (the protagonist) gives a mild shove to the other (the victim) at the end of the discussion. Protagonists and victims were either black or white. If the protagonist was white, the shove was seen as a form of dramatization or simply playing around. If the protagonist was black, the shove was more likely to be labeled as aggressive or even violent. Of course, whether or not these are *biased* interpretations depends on the comparability of the behaviors being evaluated. Since close comparability was not guaranteed in this study, we do not know if the shoves were, in fact, different and confounded with the race of the protagonist *or* if racial stereotypes were responsible for the differing interpretations (Hamilton, 1979: 69, n. 2). But even in studies where comparability is guaranteed (for reviews, see Snyder, 1981a, 1981b; Taylor, 1981), the demonstration of bias is not necessarily a demonstration of irrationality—quite the opposite. It is perfectly rational to generate *plausible* interpretations of ambiguous events on the basis of lay theories (Allport, 1954). To treat the interpretations of ambiguous events with the same confidence that one attaches to interpretations of unambiguous events when those interpretations are of some consequence to the actor would be irrational. To see these data as *not falsifying* previous theorizing is perfectly reasonable, even if they do have multiple interpretations. Obviously, it would be better were there only one interpretation. Unfortunately, no data are available currently that test the limits of the pragmatic rationality of actors in coping with their own biases.[5]

Selection/Implementation.[6] Scientists have at their disposal an array of tools for the acquisition of knowledge. Faced with a phenomenon of interest, a scientist can deploy one or more of these tools to satisfy a specific goal (or goals). Whether or not this choice of tools is pragmatically rational depends on the fit between goals and tool choice given the capacity and resource limitations faced by the scientist. Whether or not the choice will result in biased data depends on the severity of the capacity and resource limitations *and* on the scientist's awareness of those limitations.

Scientists, both professional and lay, have at their disposal three broad classes of tools, or strategies, for the discovery of knowledge: passive (nonreactive observation), active (use of informants, "experiments") and interactive (interrogation, mutual disclosure) [Berger, 1979]. Berger and Roloff (this volume) summarize much of the literature relevant to these strategies of the intuitive scientist (see also Snyder, 1981a). Here we examine in some depth two key studies that address the influences of prior social knowledge on uncertainty reduction. Our purpose is to demonstrate the biasing effects of the observer's "theories" on the behavior of others while justifying the rationality of the social actors in these studies. In effect, we are attempting to show that, though prior social knowledge may affect the adequacy of tools chosen to acquire interpersonal data, these resultant biases are understandable within the context of pragmatic rationality. The tools chosen are not so inherently flawed, nor are the data they yield always so tainted, that naive scientists appear to be simply naive.

Berger and Roloff (this volume) indicate that, of the three classes of tools noted above, the least understood are the interactive strategies. We agree with their assessment. Unequivocal studies of interactive uncertainty reduction are devilishly hard to conduct and even harder to interpret. Consider as an illustration two studies by Snyder on intrusive (Snyder and Swann, 1978a) and nonintrusive (Snyder et al., 1977) interpersonal hypothesis-testing strategies. First, to the nonintrusive strategies.

Snyder et al. (1977) explored the self-fulfilling influences of one social stereotype—physical attractiveness—on dyadic social interaction. They hypothesized that "the physically attractive may actually come to behave in a friendly, likable, sociable manner—not because they necessarily possess these dispositions, but because the behavior of others elicits and maintains behaviors taken to be manifestations of such traits" (1977: 659). To test this hypothesis, both male and female subjects were recruited, ostensibly for a study in the acquaintanceship process. Unacquainted subjects were paired by sex. They filled out biographical information sheets that were later given to their partners. In addition, male subjects were given bogus photographs, supposedly of their female partners. In reality these photographs were randomly assigned from a set of either four very attractive or four very unattractive women. Male subjects rated their initial impressions of their partners from the photograph alone in terms of their sociability, intelligence, enthusiasm, and so on. The subjects then interacted via telephone, completing impression questionnaires after the interaction. In addition, tapes of males' and females' halves of the conversations were rated separately by raters (blind to the hypotheses) along the same dimensions (that is, sociability, intelligence, and so on) as the male subjects had rated them.

Results supported the authors' hypotheses. Males did differentiate purportedly physically attractive from unattractive women in their initial impressions significantly along the dimensions of sociability (poised, humorous, adept, and so on) but not, apparently, on the basis of intelligence, enthusiasm, trustworthiness, or successfulness (1977: 660-661). Thus, the content of the implicit theory of physical attractiveness apparently includes the former set of attributes but not the latter. Further, the raters "heard" more sociability among women randomly assigned to the "attractive" rather than the "unattractive" condition in 17 of the 21 scales used to assess those related traits. They "heard" proportionally less difference (8 of 13 traits) in the behavior of the "attractive" and "unattractive" women along those dimensions that did not discriminate impressions of the "attractive" and "unattractive" partners. Note: This is a crucial comparison, for if the implicit theory of physical attractiveness is an operative factor in the formation of male subjects' impressions, then the *content* of that theory must reveal some systematic impact on those impressions. Unfortunately, Snyder et al. did not test for the statistical significance of the difference between these two key proportions (.8095 [17/21] for attributes of "attractive" individuals versus .6154 [8/13] for "unattractive" individuals). Had Snyder et al. performed the appropriate test they would have found no significant difference ($z = 1.2467$, $p > .10$, one-tailed), although the observed difference is in the anticipated direction. These results could support Snyder et al.'s conclusion that the stereotype of physical attractiveness may be self-confirming. Thus, this stereotype and, perhaps, others may create the very behaviors they are supposed to explain—that is, they may do so *if* we are willing to accept nonsignificant results (above) and *if* we believe that subjects saw this primarily as a hypothesis-testing (inductive) rather than an instrumental exercise.

Stereotypes can create their own reality only to the extent that they are not correctable through observation. Male subjects clearly had a stereotype of attractive women, as evidenced in their response to the initial impression questionnaires. Apparently they also acted differently toward the supposedly attractive woman, probably by being more friendly—a perfectly reasonable thing to do for instrumental purposes, though not necessarily for testing hypotheses about stereotypes. Did the "attractive" women provide support for the males' stereotype? The "attractive" women acted differently from their "unattractive" counterparts, proving only that they reciprocated positive sociable gestures. It does not prove that the women's behavior was taken as support for, or failure to disconfirm, existing physical attractiveness stereotypes. We do not know what cognitive impact their behavior had, and thus we do not know if social stereotypes are both incorrigible enough and untrue enough to create social reality. If the male subjects saw this encounter as primarily instrumental and did not "count" this interaction as evidence for social stereotypes or if they mentally controlled for reciprocity effects, then their actions were pragmatically rational, although perhaps not socially desirable. Although the focus-of-attention explanation of the fundamental attribution error would auger against the second compensation strategy (the ability of subjects to "control for" reciprocity effects; see Ross, 1977), we hve no direct evidence on this point. Such evidence would be useful in testing the limits of rationality of intuitive scientists and, indeed, the extent to which their perception of behavior is biased by prior knowledge. At present, the effects of prior social knowledge on nonintrusive theory testing are unclear.

Snyder and Swann (1978a) ran into similar difficulties in testing the self-fulfilling nature of more intrusive hypothesis-testing strategies (see also Snyder, 1981a; Snyder and Campbell, 1980; Snyder and Skrypnek, 1979; Snyder and Swann, 1978b). Here they investigated the effects of cuing prior knowledge on the hypothesis-testing process (induction). In particular, they wondered whether having people test one of two incompatible hypotheses about a target person's personality (for example, is a person an extravert *versus* an introvert?) would influence the kinds of probe questions they would ask, questions that might lead the target to confirm their initial hypotheses with behavior.

Snyder and Swann (1978a) performed a series of four experiments to test this hypothesis. Although the experiments differed in terms of the amount of confidence the subjects had in the applicability of the hypothesis to the other (Experiments 1 and 3), the extent to which the probe questions were spontaneously generated or supplied by the experimenters (Experiment 2), and the importance of correctly classifying the other person (Experiment 4), in each case subjects showed a marked tendency to ask questions that raters thought were leading. For example, in Experiment 1 the following question was classified as leading to extravert confirmation: "What kind of situations do you seek out if you want to meet new people?" An example of an introvert leading question is, "In what situations do you wish you could be more outgoing?" Furthermore, independent ratings of the interviewee's responses to the questions indicated a marked tendency for interviewees to project an image consistent with the interviewer's hypothesis—that is, to appear to be more or less confident, talkative, poised, and the like, consistent with the hypothesis of either extraversion or introversion.

Do these findings indicate that prior knowledge (hypotheses) creates bias through its influence on tool selection? The answer to this question is unclear, since Snyder and Swann did not report the impact of the answers to the probe questions on the interviewers' classifications, although unreported data apparently bore out the authors' hypotheses (Snyder, 1981a: 292; see also Snyder and Swann, 1978a: 1203). No statistical tests of these results were mentioned; nevertheless, they do constitute tentative evidence of the biasing effects of prior social knowledge on the choice of communicative strategies to reduce uncertainty.

Is this bias understandable in terms of the goals and capacity and resource limitations of the intuitive scientist? Snyder (1981a) seems to think it is not. He appears to be continually amazed at the inability of subjects to use the correct tools to test their hypotheses even when prompted (1981a: 289-290; see also Snyder and Campbell, 1980). For Snyder, the correct strategy is to use an equal number of questions that lead toward the two opposing hypotheses (Snyder, 1980a: 290; Snyder and Swann, 1978a: 1210, n. 4, are more hesitant). Snyder reasons that, since human behavior is highly variable (Mischel, 1968), even true extraverts have had introvertlike experiences and vice versa. Leading questions focus attention on aspects of a person's behavior consistent with the initial hypothesis, thus generating a biased sample of those experiences and leading to biased conclusions.

But if so, the intuitive scientist may be naive but is no less a scientist. The bias results from a false belief in the consistency of human behavior. Nothing in Snyder's research indicates that the interview strategy or its application is biased in any other way than being inappropriate for testing hypotheses concerning highly variable trait behavior. In a world of highly consistent individuals, *any* distribution of questions would allow for accurate classification. Intuitive scientists are probably ignorant of the true variability in human behavior, and they may fall err to confirmation biases and the fundamental attribution error due to inherent limitations on their memories or perceptual capacity (see our earlier discussion of focusing and storage/retrieval), but they are not bad scientists. Prior social knowledge produces biases in the acquisition of new data, but these biases are the understandable, and forgivable, results of inherent limitations in human information processing. They are not the result of an inexplicably counterproductive logic of discovery. What social actors would do were their beliefs about cross-situational consistency corrected remains unclear. At any rate, Snyder has identified a potentially serious source of bias in the testing of social knowledge in interactive settings, although more careful tests of the impact of that biasing information on the "theory" of the questioner are needed.

What can we say to summarize our functional analysis of intuitive theories? We, like Hanson, find prevalent biases in the acquisition and interpretation of "scientific" data—biases that flow from the use of prior social knowledge, or theories. Like Hanson, we find the distinctions between and the interrelationships among retroduction, induction, and deduction useful heuristics for characterizing the goals of the scientist, lay as well as professional. Given these approaches to interpersonal goals, the goals themselves (normative judgment, instrumental action beyond uncertainty reduction, and so forth) and some insights into the inherent capacity and resource limitations of the intuitive scientists, we can identify predictable patterns of bias. Furthermore, these are explanable patterns of bias if we accept the view of social actors as rational beings attempting to maximize uncertainty reduction given these constraints.

We readily admit that we have had to speculate on the motives and social knowledge available to the subjects in several of these experiments in order to cast them as pragmatically rational beings. Furthermore, we have by no means exhausted the list of biases that could be examined (see Taylor and Crocker, 1981). Nevertheless, the advantage of the concept of pragmatic rationality is that it can lead to hypotheses that should be tested before we denigrate the intuitive scientist. Moreover, it emphasizes the fact that uncertainty about others is reduced with respect to specifiable goals and in the context of inherent limitations in the capacities and resources available to the social actor.

Bias Correction and Social Knowledge: The "Science of Second-Guessing"

In the introduction we raised this question: Do the principles governing interpersonal uncertainly reduction affect the veridicality of newly acquired information? The preceding section has provided part of the answer, for clearly, social knowledge, construed as implicit theories or hypotheses, does appear to lead to seriously biased perceptions of others. But if this is the case, how can we function effectively in the social world? Are we really able to understand others and coordinate our actions successfully with them?

In this section we hope to offer preliminary and tentative answers to those questions by arguing that social actors have implicit theories of bias which, under the appropriate circumstances, they can utilize in order to attempt to compensate for the kinds of biases just discussed. We present the outlines of a process we call "second-guessing," an interpretive process employing implicit theories of specific others, their proclivities for generating biased information, and the nature of that bias. We view intuitive scientists as *potentially* reflective individuals who, when the stakes are high enough, ponder the sources and effects of the biased information they receive in interpersonal exchanges. Moreover, we suggest that intuitive scientists may take steps to compensate for these biases, much as professional scientists reinterpret the work of others based on the same concerns. For both types of scientists, theories concerning the sources of bias, its direction, and methods of compensating for it play key roles in the accumulation of knowledge.

Why accord intuitive scientists this kind of prior social knowledge? First and foremost, we believe that knowledge of bias in others plays an important role in interpersonal settings. Consider the following examples. Suppose that you are thinking of going to see a new movie, of hiring someone for an important job, of taking a class from a professor you do not know directly, or of going out with someone you have not met. In other words, you are faced with a situation in which the consequences of success or failure are relatively important and in which you have some opportunity to reflect before acting. In addition, in each of these situations you are forced or choose to rely on a *source* (a movie critic, letters of recommendation, the "grapevine," a friend) for information about the *target* event or person (the movie, the job candidate, and so on), because this kind of information is the only kind available or is more accessible than direct experience. Such indirect sources of information appear to be fairly common (Berger, 1979).

In each of these cases you might have reason to question either the *motivations* or the *ability* of the source to provide accurate information about the target. For instance, although we would all grant that movie critics are intelligent, knowledgeable people who have our best interests at heart, you know that a particular reviewer likes Burt Reynolds a bit too little or character sketches a bit too much for your taste. Similarly, if you know that grapevine intelligence on a professor comes from "preppies," you may not take too seriously that part of the report on heavy weekend assignments. Notice that in each case you are neither merely accepting the message at face value nor simply devaluing it. You are involved in an active effort to compensate for specific biases related to specific aspects of the message. You are engaged in transforming an inaccurate message into an accurate one—accurate by your lights, at least. Of course, any receiver may incorrectly attribute bias to a source or inaccurately compensate for it.

While we grant that this is probably not the predominant response to messages, descriptive or persuasive (Langer, 1978; Roloff, 1980), we suspect that it may be an important one. After all, people are most likely to act "mindfully," in Langer's terms, precisely in those circumstances in which they have something important to gain or lose and are ill-prepared to respond without thought (Langer, 1978: 48-49). More to the point, unless some corrective mechanisms exist for the plethora of biases documented here and elsewhere (Hastie, 1980; Nisbett and Ross,

1980; Taylor and Crocker, 1981), we would have to wonder how the social world functions at all.

Nisbett and Ross (1980: 249) underscored this point by relating the reaction of a colleague to their list of cognitive biases: "If we're so dumb, how come we made it to the moon?" This is not a fatuous question. Unless we can identify compensatory devices, cognitive or social, that mitigate the effects of even understandable biases, it is hard to square the picture of social actors painted in the pages of this book (see, particularly, Berger and Roloff's and Sillar's chapters as well as our own) with the coordinators of complex social efforts we know people to be (Planalp and Hewes, 1982).

As far as we can tell, there are at least six ways around the apparent effects of cognitive bias on the social world: (1) Cognitive biases are laboratory artifacts and nothing more. (2) They exist but are of such small magnitude that they have no serious social consequences. (3) They exist but "average out" in a social environment. (4) They exist, but we see them in ourselves and compensate for them when the stakes are high enough. (5) They exist, but, although we cannot see them or compensate for them in ourselves, we can see them and compensate for them in others when the stakes are high enough. (6) They exist, but we can both see them and compensate for them in ourselves and others when the stakes are high enough.

Nisbett and Ross (1980: Ch. 11) address the first three ways around the effects of bias on the social world. They, along with Snyder et al. (1977: 663-664), make a compelling case for dismissing options 1 and 2. Option 3, arithmetic averaging, is still a possibility but does not seem up to the task alone. For example, there is no guarantee that, in a group, a given individual will not be the focus of attention of all other group members, engendering an attributional bias (see Taylor, 1981). Options 4-6 all involve some reflexiveness on the part of social actors, either on their own errors or on those of others.

In general, social psychologists have granted to social actors awareness of motivational errors, at least in others, but have denied them knowledge of specific cognitive biases without appealing directly to empirical evidence (see Nisbett and Ross, 1980: Ch. 10). And if Ross (1977) is correct, even knowledge of motivational biases may be specious knowledge at best. Thus, we are left either with no palliatives for biased social knowledge or a set of unanswered questions: Do intuitive scientists have knowledge of the biases that they or others generate? If so, do they use that knowledge to reinterpret messages? If they do reinterpret messages, can they do so accurately? Since we have always favored confronting unanswered questions over defeat, we offer the following evidence for one set of answers to these questions, a set of answers that center on a phenomenon we call "second-guessing."

The verb "second-guess" is defined by *Webster's New Collegiate Dictionary* as follows: "to think out alternative strategies or explanations for [some event] after the event." In other words, one aspect of second-guessing involves actively reinterpreting an observation of an event or a message about some action after the action has occurred. Intuitive scientists might engage in this activity under these three interlocking conditions:

(1) when they are seeking accurate information about some *target* (another person or state of affairs);

(2) when they are forced to or chose to rely on some *source* for information concerning the target rather than relying on direct observation; and

(3) when they have reason to question the *ability* or *intention* of the source to report accurately on the target.

Implicit in these conditions are two assumptions: (1) Intuitive scientists are presumed to be capable of active involvement in interpreting the message rather than simple, passive acceptance; however, we should add that the *capacity* to be an active interpreter does not imply that people always are or should be (Planalp and Hewes, 1982). In many circumstances active interpretation may prove unnecessarily burdensome for the benefits it is likely to reap (see Langer, 1978; Roloff, 1980). (2) We assume that intuitive scientists use their theories of the motivations and/or abilities of the source to gain accurate information about the target even when the source's message is thought to be biased in some specifiable way. Thus, second-guessing is a process of interpretation involving both knowledge of sources and the ways in which knowledge of the context, personal liabilities, and/or intentions of the source affect the meaning assigned to the message.

Were these our only assumptions, second-guessing would sound much like the construct "source credibility" (see Andersen and Clevenger, 1963; McCroskey, 1966), except for the following differences. Source credibility is most often conceived of as an *evaluative orientation* toward the character and expertise of the source (McCroskey and Young, 1981). By contrast, although second-guessing may involve evaluation, it is primarily an *interpretive* process by which messages are assigned meanings that may or may not be in accord with the overt content of the messages. Thus, the output of second-guessing is a reinterpretation of a message, not just the intensification or retardation of an attitude shift. Whereas source credibility research focuses on the degree of acceptance of a message given attributions concerning the character or expertise of the source, the study of second-guessing must focus on the processes by which intuitive scientists attempt to wrest accurate information from potentially biased messages. This may involve the simple expedient of devaluing the message, as the source credibility formulation would suggest, or it may involve an effort to compensate for, to transform out, the supposed bias through the use of explicit knowledge (accurate or inaccurate) of the causes of the source's bias. Finally, in addition to the credibility construct's emphasis on the global dimensions of "goodwill" (character, intentions) and "knowledgeability" (competence, expertise) of the source, second-guessing adds specific information on the capacity and resource limitations—limitations that may unintentionally generate inaccuracy—as well as how *both* intentional and unintentional biases may be corrected. In short, second-guessing, though a first cousin to source credibility as traditionally conceived (but compare Delia, 1976), focuses directly on the interpretation assigned to messages rather than on the persuasive impact of those messages; it presents intuitive scientists as active interpreters of messages who can utilize more elaborate and more specific information about the sources and manifestations of bias than accorded them in the credibility construct.

Is Second-Guessing "Real"?

Let us break this question into two parts: Do people have intuitive theories about the sources of bias? Do people utilize that knowledge in attempts to correct for known or suspected biased messages? In answering the first question, we should keep in mind a general tendency among social scientists to ignore people's knowledge of the social world or cognitive processes as a source of viable data (Nisbett and Wilson, 1977a). Although this tendency is certainly justified under specifiable circumstances (Nisbett and Bellows, 1977; Nisbett and Wilson, 1977b; Wilson and Nisbett, 1978), it is by no means universally legitimate (Ericsson and Simon, 1980).

In a graphic demonstration of the potential accuracy of people's intuitive knowledge of psychological principles, for instance, Mischel and Mischel (see Mischel, 1979) asked 10-year-olds to guess the outcomes of a variety of classic experiments, including those on the aggression-facilitation effects of watching aggressive models, the advantages of guided live modeling over systematic desensitization, or symbolic modeling in the treatment of phobias. They understood the advantages of intermittent over consistent reinforcement in preventing the decay of learned behavior and so on, although they did not guess accurately the results of Asch's conformity experiments or Festinger's studies on cognitive dissonance (Mischel, 1979: 748). Similarly, adults have demonstrated a remarkable, though by no means complete, understanding of the sources of bias in eyewitness testimony (Loftus, 1979: Ch. 9) and have described the relationship between trait and situational causes of behavior with a degree of sophistication on a par with modern personality theorizing (Bromley, 1977).

More to the point, people demonstrate remarkable awareness of both intentional (see Hample, 1979) and unintentional sources of inaccurate messages. For example, in a recent study, Hewes and Pavitt (in progress)[7] found that undergraduates report using indirect sources (friends, the grapevine, and the like) to learn about other people for approximately 29 percent of their information (direct observation, 65 percent; other, usually mass media sources, for only 4 percent). However, they regarded indirect information as only somewhat less useful than direct information in forming impressions of others (7-point scale, "highly useful" = $\bar{X}$ [direct experience] = 5.4; $\bar{X}$ [indirect information] = 3.2) and listed a number of instances in which indirect information would prove more useful than direct. For example, 64 percent of the sample noted that indirect sources might have access to information about targets otherwise unattainable; 53 percent observed that others might offer unique and useful perspectives on a target's actions. This was true even though 65 percent of the subjects could identify at least one individual who gave them systematically biased information about others. Curiously, on the average subjects believed that these individuals were only slightly worse than people in general in providing accurate data about others (8-point scale, "always inaccurate" = 8; $\bar{X}$ [particular biased source] = 3.3; $\bar{X}$ [people in general] = 2.3), suggesting considerable sensitivity to the existence of bias and the problems created by it.

If people are aware of bias, they must have some notion of its sources and effects. And, of course, they do. For example, Hample (1979) has provided some intriguing interview and questionnaire data revealing considerable sophistication in people's knowledge concerning the causes and effects of lying, although the deception research does suggest that this knowledge may be inaccurate, or at least applied inaccurately (see Miller and Burgoon, 1981). Certainly, research on source credibility also implies the existence of such social knowledge and its use in effecting attitude change (see Andersen and Clevenger, 1963). Hewes and Pavitt's data also speak to this issue.

Since most treatments of the sources of cognitive bias (representativeness and availability heuristics, the fundamental attribution error, and so forth) do not test directly subjects' knowledge of these sources, Hewes and Pavitt asked subjects to identify and rate the importance of various sources of bias, cognitive and motivational, found in Nisbett and Ross (1980), paraphrased in plain English. For example, motivational bias was described as follows: "The sources distort the information for their own benefit." The availability heuristic (Tversky and Kahneman, 1973) became, "The sources are basing their judgments about the targets on only a few striking occurrences, rather than on the targets' regular, daily behavior," and so on for errors in choosing diagnostic behaviors on which to make judgments (Chapman, 1967; Chapman and Chapman, 1967, 1969), the representativeness heuristic (Tversky and Kahneman, 1974), the fundamental attribution error (Ross, 1977), and the simple inability to articulate knowledge about the other adequately.

Despite claims that naive scientists rely on primarily motivational, rather than cognitive, information in explaining bias (Nisbett and Ross, 1980: Ch. 10), 80 percent of Hewes and Pavitt's subjects, subjects who had never had courses in cognitive social psychology (see note 7) identified the fundamental attribution error as a source of bias and rated it as more important (7-point scale, "very important" = 1; $\bar{X}$ = 3.1) than the availability heuristic (ranked second on average ratings of importance; 91 percent identified; $\bar{X}$ = 3.2), motivational biases (ranked third; 90 percent; $\bar{X}$ = 3.3), the representativeness heuristic (ranked fourth; 80 percent; $\bar{X}$ = 3.4), and so on. In fact, even the lowest-ranked source of cognitive bias—errors in the diagnosticity of behaviors—was identified by *54 percent* of the subjects as a source of bias occurring in their own experience ($\bar{X}$ = 4.0). Thus, naive subjects demonstrated rather specific knowledge of the sources of cognitive bias, knowledge not accorded them either in discussions of source credibility or in the cognitive social psychological literature.

Certainly, some caution should be exercised in interpreting these data. Although these subjects did not have direct classroom training in the sources of bias, perhaps they heard about these sources from friends. On the other hand, subjects' responses to open-ended questions concerning these biases did not reveal the use of jargon words ("attribution," "heuristic," "availability," and the like). Furthermore, given the current, controversial nature of motivation as a source of bias (see Ross, 1977; Nisbett and Ross, 1980), even indirect exposure to these issues should have led to ranking motivational sources lower in importance than they were ranked. Nevertheless, replication with more insulated samples seems judicious. However, even given these limitations on Hewes and Pavitt's data, they, combined with the literature on lying and source credibility, strongly suggest an affirmative answer to our first question about second-guessing: People do seem to have intuitive theories about the sources of bias in messages, even cognitive sources of bias. But can they use this knowledge and, if so, how? We suggest that under circumstances that provoke mindful reflection, that is, when the need for accuracy is particularly salient and there is time for reflection, people are capable of applying this knowledge. Consider two bits of evidence in support of this conclusion.

Kruglanski et al. (1978; see also Kruglanski, 1980) offer a general theory of attributional processes designed to subsume Kelley's (1967)

ANOVA model, Jones and Davis's (1965) theory of correspondent inferences, and the like. Of particular interest to the study of second-guessing is Kruglanski et al.'s claim that people can assess the relative utility of specific kinds of evidence in testing the veridicality of attributional claims. They tested this hypothesis in their Experiment IV (1978: 323-327) by asking subjects to choose among a closed set of sources of information before accepting an expert's attribution as legitimate. Kruglanski et al. systematically varied sources of potential bias cued in descriptions of the sources. Biases manipulated included ego-defensiveness, chance interference caused by incidental emotional upsets, and failure of a scientific instrument. Subjects demonstrated laudable sophistication in identifying which of several sources of information (consistency over modalities, consensus with experts, and consistency over time) would provide normatively optimal information concerning the presence or absence of bias. In other words, subjects were aware of specific sources of bias and could, at least under optimal conditions, assess how that bias might be identified and corrected. Whether they could do this in a more natural setting, where they would have to implement these bias-testing strategies themselves, is not clear.

Kruglanski et al.'s study points to the lay scientist's ability to use potentially interactive strategies to correct for bias. Hewes and Pavitt (in progress) provide evidence that people can also employ active, cognitive strategies to correct for, or transform out, bias in messages. Of their subjects, 83 percent responded affirmatively to the question, "Do you think that you can compensate for the inaccurate information you sometimes get from sources concerning others?" Only 2 percent responded negatively. When asked in an open-ended question how they might do this, 40 percent claimed to weight purportedly biased evidence less heavily than unbiased evidence in making judgments about target events or people—a strategy consistent with both source credibility and second-guessing formulations. In addition, 68 percent of the subjects felt that they could compensate for biased messages because they understood the source(s) of that bias, and they claimed to exercise this option frequently (7-point scale, "very frequently" = 1; $\bar{X} = 2.8$)—a result strongly consistent with our view of second-guessing. Thus, for these subjects at least, second-guessing is a real phenomenon of some importance in their daily lives. Consequently, we can provide a tentative answer to our second question about second-guessing: Yes, people do seem to utilize knowledge about the sources of others' biases to correct for known or suspected bias in messages.

Are these compensatory strategies, whether social (as in Kruglanski et al., 1978) or cognitive (as in Hewes and Pavitt, in progress) adequate to the task of preventing the dissemination of bias through a social network? Can people correctly identify instances of actual bias and apply the right corrective strategies to them? Under what circumstances can they do this, and under what circumstances is it pragmatically rational to do so? These are some of the questions raised by a concern for the process of second-guessing—questions that need to be answered before this process is understood. Nevertheless, even without the answers, our discussion of second-guessing provides positive, if tentative, support for our view of the intuitive scientist as a potentially reflective seeker of social knowledge in interpersonal settings. A strong analogy between the professional and intuitive scientist seems all the more justified given the latter's apparent knowledge of cognitive sources of bias and methods by which that bias might be identified and corrected.

Conclusions

An interactant in an interpersonal setting, especially during the early stages of relational development, is faced with profound problems in acquiring knowledge about the other person. Similarly, those entering a particular role-governed setting for the first time must overcome their uncertainty about appropriate behavior if they are ever to satisfy whatever instrumental goals brought them there. In either the truly interpersonal or the "impersonal" situation (Miller and Steinberg, 1975), social actors must follow some "logic of discovery" in acquiring and interpreting new information.

We have likened the social actor's logic of discovery to that of a professional scientist, in part, because a metaphoric link between these two classes of people has proven illuminating in the past. In part, though, we believe that the comparison between the professional and intuitive scientist is more than simply metaphorical. Professional and intuitive scientists are not separate species. They both draw on common sense as a basis for their respective enterprises. As Whitehead (1929: 110) put it, "Science is rooted in what I have called the whole apparatus of common sense thought. That is the *datum* from which it starts, and to which it must recur. . . . You may polish up common sense, you may contradict it in detail, you may surprise it. But ultimately your whole task is to satisfy it."

The professional scientific enterprise is a particularly intensive, self-reflective, publicly articulated, rigorous, and tidy version of the knowledge acquisition, testing, and data interpretation tasks faced by all of us in everyday life. For example, just as theories are the *sine qua non* of the professional scientist, so are expectations and intuitive theories for the lay scientist. We have demonstrated several points of analogy between scientific and intuitive theories, and we have posited others. We believe this analogizing is useful. First, it helps to unify the plethora of terms for and conceptualizations of cognitive representations of social knowledge ("schemata" and the like). In addition, the analogy allows us to go beyond previous descriptions of cognitive representations by placing needed structure on them. As Taylor and Crocker (1981) note in their discussion of the cognitive "schema," currently this concept is pretty much defined inductively by the biases it has been used to explain. Falsification of the existence of schemata is impossible under this condition. By likening schemata to scientific theories in somewhat greater detail than in previous treatments, we believe we have given them more structure, making them that much more falsifiable. Finally, the analogy between intuitive and scientific theories helps identify aspects of cognitive representation too little explored. As an illustration, although there has been considerable effort to study the *process* of inferencing, understanding the "psycho-logics" that warrant inferences has advanced little since Abelson's early efforts (Abelson, 1968; Leff and Hewes, 1981). Since it is precisely these implicational processes that separate schemata from simple expectations, a better understanding of them is crucial.

But the points of similarity between the formal and informal sciences should not obscure the differences. The process of social uncertainty reduction operates in the context of competing scientific and nonscientific goals, limitations on cognitive capacities, and shortages of effective passive (observational) and active resources (communication strategies) for acquiring requisite data. The consequences of these practical constraints are a set of biases—biases that can be explained by these constraints and judged rational or irrational against them. This conception of "pragmatic rationality" permits us to identify disparities between professional and lay scientists while making those disparities comprehensible. Viewing lay scientists as pragmatically rational aids us in generating hypotheses concerning the interactions between social and scientific goals, alternative inferential strategies for reducing uncertainty (retroduction, induction, deduction), and their implications for the study of biases in uncertainty reduction. It also points to the existence of types of social knowledge that permit social actors to cope, potentially at least, with consequences of biased messages (second-guessing).

In conclusion, the task of uncertainty reduction in interpersonal settings is complex. We have tried to picture sympathetically the abilities and knowledge that social actors employ in undertaking this task. Our purpose was not to pen a paean to the Common Person. Instead we hoped to demonstrate that social actors can utilize quite elaborate forms of social knowledge when they explain social events and that this social knowledge influences materially the course of uncertainty reduction. Any theory of interpersonal uncertainty reduction that fails to acknowledge the influence of prior knowledge, that does not specify the nature and functions of that knowledge, that ignores either the mindful or the mindless application of that knowledge, and that does not explain the sources of biased knowledge is an incomplete theory at best.

Notes

1. Difficulties in understanding exactly how observed events are categorized as instances of implicit theories should not be underestimated. It requires precise specification of both how knowledge is represented in memory and how incoming information is processed (Anderson, 1978; Ebbesen and Allen, 1979; Palmer, 1978). Recently the problem has become more complicated by the recognition that incoming information neither fits nor fails to fit a category, but does so by degrees (Cantor and Mischel, 1977, 1979; Rosch and Mervis, 1975; Zadeh, 1965). Furthermore, it seems too simple to presume that observed data suggest the relevant category (or theory) or that the theory suggests which data are relevant. Instead, both theory-driven and data-driven processes operate simultaneously to achieve an acceptable fit (Bobrow and Norman, 1975; Neisser, 1976; Norman, 1976: Ch. 3).

2. The term "frame" is also used to refer to knowledge that is self-contained to some extent or has some distinct boundary, like a picture frame. Beyond the common emphasis on boundaries, "frame" takes on two different meanings. Computer scientists use it to refer to general-purpose data structures (Kuipers, 1975; Minsky, 1975), whereas Goffman (1974) uses it to refer to organized social experience. These two uses are probably not incompatible, but neither are they integrated, so the term "frame" cannot be distinguished from other types of implicit theories outside of specific research programs.

3. Note that if intuitive scientists were to allocate effort to correcting biases by focusing on the environmental causes of another's behavior, we might expect that they could do so, at some cost in data-gathering efficiency. If they cannot, then simple limitations in attentional capacity are not the sole explanation for the fundamental attribution error.

4. We have collapsed the interrelated functions of storage and retrieval in our discussion of forgivable errors. These two functions, while separable conceptually and empirically, are often associated with the same classes of biases (see Hamilton, 1981: 118-120; Taylor and Crocker, 1981). Storage, retrieval, and even integration (covered in the next section) are highly integrated components of the constructive processes of human memory (Bartlett, 1932; Paris and Lindauer, 1977; Piaget and Inhelder, 1973), all of which probably contribute to a variety biases.

5. We return to a related issue in the section on "second-guessing" later in the chapter.

6. We have collapsed those two cognitive functions since there are no studies that identify whether biases arise in the process by which an observational or interactional strategy is selected or in the process by which it is implemented in action.

7. Hewes and Pavitt (in progress) surveyed 75 freshman and sophomores at the University of Wisconsin—Madison. In order to circumvent the possibility that these subjects were familiar with social psychological treatments oι cognitive bias, questionnaires were eliminated from those subjects (1) who had taken a class in social psychology, sociological social psychology, or communication theory and/or (2) who used the

appropriate scientific jargon ("fundamental attribution error," "representativeness heuristic," "capacity limitations," and so on) in describing sources of bias in others. This resulted in a sample of 67 subjects on whose responses all the results are based.

References

Abelson, R. Psychological implication. In R. Abelson et al. (Eds.), *Theories of cognitive consistency: A sourcebook*. Chicago: Rand McNally, 1968.

Abelson, R. Psychological status of the script concept. *American Psychologist*, 1981, *36*, 715-729.

Allport, G. *The nature of prejudice*. Reading, MA: Addison-Wesley, 1954.

Andersen, K., and Clevenger, T., Jr. A summary of experimental research in ethos. *Speech Monographs*, 1963, *30*, 59-78.

Anderson, J. *Language, memory and thought*. Hillsdale, NJ: Erlbaum, 1976.

Anderson, J. Arguments concerning representations for mental imagery. *Psychological Review*, 1978, *85*, 249-277.

Anderson, J. Concepts, propositions, and schemata: What are the cognitive units? In J. Flowers (Ed.), *Nebraska Symposium on Motiviation* (Vol. 28). Lincoln: University of Nebraska Press, 1981.

Anderson, R. The notion of schemata and the educational enterprise: General discussion of the conference. In R. Anderson, R. Spiro, and W. Montague (Eds.), *Schooling and the acquisition of knowledge*. Hillsdale, NJ: Erlbaum, 1977.

Bartlett, F. *Remembering*. Cambridge: Cambridge University Press, 1932.

Bem, D., and Allen, A. On predicting some of the people some of the time: The search for cross-situational consistencies in behavior. *Psychological Review*, 1974, *31*, 506-520.

Berger, C. Beyond initial interaction: Uncertainty, understanding, and the development of interpersonal relationships. In H. Giles and R. St. Clair (Eds.), *Language and social psychology*. Baltimore: University Park Press, 1979.

Berger, C., and Calabrese, R. Some explorations in initial interaction and beyond: Toward a developmental theory of interpersonal communication. *Human Communication Research*, 1975, *1*, 99-112.

Berger, C., Gardner, R., Parks, M., Schulman, L., and Miller, G. Interpersonal epistemology and interpersonal communication. In G. Miller (Ed.), *Explorations in interpersonal communication*. Beverly Hills, CA: Sage, 1976.

Berger, C., Weber, M., Munley, M., and Dixon, J. Interpersonal relationship levels and interpersonal attraction. In B. Ruben (Ed.), *Communication Yearbook 1*. New Brunswick, NJ: Transaction, 1977.

Berscheid, E., and Graziano, W. The initiation of social relationships and interpersonal attraction. In R. Burgess and T. Huston (Eds.), *Social exchange in developing relationships*. New York: Academic Press, 1979.

Black, J., and Wilensky, R. An evaluation of story grammars. *Cognitive Science*, 1979, *3*, 213-230.

Bobrow, D., and Norman, D. Some principles of memory schemata. In D. Bobrow and A. Collins (Eds.), *Representation and understanding: Studies in cognitive science*. New York: Academic Press, 1975.

Bower, G., Black, J., and Turner, T. Scripts in memory for text. *Cognitive Psychology*, 1979, *11*, 177-220.

Brachman, R. On the epistemological status of semantic networks. In N. Finder (Ed.), *Associative networks: Representation and use of knowledge by computers*. New York: Academic Press, 1979.

Bransford, J., and Franks, J. The abstraction of linguistic ideas. *Cognitive Psychology*, 1971, *2*, 331-350.

Bransford, J., and McCarrell, N. A sketch of a cognitive approach to cognitive approach to comprehension. In W. Weimer and D. Palermo (Eds.), *Cognition and the symbolic processes.* Hillsdale NJ: Erlbaum, 1974.

Bromley, D. *Personality description in ordinary language.* New York: John Wiley, 1977.

Brooks, L. Nonanalytic concept formation and memory for instances. In E. Rosch and B. Lloyd (Eds.) *Cognition and categorization.* Hillsdale, NJ: Erlbaum, 1978.

Campbell, N. *Physics: The elements.* Cambridge: Cambridge University Press, 1920.

Cantor, N., and Mischel, W. Traits as prototypes: Effects on recognition memory. *Journal of Personality and Social Psychology,* 1977, *35,* 38-48.

Cantor, N., and Mischel, W. Prototypes in person perception. In L. Berkowitz (Ed.), *Advances in experimental social psychology* (Vol. 12). New York: Academic Press, 1979.

Chanowitz, B., and Langer, E. *Premature cognitive commitments: Causes and consequences.* Unpublished manuscript, Harvard University, 1978.

Chapman, L. Illusory correlation in observational report. *Journal of Verbal Learning and Verbal Behavior,* 1967, *6,* 151-155.

Chapman, L., and Chapman, J. Genesis of popular but erroneous diagnostic observations. *Journal of Abnormal Psychology,* 1967, *72,* 193-204.

Chapman, L., and Chapman, J. Illusory correlation as an obstacle to the use of valid psychodiagnostic signs. *Journal of Abnormal Psychology,* 1969, *74,* 271-280.

Chiesi, H., Spilich, G., and Voss, J. Acquisition of domain-related information in relation to high and low domain knowledge. *Journal of Verbal Learning and Verbal Behavior,* 1979, *18,* 257-273.

Cicourel, A. Interpretation and summarization: Issues in the child's acquisition of social structure. In J. Glick and K. Clarke-Stewart (Eds.), *The development of social understanding.* New York: Gardner Press, 1978.

Clark, R., and Delia, J. Topoi and rhetorical competence. *Quarterly Journal of Speech,* 1979, *65,* 187-206.

Cohen, C., and Ebbesen, E. Observational goals and schema activation: A theoretical framework for behavior perception. *Journal of Experimental Social Psychology,* 1979, *15,* 305-329.

Craik, F. Human memory. *Annual Review of Psychology,* 1979, *30,* 63-102.

Delia, J. A constructivist analysis of the concept of credibility. *Quarterly Journal of Speech,* 1976, *62,* 361-375.

Delia, J. Constructivism and the study of human communication. *Quarterly Journal of Speech,* 1977, *63,* 66-83.

Duncan, B. Differential social perception and attribution of intergroup violence: Testing the lower limits of stereotyping blacks. *Journal of Personality and Social Psychology,* 1976, *34,* 590-598.

Ebbesen, E., and Allen, R. Cognitive processes in implicit personality trait inferences. *Journal of Personality and Social Psychology,* 1979, *37,* 471-488.

Ericsson, K., and Simon, H. Verbal reports as data. *Psychological Review,* 1980, *87,* 215-251.

Feyerabend, P. *Against method.* London: Versa, 1975.

Fiske, S., and Kinder, D. Involvement, expertise and schema use: Evidence from political cognition. In N. Cantor and J. Kihlstrom (Eds.), *Cognition, social interaction, and personality.* Hillsdale, NJ: Erlbaum, 1981.

Fiske, S., and Linville, P. What does the schema concept buy us? *Personality and Social Psychology Bulletin,* 1980, *6,* 543-557.

Garfinkel, H. The rational properties of scientific and common-sense activities. In A. Giddens (Ed.), *Positivism and sociology.* London: Heinemann, 1974.

Goffman, E. *Strategic interaction.* Philadelphia: University of Pennsylvania Press, 1969.

Goffman, E. *Frame analysis.* New York: Harper & Row, 1974.

Habermas, J. *Knowledge and human interests.* Boston: Beacon Press, 1971.

Hamilton, D. A cognitive-attributional analysis of stereotyping. In L. Berkowitz (Ed.), *Advances in experimental social psychology* (Vol. 12). New York: Academic Press, 1979.

Hamilton, D. Illusory correlation as a basis for stereotyping. In D. Hamilton (Ed.), *Cognitive processes in stereotyping and intergroup behavior.* Hillsdale, NJ: Erlbaum, 1981.

Hamilton, V. Intuitive psychologist or intuitive lawyer? Alternative models of the attribution process. *Journal of Personality and Social Psychology,* 1980, *39,* 767-772.

Hample, D. *The purposes and effects of lying.* Presented to the Speech Communication Association Convention, San Antonio, Texas, 1979.

Hanson, N. *Patterns of discovery.* Cambridge: Cambridge University Press, 1958.

Hanson, N. Is there a logic of scientific discovery? In H. Feigl and G. Maxwell (Eds.), *Current issues in the philosophy of science.* New York: Holt, Rinehart & Winston, 1961.

Hastie, R. Schematic principles in human memory. In E. Higgins, C. Herman, and M. Zanna (Eds.), *Social cognition: The Ontario Symposium* (Vol. 1). Hillsdale, NJ: Erlbaum, 1981.

Head, H. *Studies in neurology* (Vol. II). London: Hodder & Stoughton/Oxford University Press, 1920.

Heider, F. *The psychology of interpersonal relations.* New York: John Wiley, 1958.

Hempel, C. *Fundamentals of concept formation in empirical science.* Chicago: University of Chicago Press, 1952.

Henle, M. On the relation between logic and thinking. *Psychological Review,* 1962, *69,* 366-378.

Hewes, D. An axiomatized, stochastic model of the behavioral effects of message campaigns. In D. Cushman and R. McPhee (Eds.), *Message-attitude-behavior relationship.* New York: Academic Press, 1980. (a)

Hewes, D. Stochastic modeling of communication processes. In P. Monge and J. Cappella (Eds.), *Multivariate techniques in human communication research.* New York: Academic Press, 1980. (b)

Hewes, D., and Haight, L. The cross-situational consistency of communicative behaviors: A preliminary investigation. *Communication Research,* 1979, *6,* 243-270.

Hewes, D., and Pavitt, C. *The "science" of "second-guessing."* Unpublished manuscript, University of Illinois, in progress.

Housel, T., and Acker, S. *Schema theory: Can it connect communication's discourse?* Presented at the International Communication Association Convention, Philadelphia, 1979.

Jackson, S., and Jacobs, S. Structure of conversational argument: Pragmatic bases for the enthymeme. *Quarterly Journal of Speech,* 1980, *66,* 251-265.

Jennings, D., Amabile, T., and Ross, L. Informal covariation assessment: Data-based vs. theory-based judgments. In A. Tversky, D. Kahneman, and P. Slovic (Eds.), *Judgment under uncertainty: Heuristics and biases.* New York: Cambridge University Press, forthcoming.

Jones, E., and Davis, K. From acts to dispositions: The attribution process in person perception. In L. Berkowitz (Ed.), *Advances in experimental social psychology* (Vol. 2). New York: Academic Press, 1965.

Kahneman, D. *Attention and effort.* Englewood Cliffs, NJ: Prentice-hall, 1973.

Kant, I. [*Critique of pure reason*] (J. Meiklejohn, trans.). New York: Collier, 1902.

Kaplan, A. *The conduct of inquiry.* Scranton, PA: Chandler, 1964.

Keenan, J. Psychological issues concerning implication: Comments on "Psychology of pragmatic implication: Information processing between the lines" by Harris and Monaco. *Journal of Experimental Psychology: General*, 1978, *107*, 23-27.

Kelley, H. Attribution theory in social psychology. In D. Levine (Ed.), *Nebraska Symposium on Motivation* (Vol. 15). Lincoln: University of Nebraska Press, 1967.

Kelley, H. *Causal schemata and the attribution process.* Morristown, NJ: General Learning, 1972.

Kelley, H., and Michela, J. Attribution theory and research. *Annual Review of Psychology*, 1980, *31*, 457-501.

Kelly, G. *A theory of personality.* New York: Norton, 1955.

Kruglanski, A. Lay epistemo-logic—Process and contents: Another look at attribution theory. *Psychological Review*, 1980, *87*, 70-87.

Kruglanski, A., Hamel, I., Maides, S., and Schwartz, J. Attribution theory as a special case of lay epistemology. In J. H. Harvey, W. J. Ickes, and R. F. Kidd (Eds.), *New directions in attribution research* (Vol. 2). Hillsdale, NJ: Erlbaum, 1978.

Kuhn, T. *The structure of scientific revolutions* (2nd ed.). Chicago: University of Chicago Press, 1970.

Kuipers, B. A frame for frames: Representing knowledge for recognition. In D. Bobrow and A. Collins (Eds.), *Representation and understanding.* New York: Academic Press, 1975.

Langer, E. Rethinking the role of thought in social interaction. In J. H. Harvey, W. J. Ickes, and R. F. Kidd (Eds.), *New directions in attribution research* (Vol. 2). Hillsdale, NJ: Erlbaum, 1978.

Leatherdale, W. *The role of analogy, model and metaphor in science.* Amsterdam: North-Holland, 1974.

Leff, M., and Hewes, D. Topical invention and group communication: Towards a sociology of inference. In G. Ziegelmueller and J. Rhodes (Eds.), *Dimensions of argument.* Annandale, VA: Speech Communication Association, 1981.

Loftus, E. *Eyewitness testimony.* Cambridge, MA: Harvard University Press, 1979.

Luria, A. *Cognitive development: Its cultural and social foundations.* Cambridge, MA: Harvard University Press, 1976.

Lyman, S., and Scott, M. *A sociology of the absurd.* Chicago: Scott, Foresman, 1970.

Mandler, J. A code in the node: The use of a story schema in retrieval. *Discourse Processes*, 1978, *1*, 14-35.

Mandler, J., and Johnson, N. Remembrance of things parsed: Story structure and recall. *Cognitive Psychology*, 1977, *9*, 111-151.

Mandler, J., and Johnson, N. On throwing out the baby with the bathwater: A reply to Black and Wilensky's evaluation of story grammars. *Cognitive Science*, 1980, *4*, 305-312.

Markus, H. Self-schemata and processing information about the self. *Journal of Personality and Social Psychology*, 1977, *35*, 63-78.

McCroskey, J. Scales for the measurement of ethos. *Speech Monographs*, 1966, *33*, 65-72.

McCroskey, J., and Young, T. Ethos and credibility: The construct and its measurement after three decades. *Central States Speech Journal*, 1981, *32*, 24-34.

Miller, G., and Burgoon, J. Factors affecting assessments of witness credibility. In R. Bray and N. Kerr (Eds.), *The psychology of the courtroom.* New York: Academic Press, 1981.

Miller, G., Galanter, E. Pribam, K. H. *Plans and the structure of behavior.* New York: Holt, Rinehart & Winston, 1960.

Miller, G., and Steinberg, M. *Between people: A new analysis of interpersonal communication*. Palo Alto, CA: Science Research Associates, 1975.

Minsky, M. Frame-system theory. In R. Schank and B. Nash-Weber (Eds.), *Theoretical issues in natural language processing*. Presented at a conference at MIT, June 1975.

Mischel, W. *Personality and assessment*. New York: John Wiley, 1968.

Mischel, W. Toward a cognitive social learning reconceptualization of personality. *Psychological Review*, 1973, *80*, 252-283.

Mischel, W. On the interface of cognition and personality: Beyond the person-situation debate. *American Psychologist*, 1979, *34*, 740-754.

Neisser, U. *Cognition and reality*. San Francisco: Freeman, 1976.

Nisbett, R., and Bellows, N. Verbal reports about causal influences on social judgments: Private access versus public theories. *Journal of Personality and Social Psychology*, 1977, *35*, 613-624.

Nisbett, R., and Ross, L. *Human inference: Strategies and shortcomings of social judgment*. Englewood Cliffs, NJ: Prentice-Hall, 1980.

Nisbett, R., and Wilson, T. Telling more than we can know: Verbal reports on mental processes. *Psychological Review*, 1977, *84*, 231-259.

Nisbett, R., and Wilson, T. The halo effect: Evidence for unconscious alteration of judgments. *Journal of Personality and Social Psychology*, 1977, *35*, 250-256. (b)

Norman, D. *Memory and attention* (2nd ed.). New York: John Wiley, 1976.

Ortony, A. Remembering, understanding, and representation. *Cognitive Science*, 1978, *2*, 53-69.

Palmer, S. Fundamental aspects of cognitive representation. In E. Rosch and B. Lloyd (Eds.), *Cognition and categorization*. Hillsdale, NJ: Erlbaum, 1978.

Paris, S., and Lindauer, B. Constructive aspects of children's comprehension and memory. In R. Kail and J. Hagen (Eds.), *Perspectives on the development of memory and cognition*. New York: John Wiley, 1977.

Peirce, C. *Collected papers* [Vols. V, VII] (C. Hartshorne and P. Weiss, Eds.). Cambridge, MA: Harvard University Press, 1931-1935.

Piaget, J. *The origins of intelligence in children* [2nd ed.] (M. Cook, trans.). New York: Norton, 1963.

Piaget, J. and Inhelder, B. *Memory and intelligence*. New York: Basic Books, 1973.

Planalp, S. *Relational schemata: An interpretive approach to relationships*. Unpublished doctoral dissertation, University of Wisconsin—Madison, forthcoming.

Planalp, S., and Hewes, D. A cognitive approach to communication theory: Cogito ergo dico? In M. Burgoon (Ed.), *Communication Yearbook 5*. New Brunswick, NJ: Transaction, 1982.

Planalp, S., and Tracy, K. Not to change the topic but . . . : A cognitive approach to the management of conversation. In D. Nimmo (Ed.), *Communication Yearbook 4*. New Brunswick, NJ: Transaction, 1980.

Pollard-Gott, L., McCloskey, M., and Todres, A. Subjective story structure. *Discourse Processes*, 1979, *2*, 251-281.

Popper, K. *The open society and its enemies* (4th ed.). London: Routledge & Kegan Paul, 1962.

Rands, M., and Levinger, G. Implicit theories of relationship: An intergenerational study. *Journal of Personality and Social Psychology*, 1979, *37*, 645-661.

Roloff, M. Self-awareness and the persuasion process: Do we really *know* what we are doing? In M. Roloff and G. Miller (Eds.), *Persuasion: New directions in theory and research*. Beverly Hills, CA: Sage, 1980.

Rosch, E., and Mervis, C. Family resemblances: Studies in the internal structure of categories. *Cognitive Psychology*, 1975, *7*, 573-605.

Rosenberg, S., and Sedlak, A. Structural representations of implicit personality theory. In L. Berkowitz (Ed.), *Advances in experimental social psychology* (Vol. 6). New York: Academic Press, 1972.

Ross, L. The intuitive psychologist and his shortcomings: Distortions in the attribution process. In L. Berkowitz (Ed.), *Advances in experimental social psychology* (Vol. 10). New York: Academic Press, 1977.

Rumelhart, D. Schemata: The building blocks of cognition. In R. Spiro, B. Bruce, and W. Brewer (Eds.), *Theoretical issues in reading comprehension*. Hillsdale, NJ: Erlbaum, 1980. (a)

Rumelhart, D. On evaluating story grammars. *Cognitive Science*, 1980, *4*, 313-316. (b)

Rumelhart, D., and Ortony, A. The representation of knowledge in memory. In R. Anderson, R. Spiro, and W. Montague (Eds.), *Schooling and the acquisition of knowledge*. Hillsdale, NJ: Erlbaum, 1977.

Schank, R., and Abelson, R. *Scripts, plans, goals and understanding*. Hillsdale, NJ: Erlbaum, 1977.

Schneider, D. Implicit personality theory: A review. *Psychological Bulletin*, 1973, *79*, 294-309.

Seibold, D., and Spitzberg, B. Attribution theory and research: Formalization, review, and implications for communication. In B. Dervin and M. Voigt (Eds.), *Progress in communication sciences* (Vol. 3). Norwood, NJ: Ablex, 1981.

Shaw, M., and Costanzo, P. Theories of social psychology. New York: McGraw-Hill, 1970.

Sillars, A. The stranger and the spouse as target persons for compliance-gaining strategies: A subjective expected utility model. *Human Communication Research*, 1980, *6*, 265-279.

Simon, H. Discussion: Cognition and social behavior. In J. Carroll and J. Payne (Eds.), *Cognition and social behavior*. Hillsdale, NJ: Erlbaum, 1976.

Snyder, M. Seek, and ye shall find: Testing hypotheses about other people. In E. Higgins, C. Herman, and M. Zanna (Eds.), *Social cognition: The Ontario Symposium* (Vol. 1). Hillsdale, NJ: Erlbaum, 1981. (a)

Snyder, M. On the influence of individuals on situations. In N. Cantor and J. Kihlstrom (Eds.), *Personality, cognition and social interaction*. Hillsdale, NJ: Erlbaum, 1981. (b)

Snyder, M., and Campbell, B. Testing hypotheses about other people: The role of the hypothesis. *Personality and Social Psychology Bulletin*, 1980, *6*, 421-426.

Snyder, M., and Skrypnek, B. *Testing hypotheses about the self: Assessments of job suitability*. Unpublished manuscript, University of Minnesota, 1979.

Snyder, M., and Swann, W., Jr. Hypothesis-testing processes in social interaction. *Journal of Personality and Social Psychology*, 1978, *36*, 1202-1212. (a)

Snyder, M., and Swann, W., Jr. Behavioral confirmation in social interaction: From social perception to social reality. *Journal of Experimental Social Psychology*, 1978, *14*, 148-162. (b)

Snyder, M., Tanke, E., and Berscheid, E. Social perception and interpersonal behavior: On the self-fulfilling nature of social stereotypes. *Journal of Personality and Social Psychology*, 1977, *9*, 656-666.

Spilich, G., Vesonder, G., Chiesi, H., and Voss, J. Text processing of domain-related information for individuals with high and low domain knowledge. *Journal of Verbal Learning and Verbal Behavior*, 1979, *18*, 275-290.

Spiro, R. Remembering information from text: The "state of schema" approach. In R. Anderson, R. Spiro, and W. Montague (Eds.), *Schooling and the acquisition of knowledge*. New York: John Wiley, 1977.

Spiro, R. Accommodative reconstruction in prose recall. *Journal of Verbal Learning and Verbal Behavior*, 1980, *19*, 84-95.

Storms, M. Videotape and the attribution process: Reversing actors' and observers' points of view. *Journal of Personality and Social Psychology*, 1973, *27*, 165-175.

Suppe, F. *The structure of scientific theories*. Urbana: University of Illinois Press, 1974.

Taylor, S. A categorization approach to stereotyping. Pp. 83-116 in D. Hamilton (Ed.), *Cognitive processes in stereotyping and intergroup behavior*. Hillsdale, NJ: Erlbaum, 1981.

Taylor, S. A categorization approach to stereotyping. In D. Hamilton (Ed.), *Cognitive processes in stereotyping and intergroup behavior*. Hillsdale, NJ: Erlbaum, 1981.

Taylor, S., Crocker, J., and D'Agostino, J. Schematic bases of social problem-solving. *Personality and Social Psychology Bulletin*, 1978, *4*, 447-451.

Taylor, S., and Fiske, S. Point of view and perceptions of causality. *Journal of Personality and Social Psychology*, 1975, *32*, 439-445.

Taylor, S., and Fiske, S. Salience, attention and attribution: Top of the head phenomena. In L. Berkowitz (Ed.), *Advances in experimental social psychology* (Vol. 11). New York: Academic Press, 1978.

Thayer, J. *Preliminary treatise on evidence at the common law*. Boston: Little, Brown, 1898.

Thorndyke, P. Cognitive structures in comprehension and memory of narrative discourse. *Cognitive Psychology*, 1977, *9*, 77-110.

Toulmin, S. *The philosophy of science*. London: Hutchinson, 1953.

Tracy, K. On getting the point: Distinguishing "issues" from "events," an aspect of conversational coherence. In M. Burgoon (Ed.), *Communication Yearbook 5*. New Brunswick, NJ: Transaction, 1981.

Turner, M. *Philosophy and the science of behavior*. New York: Appleton-Century-Crofts, 1967.

Tversky, A., and Kahneman, D. Availability: A heuristic for judging frequency and probability. *Cognitive Psychology*, 1973, *5*, 207-232.

Tversky, A., and Kahneman, D. Judgment under uncertainty: Heuristics and biases. *Science*, 1974, *185*, 1124-1131.

Wason, P., and Johnson-Laird, P. *Psychology of reasoning*. Cambridge, MA: Harvard University Press, 1972.

Wegner, D., and Vallacher, R. *Implicit psychology*. New York: Oxford University Press, 1977.

Whitehead, A. *The aims of education and other essays*. New York: New American Library, 1929.

Wilson, T., and Nisbett, R. The accuracy of verbal reports about the effects of stimuli on evaluations and behavior. *Social Psychology*, 1978, *41*, 118-131.

Wish, M., and Kaplan, S. Toward an implicit theory of interpersonal communication. *Sociometry*, 1977, *40*, 234-246.

Wyer, R., Jr. The acquisition and use of social knowledge: Basic postulates and representative research. *Personality and Social Psychology Bulletin*, 1980, *6*, 558-573.

Wyer, R., Jr., and Srull, T. The processing of social stimulus information: A conceptual integration. In R. Hastie et al. (Eds.), *Person memory: The cognitive basis of social perception*. Hillsdale, NJ: Erlbaum, 1980.

Zadeh, L. Fuzzy sets. *Information and Control*, 1965, *3*, 338-353.

5

Thinking about Friends and Lovers

SOCIAL COGNITION AND RELATIONAL TRAJECTORIES

Charles R. Berger
Michael E. Roloff

*Why should I disparage my parts by thinking about
what to say? None but dull rogues think.*

William Congreve, *The Double Dealer,* Act IV, Scene ii

As we pointed out in Chapter 1, the study of social cognition spans a number of relatively discrete areas of research. Although the current vogue is to refer to social cognition as if it were some kind of monolithic field of inquiry, researchers who identify themselves as interested in social cognition are quite diverse in their research interests and theoretical predispositions. One potential result of this diversity may be the proliferation of a number of isolated theoretical positions and research traditions and a lack of integration of these various positions and interests. Each research area is "mined" until it "runs dry," and then the researchers involved in the area move on to potentially more fruitful lodes.

One way to avoid this kind of "strip-mining" approach to inquiry is to try to focus the diverse perspectives of social cognition on some kind of communication process to see how each of these perspectives might relate to the process under consideration and how the various perspectives might relate to each other. This kind of focusing has the advantages of exposing potential links between research areas and making manifest those research areas where little or no effort is being expended. In this chapter, we have chosen the arena of *relationship development* as a communication process upon which to focus. We will show how various theoretical and research traditions within social cognition might explain how relationships are formed, how they are maintained, and why they decay. We also hope to demonstrate how various social cognition

151

perspectives can be related to each other within the relationship development context. Finally, we will explore some of the implications of these social cognition perspectives for the conduct of communication inquiry.

This chapter will not present a new theory of social cognition and communication. It will demonstrate, however, the critical importance of the study of social cognition for the understanding of relationship development processes. We are not contending that the only way to study relationship development is from the perspective of social cognition. What we are arguing is that a full understanding of relationship growth and decline relies heavily on an understanding of how persons seek, process, recall, and act on social information that they gain from their environments and the store of knowledge they bring with them to the social situation.

The plan of this chapter is to track relationships through various stages and to show how various social cognitive processes are important to each stage of a relationship. We will start with a situation in which persons anticipate interaction with others and the effects that anticipation has on information processing. We will then assume that persons have established some kind of ongoing relationship and consider some important cognitive processes that might occur at this relationship stage. We will then examine some of the social cognitive processes that might be implicated in relationship decline. Here we will also consider problems associated with retrospective accounts of social interactions. Finally, we will examine some implications of our discussion for the study of communication and relationship development.

Anticipation: It's Getting Me Down—
It's Keeping Me Waiting

There are a number of ways anticipated interaction might influence the processing of social information. First, when persons know they will be interacting with target others sometime in the near future, that knowledge might prompt the persons to seek information about the target persons from others. Second, anticipated interaction with a target other might call up a kind of stereotype or prototype of the target person based on the information that the person has about the target. Such stereotypes and prototypes might well have an impact on the initial stages of the actual encounter, but their effects might dissipate as the person gains more personal information about the target from direct interaction. Finally, if two persons who are relative strangers interact and know that they will be meeting again, they may alter their actions in such a way that they lower the likelihood that their current interaction will create some kind of ill will between them. Kiesler (1969) has pointed out that commitment to future interaction may have the effect of inducing interactants to suppress certain actions. Moreover, Goffman (1959) has discussed the information control strategies that persons use to project a particular self in social situations. In later work, Goffman (1969) explicated the kinds of moves and countermoves interactants use to uncover each other's actual intentions in social situations. Thus, anticipation of future interaction may significantly influence the information that persons make available to each other for processing.

At least two studies have shown that anticipated interaction influences the ways persons seek and process information about those with whom they anticipate interaction. First, Berscheid et al. (1976) asked students to agree to allow the experimenters to determine randomly their dating choices for a period of five weeks. In the high-exclusiveness condition, subjects were led to believe that they would be dating the same person for the five-week period. Subjects in the low-exclusiveness condition were told that they would date a different person each week for the five weeks. Subjects in both groups were told that they could watch a videotape in which their prospective date was discussing an issue with two other persons. The videotape apparatus was set up in such a way that subjects could select which of the three discussants they wished to view. After viewing the discussion, a number of measures were administered.

The results of this study revealed that anticipated dates were awarded more attention in terms of viewing time than were discussants who were nondates. Also, dates of the high-exclusiveness group were given more attention than were dates of the low-exclusiveness group. Subjects recalled more about their anticipated dates than they did about other discussion participants, although there was no significant difference between the two exclusiveness groups. Trait ratings and confidence ratings of dates were more extreme than were the same ratings for nondates. No significant exclusiveness effects were found in these comparisons. Finally, dates were rated as more attractive than nondates. Again, the exclusiveness effect was not significant.

In a second study, Harvey et al. (1980) had persons view a videotape of a group discussion. Before viewing the tape, some subjects were told that they would be interacting with a particular group member after the videotape was finished. Other subjects were not given these instructions.

Comparisons between these two groups showed that those who anticipated interaction remembered more about the target person than did those who did not believe that they would interact with the person.

These studies clearly demonstrate that when persons anticipate interaction with a total stranger and they have access to information about that person, they will spend more time gathering information about that person and will process that information more deeply than when they anticipate no interaction with the person. Of course, the Berscheid et al. (1976) study not only dealt with the effects of anticipated interaction but also demonstrated some limited effects of outcome dependence. Those persons who expected to date the same person for the entire five-week period paid more attention to their prospective dates than did those who believed they would be dating the person on the videotape for one week. It is interesting to note, however, that no effects beyond attention differences were observed for the exclusiveness manipulation.

In a study related to the above experiment, Calabrese (1975) paired strangers and had them "get acquainted" for a period of 13 minutes. During this time their conversations were unobtrusively tape-recorded. In addition, half of the dyads were led to believe that they would be interacting in the future, while the other half were told that they would not converse again. Analyses of the tapes revealed that persons who anticipated future interaction with each other exchanged significantly more background and demographic information than did persons who did not anticipate future interactions. Although Calabrese's study did not assess memory and attribution differences between the two groups, his findings suggest that anticipated interaction may have the effect of inducing persons to make more information available to each other during their current interaction. Of course, there may be circumstances under which persons might inhibit information exchange under conditions of anticipated interaction.

While the Calabrese (1975) study demonstrated a quantitative difference in information exchange as a result of anticipated interaction, it did not address the issue of potential differences in the *types* of information that persons might seek depending on anticipated interaction. One study has examined the differences in the kinds of *visual information* that persons prefer as a function of anticipated interaction. Berger and Douglas (1981) led some persons to believe that they would be interacting with a target person. These subjects were ushered to a room and actually saw the target person sitting at a table reading a book. The subjects were told that before they would interact with the target person, they would have the opportunity to view a series of slide pictures of the target person in a variety of situations. The subjects were also told that after viewing the slides, they would have a conversation with the target person in which their task was to make as favorable an impression as possible on the target person during the conversation. Another group of subjects was not told anything about the target person.

All subjects were asked to judge the information value of a series of slides of the target person in a variety of solitary and social situations. Subjects were asked to indicate which of two situations pictured in two slides would give them the most information about the target person if they could unobtrusively observe the target person in the situations shown. These paired comparison judgments were subjected to multi-dimensional scaling procedures (MDPREF; Carroll, 1972) in order to ascertain the dimensions underlying the preference judgments. Analyses revealed a dimension related to the *social or solitary* nature of the situation shown. Persons generally preferred slides in which the target person was actively involved in interaction with others as opposed to solitary situations. A second factor dealt with the level of *formality* of the situations shown. Here there was considerably more variability in preferences; however, those who anticipated interaction with the target person showed a stronger preference for informal pictures than did those who did not anticipate interaction with the target. Those who antici-pated interaction with the target found the informal slides more informative. No differences were observed between the two groups on the social-solitary dimension, however. After the slide judgments were made, subjects indicated the extent to which they felt *similar* to the target person. Those who anticipated interacting with the target person indicated that they felt more similar to the target.

The findings of this study give us further insight into the kinds of information-processing strategies persons use when they anticipate interacting with others. Observing a total stranger in a social context in which there are fewer constraints on action is more likely to tell an observer more about the person being observed than is observing the target person in a more formal context. It is not that observations of persons in formal contexts tell us nothing about the persons in them, but observing persons in environments that allow more choices of action will probably afford us more information about persons *as individuals*. Thus, the strategy of preferring to view the target person in informal contexts by those who anticipated interaction with the target appears to be an optimal one. This study also suggests, along with the Berscheid et al. (1976) study discussed previously, that anticipated interaction with a stranger has the effect of increasing felt similarity with the stranger and may increase the attractiveness of the stranger.

Some studies have demonstrated that anticipated interaction influences the kinds of attributions one person will make about another. For example, Miller et al. (1978) found that persons who either actively interacted with another or anticipated interacting with the other after observing him or her felt that they learned more about the person's personality dispositions than did those who passively observed the target person. Knight and Vallacher (1981) demonstrated how anticipated interaction and actual interaction can influence attributions made about a target person. In this experiment, persons were exposed to the same stimulus videotape but were led to believe that they were (1) watching a tape, (2) watching a tape of someone with whom they would be interacting, or (3) having an interaction with the person on the television monitor. During the course of what was allegedly an interview, the interviewer who was on the tape made either positive or negative remarks about the interviewee. After observing these positive or negative performances by the interviewer, subjects evaluated the interviewer. With respect to causal attribution, an interaction was found between the interviewer affect conditions and the degree to which the subject was engaged with the interviewer. Those who anticipated interaction with the positive interviewer attributed his behavior to his disposition, while those who thought they were actually interacting with the positive interviewer attributed his behavior to the situation. The results for the negative interviewer were reversed. Those who anticipated interaction attributed the negativism to the situation, while those who thought they were interacting with the interviewer attributed his negativism to his disposition.

A study by Kiesler et al. (1967) examined the impact of deviance and expected interaction on interpersonal attraction. Some subjects were led to expect further interaction with a particular target person, while other subjects were not. The target person either conformed to the norms of the situation or deviated significantly from them. After exposure to these conditions, subjects were asked to indicate how attractive they found the target person. Persons who anticipated future interaction with the norm violator found him to be less attractive than did persons who anticipated no future interaction with him. The level of attraction of the norm conformer was higher for those who anticipated interacting with him in the future.

Pallak et al. (1972) explored the impact of commitment to future interaction on agreement with a persuasive message. Subjects were led to expect interaction with either the same or a different partner in three upcoming sessions. All subjects received a persuasive message from the partner that varied in the degree to which it deviated from the subjects' initial attitudes. Their results indicated that commitment to future interaction with a source of a persuasive message facilitated agreement with the message, regardless of its extremity, when compared with commitment to communicate with a different partner.

Commitment to future interaction has also been found to influence outcomes in bargaining situations. In general, anticipating future interaction with a bargaining opponent increases the probability of cooperation (Shure and Meeker, 1968; Slusher et al., 1974). However, this finding has specific limits. Marlowe et al. (1966) observed that greater cooperation resulted from commitment when a subject expected to meet a "self-effacing other"; however, subjects expecting to meet an "egotistical" partner evidenced greater competition than when not expecting interaction. Gruder (1969, 1971) similarly found greater cooperation only occurred when a person anticipated meeting a "fair" partner; greater competition was evidenced when a person anticipated meeting an "exploitative" partner. Roering et al. (1975) discovered that more cooperation was evidenced when anticipated interaction existed *and* when the subject anticipated a companionable interaction rather than a competitive one. More recently, Slusher et al. (1978) reported that cooperation was a joint function of three variables: anticipated interaction, relative power, and the structure of the bargaining situations. Low-power subjects were more cooperative as a result of commitment to future interaction when playing Chicken or No Conflict bargaining games. High-power subjects were more cooperative as a result of commitment to future interaction when playing a Prisoner's Dilemma bargaining game.

There is some evidence to suggest that individual difference variables exert an impact on information processing in the anticipated interaction paradigm. For example, in the aforementioned Berscheid et al. (1976) study, a measure of self-monitoring (Snyder, 1974) was administered to all participants. According to Snyder (1974, 1979), since high self-monitors are more concerned with making favorable impressions on others, they are more sensitive to cues that others provide in order to guide their self-presentations. By contrast, low self-monitors are more likely to "say it the way they feel it," regardless of the social consequences. These characteristic differences led Berscheid et al. (1976) to suggest that self-monitoring differences should be manifested on the various dependent variables of their study. Although they found that high self-monitors spent no more time looking at their prospective dates, they did find that high self-monitors recalled more details about their prospective dates and found their prospective dates more attractive than did their low self-monitoring counterparts. The differential memory effects found in this study are consistent with Snyder's (1974, 1979) characterizations of high self-monitors.

A measure of self-monitoring was also included in the previously discussed Berger and Douglas (1981) study dealing with visual information. Here it was found that high self-monitors showed stronger preferences for the informal slide pictures than did lows. This finding may indicate that high self-monitors are more likely to employ optimal information acquisition strategies than are low self-monitors, even when both anticipate interaction with the same target person. Interestingly, no interaction between anticipated interaction and self-monitoring on preferences for the informal slides was observed in this study.

Two additional studies have shown information-seeking differences between high and low self-monitors. Snyder (1974) found that among persons who anticipated participating in a group discussion, who were given access to information about the population from which the group was formed, high self-monitors spent more time looking at the information than did lows. Elliott (1979) reported that high self-monitors spent more money than lows so that they could buy information about a person to whom they were asked to misrepresent their opinions on a particular issue. These two studies, as well as the Berger and Douglas (1981) and the Berscheid et al. (1976) studies, generally support the view that when high self-monitors anticipate interactions with others whom they do not know, they will more carefully construe information about the target persons than will low self-monitors who also anticipate such interactions. In addition, it appears that high self-monitors may attend to different kinds of information about prospective interactants. It may be that high self-monitors select information that will help them to optimize their chances of making favorable impressions on target persons. This possibility deserves research attention.

Duval and Wicklund (1972: 172) argued that anticipated interaction can lead to objective self-awareness because the individual anticipates future scrutiny by others: "When exposing himself to information, the person who expects to convey that information to others should be more objectively self-aware than the person who simply expects to absorb the same information passively—the reasons being that the communicator anticipates focused attention from his audience, and this anticipation will cause him to focus on the correctness and consistency of the material to be communicated."

A variety of studies have found that anticipation of being a source of information creates greater concern for consistency. Davis and Wicklund (cited in Duval and Wicklund, 1972: 180-184) found that anticipated interaction resulted in greater integration of contradictory information than not expecting interaction. Brock and Blackwood (1962) reported that subjects *anticipating* delivering a counterattitudinal message changed their attitude in advance of delivering the message more than subjects who did not. This effect was particularly pronounced for subjects who had little justification for engaging in the counterattitudinal behavior. Jellison and Mills (1969) and Greenwald (1969) found that subjects who commit themselves to expressing public stands on an issue tend to increase the extremity of their position in advance of their statements.

When a person anticipates being the receiver of information, changes in self-related variables also are found. Subjects who anticipate receiving a counterattitudinal message will shift their attitudes prior to receiving the message (Deaux, 1968; McGuire, 1966; McGuire and Millman, 1965; McGuire and Papageorgis, 1962; Newtson and Czerlinsky, 1974; Papageorgis, 1967; Sears et al., 1964). Other research has demonstrated that this generalization is limited by specific conditions (see Apsler and Sears, 1968; Cooper and Jones, 1970; Dinner et al., 1972; Wicklund et al., 1967).

Anticipated interaction has also been found to influence how we process information about the topic that is the focus of interaction. Zajonc (1960) found that subjects who expected to *transmit* information tend to have cognitive structures about the information that were more differentiated, complex, and unified than those of subjects who only expected to *receive* further information about the topic. Similarly, Cohen (1961) reported that subjects expecting to transmit incoming contradictory information tended to organize the information according to one consistent point of view more than did subjects who simply expected to receive the information. Brock and Fromkin (1968) found that subjects who expected to transmit information tended to spend more time listening to information that supported their initial impressions of an object than did those who only expected to receive further information. Recently, Ford and Weldon (1981) found that subjects who anticipated justifying their judgments about a person and were forewarned to memorize certain traits of the person tended to spend more time making a judgment about the person than did subjects who did not anticipate transmitting such information.

Transmission sets are further influenced by the specific instructions as to what is important in a task (Jeffery and Mischel, 1979). Chaiken (1980) found that subjects anticipating the transmission of information that was gained from a persuasive communication desired to be better informed about the topic, recalled more of the arguments in the message, reported thinking more about the arguments, and spent more time reading the message than did subjects who anticipated interacting on a different logic. In addition, subjects who anticipated interacting on the same topic based their agreement with the message on the number of supporting arguments, whereas those anticipating inter- action on a different topic based agreement on the perceived source's likability.

In this section we have examined a number of studies suggesting that when persons anticipate interaction with strangers or when persons expect to interact in the future with a person with whom they are currently interacting, the amounts and kinds of visual and verbal information about the person that they seek and heed are affected. Once this information is heeded, anticipated interaction influences the ways the information is integrated. Moreover, individual differences influence this process. High self-monitors seem to seek more information than lows, and they process it in such ways that it is more available to them in memory. What these studies do *not* tell us is what *types* of information are sought under conditions of anticipated interaction and how the information is ultimately related to *actions* by the individual when he or she actually *encounters* the target person. Finally, an important issue in this line of research concerns the use to which information about a target person is put. There are at least two possibilities. First, persons might use the information to call up existing knowledge structures, such as prototypes or stereotypes. Thus, when a person finds that he or she will be interacting with a person from a particular occupational category, that piece of information might be used to instantiate a kind of generic prototype of members of that particular occupational group. A second possibility is that information provided about a target person might be linked in such a way that a unique or individuated characterization of the target person is built. Obviously, the building of a unique characterization requires more information, time, and cognitive energy than does the prototype accessing process. Whether the first or second possibility occurs may depend on the nature of the anticipated interaction. For routine interactions, the prototype may suffice; for more idiosyncratic encounters, more individuated characterizations might be necessary. These possibilities suggest that future work in this area should take into account the nature of the anticipated interaction in relation to the information provided about the target person.

Relationship Development: The Initial Stages

In the previous sections, we examined some of the effects that antici- pated interaction has on the acquisition, processing, and recall of social information. In this section, we assume that persons have met for the first time and are engaging in initial interactions. Both Altman and Taylor (1973) and Berger (1973) have pointed out that typical initial encounters are characterized by exchanges of noncontroversial, factually oriented background and demographic information. Berger (1973) and Calabrese (1975) found that the first two minutes of initial interactions were dominated with exchanges of background information. After this point, these exchanges tended to decrease and exchanges of attitudinal information and information related to hobbies and interests increased. The first few minutes of initial interactions also tend to consist of a number of rapid exchanges of a question-answer format. In his analysis of conversations between strangers, Motl (1980) found significantly more floor exchanges during the first two minutes of initial interactions than were manifested later in the interactions. In general, then, the information environments generated by participants in initial interactions tend to be rich in factual background information that is exchanged rather rapidly.

We should point out that the above characterization of initial interactions has its exceptions. For example, two persons might meet for the first time in an environment that leads them both to predict that they share similar perspectives on an issue or share similar interests; for instance, they both may be attending a political rally for the same candidate or they may be at a meeting of amateur radio operators. Initial encounters in such environments may allow strangers to forego initial demographic exchanges in favor of conversation about the topic or interest at hand. Exchanges of personal background information may occur after initial exchanges related to their purpose for being together.

Assuming the more typical pattern of initial interaction, it is interesting to consider why background information of that kind is exchanged first rather than some other kind of information. After all, persons could open conversations by announcing their yearly incomes or their attitudes toward abortion. There are several possible answers to the question of sequencing. First, it might be argued that persons exchange background information merely to pass the time in a relatively innocuous manner. Second, exchanges of background information are noncontroversial and are not likely to engender conflict between conversational participants. When a person announces, "I'm from Philadelphia," it is difficult to disagree with the person, regardless of one's feelings about Philadelphia. Finally, as a study by Berger (1975) demonstrated, information disclosed early in a relationship may be used in at least two different ways. First, the information might be used to make predictions about the person disclosing it. Knowing that a person is a professor at a university is likely to lead to predictions that are quite different from those that would be made if one knew that person to be a sanitary engineer. These predictions do, of course, have extremely significant communicative consequences. For example, in Japan and Korea it is not uncommon for businessmen who meet for the first time to exchange business cards before saying much more than hello to each other. It is critical for persons to know each other's status in such countries because language choices are highly dependent on the relative statuses of conversational participants. Using the improper form of address could be either insulting or a sign of ignorance on the part of the user. There are other ways background information may be used to guide subsequent conduct. Given a particular configuration of background information about another, one might make certain assumptions about the person's attitudes on issues that have not been discussed. If one wishes to avoid disagreement or to show agreement, he or she might avoid or bring up issues to be discussed depending on whether predictions of dissimilarity or similarity are made on the basis of background characteristics.

A second way initial information might be used is to explain subsequent events in interactions. Berger (1975) found that when subjects heard conversations in which persons agreed or disagreed over attitudinal issues and the subjects were led to believe that the conversational participants were from similar of dissimilar backgrounds, those subjects who heard the persons disagree attributed their disagreements to their dissimilar backgrounds, while persons who heard the conversational participants agree tended to attribute their agreement to similarity in their backgrounds. When persons heard disagreement in conversations between individuals with similar backgrounds or agreement in conversations between individuals with dissimilar backgrounds, attributions for attitudinal agreements and disagreements shifted from background characteristics to personality attributes. Thus, background information was employed to explain later attitudinal agreements and disagreements when it was consistent with the hypothesis that persons with similar backgrounds tend to agree with each other and those from dissimilar backgrounds tend to disagree. However, when the conversational pattern was inconsistent with this hypothesis and persons were asked to make attributions for agreement and disagreement, the background information tended to be ignored for the purpose of formulating causal attributions. Attributions to general personality differences were more frequent in these situations.

Another study demonstrating the effects of information sequencing on interpersonal perceptions was reported by Jones and Gordon (1972). This study involved an interview situation in which certain critical information was disclosed by the interviewee either early or late in the interview. Subjects listened to tape-recorded interviews in which a prospective applicant to a college disclosed either a positive or a negative piece of information about life experiences for which he was either responsible or not responsible. This information was disclosed either early or late in the interview. After listening to one of the variations of the tapes, subjects rated the attractiveness of the interviewee. This study found that persons generally evaluated the interviewee more negatively when he disclosed positive information about himself early as opposed to late in the interview, whereas the impact of negative information on evaluations depended on whether or not the interviewee was responsible for the negative event. When he was responsible, early disclosure increased his attractiveness. When he was not responsible, later disclosure produced more attractiveness. Although this study dealt with affective reactions to different patterns of information sequencing, it does demonstrate that persons may have expectations about the appropriate sequencing of information in social interaction situations. Conformity to or deviation from these kinds of expectations might influence the encoding, processing, and retrieval of the conversation.

Hypothesis Testing

In addition to the above research concerned with initial interactions is the work of Snyder and his colleagues on hypothesis testing (Snyder, 1981; Snyder and Campbell, 1980; Snyder and Cantor, 1979; Snyder and Swann, 1978). The aim of these studies was to determine the kinds of information persons will seek when they are attempting to test a hypothesis about a target person. In one of these studies (Snyder and Swann, 1978), subjects were given prototypic descriptions of extraverted or introverted persons. They were then given the task of determining whether a target person was extraverted or introverted, depending on which of the hypotheses they were assigned to test. Subjects were then given a list of questions they could ask the target in order to determine whether the target person possessed the hypothesized trait. From the list, subjects were asked to select questions that would provide them with the data necessary to test their hypotheses. Unknown to the subjects, the questions were formulated in such a way that some of them were aimed at detecting extraversion while others were focused on introversion. A set of "neutral" questions was also in the list. Subjects were limited as to the number of questions they could select.

Snyder and Swann (1978) found that subjects generally chose questions that would *confirm* their hypotheses. That is, those assigned to determine whether the target was extraverted tended to choose to ask questions that would confirm the presence of extraversion in the target person, while those assigned to test the introversion hypothesis tended to choose questions that would confirm introversion. Snyder and Swann (1978) suggested that a person testing such a hypothesis could use two strategies in addition to confirmation. First, one might ask questions aimed at disconfirming the hypothesis. Second, one might search for both confirming and disconfirming evidence for the hypothesis. No evidence was found to support the assertion that persons generally employ these latter two possible strategies.

In addition to the above findings, the Snyder and Swann (1978) study indicated that in actual face-to-face interactions, the search for confirmatory rather than disconfirming evidence was also manifested. Furthermore, one of their experiments revealed that the target person behaved in ways consistent with the hypothesis the subject was testing. Subjects who were testing their target persons for extraversion apparently induced their target persons to behave in ways that were judged to be extraverted by a panel of independent judges, while subjects who were given the task of testing the introversion hypothesis apparently constrained the behavior of their targets in such ways as to make them appear to be more introverted to a panel of independent judges. Thus, not only do persons seek information that will confirm rather than disconfirm a hypothesis they hold about another, they also may somehow induce persons to behave in ways that will confirm their hypotheses.

Snyder and Cantor (1979) performed a series of similar experiments in which persons were given prototypic information at one point in time and were asked to test a similar hypothesis about another at a later point in time. These studies found results similar to those of the Snyder and Swann (1978) experiments. Persons tended to retrieve information that would confirm rather than disconfirm their hypotheses. One possible critique of these studies is that, since persons were given the type of prototypic information that was consistent with the hypotheses they were asked to test, they would have been inordinately biased in the direction of seeking confirmatory information. Snyder and Campbell (1980) examined this possibility by asking their subjects to determine whether a given target person was either extraverted or introverted. However, within each of these conditions, some persons were provided with prototypic information that was consistent with the trait for which they were testing, while others were provided with both extraverted and introverted prototypic information. Even when subjects were provided with both types of information, they chose to ask questions that would produce data confirming their hypotheses and not questions that would disconfirm their hypotheses. Although the interpretation of these hypothesis-testing studies appears to be straightforward, Hewes and Planalp (this volume) suggest that if persons generally assume that others have relatively consistent personality traits, the strategy of asking confirmatory questions may be a reasonable one.

Knowledge-Gaining Strategies

In a sense, the hypothesis-testing research discussed above is not a very good analog to the beginnings of initial interactions. In most initial interactions, persons are not given an explicit hypothesis to test about the person whom they will meet! As the interaction unfolds, hypotheses may be developed and subsequently tested; however, we assume that the process of developing hypotheses to test takes some time. Perhaps an even more basic question to pose about social cognition in initial interactions concerns the issue of what strategies persons use to acquire information about those with whom they are interacting—assuming, of course, that they are interested in learning something about the target persons. Note that in posing this question we do not assume that the knowledge seeker has any particular hypotheses in mind. He or she may simply wish to learn "something" about the target person for any number of reasons. For the moment we will ignore the issue of how these reasons might influence what information is sought or the strategies used to gather it. We suspect that the goals a person has during interaction significantly affect the type of information he or she will seek and the strategies he or she will use to obtain it.

Berger (1979) has suggested a taxonomy of knowledge-gaining strategies consisting of three general categories. First, there are strategies the observer might use that involve no direct interaction with the target person. The knowledge seeker might simply observe the target unobtrusively. These strategies Berger (1979) labeled *passive*. This label does not imply that perception and cognition are passive processes; it merely indicates that the observer assumes a passive role with respect to the target person. A second class of strategies is called *active*. Active strategies also do not involve direct interaction between the target and the observer, but the observer does structure the physical or social environment of the target person in order to learn something about him or her. Frequently, social scientists arrange social environments in different ways and observe how subjects respond to these variations. In everyday life, interviewers may manipulate situations to see how prospective employees react to stress. In the active mode, the observer manipulates the environment and then observes how the target responds to it. By contrast, *interactive* strategies involve direct interaction between the observer and the target person. The knowledge seeker becomes a participant observer.

In a series of investigations aimed at illuminating the passive strategies (Berger and Perkins, 1978, 1979; Berger and Douglas, 1981), subjects were asked to judge the information utility of slide pictures of a target person in a variety of social and solitary situations under a variety of conditions. These studies reveal that when persons are asked to assume that they want to "get to know" the target person, they consistently judge social slides to be more informative than solitary ones, and within the domain of social situations they generally prefer ones where the target person is actively involved with the others present. These marked preferences for active social situations are not the product of the assumption that as observers persons would overhear what the target person is saying to the others pictured (Berger and Perkins, 1979). Rather, it seems that the visual activity cues are judged to be more significant sources of information about the target person. In addition to the social activity dimension, Berger and Douglas (1981) found that persons also employed a formal-informal dimension in making information utility judgments. As noted earlier in this chapter, persons who anticipated interaction with the target person showed a greater preference for these informal slides.

Although there has been little research done directly to explore the active strategies, there would appear to be good theoretical and practical reasons to explore such strategies. Attribution theorists, as discussed by Sillars (this volume), have assumed that persons act as if they are naive scientists trying to understand the causes for their own and others' actions. However, much of the research done in this vein has placed subjects in relatively passive roles. For example, the line of research stimulated by McArthur (1972) involves having subjects respond to hypothetical situations. Only recently has attention been paid to such questions as how much information persons will seek when they are asked to make an attribution (Major, 1980) or what prompts attribution processes in the first place (Pyszcynski and Greenberg, 1981). We suggest that it might be useful to extend the naive scientist notion to the study of how persons actively manipulate aspects of others' physical and social environments (much as a social scientist would) in order to gain knowledge about the others. Here several questions suggest themselves. First, what is it that gets manipulated? What is the independent variable? What responses does the observer look for? What is the dependent variable? Does the observer employ simple or complex designs? Does he or she allow for interaction effects? Are multiple response variables observed? Finally, how are observations accumulated through time? While Kelley (1967, 1972) has used the ANOVA cube as a model for a cognitive structure, attribution theorists have not done much in the way of pushing the person-as-naive-scientist metaphor in the direction of examining the ways in which observers actively manipulate variables and observe responses to their manipulations.

There is considerable extant research that bears directly on interactive strategies. Studies of initial interactions between strangers (Frankfurt, 1965; Calabrese, 1975; Motl, 1980) reveal that in the first few minutes of an encounter, question asking is frequent. As the interaction progresses, question asking decreases. While asking questions is a rather obvious way to gain knowledge about another person, what is somewhat less obvious is the issue of the limits that social conventions place on question asking. Asking too many questions might turn an informal social interaction into an interview. One interesting issue involves the number of questions per unit of time persons are allowed to ask in the interaction context. Furthermore, once this number has been exhausted, what other strategies might then be employed to gain knowledge?

One possible alternative to question asking is self-disclosure. A number of studies (for example, Jourard, 1971; Sermat and Smyth, 1973; Worthy et al., 1969) have demonstrated that persons tend to reciprocate self-disclosures in terms of intimacy and frequency. Thus, one way to find out some particular piece of information about another is to disclose the same or similar information about oneself.

While the interactive strategies discussed above deal with the means by which persons might gain information about another, they do not address the *types* of information that might be sought. A study reported by Swann et al. (1981) bears directly on this issue. These investigators tested the hypothesis that when persons are deprived of control, they will be more inclined to seek information about others. Their study revealed that when persons were deprived of control in a task, they sought more *diagnostic information* about a stranger with whom they anticipated interaction than did persons who were not deprived of control on the first task.

The relationship between deprivation of control and information seeking found in the Swann et al. (1981) study raises the issue of antecedents to knowledge gaining. Berger (1979) suggested at least three such antecedents. First, he argued that persons would want to gain information about another if the other controlled rewards or punishments for the person. Second, he suggested that persons would seek information if they thought they would have to interact with the other sometime in the future. It was assumed that such information would make subsequent interactions easier to manage. Finally, it was suggested that observing deviance in another person might prompt attempts to gain knowledge about him or her in order to make the deviant conduct more understandable. In a sense, the Swann et al. (1981) investigation falls under the first of these antecedents. It is likely that most persons prefer to control their outcomes in social interactions if at all possible, especially if the outcomes have significant material or emotional consequences for the individual. When the stakes are high, we would expect the individual to exert considerable time and effort to gather what he or she deems to be highly diagnostic information in order to maximize the likelihood of obtaining positive outcomes.

Impression Formation

Since the seminal work of Asch (1946) on impression formation, considerable research attention has been paid to the ways persons form overall impressions based on various configurations of information inputs. One of the more coherent lines of research in this tradition is that of Anderson (1974), done under the rubric of information integration theory. Over a number of years, Anderson has attempted to determine how persons take descriptions of others in the form of adjective lists and integrate these adjectival descriptions to form an overall judgment of their liking for the person. Adjectives are scaled for their positiveness or negativeness, and attempts have been made to predict terminal judgments of liking based on various combinations of adjectives. Space does not permit an exhaustive review of this long line of research; however, Anderson (1974) has found that among a number of alternative models that might be used to predict a final judgment—for example, an additive model versus an averaging model—a weighted averaging model appears to be one of the better predictors of a final judgment. This finding implies that in order for impressions to be changed in a more positive or negative direction, adjectives having scale values that exceed the existing average would have to be integrated with the existing adjective set. Under the additive model, any additional positive or negative adjective would predict a shift in the direction of its valence.

Some researchers have focused on the structures people use to describe others, or what has been termed implicit theories of personality. Research suggests that people see certain personality traits clustering together. A number of studies have found five dimensions underlying trait judgments: extraversion, agreeableness, conscientiousness, emotional stability, and culture (Tupes and Christal, 1961; Norman, 1963; D'Andrade, 1965; Passini and Norman, 1966; Hakel,

1969). Alternatively, Rosenberg et al. (1968) and Rosenberg and Sedlack (1972) discovered that people judge others based on two evaluative criteria: intellectual and social activity. Since this research indicates that people infer that an individual has certain traits consistent with others, one could anticipate that interpersonal judgments are relatively quick. Once a trait is perceived, other traits are automatically assumed to be present or absent. However, recent research tends to modify this position.

Ebbesen and Allen (1979) have argued that interpersonal judgments are made in two stages. The first stage is relatively quick and consists of a recall of global descriptions of a person. The second is a much longer process in which a thorough search of information related to the person takes place. Ebbeson and Allen found that people took less time to affirm and more time to deny that two traits were related if the traits were semantically similar. Conversely, when people make judgments that require greater recall of information to affirm that the two traits are related, subjects take greater time to affirm than deny. Thus, decisions are made rapidly only in certain situations.

Allen and Ebbesen (1981) investigated the judgments subjects made about a target individual after having viewed a videotape of the target. The subjects attempted to recall specific behavioral actions of the target and inferred abstract personality traits associated with the target. Based on reaction time and accuracy of recall, they found that people spend a considerable amount of time making both types of judgments, although they tended to spend more time making judgments about personality traits. In addition, people make judgments about personality traits that are correlated with measures of their implicit theories of personality, while judgments about specific behavior are uncorrelated with the theories. Thus, implicit personality theories may be most useful for certain kinds of judgments, but in other cases, close scrutiny of memory takes place.

Research done in the constructivist tradition, which is outlined by Delia and O'Keefe (this volume), has revealed that cognitive complexity exerts an impact on the kinds of impressions persons form of each other. Following the seminal work of Kelly (1955), cognitive complexity is viewed as a construct that varies along a number of dimensions. Persons with high levels of cognitive complexity are those who view a given domain of experience with many dimensions rather than a few. Highly complex persons might also interrelate these dimensions to a greater extent than their low-complexity counterparts. A study reported by Delia et al. (1974) showed that persons scoring high in cognitive complexity generated more complex impressions of a stranger than did persons low in complexity. In a later study, the same research team (Delia et al., 1979) demonstrated that when persons with high levels of cognitive complexity interacted with strangers, they were more likely to engage in conversation related to themselves and the other person present. Persons with low complexity levels were more likely to talk about topics external to the interaction in the initial interaction context. These studies indicate that individual difference variables like cognitive complexity can exert some influence on the kinds of impressions that persons form of each other when they interact for the first time. Moreover, these different cognitive styles appear to have an impact on the content of conversations in initial interactions.

There are a host of studies which demonstrate the effects of various linguistic and paralinguistic variables on impressions and evaluations of others (Giles and Powesland, 1975; Street and Giles, this volume; Berger and Bradac, forthcoming). There is ample evidence that dialect, accent, speech rate, pitch, and other speech variables can exert considerable impact on the impressions that persons make upon each other. Giles and Powesland (1975) have suggested that under some conditions persons with differing speech styles will become more similar to each other (convergence), while under other conditions, persons will emphasize their differences through speech (divergence). Convergence tends to be associated with attraction and cooperation. Divergence appears to be an indicant of conflict and competition. Giles and Powesland (1975) also suggest that some speech features, like language code, are most probably consciously altered. Other features of speech, like rate and intensity, are most probably varied unconsciously. The problem of the degree to which speech is consciously controlled will be considered later in this chapter.

We believe that more work needs to be done by communication researchers to link various language and speech variables to the processes of forming impressions of others. Because linguistic stimuli are more complex than adjective lists, studying impression formation with linguistic stimuli poses more difficult control problems. However, we feel that the loss of some control is more than offset by the gains in ecological validity. We believe that persons are rarely presented with adjective lists in their everyday lives and asked to form impressions from them; by contrast, persons do encounter numerous strangers who do manifest differing speech styles. It is our bet that more can be learned about impression formation from the study of these styles than from the elegant but fairly unrealistic adjective list techniques.

Relational Escalation: To Know Him/Her
Is To Love Him/Her?

It is obvious that while we encounter numerous strangers during our lives, only a very small percentage of those we encounter become friends, close friends, or lovers. The question we will consider in this section concerns how one might explain relational growth or increased attraction. Of course, when we invoke constructs like interpersonal attraction, we have moved from the cognitive to the affective domain; however, there has been and continues to be an interest in trying to relate the two via consistency theory (Rosenberg, 1960), self-perception theory (Bem, 1972), and schema theory (Tomkins, 1978).

Most accounts of relational escalation rely on some variant of social exchange theory (Roloff, 1981). For example, Altman and Taylor's (1973) social penetration theory asserts that relationships grow and decline depending on the relative ratios of rewards and costs in the relationship. When rewards exceed costs, growth tends to occur. When costs exceed rewards, pressures for relational dissolution increase. These authors also point out that it is not only current rewards and costs that enter into these calculations. They claim that persons develop a kind of bank account of previous rewards and costs, and they also forecast what future rewards and costs might be. Thus, a person might remain in what is now a relatively costly relationship because he or she has either experienced considerable rewards from the relationship in the past or anticipates that the relationship will become more rewarding in the future.

Although couched in different terminology, the reinforcement-affect theory of Byrne (1971) takes a similar position. Byrne (1971) argues that interpersonal attraction is a simple, positive linear function of the degree to which a person is reinforced by another. Reinforcements may come in a variety of forms, but the form most studied by Byrne has been attitude similarity. Byrne (1971) has demonstrated not only that attraction is a positive linear function of perceived attitude similarity, but also that statements of attitude similarity appear to take on the properties of reinforcers in modifying response rates. This line of research has also demonstrated that attributes like physical attractiveness act to enhance attraction.

The social exchange approaches and the reinforcement-affect position would seem to provide both an exhaustive and parsimonious account of relational escalation and relational disintegration. However, we feel that this is far from the case. Persons with similar attitudes on important issues who marry do get divorced, and those with dissimilar attitudes on issues can develop lifelong friendships. Moreover, neither social exchange nor reinforcement-affect theories can stipulate on an a priori basis what is likely to be rewarding or reinforcing and what is likely to be costly in a given context. It is only after the fact that "rewards" and "costs" can be identified. Furthermore, there is a hint of tautology when these theories are invoked to explain relationship growth or decline. If we ask why certain relationships flourished, the theories merely assert that rewards must have exceeded costs or there must have been powerful reinforcers at work in the situation. If we ask why relationships fail, we are informed that it is because costs must have exceeded rewards or reinforcements must have been minimal or nonexistent. It is not at all clear exactly what purchase such theories give us in explaining relationship growth and decline. Indeed, they *sound* plausible and may even *feel* plausible, but we are not convinced that they provide as complete an explanation as one would wish.

Duck (1973) has provided an alternative explanation of friendship development from the constructivist perspective. Employing Kelly's (1955) theory of personal constructs as a base, he has adduced evidence supporting the view that attitude similarity may be only an intermediate step in the development of a close friendship. His data suggest that persons will develop close friendships with those who are *conceptually* similar to themselves. Conceptual similarity is operationally defined using Kelly's Role Construct Repertory Test. On the basis of several studies, Duck (1973) suggests that friendships may be developed through a series of filters. Initially, factors such as physical attractiveness might be important. Next, attitude similarity might be used as a basis for making further judgments. Finally, the degree to which persons are conceptually similar may be the last filter through which the relationship must pass.

There are related studies that provide a potential explanation for some of Duck's (1973) findings. Runkle (1956) reported that students who were cognitively similar or *collinear* with respect to their instructors tended to perform better on examinations than did students who were not collinear with their instructors. It was assumed that these differences were mediated by communication efficiency; that is, students who were collinear experienced less difficulty understanding their instructors than did students who were not collinear. In a more direct test of the communication efficiency hypothesis, Padgett and Wolosin (1980) compared the communication efficiency of collinear and noncollinear dyads. Their results demonstrated the superiority of the collinear dyads. These collinearity studies suggest that one reason cognitively similar persons develop close friendships is that they literally understand each other better than do cognitively dissimilar persons. A closely related point is that when noncollinear persons interact with each other, they may have to expend considerable time and effort trying to understand each other. Such expenditures might act to lower the attractiveness of the potential relationship partner.

Although the collinearity studies did not employ spontaneous face-to-face interaction situations, one self-monitoring study (Ickes and Barnes, 1977) examined some dimensions of actual interactions between dyads with similar or different levels of self-monitoring. Among the several differences they reported was the finding that dyads composed of one high self-monitor and one low self-monitor displayed more breaks in their conversations than did dyads composed of other combinations of self-monitors. In addition, after the interactions, high self-monitors who were paired with low self-monitors reported that they felt more uneasy in their conversations than did high self-monitors who were paired with persons who were either high or moderate in self-monitoring. These findings provide some support for the generalization that cognitively dissimilar persons are more likely to experience interaction difficulties. If this is the case, it is but a small inferential leap to conclude that cognitively dissimilar persons are less likely to develop close relationships with each other.

There is a need to test more directly the relationship between cognitive similarity and communication in ongoing relationships. While the collinearity research is suggestive, it has not involved direct interactions between persons. The Ickes and Barnes (1977) study is relevant to this general issue, but the status of the self-monitoring measure as an index of some kind of cognitive process is in some doubt. Two studies have found the measure to be multidimensional (Briggs et al., 1980; Gabrenya and Arkin, 1980), and Snyder, (1974, 1979) has not provided a very detailed theoretical explication of the construct. Thus, the Ickes and Barnes (1977) findings are somewhat difficult to extrapolate to the present context. Nevertheless, we feel that this general line of inquiry provides a potentially more complete explanation of relational escalation than do the social exchange theories. Moreover, given the relationships that collinearity researchers have found between cognitive similarity and communication, it is surprising that few researchers in the communication discipline have pursued research in this area. We hope that the potential relationships among collinearity, communication efficiency and relationship development receive more attention from communication researchers in the future.

Ongoing Relationships

Whether a relationship remains at the level of acquaintance or escalates to a more intimate level, we would argue that repeated exposure to a given person or group of persons over time is likely to have cognitive consequences for the individual in terms of the way in which information about the person or group is processed. We assume that even in intimate relationships, such as those associated with marriage, a number of communicative routines develop that are enacted with relatively great frequency, so that a high proportion of everyday interaction is quite routine. Although the picture we have painted so far appears to characterize most interaction as commonplace and potentially boring, we would urge the reader to think about his or her relationships and the kinds of problems never-ending uniqueness would introduce into these interactions. Persons prefer predictability to unpredictability, especially in relationships that "count." Predictability requires both patterns and expectations that are met most of the time. Thus, the evolution of stable and repetitive patterns of interaction in a relationship is not necessarily negative.

Scripts and Schemata

There are a number of researchers who have coined terms to describe knowledge structures that are necessary for the understanding of various facets of experience. For example, Minsky (1975) used the term "frames" to refer to knowledge structures that organize generic experience about objects. Rumelhart (1976) referred to "schemata" as knowledge structures necessary for the understanding of textual passages. Abelson (1976: 33) defined cognitive "scripts" as "a coherent sequence of events expected by the individual, involving him as either a participant or as an observer." According to Abelson, scripts are learned throughout one's lifetime through direct participation in event sequences or by observing event sequences. The basic unit of a script is a vignette. Vignettes are likened to the individual panels of a cartoon strip; they contain a picture and a caption. Scripts can vary in their levels of abstraction. Some scripts might refer directly to particular events, while others might refer to abstract classes of events. For example, a child might develop a script for greeting Mr. Jones when he comes to visit. This script might later be abstracted by means of an appropriate name change, for greeting any adult. Schank and Abelson (1977) have pointed out that the human understander comes equipped with thousands of scripts. Moreover, they also assert that scripts are not the only knowledge structures necessary for the understanding of experience. Their construct is intended to refer only to that portion of experience that is represented verbally. The main thrust of their research has been to develop computer programs that will represent scripts and thus models of human knowledge structures.

There are a number of studies that demonstrate the importance of scripts to the understanding of event sequences. Chiesi et al. (1979) found that persons who had greater knowledge of baseball principles and terms were better able to recognize changes in the game that were important to its outcome. In this study it was assumed that persons with higher knowledge levels had better formulated scripts for processing baseball games. This study also indicated that high-knowledge persons were better able to recall events in their normal order. In a related investigation, Spilich et al. (1979) found that persons with a high knowledge of baseball not only displayed better recall of action sequences within events, but also were better able to recall the events in the correct order. Although these two studies show the superior performance of persons who have well-developed scripts in terms of recall, a study by Bower et al. (1979) reported that when persons were asked to recall scripted actions after being presented with event sequences, they frequently included actions that were *implied* by the script but not actually part of the material that they were being asked to recall. Persons "filled in" information that was part of the script but was not part of the information sequence to which they were initially exposed. Thus, well-developed scripts can produce distortions in recall.

Two studies have provided evidence in support of the script pointer + tag hypothesis advanced by Schank and Abelson (1977). This hypothesis asserts that persons develop specific memory representations of activities that are enacted or read. These specific representations contain a script pointer to a generic script that seems to fit best with the action sequence being observed. It also contains provision for actions that are unrelated to the script. These are called tagged actions. The script pointer + tag hypothesis asserts that tagged actions, or actions that are inconsistent with the script, should be better remembered than actions that are consistent with the script. One of the experiments reported by Bower et al. (1979) provided support for the hypothesis, and a study by Graesser et al. (1979) did as well.

When persons become involved in ongoing relationships, they can either understand them from the perspective of existing scripts or develop a new script so that they are able to anticipate what is likely to happen in the relationship. In either case, once a script has been formulated, there is a very real danger that erroneous assumptions are likely to be made regarding the actions of the other person. As we have seen, persons tend to remember actions that a script suggests should occur but that actually do not occur. This may explain why conflict in close, ongoing relationships is difficult to deal with sometimes. There is little doubt that conflict episodes can and do become scripted. If this is so, then both parties in the conflict are likely to *assume* that the other has acted in a particular way or that the other meant something by a particular action that he or she actually did not mean. Once these scripts become automated, they may be played out over and over again, even when the parties in the interaction do not wish to continue to play them out. The difficulty here is developing a new script with which to understand the situation.

Schank and Abelson (1977) point out that once scripts have been well developed, they can be instantiated without thinking. This possibility obviously aggravates the kinds of conflict scripts that persons develop in interpersonal relationships. The action sequence will begin without either party actually being aware of where it is going until they are well into the shouting phase of the conflict. Although scripts enable us to "understand" event sequences that transpire around us, they also make us less attentive to the details of the interaction. This might, in turn, lead to considerable misunderstanding between interaction partners.

Mindlessness

Operating from the framework of the cognitive script concept, Langer (1978) has suggested that when persons enact behavior sequences repeatedly and overlearn these sequences, they are able to perform them without thinking about what they are doing, or they are able to perform the behavior and think about something else at the same time. Langer (1978) has termed the disjunction between thought and action "mindlessness." She contends that many models of social interaction carry with them the assumption that persons are highly aware of what they are doing during most social interaction sequences. She argues, to the contrary, that since most daily social interactions are highly routine, persons are most apt to be thinking about something else or to be thinking about nothing as they carry out these routine interactions.

A study by Langer et al. (1978) illustrates this possibility. In one of the experiments reported in this study, persons who were just about to use a photocopier were approached by a confederate of the experimenter. The confederate asked the person who was about to use the machine if he or she could use it first. There were two variations of the request. First, some of the persons were informed that the confederate had to make 5 copies (small favor); while others were told that the confederate had to make 20 copies (large favor). In addition, the request was followed by one of the following justifications: (1) realistic, (2) placebic, or (3) none.

In the realistic condition, persons were told that the confederate needed to make copies first because he or she was in a hurry. In the placebic justification condition, those waiting were told that the person needed to use the machine first to make some copies. Obviously, this justification is really no justification at all. Finally, a third group of persons were simply given the request with no justification. Langer et al. (1978) reasoned that persons in the small favor condition would be relatively mindless with respect to what the confederate said after making the request because of the small magnitude of the request. By contrast, those persons in the large favor condition would pay closer attention to the justification given for wanting to get ahead to make copies. This increased attention was expected to decrease the effectiveness of the placebic justification. The findings of the study provided strong support for this reasoning. Within the small favor condition, 94 percent of those who were given a realistic justification and 93 percent of those given a placebic justification let the confederate make copies first. Only 60 percent of those given no justification complied. Within the large favor condition, however, 42 percent of those given the realistic justification complied, while only 24 percent given the placebic justification did so. In the no justification condition, 24 percent complied. As predicted, the placebic justification lost its justificatory value when persons were made mindful by being asked for a large favor.

In another experiment reported by Langer et al. (1978), memoranda sent to secretaries were examined to determine in what form they were generally written. This survey revealed that the memos were usually couched in terms of a *request* rather than a demand and were generally *unsigned* by the sender rather than signed. Langer et al. (1978) reasoned that if memos in the form of an unsigned request were sent to secretaries, they would be more likely to be mindless with respect to the message contained in the memo than they would be if they received memos of a structurally different form, for example, a signed demand. In order to test this hypothesis, Langer et al. constructed an absurd message and transmitted it to secretaries in the form of a memo. The message requested that the secretary return the memo to a nonexistent room number. The memos were constructed in four different forms: (1) signed demand, (2) unsigned demand, (3) signed request, and (4) unsigned request. The researchers were able to intercept the memos that were returned in order to assess the degree of compliance with the request. The results of this study again provided strong support for the mindlessness hypothesis. Of those secretaries who received the memo in its usual form (unsigned request), 90 percent returned the message as requested. Only 60 percent of those secretaries who received the most structurally deviant form of the message (signed demand) actually complied with the demand. Because of the deviant nature of the structure of the message the secretaries were made more mindful and became more aware of the absurd nature of the request being made. These findings comport with those of Bower et al. (1979) and Graesser et al. (1979) discussed in connection with scripts. Recall that in these studies actions that deviated from the scripted sequence were more likely to be recalled or recognized than actions that were consistent with the script. Moreover, the Langer et al. (1978) findings are also consistent with those of Pyszcynski and Greenberg (1981), who found that persons engaged in attribution generation only when their expectations were violated. When persons' expectations were met, their attributional activities were minimal.

While we have emphasized the potentially deleterious effects of mindlessness on ongoing social interaction, there are conditions under which mindlessness can have facilitating effects on interaction. For example, Langer and Weinman (1981) had subjects discuss either an issue in which they had previously engaged in discussions with others or a novel issue. Some subjects were merely asked to discuss the issue. Other subjects were either explicitly encouraged to think about the issue before discussing it or were given time in which they could elect to think about the issue. Subjects discussed the issue while being tape-recorded. Analyses of the subjects' talk indicated that persons who had time to think about the familiar issue or persons who were explicitly encouraged to think about the familiar issue manifested more filled pauses in their speech than did persons who were not given time to think about the issue. By contrast, persons who were asked to discuss the novel issue and given time in which they could think or explicitly encouraged to think showed significantly fewer pauses than did persons who were given no time in which to think about the issue.

The above study demonstrates not only how mindlessness can actually facilitate performance on overlearned tasks, but also how mindlessness can operate on the "output" side of the individual. Up to this point, much of the mindlessness research we have considered involves placing the subject in a relatively passive role, that is, reading stimulus materials, responding to requests, or responding to memos. The Langer and Weinman study shows how mindlessness can be manifested in communicative behavior. This study brings to mind a distinction made by Berger and Roloff (1980) between thoughtful and thoughtless speech. Like Langer, Berger and Roloff (1980) point out that persons who study communication and others seem to assume that "all utterances are created equal." That is, the cognitive machinery responsible for the generation of utterances is considered somehow constant. While the physiology of speech is no doubt a "constant," the degree to which persons attend to their speech varies across situations and persons. Frequently persons say things that are only marginally under their conscious control. At other times, speech may be the product of considerable thought and conscious calculation. However, simply because persons have the capabilities of conscious calculation and reasoned choice does not mean ipso facto that they use these powers frequently. The mindlessness research would suggest that speech may be more often of the thoughtless variety than of the thoughtful variety. An important question for communication researchers in this regard is how one might discriminate between speech that is thoughtful and speech that is relatively thoughtless. The Langer and Weinman study provides the beginnings of an answer to that question, but certainly there are other verbal and nonverbal indicators of mindlessness.

Another important question wtih respect to communication and mindlessness concerns how mindlessness is recognized in ongoing interactions. In informal discussion with students regarding mindlessness in interactions, the first author has found that most students can recall numerous instances in which they have talked to another person while paying little attention to what is being said by the person or by themselves. It is not merely a question of not listening to the other. It is also a question of not monitoring oneself. One interesting facet of this phenomenon is that persons apparently can be mindless with respect to the conduct of both the other and themselves and yet present themselves in such a way that the other believes that they are highly involved in the conversation. It seems that persons can give off cues that indicate involvement in the interaction while being almost totally disengaged from it. How this is accomplished and how persons detect this kind of inattention are issues worth at least some research attention.

Relational Termination and Retrospection: You Know You Done Me Wrong

In this section we assume that a given relationship has escalated to the point where persons consider each other very close friends or lovers. The question with which we will deal here concerns the kinds of social cognitive factors that might play a role in both the disintegration of and retrospective accounting for such relationships. We recognize that there are a host of noncognitive factors that can be responsible for the dissolution of relationships, especially friendships. For example, mere proximity (Festinger et al., 1950) can determine friendship formation and sociometric choice. When distance intervenes between persons, there is the increased probability that they will not be able to sustain their relationships. Of course, even in this case we might entertain the notion that physical distance has a psychological counterpart which might influence the course of a relationship. Nevertheless, we assume that cognitive factors can and do play a significant role in relationship deterioration and even more in the retrospective accounting for the course of the relationship.

Relational Deterioration

In the previous section, we pointed to the potentially negative impact of overlearned behavior or cognitive scripts on mutual understanding between relational partners. We argued that when behavior becomes scripted, the probability of misunderstandings occurring increases, which leads to greater interpersonal conflict. In addition to this possibility is the so-called negativity effect in the evaluation of others. Kanouse (1971) and Kanouse and Hanson (1971) have pointed to evidence suggesting that persons tend to weigh negative attributes of others more heavily than they weigh positive attributes in forming an overall impression. Wegner and Vallacher (1977) have proffered two potential explanations for these effects. One of these, which they label *figure-ground*, states that since persons expect to experience good things in their everyday lives, including the actions of others, when a person displays negative attributes, these characteristics stand out and assume an inordinate weight in the overall impression formed. A second explanation of this effect they label *vigilance*. This explanation suggests that for the sake of survival and in order to avoid threat, persons are more sensitive to the potential dangers that others might pose and less sensitive to the positive actions in which others might engage.

In the present context the negativity effect is important regardless of the explanation for it. Since persons in close interpersonal relationships generally spend considerable time with each other and are privy to a wider sample of each other's actions across social contexts, we would expect that on the basis of chance alone they would be more likely to become aware of each other's negative attributes (for example, he belches audibly after consuming a can of soda, while she chews gum with her mouth open). The fact that such socially undesirable actions may be suppressed in public and only displayed in the privacy of the household *may* make them appear to be more negative than they would ordinarily be; that is, "If you really cared about me you wouldn't do such gross and disgusting things in my presence," or "You wouldn't do that in front of your friends. What about *me?*"

Yet another facet of this problem concerns the kinds of behavioral norms that tend to govern dating behavior. When persons are in a dating relationship, they tend to make an effort to present themselves in the most positive way possible. One makes a definite attempt to suppress one's potentially negative attributes. However, once persons are living together either by dint of marriage or informal agreement, it becomes more difficult to mask negative attributes. Not only does the situation of living together make it more difficult to gloss over such negative characteristics, but also the persons themselves may feel that they have the "right" to relax their self-presentations and let some of the more negative characteristics manifest themselves. This contrast between the dating situation and the situation of living together may well trigger feelings of disappointment, deception, and lack of consideration. It is important to note with respect to the negativity effect that even though many persons may display more positive than negative attributes, the negative ones may predominate. Thus, even when persons make commitments to change their ways and in fact do achieve such changes, these changes may not be enough to overcome the deleterious effects of the relatively few negative attributes they possess.

Another cognitively oriented explanation of relational deterioration is rooted in the work on cognitive similarity discussed previously. We noted that Duck (1973) has contended that friendships tend to develop through stages and that only persons who are conceptually similar are likely to develop lasting friendships. It is, of course, possible that, on the basis of attitude similarity on issues that are salient to both parties, relationships may escalate to a highly intimate level. In fact, this kind of escalation may occur simply on the basis of physical attractiveness. However, what may happen in these relatively rapidly escalating relationships is that the interactants may turn out to be conceptually dissimilar. On the basis of our previous discussion, we would expect such cognitive dissimilarity to lead to difficulties in mutual understanding and the expenditure of considerable energy to try to achieve understanding. We would expect that, over time, persons would grow weary of such relationships and terminate them out of sheer exhaustion.

Retrospective Accounting

Although there is not a great deal of research directed at cognitive phenomena that are contemporaneous with relationship deterioration and termination, there is a considerable amount of literature devoted to the retrospective accounting for conflict and relationship termination. In a classic early study, Goode (1956) interviewed a large sample of recently divorced women to determine the ways in which they viewed their divorces. He cautioned that one could not accept verbal accounts of the causes for divorce at face value. Thus, while persons might attribute divorce to disagreements about money or to sexual incompatibility (two frequently mentioned reasons in such studies), the actual causes for the divorce might be rooted in factors of which neither partner is aware. Later research has focused mainly on the kinds of reasons persons have given for relational difficulties and relational termination, regardless of their accuracy in terms of actual causes.

One consistent finding emerging from this later literature supports what has been labeled the fundamental attribution error. Heider (1958) noted that for the observer, the behavior of the person being observed tends to engulf the observer's perceptual field to such a degree that the observer underestimates the role of situational factors. Nisbett and Ross (1980) and Ross (1977) have extensively discussed this attribution error and reviewed evidence of its existence. Closely related to this phenomenon is the notion that actors and observers differ in their perceptions of the causes of behavior (Jones and Nisbett, 1972). Actors tend to attribute their actions to situational factors, while observers tend to attribute the actors' actions to factors that reside in the actors themselves. Storms (1973) demonstrated that by changing perspectives through the use of videotape, this attribution bias could be reversed.

Given the fundamental attribution error and the divergent perspectives of actors and observers concerning causes of behavior, it should come as no surprise that persons who are asked for accounts of why conflicts in their relationships occurred or why their relationships with others terminated tend to attribute the cause of relational problems and termination to their current or former partners (Harvey et al., 1978; Kelley, 1979; Orvis et al., 1976; Sillars, 1980). These attributions are frequently couched in terms of dispositional properties of individuals. In comparing two attribution-of-conflict studies involving heterosexual couples (Cunningham et al. and Tiggle et al., cited in Kelley, 1979), Kelley (1979) points out that when couples are left to themselves to enumerate their relational complaints, they will generally couch their complaints in terms of undesirable personal dispositions of the other and ignore potential situational causes of their relational difficulties. Kelley (1979) notes that the tendency to make dispositional attributions to the other thwarts attempts to modify *specific behaviors*, since interactants cannot apparently think, or at least verbalize their problem, in these terms. Moreover, Sillars (1980) has shown how such attributions can influence the kinds of strategies persons use to deal with conflict. Obviously, if the other person is to blame because he or she has a personality disposition that is immutable, there is probably little use in trying to negotiate in order to overcome difficulties. Conflict management strategies such as avoidance are probably perceived as more functional under these conditions.

In the above discussion we considered some biases that would influence the kinds of retrospective reports persons might make about past relationships or about conflict episodes. We now consider an even more fundamental issue with regard to retrospective accounts: the ability of persons to give accurate verbal reports about cognitive processes they have used to make certain decisions regarding relationships. For example, when a recently divorced person is asked how or why he or she decided to get divorced and the person gives one or several reasons, are the verbal responses given by the person representative of the mental processes the person actually employed at the time or are they explanations that the person has heard others give for their relational mishaps? Nisbett and his colleagues (Nisbett and Bellows, 1977; Nisbett and Wilson, 1977a, 1977b; Wilson, 1979; Wilson and Nisbett, 1978) have reviewed a number of studies and conducted their own research, which suggests that under certain conditions persons may not be aware of the critical stimulus that caused a response, they may not be aware of the critical response itself, or, if they are aware of both the critical stimulus and the response, they may fail to see the connection between the two. A further argument asserts that when persons are able to report accurately about the causes of their behavior, their explanations are simply the result of a fortuitous congruity between an a priori causal theory that they hold and the actual causes of their behavior. One general implication to be drawn from this line of research is that verbal reports about mental processes are not likely to be representative of the processes that were actually employed to make a judgment or to reach a decision.

There have been a number of direct challenges to the Nisbett position. Smith and Miller (1978) contend that the designs of many of the experiments used to demonstrate these effects did not allow subjects access to all of the relevant information. Moreover, they point to the vagueness of the notion of a mental process as used by Nisbett. These arguments have been countered by Nisbett and Ross (1980). Another line of attack on the Nisbett research has come from Ericsson and Simon (1980). These researchers suggest a number of variables that influence the extent to which persons can retrieve from memory information regarding such processes. They also suggest procedures that might be used to elicit information about mental processes. Finally, Wright and Rip (1981) have reported two experiments that support the proposition that, under conditions which encourage accurate reporting, persons can give relatively accurate accounts of how they weighed various factors in arriving at a series of preference judgments.

Research on implicit theories of interpersonal communication and relations also provides insights into this area. Wish et al. (1976) found that people have implicit theories of interpersonal relations similar to the implicit theories of personality described earlier (e.g., Schneider, 1973). These implicit relational theories were composed of four dimensions: cooperative and friendly versus competitive and hostile; equal versus unequal; intense versus superficial; and informal versus task-oriented and formal. The dimensions were found to be differentially associated with relational types. In a follow-up, Wish and Kaplan (1977) found implicit theories of interpersonal communication. Five dimensions of these theories were observed: cooperation, intensity, dominance, formality, and task orientation. Again, the dimensions were found to vary with relational types and situations. More recently, Knapp et al. (1980) discovered that people characterize a variety of interpersonal relationships according to three communication behaviors: personalism, synchrony, and difficulty. The communication behaviors could be used to differentiate the various types of relationships.

An important point of this research is that people have expectations about their relationships and the types of behaviors that occur within them. If the person *perceives* certain behaviors occurring between self and other, then the person may attribute a relational label to it. If the person attributes a relational term to the association with another, then the person may assume certain behaviors have and will occur. These theories may provide people with explanations of why their relationships have failed. Since marriages are expected to involve personal and synchronized communication, the failure of a marriage may be explained by the absence of these two traits, whether they were actually there or not. Thus, interpersonal judgments about relational deterioration may have little correspondence to reality.

At this point, it seems reasonable to conclude that under some conditions, persons can give relatively accurate retrospective accounts about how they arrived at decisions and evaluations of various kinds; however, there seem to be a number of circumstances in which persons are either unable to retrieve the critical information or, if they can retrieve it, they are not willing to verbalize it for self-presentational reasons. It appears that the Nisbett position may be a bit too extreme regarding the limitations of persons in providing accurate retrospective accounts. However, even if we adopt a more moderate position, there is still cause for concern regarding the meaning of retrospective reports of prior relationships. In most contexts, when a person is asked why his or her close relationship "broke up," the person asking the question is inviting responses that are heavily influenced by impression management. Thus, even if the person being questioned knows very well why the divorce occurred, he or she may not be willing to reveal this information if it is potentially embarrassing to himself or herself. This possibility may explain why so many persons seem to attribute relational failures to the negative dispositions of their partners. However, even if we set aside impression management as a potential deterrent to accurate reporting, there is still the problem of the time delay between the events in question and the interrogation of memory for those events. Asking persons months after they have had conflicts or terminated relationships why these events occurred or how they decided to end the relationship sets up conditions favorable to the reporting of cultural theories of relational disintegration rather than accurate narratives of decision processes. After all, if the interviewee is asked a question, he or she is likely to feel some obligation to answer it, even if he or she may be unable to remember much about how a decision was made. Therefore, a culturally acceptable theory may be the most available response to give in the situation.

One procedure for overcoming the retrieval problem outlined above might be to interview persons who are in the *process* of breaking up their relationships rather than waiting until their relationships have terminated. Of course, in the case of very close relationships, the period of decision making may be very protracted. For some relationships, it might be a matter of years before a decision to end the relationship is reached. However, since many divorces occur within the first few years of marriage, it might be possible to conduct studies that could at least sample decision processes within this time frame. Furthermore, since dating relationships are frequently of shorter duration, these also might be studied in progress.

Conclusion

In this chapter we have sought to demonstrate how selected issues and research lines concerning social cognition are relevant to the study of the formation and decay of interpersonal relationships. We believe that the relationship development perspective illustrates both strengths and weaknesses of some of these research traditions. We have also discovered some gaps in both theory and research that could be filled by communication research.

Miller (1978) discussed a number of alternative ways to approach the study of interpersonal communication. Among the various approaches he considered, he argued that the relationship development alternative appeared to have the most heuristic potential. Consistent with Miller's analysis, we believe that the relationship development area provides an interesting source of questions for the researcher interested in social cognition as well as an important arena for testing hypotheses derived from social cognition theories. We hope that more research will be conducted at the intersection of these two research concerns.

References

Abelson, R. P. Script processing in attitude formation and decision making. In J. S. Carroll and J. W. Payne (Eds.), *Cognition and social behavior*. Hillsdale, NJ: Erlbaum, 1976.

Allen, R., and Ebbesen, E. Cognitive processes in person perceptions: Retrieval of personality traits and behavioral information. *Journal of Experimental Social Psychology*, 1981, *17*, 119-141.

Altman, I., and Taylor, D. A. *Social penetration: The development of interpersonal relationships*. New York: Holt, Rinehart & Winston, 1973.

Anderson, N. H. Cognitive algebra. In L. Berkowitz (Ed.), *Advances in experimental social psychology* (Vol. 7). New York: Academic Press, 1974.

Apsler, R., and Sears, D. Warning, personal involvement, and attitude change. *Journal of Personality and Social Psychology*, 1968, *9*, 162-166.

Asch, S. E. Forming impressions of personality. *Journal of Abnormal and Social Psychology*, 1946, *41*, 258-290.

Bem, D. J. Self-perception theory. In L. Berkowitz (Ed.), *Advances in experimental social psychology* (Vol. 6). New York: Academic Press, 1972.

Berger, C. R. *The acquaintance process revisited: Explorations in initial interaction*. Presented at the annual convention of the Speech Communication Association, New York, 1973.

Berger, C. R. Proactive and retroactive attribution processes in interpersonal communications. *Human Communication Research*, 1975, *2*, 33-50.

Berger, C. R. Beyond initial interaction: Uncertainty, understanding, and the development of interpersonal relationships. In H. Giles and R. St. Clair (Eds.), *Language and social psychology*. Oxford: Blackwell, 1979.

Berger, C. R., and Bradac, J. J. *Language and social knowledge: Uncertainty in interpersonal relations*. London: Edward Arnold, forthcoming.

Berger, C. R., and Douglas, W. Studies in interpersonal epistemology: III. Anticipated interaction, self-monitoring, and observational context selection. *Communication Monographs*, 1981, *48*, 183-196.

Berger, C. R., and Perkins, J. W. Studies in interpersonal epistemology I: Situational attributes in observational context selection. In B. D. Ruben (Ed.), *Communication Yearbook 2*. New Brunswick, NJ: Transaction, 1978.

Berger, C. R., and Perkins, J. W. *Studies in interpersonal epistemology II: Self-monitoring, involvement, facial affect, similarity and observational context selection*. Presented at the annual convention of the Speech Communication Association, San Antonio, Texas, 1979.

Berger, C. R., and Roloff, M. E. Social cognition, self-awareness, and interpersonal communication. In B. Dervin and M. J. Voigt (Eds.), *Progress in communication sciences* (Vol. II). Norwood, NJ: Ablex, 1980.

Berscheid, E., Graziano, W., Monson, T., and Dermer, M. Outcome dependency: Attention, attribution, and attraction. *Journal of Personality and Social Psychology*, 1976, *34*, 978-989.

Bower, G. H., Black, J. B., and Turner, T. J. Scripts in memory for text. *Cognitive Psychology*, 1979, *11*, 177-220.

Briggs, S., Cheek, J., and Buss, A. An analysis of the self-monitoring scale. *Journal of Personality and Social Psychology*, 1980, *38*, 679-686.

Brock, T., and Blackwood, J. Dissonance reduction, social comparison, and modification of others' opinions. *Journal of Abnormal and Social Psychology*, 1962, *65*, 319-324.

Brock, T., and Fromkin, H. Cognitive tuning set and behavioral receptivity to discrepant information. *Journal of Personality*, 1968, *36*, 108-125.

Byrne, D. *The attraction paradigm.* New York: Academic Press, 1971.

Calabrese, R. J. *The effects of privacy and probability of future interaction on initial interaction patterns.* Unpublished doctoral dissertation, Northwestern University, 1975.

Carroll, J. D. Individual differences and multidimensional scaling. In R. N. Shepard, A. K. Romney, and S. B. Nerlove (Eds.), *Multidimensional scaling: Theory and applications in the social sciences, Volume I: Theory.* New York: Seminar Press, 1972.

Chaiken, S. Heuristic versus systematic information processing and the use of source versus message cues in persuasion. *Journal of Personality and Social Psychology*, 1980, *39*, 752-766.

Chiesi, H. L., Spilich, G. J., and Voss, J. F. Acquisition of domain-related information in relation to high and low domain knowledge. *Journal of Verbal Learning and Verbal Behavior*, 1979, *18*, 257-273.

Cialdini, R., Levy, A., Herman, C., Kozlowski, L., and Petty, R. Elastic shifts of opinion: Determinants of direction and durability. *Journal of Personality and Social Psychology*, 1976, *34*, 663-672.

Cohen, A. Cognitive tuning as a factor affecting impression formation. *Journal of Personality*, 1961, *29*, 235-245.

Cooper, J., and Jones, R. Self-esteem and consistency as determinants of anticipatory opinion change. *Journal of Personality and Social Psychology*, 1970, *14*, 312-320.

D'Andrade, R. Trait psychology and componential analysis. *American Anthropologist*, 1965, *67*, 215-228.

Davis, D., and Wicklund, R. An objective self-awareness analysis of communication sets. Pp. 180-184 in S. Duval and R. Wicklund (Eds.), *A theory of objective self-awareness.* New York: Academic Press, 1972.

Deaux, K. Variations in warning, information preference and anticipatory attitude change. *Journal of Personality and Social Psychology*, 1968, *9*, 157-161.

Deaux, K. Anticipatory attitude change: A direct test of the self-esteem hypothesis. *Journal of Experimental Social Psychology*, 1972, *8*, 143-155.

Delia, J. G., Clark, R. A., and Switzer, D. E. Cognitive complexity and impression formation in informal social interaction. *Speech Monographs*, 1974, *41*, 299-308.

Delia, J. G., Clark, R. A., and Switzer, D. E. The content of informal conversations as a function of interactants' interpersonal cognitive complexity. *Communication Monographs*, 1979, *46*, 274-281.

Dinner, S., Lewkowicz, B., and Cooper, J. Anticipatory attitude change as a function of self-esteem and issue familiarity. *Journal of Personality and Social Psychology*, 1972, *24*, 407-412.

Duck, S. W. *Personal relationships and personal constructs: A study of friendship formation*. New York: John Wiley, 1973.

Duval, S., and Wicklund, R. *A theory of objective self-awareness*. New York: Academic Press, 1972.

Ebbesen, E., and Allen, R. Cognitive processes in implicit personality trait inferences. *Journal of Personality and Social Psychology*, 1979, *37*, 471-488.

Elliott, G. C. Some effects of deception and level of self-monitoring on planning and reacting to self-presentation. *Journal of Personality and Social Psychology*, 1979, *37*, 1282-1292.

Ericsson, K. A., and Simon, H. A. Verbal reports as data. *Psychological Review*, 1980, *87*, 215-251.

Festinger, L., Schachter, S., and Back, K. *Social pressures in informal groups: A study of human factors in housing*. New York: Harper & Row, 1950.

Ford, J., and Weldon, E. Forewarning and accountability: Effects on memory-based interpersonal judgments. *Personality and Social Psychology Bulletin*, 1981, *7*, 264-268.

Frankfurt, L. The role of some individual and interpersonal factors on the acquaintance process. Unpublished doctoral dissertation, American University, 1965.

Gabrenya, W. K., Jr., and Arkin, R. M. Self-monitoring scale: Factor structure and correlates. *Personality and Social Psychology Bulletin*, 1980, *6*, 13-22.

Giles, H., and Powesland, P. F. *Speech style and social evaluation*. New York: Academic Press, 1975.

Goffman, E. *The presentation of self in everyday life*. Garden City, NY: Doubleday, 1959.

Goffman, E. *Strategic interaction*. Philadelphia: University of Pennsylvania Press, 1969.

Goode, W. J. *After divorce*. New York: Free Press, 1956.

Graesser, A. C., Gordon, S. E., and Sawyer, J. D. Recognition memory for typical and atypical actions in scripted activities: Tests of the script pointer + tag hypothesis. *Journal of Verbal Learning and Verbal Behavior*, 1979, *18*, 319-332.

Greenwald, A. The open-mindedness of the counterattitudinal role player. *Journal of Experimental Social Psychology*, 1969, *5*, 375-388.

Gruder, C. Effects of perceptions on opponent's bargaining style and accountability to opponent and partner on interpersonal mixed-motive bargaining. (Doctoral dissertation, University of North Carolina, Chapel Hill). Dissertation Abstracts, 1969, *29*, 4555A-4556A.

Gruder, C. Relationships with opponent and partner in mixed-motive bargaining. *Journal of Conflict Resolution*, 1971, *15*, 403-416.

Hakel, M. Significance of implicit personality theories for personality research and theory. *Proceedings of the American Psychological Association*. Washington, DC: American Psychological Association, 1969.

Harvey, J. H., Wells, G. L., and Alvarez, M. D. Attribution in the context of conflict and separation in close relationships. In J. H. Harvey, W. J. Ickes, and R. F. Kidd (Eds.), *New directions in attribution research* (Vol. 2). Hillsdale, NJ: Erlbaum, 1978.

Harvey, J. H., Yarkin, K. L., Lightner, J. M., and Town, J. P. Unsolicited interpretation and recall of interpersonal events. *Journal of Personality and Social Psychology*, 1980, *38*, 551-568.

Heider, F. *The psychology of interpersonal relations*. New York: John Wiley, 1958.

Ickes, W. J., and Barnes, R. D. The role of sex and self-monitoring in unstructured dyadic interactions. *Journal of Personality and Social Psychology*, 1977, *35*, 315-330.

Jeffery, K., and Mischel, W. Effects of purpose on the organization and recall of information in person perception. *Journal of Personality*, 1979, *47*, 397-419.

Jellison, J., and Mills, J. Effect of public commitment upon opinions. *Journal of Experimental Social Psychology*, 1969, *5*, 340-346.

Jones, E. E., and Gordon, E. M. Timing of self-disclosure and its effects on personal attraction. *Journal of Personality and Social Psychology*, 1972, *24*, 358-365.

Jones, E. E., and Nisbett, R. E. The actor and the observer: Divergent perceptions of the causes of behavior. In E. E. Jones, D. E. Kanouse, H. H. Kelley, R. E. Nisbett, S. Valins, and B. Weiner (Eds.), *Attribution: Perceiving the causes of behavior*. Morristown, NJ: General Learning, 1972.

Jourard, S. *Self-disclosure: An experimental analysis of the transparent self*. New York: John Wiley, 1971.

Kanouse, D. E. *Language, labeling and attribution*. Morristown, NJ: General Learning, 1971.

Kanouse, D. E., and Hanson, L. R. *Negativity in evaluations*. Morristown, NJ: General Learning, 1971.

Kelley, H. H. Attribution theory in social psychology. In D. Levine (Ed.), *Nebraska Symposium on Motivation* (Vol. 15). Lincoln: University of Nebraska Press, 1967.

Kelley, H. H. Causal schemata and the attribution process. Morristown, NJ: General Learning, 1972.

Kelley, H. H. *Personal relationships: Their structures and processes*. Hillsdale, NJ: Erlbaum, 1979.

Kelly, G. A. *A theory of personality: The psychology of personal constructs*. New York: Norton, 1955.

Kiesler, C. A. Group pressure and conformity. In J. Mills (Ed.), *Advanced experimental social psychology*. New York: Macmillan, 1969.

Kiesler, C. A., Kiesler, S. B., and Pallak, M. S. The effects of commitment to future interaction on reactions to norm violations. *Journal of Personality*, 1967, *35*, 585-599.

Knapp, M., Ellis, D., and Williams, B. Perceptions of communication behavior associated with relationship terms. *Communication Monographs*, 1980, *47*, 262-278.

Knight, J. A., and Vallacher, R. R. Interpersonal engagement in social perception: The consequences of getting into the action. *Journal of Personality and Social Psychology*, 1981, *40*, 990-999.

Langer, E. J. Rethinking the role of thought in social interaction. In J. H. Harvey, W. J. Ickes, and R. F. Kidd (Eds.), *New directions in attribution research* (Vol. 2). Hillsdale, NJ: Erlbaum, 1978.

Langer, E. J., Blank, A., and Chanowitz, B. The mindlessness of ostensibly thoughtful action: The role of "placebic" information in interpersonal interaction. *Journal of Personality and Social Psychology*, 1978, *36*, 635-642.

Langer, E. J., and Weinman, C. When thinking disrupts performance: Mindfulness on an overlearned task. *Personality and Social Psychology Bulletin*, 1981, *7*, 240-243.

Major, B. Information acquisition and attribution processes. *Journal of Personality and Social Psychology*, 1980, *39*, 1010-1023.

Marlowe, D., Gergen, K., and Doob, A. Opponent's personality, expectation of social interaction, and interpersonal bargaining. *Journal of Personality and Social Psychology*, 1966, *3*, 206-213.

McArthur, L. A. The how and what of why: Some determinants and consequences of causal attribution. *Journal of Personality and Social Psychology*, 1972, *22*, 171-193.

McGuire, W. Attitudes and opinions. *Annual Review of Psychology*, 1966, *17*, 475-515.

McGuire, W., and Millman, S. Anticipatory belief lowering following forewarning of a persuasive attack. *Journal of Personality and Social Psychology*, 1965, *2*, 471-479.

McGuire, W., and Papageorgis, D. Effectiveness of forewarning in developing resistance to persuasion. *Public Opinion Quarterly*, 1962, *26*, 24-34.

Michelini, R. Effects of prior interaction, contact, strategy, and expectation of meeting on game behavior and sentiment. *Journal of Conflict Resolution*, 1971, *15*, 97-103.

Miller, D. T., Norman, S. A., and Wright, E. Distortion in person perception as a consequence of effective control. *Journal of Personality and Social Psychology*, 1978, *36*, 598-607.

Miller, G. R. The current status of theory and research in interpersonal communication. *Human Communication Research*, 1978, *4*, 164-178.

Minsky, M. A framework for representing knowledge. In P. H. Winston (Ed.), *The psychology of computer vision*. New York: McGraw-Hill, 1975.

Motl, J. R. Attitudes, attraction, and nonverbal indicators of uncertainty in initial interaction. Unpublished doctoral dissertation, Northwestern University, 1980.

Newtson, D., and Czerlinsky, T. Adjustment of attitude communications for contrasts by extreme audiences. *Journal of Personality and Social Psychology*, 1974, *30*, 829-837.

Nisbett, R. E., and Bellows, N. Verbal reports about causal influences on social judgments: Private access versus public theories. *Journal of Personality and Social Psychology*, 1977, *35*, 613-624.

Nisbett, R. E., and Ross, L. *Human inference: Strategies and shortcomings of social judgment*. Englewood Cliffs, NJ: Prentice-Hall, 1980.

Nisbett, R. E., and Wilson, T. D. Telling more than we can know: Verbal reports on mental processes. *Psychological Review*, 1977, *84*, 231-259. (a)

Nisbett, R. E., and Wilson, T. D. The halo effect: Evidence for the unconscious alteration of judgments. *Journal of Personality and Social Psychology*, 1977, *35*, 250-256. (b)

Norman, W. Toward an adequate taxonomy of personality attributes: Replicated factor structure in peer nomination personality ratings. *Journal of Abnormal and Social Psychology*, 1963, *66*, 574-583.

Orvis, B. R., Kelley, H. H., and Butler, D. Attributional conflict in young couples. In J. H. Harvey, W. J. Ickes, and R. F. Kidd (Eds.), *New directions in attribution research* (Vol. 1). Hillsdale, NJ: Erlbaum, 1976.

Padgett, V. R., and Wolosin, R. J. Cognitive similarity in dyadic communication. *Journal of Personality and Social Psychology*, 1980, *39*, 654-659.

Pallak, M., Mueller, M., Dollar, K., and Pallak, J. Effect of commitment on responsiveness to an extreme consonant communication. *Journal of Personality and Social Psychology*, 1972, *23*, 429-436.

Papageorgis, D. Anticipation of exposure to persuasive messages and belief change. *Journal of Personality and Social Psychology*, 1967, *5*, 490-496.

Passini, F., and Norman, W. A universal conception of personality structure? *Journal of Personality and Social Psychology*, 1966, *4*, 44-49.

Pyszcynski, T. A., and Greenberg, J. Role of disconfirmed expectancies in the instigation of attributional processing. *Journal of Personality and Social Psychology*, 1981, *40*, 31-38.

Roering, K., Slusher, E., and Schooler, R. Commitment of future interaction in marketing transactions. *Journal of Applied Psychology*, 1975, *60*, 286-288.

Roloff, M. E. *Interpersonal communication: The social exchange approach*. Beverly Hills, CA: Sage, 1981.

Rosenberg, M. J. An analysis of affective-cognitive consistency. In C. I. Hovland and M. J. Rosenberg (Eds.), *Attitude organization and change*. New Haven, CT: Yale University Press, 1960.

Rosenberg, S., Nelson, C., and Vivekananthan, P. A multi-dimensional approach to the structure of personality impressions. *Journal of Personality and Social Psychology*, 1968, *9*, 283-294.

Rosenberg, S., and Sedlack, A. Structural representations of implicit personality theory. Pp. 235-298 in L. Berkowitz (Ed.), *Advances in experimental social psychology* (Vol. 6). New York: Academic Press, 1972.

Ross, L. The intuitive psychologist and his shortcomings. In L. Berkowitz (Ed.), *Advances in experimental social psychology* (Vol. 10). New York: Academic Press, 1977.

Rumelhart, D. E. Understanding and summarizing brief stories. In D. La Berge and S. J. Samuels (Eds.), *Basic processing in reading: Perception and comprehension.* Hillsdale, NJ: Erlbaum, 1976.

Runkel, P. Cognitive similarity in facilitating communication. *Sociometry,* 1956, *19,* 178-191.

Schank, R. C., and Abelson, R. P. *Scripts, plans, goals and understanding.* Hillsdale, NJ: Erlbaum, 1977.

Schneider, D. Implicit personality theory: A review. *Psychological Bulletin,* 1973, *79,* 294-309.

Sears, D., Freedman, J., and O'Connor, E. The effects of anticipated debate and commitment on the polarization of audience opinion. *Public Opinion Quarterly,* 1964, *28,* 615-627.

Sermat, V., and Smyth, M. Content analysis of verbal communication in the development of a relationship: Conditions influencing self-disclosure. *Journal of Personality and Social Psychology,* 1973, *26,* 332-346.

Shure, G., and Meeker, R. Empirical demonstration of normative behavior in the Prisoner's Dilemma. In *Proceedings of the American Psychological Association.* Washington, DC: American Psychological Association, 1968.

Sillars, A. L. Attributions and communication in roommate conflicts. *Communication Monographs,* 1980, *47,* 180-200.

Slusher, E., Roering, K., and Rose, G. The effects of commitment to future interaction in single plays of three games. *Behavioral Science,* 1974, *19,* 119-132.

Slusher, E., Rose, G., and Roering, K. Commitment to future interaction and relative power under conditions of interdependence. *Journal of Conflict Resolution,* 1978, *22,* 282-298.

Smith, E. R., and Miller, E. R. Limits on perception of cognitive processes: A reply to Nisbett and Wilson. *Psychological Review,* 1978, *85,* 355-362.

Snyder M. Self-monitoring of expressive behavior. *Journal of Personality and Social Psychology,* 1974, *30,* 526-537.

Snyder, M. Self-monitoring processes. In L. Berkowitz (Ed.), *Advances in experimental social psychology* (Vol. 12). New York: Academic Press, 1979.

Snyder, M. Seek, and ye shall find: Testing hypotheses about other people. In E. T. Higgins, C. P. Herman, and M. P. Zanna (Eds.), *Social cognition: The Ontario Symposium on Personality and Social Psychology.* Hillsdale, NJ: Erlbaum, 1981.

Snyder, M., and Campbell, B. Testing hypotheses about other people: The role of the hypothesis. *Personality and Social Psychology Bulletin,* 1980, *6,* 421-426.

Snyder, M., and Cantor, N. Testing hypotheses about other people: The use of historical knowledge. *Journal of Experimental Social Psychology,* 1979, *15,* 330-342.

Snyder, M., and Swann, W.B., Jr. Hypothesis-testing processes in social interaction. *Journal of Personality and Social Psychology,* 1978, *36,* 1202-1212.

Spilich, G. J., Vesonder, G. T., Chiesi, H. L., and Voss, J. F. Text processing of domain-related information for individuals with high and low domain knowledge. *Journal of Verbal Learning and Verbal Behavior,* 1979, *18,* 275-290.

Storms, M. D. Videotape and the attribution process: Reversing actors' and observers' points of view. *Journal of Personality and Social Psychology,* 1973, *27,* 165-175.

Swann, W.B., Jr., Stephenson, B., and Pittman, T. S. Curiosity and control: On the determinants of the search for social knowledge. *Journal of Personality and Social Psychology,* 1981, *40,* 635-642.

Tompkins, S. S. Script theory: Differential magnification of affects. In H. E. Howe, Jr., and R. A. Dienstbier (Eds.), *Nebraska Symposium on Motivation* (Vol. 27). Lincoln: University of Nebraska Press, 1978.

Tupes, E., and Christal, R. Recurrent personality factors based on trait ratings. *USAF Aeronautical Systems Divsion, Technical Report*, 1961, 61-97.

Wegner, D. M., and Vallacher, R. R. *Implicit psychology: An introduction to social cognition*. New York: Oxford University Press, 1977.

Wetzel, C., Wilson, T., and Kort, J. The halo effect revisited: Forewarned is not forearmed. *Journal of Experimental Social Psychology*, 1981, *17*, 427-439.

Wicklund, R., Cooper, J., and Linder, D. Effects of expected effort on attitude change prior to exposure. *Journal of Experimental Social Psychology*, 1967, *3*, 116-128.

Wilson, T. D., and Nisbett, R. E. The accuracy of verbal reports about the effects of stimuli on evaluations and behavior. *Social Psychology*, 1978, *41*, 118-131.

Wilson, W. R. Feeling more than we can know: Exposure effects without learning. *Journal of Personality and Social Psychology,* 1979, *37*, 811-821.

Wish, M., and Kaplan, S. Toward an implicit theory of interpersonal communication. *Sociometry*, 1977, *40*, 234-246.

Wish, M., Deutsch, M., and Kaplan, S. Perceived dimensions of interpersonal relations. *Journal of Personality and Social Psychology*, 1976, *33*, 409-420.

Worthy, M., Gary, A., and Kahn, G. Self-disclosure as an exchange process. *Journal of Personality and Social Psychology*, 1969, *13*, 59-64.

Wright, P., and Rip, P. D. Retrospective reports on the causes of decisions. *Journal of Personality and Social Psychology*, 1981, *40*, 601-614.

Zajonc, R. The process of cognitive tuning in communication. *Journal of Abnormal and Social Psychology*, 1960, *61*, 159-161.

6

Speech Accommodation Theory

A SOCIAL COGNITIVE APPROACH TO LANGUAGE AND SPEECH BEHAVIOR

Richard L. Street, Jr.
Howard Giles

During social interaction, participants create an interpersonal system characterized by accommodative (Giles and Powesland, 1975) and mutually influential (Hewes, 1979) behavior. One of the most fundamental yet least understood processes of such systems concerns the manner by which interactants structure their speech patterns and rhythms. Formal and informal interaction consists of linguistic codes and of sound-silence sequences that vary in intensity, duration, frequency, and tempo. Speech behaviors contributing to these latter sequences are called "noncontent" speech behaviors in that they concern "how" speech is produced rather than "what" is said (Natale, 1975a; Giles and Smith, 1979; Street, 1982). Representative of this class are pause and vocalization durations, speech rate, vocal pitch and intensity, and pronunciation. Researchers have long noted that interactants influence one another's speech on these dimensions (Chapple, 1940), tending to make mutual adjustments toward similarity (Jaffe and Feldstein, 1970; Matarazzo and Wiens, 1972; Giles, 1977, 1980; Cappella and Planalp, 1981). These moves toward similarity have been variously labeled "convergence" (Natale, 1975a; Giles, 1977), "congruence" (Feldstein, 1972; Welkowitz et al., 1976), "reciprocity" (Argyle, 1969; Cappella, 1981), "synchrony" (Webb, 1972), "symmetry" (Meltzer et al., 1971), and "pattern matching" (Cassotta et al., 1967). However, in some situations interactants change their speech to become more dissimilar or to "diverge" (see Giles, 1977, 1980, and Street, 1982, for reviews).

Authors' Note: *The authors wish to thank Richard Bourhis, Dean Hewes, and Bob Hopper for helpful comments on earlier versions of this chapter.*

While research in this area is rich, theoretical accounts of these processes remain relatively underdeveloped (Feldstein and Welkowitz, 1978). The problem appears twofold: (1) Theoretical development is rarely characterized by comparisons and contrasts of competing explanations and predictions of other views, and (2) The models fail adequately to specify both the processes by which speech adjustments occur and the generative mechanism underlying these adjustments. Regarding the latter problem, we contend that any theory of inter-speaker influence among language and noncontent speech shifts must account for function and process—that is, *why* interactants enact certain speech modifications and *how* they are accomplished.

In this chapter we discuss the relative merits of four theoretical frameworks for understanding mutual influence in communication. They are Webb's (1972) adaptation of Fiske and Maddi's (1961) activation level model, Natale's (1975a) communication model, Cappella's (1981; Cappella and Greene, 1981) adaptation of Stern's (1974) discrepancy-arousal model, and Giles's (1977, 1980; Giles and Powesland, 1975; Thakerar et al., 1982) speech accommodation theory. We shall, however, devote much of our attention to outlining the main propositions of and research related to the last of these—speech accommodation theory (SAT). Our emphasis on SAT is due not only to our belief that it more thoroughly accounts for the complexity of the phenomena addressed but also to its value in acknowledging the explanatory roles of social cognitive processes and functions.

A Review of Three Theories

Webb's (1972) Adaptation of the Activation-Level Model

Utilizing Fiske and Maddi's (1961) activation-level model, Webb explains noncontent speech convergence as resulting from an interaction between a communicator's speech behavior and ambient stimuli in the environment. Convergence is an automatic process in which increases and decreases in the intensity, frequency, and timing of ambient stimuli result in temporarily increased or decreased somatic arousal, which becomes manifest in kind through noncontent speech shifts. Thus, interactants would respond in a similar manner not only to one another's speech behaviors, but also to impersonal stimuli. Heckel et al. (1963) and Brister (1968) demonstrated that speakers significantly increased speech rates when listening to fast music as opposed to slow or no music. Bender and Brister (1968) observed that subjects' written responses in a sentence completion task were positively correlated to the number of stimulus words. Though arguing that a perceptual-physi-ological mechanism automates noncontent speech convergence toward the intensity, duration, and tempo of social and nonsocial stimuli, Webb admits the possibility of personality and role-relationship variables that may influence matching processes. However, he does not elaborate on these.

Natale's (1975) Communication Model

Based on the work of Lane and Tranel (1971), Natale (1975a) has forwarded the "communication model." He posits that conversants use a public feedback system to monitor, primarily at subconscious levels, the intensity and temporal patterns of partners' vocal behaviors. Interactants utilize one another's vocal levels as guidelines for choosing the optimum format for messages. Mutually adjusting to similar speech patterns in turn enhances message understanding. The more speakers desire communication effectiveness, the more similar are their speech patterns. Natale bases the notion of motives for communication effectiveness as generating convergent responses on two studies indicat-ing increased noise compensation among speakers placing greater emphasis on intelligibility (Gardner, 1966) and attaching greater importance to the message (Black, 1949). Natale cites indirect support from the developmental literature, claiming that infants converge vocal pitch toward adults in an apparent attempt to communicate (see also Jakobson, 1968; Crystal, 1975; Helfrich, 1979).

Finally, Natale notes that personal and social-situational factors may influence convergence processes. Personal factors influencing non-content speech shifts include individuals' attitudes and modes (Mat-arazzo, 1973) as well as personality variables such as social desirability (Natale, 1975a). Social-situational factors appear to relate to normative constraints. In such settings, communicators may have a "perceptual set" that dictates responses calling for speech differences. As an example, Natale cites a study by Matarazzo et al. (1968) in which therapists' and patients' talk durations were inversely related, pre-sumably to allow for greater verbal productivity from the patients.

Whereas the two models discussed above concerned convergence only, Cappella's model is more inclusive, addressing noncontent speech moves toward increased similarity and dissimilarity.

Cappella's Adaptation of Stern's (1974) Discrepancy-Arousal Model

In a series of papers, Cappella and others (Cappella, 1981; Cappella and Planalp, 1981; Cappella and Greene, 1982) have modified Stern's

(1974) discrepancy-arousal theory to include expressive behaviors, or behaviors indicating involvement with another person (affiliation) and in the situation (activity). Expressive behaviors include nonverbal and verbal behaviors such as eye gaze, distance, smiling and laughter, body orientation and movement, touch, verbal intimacy, and, of interest in this chapter, noncontent speech behaviors.

The discrepancy-arousal model attempts to account for convergent, divergent, and no change responses. Expressive behaviors serve primarily affective functions and are modified in particular directions to maintain desired levels. There are three main causal linkages in the model. Consider the case of an interaction between persons A and B, using speech rate as an example. First, the behavior-arousal linkage depicts B's arousal as a function of the discrepancy between A's behavior and B's expectations about A's behavior. The extent to which A's behavior is beyond (that is, greater or less than) B's expectation range is monotonically related to B's arousal level. Thus, if B expects a moderate speech rate and A's rate is relatively fast or slow, B will experience a high degree of arousal. If A's rate is moderate and within the acceptance region, a moderate arousal level will be experienced.

Second, arousal in turn leads to affect. High arousal levels generate negative affect; moderate levels produce positive affect; minimal levels are affectively neutral. Thus, very fast or very slow rates are experienced by B as affectively negative, whereas moderate rates are affectively positive. In addition, the model also predicts that little or no discrepancy, for example, exact similarity, would produce less positive affect than moderate discrepancies.

Third, affect determines the nature of the response. If A's behavior is perceived within B's expectation region, B experiences positive affect and will likely reciprocate (or converge toward) A's behavior. On the other hand, if A's behavior falls outside the acceptance region, B will compensate for (or diverge from) A's behavior. For example, if A is speaking too fast, B will slow down his or her speech rate.

Cappella's literature review is both comprehensive and impressive. As he admits, much of the evidence is circumstantial, though encouraging. Unfortunately, the most convincing data regard distance, gaze, and verbal immediacy rather than noncontent dimensions of speech. Finally, Cappella mentions that personal characteristics such as life stress, affective orientation toward another, sensation seeking, and self-monitoring may influence the "width" of interactants' acceptance regions.

A Critique of the Foregoing Models

General Limitations. We contend these three models suffer from at least four limitations. The first concerns the tendency for the Webb, the

Natale, and, to a lesser extent, the Cappella models to be somewhat overly speaker-oriented. In other words, they do not have much theoretical recourse to the types of reactions their speech modifications produce in their listeners. This is, in fact, a curious oversight given over four decades of research into the social meanings of various vocal and linguistic characteristics (for recent reviews, see Scherer and Giles, 1979; Ryan and Giles, 1982). Moreover, many studies across a range of linguistic features have shown (with certain important exceptions to be discussed later) that convergence is positively but divergence negatively received and reacted to by recipients. In other words, it is conceivable that language and noncontent speech moves may not be consciously generated but are purposive and have functional value. At the very least, we require a theory that takes into account in a more rounded fashion the social consequences of speech shifts on the part of the listener as well as the interpretive, anticipated value of these for the speaker him- or herself.

The second limitation of the three models is their lack of appreciation of the fact that a one-to-one, so-called interpersonal encounter can be an intergroup situation (Brown and Turner, 1981), with all the attending processes that such a contextual construal involves. Until recently, there has been an "individualistic" bias in the social psychology of intergroup relations in the sense that intraindividual and interindividual factors have been transported into the intergroup arena in an attempt to elucidate the underlying processes (Turner and Giles, 1981a). For example, notions of authoritarianism, frustration-aggression, and belief dissimilarity have been used to examine intergroup discrimination and prejudice. Recent research (see Turner, 1981) has shown not only that these factors *cannot* account for intergroup discrimination under minimal categorization conditions, but also that processes of a *different* order, such as social identification, are operating at the intergroup level of analysis. In order to elaborate, let us consider the two extremes of interaction discussed by Tajfel and Turner (1979: 34):

> At one extreme is the interaction between two or more individuals which is *fully* determined by their interpersonal relationships and individual characteristics and not at all affected by various social groups to which they respectively belong. The other extreme consists of interaction between two or more individuals which are *fully* determined by their respective memberships [in] various social groups and are not at all affected by the inter-individual personal relationships between the people involved.

These two extremes are considered as lying at either end of a bipolar continuum labeled interindividual and intergroup encounters respectively (see Stephenson, 1981, for the more plausible proposal that they are two orthogonal continua). In has been argued (Tajfel and Turner, 1979: 34) that the *more* members of a group conceive of an encounter to be toward the intergroup pole,

> the more uniformity will they show in their behavior towards members of the relevant outgroup . . . [and] the more they will tend to treat members of the outgroup as undifferentiated items in a unified social category rather than in terms of their individual characteristics.

Tajfel and his associates (Tajfel, 1978, 1982) have been concerned with developing a theory for understanding this unique intergroup end of the continuum. In essence, it suggests that when individuals identify with a social group, they desire to derive satisfaction from their membership in it; that is, they wish to possess a positive rather than a negative group identity. The realization of the affect associated with in-group identity comes through making intergroup comparisons of the position of one's own group with that of the other on certain valued dimensions, such as power, resources, and capabilities. Much of the theory and the empirical research deriving from it is concerned with the conditions necessary and strategies used for achieving a positive in-group identity. Given that speech style, dialects, and languages can be important dimensions of identity for many social groupings, particular class and ethnic categories, and even, perhaps, certain women (Kramarae, 1981), we have argued elsewhere (Bourhis, 1979; Giles, 1978, 1979; Giles and Johnson, 1981) that language in its broadest senses would be an extremely important set of features along which speakers may wish to differentiate from each other in an intergroup context.

Regarding speech behavior adjustments, by diverging and emphasizing their own language, dialect, noncontent, and nonverbal features (von Raffler-Engel, 1980), discourse structures, or even isolated words (Tannen, 1981), individuals who define themselves cognitively as category members at the time of interaction often accentuate differences between themselves and an out-group member on salient, valued dimensions of their group identity in order to achieve a "positive psycholinguistic distinctiveness" (Giles et al., 1977). Regarding listener evaluation, when defining the situation in intergroup terms, perceivers may focus more attention and be aware of certain speech behaviors like rate and accent (Giles and Smith, 1979) which within interindividual contexts occur largely unnoticed (Thakerar et al., 1982; Street, 1982; Putman and Street, forthcoming). A comprehensive theory of speech modifications therefore needs to take into account not only the linguistic consequences of interindividual definitions of a social encounter (for a more detailed discussion, see Bradac, 1982; Giles et al., forthcoming; Smith et al., 1982), but also potential intergroup situations.

The models of Webb and Natale fail in this respect by considering speech adjustments only in terms of interlocuters' speech behaviors (for example, person A's faster rate leads to a faster rate by person B) without taking into account situational definitions. One could argue that Cappella's model incorporates situational definitions regarding the "expectations" that influence preference regions. But it remains uncertain how definitions of intergroup situations influence discrepancy-arousal predictions of speech modifications. For example, if one perceives an intergroup encounter positively and that respective group memberships are acceptable, preference regions for interlocuters' speech would center on their characteristic speech styles. However, one would not *reciprocate* the out-group members' speech; rather, one would maintain, and appropriately so, speech differences. If the intergroup encounter is perceived as threatening, one might either increase speech dissimilarities (for dissociation) or increase speech similarity (for example, to be condescending or competitive; see Giles, 1980; Thakerar et al., 1982). In short, the speech behavior exhibited in intergroup settings can be more adequately explained by communicators' intentions (such as dissociation or positive group identity) than by arousal changes resulting from discrepancies among speech behaviors.

The third problem issue revolves around the fact that the models of Webb, Natale, and Cappella assume implicitly that objective speech features (as indicated by mechanical instrumentation such as stopwatches and computers) are indeed those that listeners perceive and to which they respond in speech. Language attitudes research, however, indicates that this assumption is often untenable. Street and Hopper (1982) proposed a speech-style evaluation model emphasizing a distinction between *perceived* and *objective* message characteristics and listeners' subsequent evaluative and behavioral responses. However, we would expect that, while perceived and objective messages are *usually* similar, interactants may have goals or perceptual biases that distort the perception of objective speech behavior. Certain perceived attitudinal or demographic differences between communicators may create perceptions of more speech differences or similarities than actually exist. For example, Williams et al. (1972) observed that, when white subjects viewed videotapes showing black children but using the voices of white children, the children's speech was perceived as more nonstandard and less confident than the same speech from a white mouth. Probably due to more experience, black teachers tended to make more distinctions in the perception of black speech (Williams, 1976; Robinson, 1979).

Nisbett and Wilson (1977a) noted that a European speaker was rated as having a heavier accent when he had a cold, distant style as opposed to a warm, friendly style. Scherer (1979) stated listeners tend to perceive "dominant" speakers as typically louder than they actually are. Bourhis et al. (1979) found that when a francophone speaker threatened the identity of Flemish listeners, the listeners rated the speaker as sounding more francophone than when the speaker presented nonthreatening messages. Larsen et al. (1977) reported that hearers view the speech of a speaker with a lisp as more similar to their own when the speaker is given high as opposed to low social cost characteristics. Others have found that informants often overreport (Trudgill, 1975) and underreport (Labov, 1966) standard speech usages.

The incongruity between objective and perceived speech has also been noted among noncontent speech shifts. Thakerar and Giles (1981) reported that, when a speaker presenting a one-minute monologue was ascribed with high status, he was perceived as having a more standard accent and talking faster than when the same speaker was given low status. Given the relatively consistent linear relationship between both speech rate (Brown, 1980) and standardization of accent (Giles and Powesland, 1975) to competency judgments in contextually sterile monologue conditions (Giles et al., 1981), Thakerar and Giles interpreted their results as support for a stereotype that high-status speakers talk faster and use more standard phonological variants than is actually the case. Consistent with this notion, Thakerar et al. (1982) observed that, in high-low status dyads, the high-status participants slowed their speech rates and made their accents less standard, while the low-status parties increased rate and produced more standardized accents. On objective measures, the dyads were actually diverging on these dimensions, but they *thought* they were converging. Believing their speech patterns were congruent had a greater impact on their behavioral and evaluative responses than on their actual behaviors.

In short, though one would generally expect similarity between perceived and observed noncontent speech features, interactants may have goals or perceptual constructs that can influence speech-processing behavior in several ways: by focusing perceivers' attention on aspects of behavior salient to a stereotype or prototype, by leading perceivers' to interpret behavior in a biased manner (to achieve desired outcomes, for example), and by allowing selective retention of information about the other person (Hamilton, 1979; Tajfel, 1982; Street and Hopper, 1982). This biased scanning often results in communicators "seeing" things not actually in the stimulus field. Hence, what we require is a theory that focuses on interactants' *perceptions* of each others' speech patterns rather than one that doggedly waves the old objective reality banner.

Finally, the fourth issue with which the previous three models have difficulty seems to be the range of speech behaviors that they believe to be within their brief. For instance, Webb and Natale confine their theoretical discussions to certain specific noncontent speech behaviors, while Cappella extends his framework to only the so-called expressive behaviors. Nevertheless, it is obvious that convergence as well as divergence (Drake, 1980) can occur at other levels of speech analysis. For instance, people—even at 2 years of age (Harrison and Piette, 1980) —adjust their languages (Fishman, 1966; Scotton and Ury, 1977), conversational structures (Tannen, 1981), content (Higgins, 1980), accent and grammar (Giles, 1973), and even phonological variables (Coupland, forthcoming; Trudgill, forthcoming) when talking to certain others.

Explicating a wide array of speech behaviors within one theoretical framework is indeed appealing. We realize, of course, that speakers differ in the extent to which they modify certain speech behaviors, just as listeners differ in the manner in which they perceive similar speech patterns. Cappella's reviews (1981; Cappella and Greene, 1982; Cappella and Planalp, 1981) indicate that some speech behaviors (such as switching pauses) show more interspeaker influence than do others (for example, turn length; see also Lauver et al., 1971). Phonologically also, Trudgill (forthcoming) has shown that speakers converge certain variants but not others, while Segalowitz and Gatbonton (1977) have suggested the same with regard to divergence. Moreover, one must bear in mind that certain content and noncontent speech levels remain relatively consistent within and across conversations (Cappella and Planalp, 1981; Scherer, 1979). In a similar vein, some behaviors (such as speech rate and response latency) have greater evaluative potencies than others (such as turn length; see Giles, 1979; Street, 1982; Putman and Street, forthcoming). The manner in which interactants evaluatively and behaviorally respond to their partners' speech adjustments will in part depend on their perceptions of the relative importance and acceptability of individual speech behaviors. Nevertheless, despite all of this, it does seem that we should be capable of devising one theoretical framework that can take care of mutual influence and incorporates ultimately sufficient refinements so that far more speech parameters are embraced by it.

Thus far, we can see some serious theoretical problems underlying the level of sophistication of the previous three models, both separately and as a whole. For instance, according to Webb, convergence is an automatic process stemming from somatic arousal in the organism and manifested in speech behavior matching the intensity, frequency, and duration of ambient stimuli. As Feldstein and Welkowitz (1978) note, this conception is too simplistic to be useful. Nevertheless, and assuming the strength of the unpublished data to support this point, why do people also converge to external, *non*social stimuli, such as music tempo? According to Natale (1975a), since convergence stems from nonconscious cognitive processes, it is possible that environmental stimuli other than speech may "leak" into the public feedback system, creating rather automatic convergent effects. Given the ever-present nature of the public feedback loop monitoring the social environment, it would be surprising not to discover occasional leakage into the system. One would also expect this leakage to facilitate noncontent speech responses in kind and be more prominent when the speaker is not highly cognitively involved in the interaction, such as during casual conversations with intimate partners. Certainly actors could control such influences in contexts requiring greater cognitive effort. In addition, and as is the case with the communication model as well, the adaption of the activation-level model does not account for divergent or no change responses. In these senses, both Webb's and Natale's models are found wanting, despite the intuitive cognitive appeal of the latter. While we conceive of Cappella's arguments as more thorough as well as claiming to account for convergence, no change, and divergence, we do consider difficulties of his discrepancy-arousal model to be apparent. These relate to (1) the relationship between noncontent speech discrepancy and arousal, and (2) the extent to which cognition mediates the production of reciprocal (convergent) and compensatory (divergent) adjustments in speech. These issues are central to the controversy over whether arousal or social cognitive processes are the generative mechanism underlying speech behavior modifications.

The Discrepancy-Arousal Link. Cappella posits a series of causal linkages, discrepancy-arousal-affect-adjustment, between the reception of a partner's noncontent speech and the production of one's own. The discrepancy between another's speech and the receiver's acceptance level for this speech is monotonically related to arousal. Much discrepancy is overly arousing, generating negative affect, while moderate discrepancy is moderately arousing, producing positive affect. Evidence for this claim comes mostly from research on infants and visual, not speech, stimuli. Our major concern with the discrepancy-arousal model involves its prediction that little or no discrepancy leads to no arousal and is affectively neutral. The implication is that, to be experienced most positively, interactants would move speech toward moderate discrepancy levels rather than toward similarity. Given the literature that interactants tend to become more similar on noncontent speech dimensions, this prediction seems unlikely. In his discussion of this issue, Cappella remains somewhat unclear. Whereas the model predicts that similarity may be underarousing, he indicates that behaviors within the acceptance region, which presumably contains the actor's own speech behavior in most cases, reflect appropriate responsiveness and thus have a positive effect on attraction. (For support, Cappella cites a study by Smith et al., 1975, reporting a curvilinear relationship between speech rate and ratings of benevolence.) Indeed, arousal levels (especially in the extremes) can influence speech behavior; for instance, high-anxiety subjects often talk faster with more disfluencies than those with moderate or low anxiety (Murray, 1971). But whether speech behavior *discrepancy* influences arousal and affect in the form of a butterfly curve remains untested. Moreover, the important interactive effects of different levels of anxiety at least stereotypically associated with certain social situations (for example, a job interview as opposed to a casual chat in a pub) are left unexplored and thereby assumed irrelevant. Nevertheless, one might predict that large discrepancies from speech expectancies might have less arousal force and thereby possess less negative affectivity had they been perceived in a more than less inherently arousing social context.

The Role of Cognitive Mediation. Cappella contends that partners' responses within the expectancy/acceptance region are reciprocated, while those outside are compensated as a function of activation level. While acknowledging the role of cognition as setting the expectancy levels, Cappella denies that such adjustments are purposive. However, the causal role of arousal remains relatively unclear. For example, are speakers merely passively reacting to an environmental state through experiencing arousal and affect? or does the behavioral response of convergence function to maintain a pleasurable level of moderate arousal while divergence can function to obliterate the negative affect of speech discrepancy? or are speakers trying purposively, but nonconsciously, to show approval or disapproval and maintain or bring partners' speech behaviors within the acceptance region? Two studies indicate that at least some compensation may be goal-oriented. Matarazzo et al. (1968) and Street et al. (1981) have contended that some interactants may have therapeutic or response sets to encourage speech behavior levels in others. These studies respectively observed inverse relationships between the amount of talk by therapists and adults to that of patients and children.

At the intergroup level also, Cappella's model intuitively appears problematic. Consider the following illustrations. Imagine meeting someone from a hostile out-group, be it class, ethnic, religious, or occupational. More often than not, that person's speech patterns will probably fall into the expectancy region you anticipate. Yet, in contrast to the discrepancy-arousal model, would not high rather than a moderate arousal ensue?

Speech in this case would be arousing because of what it represents (hostile out-group) rather than because it is discrepant with an expected level. Even if the situation is not highly arousing, surely defining it as an intergroup one in which in-group loyalties are paramount would lead to *divergence* on (even expressive) vocal and verbal features characteristic of category memberships rather than the convergence, or perhaps no change, predictions of Cappella's model? Similarly, imagine meeting someone whom you expect, according to all relevant criteria, to be English, soft-spoken, grammatically complex, and gestureless. Nevertheless, to your complete surprise you find him Welsh, rather loud, informal, colloquial, and gesturally flamboyant. You yourself are similarly vocally inclined and value such unexpected characteristics, which for you produce moderate or even, given the shock, high arousal. Yet you interpret this encounter, and its attending high arousal if it exists, positively, and you converge along the above-mentioned speech parameters. Finally, imagine a Britisher emigrating to the United States. He or she expects to find, and not surprisingly does find, the inhabitants of the host community sounding "American-like" and very expressive. Many Britishers will desire to integrate quickly, communicate effectively, and thereby attenuate their "UK-like" features and become more expressive. Some, on the other hand, may construe the situation in quite different cognitive and affective domains. They will not be highly aroused but instead (again, contrary to Cappella's model) will accentuate their UK-like features, expressionlessness and "stiff upper lip," in the full knowledge that in some situations and for certain Americans, such Englishness will be positively received as cultured and independent, and will allow them to be excused if they break social norms.

We have presented various problems and limitations that we consider the models of Webb, Natale, and Cappella to possess. We shall now introduce speech accommodation theory (SAT), which we believe to be a significant advance over the foregoing to the extent that it (1) acknowledges social cognitive processes, (2) has the potential for further scope in those directions, (3) incorporates the social consequences as well as the determinants of speech adjustments, (4) is applicable to many linguistic levels of analysis, from the more intercultural language and dialect switching to the more intracultural conversational and non-content speech domains, (5) attends to intergroup phenomena and processes, and (6) has had applications to a wide range of speech domains, including those of language and sex (Kramarae, 1981), language and social class (Edwards and Giles, forthcoming), language erosion and assimilation (Giles and Johnson, 1981), and second language (Beebe and Zuengler, in press; Giles and Byrne, in press) and foreign language learning contexts in the East as well as the West (Hildebrandt and Giles, 1980).

Speech Accommodation Theory

Of the theories mentioned, speech accommodation has received the most empirical attention. Giles and his associates (1977, 1980; Giles and Powesland, 1975; Giles et al., 1977; Thakerar et al., 1982) have forwarded the speech accommodation theory to account for speech convergence, maintenance, and divergence, as well as other speech strategies (such as complementarity and competitiveness) in various communication contexts. A vast majority of this research has focused on intercultural encounters (see, for example, Simard et al., 1976; Bourhis and Giles, 1977; Bourhis et al., 1979; Giles and Smith, 1979), but recently accommodation theory has been applied to intracultural-interpersonal contexts in England (Thakerar et al., 1982) and the United States (Street, 1982; Putman and Street, forthcoming).

Speech accommodation theory is derived from similarity-attraction, social exchange, causal attribution, and social identity principles. A basic postulate is that communicators are motivated to adjust their speech styles with respect to one another as a means of expressing values, attitudes, and intentions. In addition, it is the individual's perception of another's speech that will determine his or her behavioral and evaluative response. Since the importance of the perceived versus objective message characteristics has already been discussed, we consider evidence supporting speech accommodation theory under two headings: (1) intentions and speech adjustments, and (2) evaluations of speech adjustments. The six basic propositions constituting SAT are introduced subsequent to an overview of the framework.

Intentions and Speech Adjustments

Convergence. Assuming no strong or competing sociolinguistic norms dictating appropriate speech usage in given contexts (see Bourhis, 1979; Bourhis and Genesee, 1980; Ball et al., forthcoming), convergence expresses a speaker's conscious or nonconscious desire for social integration, seeking or showing approval, identification, or communicative effectiveness with another. Indeed, participants in an encounter could be displaying mutual, symmetrical convergences, albeit to differing degrees (Platt, 1977) and for different pruposes. For instance, Thakerar et al. (1982) present data suggesting that high-status speakers converge to low-status participants by means of slowing down their speech and nonstandardizing their accents principally for cognitive reasons, whereas the latter quicken their rates and standardize their accents for mainly affective purposes (cognitive organization and identity maintenance functions, respectively; see Giles et al., 1979). Of course, such convergences can occur only if the speaker has the repertoire flexibility for such adjustments to take place realistically and over the long term. Trudgill (forthcoming) reckons that lexical shifts probably precede grammatical and phonological convergences. Regarding phonological shifts, Trudgill (forthcoming) further states that these may be inhibited

> by difficulties in restructuring underlying forms and detailed phonological constraints; by phototactic constraints; by the need to avoid losses of contrast; and by a desire to avoid very strongly stereotyped features. These contrasts may well lead to the possibility that there are generalizations and predictions that can be made about the routes followed by speakers during accommodation. In addition to this, however, there is evidence that indicates that, at both phonological and grammatical levels, different speakers are very likely to follow different routes and adopt different strategies of accommodation.

Evidence for the motivational impetus behind convergence is convincing within the domain of language and dialect choice. The vast literature on language and dialect assimilation of immigrant groups in alien dominant cultures (see, for example, Fishman, 1966) can be viewed from the accommodation perspective. Typically, language shifts are unilateral, the subordinate group converging in their language use to the powerful dominant group in order to obtain identity and approval (Taylor et al., 1978; Bourhis and Giles, 1977).

Research reported by Aboud (1976) suggests that even 6-year-olds are aware of power and status differences in language usage (see also Day, 1982). Aboud and her associates studied the communication patterns of Chicano and Anglo-American children, who, of course, represent respectively low and high power groups. These children were asked to explain how to play a game they had just learned to two listeners of their own age. The authors found that 71 percent of the Spanish-dominant Chicanos converged by adopting the language of their English listeners. Only 17 percent of the English-dominant Anglos accommodated to the Spanish listeners, despite the fact that half of them were in a bilingual program. None of the nonconvergers used any alternative forms of accommodation (see Giles et al., 1973), such as saying a few key words in Spanish or apologizing for their supposed lack of Spanish fluency. In a similar study involving the investigation of Spanish-English code switching, Valdes-Fallis (1977) found that bilingual Mexican American women tended to follow a language switch initiated by a male and also tended to imitate the relative frequency of language switching as well as the kinds of switching patterns selected by a male speaker throughout the conversation. Bilingual accommodation was notably more limited or nonexistent in speech exchanges between two females. Such a finding again confirms SAT predictions based on the higher values and social power that are traditionally associated with males rather than with females. Similarly, it has been shown that the more an individual desires another's approval, the more the latter's voice will sound similar to the former's. Larsen et al. (1977) found that speakers who anticipated interaction with a prestigious, authoritative figure perceived his speech as sounding more similar to their own than did subjects who were told little about him and who did not expect to meet him (see Berger and Roloff, this volume). This perception of a reduced language barrier between oneself and another no doubt facilitates the convergence process, since the recipient will appear to be a more attainable target to shift toward.

The data linking noncontent speech convergence to goals of approval seeking and showing, of communication effectiveness, of increasing attraction, and of social identification are indirect though encouraging. Persons with a high need for social desirability have been observed to converge more on vocal intensity and pause durations than those with a low need for social approval (Natale, 1975a, 1975b). Interactants perceiving themselves as attitudinally similar tended to converge more on pause duration (Welkowitz and Feldstein, 1969, 1970) and vocal intensity (Welkowitz et al., 1972) than did interactants perceiving themselves as dissimilar. During subsequent interactions, Jaffe and Feldstein (1970) and Welkowitz and Feldstein (1969) have noted that the same conversants progressively converged on pause durations. Putman and Street (forthcoming) recently attempted to examine the relationship between interviewees' efforts to create impressions of likable (and not likable) and competent (and not competent). Likable interviewees tended to converge speech rate and turn duration toward that of the interviewers, whereas not likable interviewees slightly diverged on these behaviors. However, only the convergence score for speech rate reached statistical significance. Speech accommodation was unrelated to efforts to appear competent or not.

Additional evidence is found in the developmental literature. Jakobson (1968; see also Helfrich, 1979) argued that infants, in their apparent desire to communicate, attempt to match the vocal intensity of their adult interaction partners. Welkowitz et al. (1976) and Street et al. (1981) have suggested that noncontent speech convergence represents a form of socialized speech, since such speech shifts are coordinated with a listener's speech behavior.

Maintenance, Divergence and Other Speech Shifts. In some situations, interactants may wish to maintain deliberately a definite social distance between themselves and others, thereby establishing their own valued autonomy and independence; this can occur even in non-role-related situations. Such a strategy of what we would prefer to term "speech maintenance" (Bourhis, 1979) is most likely to occur when others in the situation are deemed to be members of undesirable groups, considered to hold noxious attitudes, or display a deplorable appearance. Under other, probably more dissociative conditions, speakers may wish to accentuate even further the differences between themselves and others (Tajfel and Wilkes, 1963; Lambert and Lambert, 1972), either by imagining that they speak differently from them in a valued direction (Wolff, 1959; Parkin, 1977) or by actually *diverging* from others on various speech dimensions (Bourhis and Giles, 1977; Bourhis et al., 1979). Speech divergence in interindividual encounters may be mediated by different cognitive mechanisms such that in some situations, the social dissociation can be regarded as either (1) a linguistic reactance (Brehm, 1972) to a perceived threat of loss of freedom (see Ryan, 1979), or (2) a linguistic "boomerang" effect (Cialdini et al., 1976; Kiesler and Jones, 1971) to anticipating dealing with an antithetical (and persuasive) speaker on an issue to which one is committed (see Bond and Yang, forthcoming), and/or (3) a linguistic "balancing act" (Heider, 1958) when at cognitive variance with significant others. In each case however, divergence should only occur when the threatened loss of freedom, commitment to particular issues, and imbalance have sociolinguistic correlates (for example, beliefs in the value of trade unions are associated stereotypically with nonstandard phonological variants; Powesland and Giles, 1975). As in the case of speech convergence, an important facet of SAT is that divergence should be manifested in a shift away from the linguistic attributes *believed* characteristic of the other.

Most of our thinking on divergence in particular has been influenced greatly by the theoretical ideas of Tajfel and Turner (1979) on the social psychology of intergroup behavior (see also Turner and Giles, 1981b). In line with the section of this chapter in which the interindividual/intergroup continuum was introduced, we conceive of divergence as a strategy of psycholinguistic distinctiveness serving to enhance the positive identity of individuals who believe they are participating in an intergroup encounter (Bourhis, 1979; Giles, 1978, 1979; Giles et al., 1977). In this sense, the nature, magnitude, and rate of divergence are believed to be influenced by intergroup factors. For instance, Taylor and Royer (1980) found that speakers would anticipate greater divergence from an outgroup speaker after discussion about the issues involved with their in-group than on their own; such linguistic polarization (Myers and Lamb, 1976) was attributed by the group members themselves to feelings of in-group belongingness. In an attempt to flush out the necessary and sufficient conditions for divergence (as well as other forms of linguistic differentiation) to occur, Giles and Johnson (1981) proposed that this speech strategy is most likely to be symmetrically forthcoming when the interacting individuals (1) consider the situation to be defined in intergroup terms and react to each other as representatives of different social categories rather than as different personalities, (2) identify strongly with their in-groups which consider linguistic attributes to be important dimensions of their social identities, (3) are aware of cognitive alternatives (Tajfel, 1978) to their groups' status positions, (4) perceive their in-groups to have many sociostructural forces in their favor (so-called high perceived vitality; Bourhis et al., 1981), (5) perceive their in-group boundaries to be hard and closed, (6) identify strongly with few other social categories, (7) perceive little overlap with each other in terms of other social category memberships, (8) consider that the social identities deriving from the other social category memberships are relatively inadequate, and (9) perceive their status within the current contextually prevalent group membership to be higher than their intragroup status in their other social category memberships.

As with speech convergence, speech divergence among language, dialect, and accent choices has been empirically as well as theoretically developed more on the affective, identity maintenance function side than on the cognitive organizational side (Giles et al., 1979). Nevertheless, it can have its more (perhaps evaluatively positive) cognitive organization functions (Taylor and Giles, 1979) rather than being only an expression of attitudes. Indeed, like convergence, divergence can also be enacted on certain noncontent dimensions so as to help the interlocutor put order and meaning into the interaction and provide a mutually understood basis for effective communciation. For instance, one of the authors may in Britain emphasize his American speech style in order to provide information to a British colleague of what assumptions can be made about knowledge of local norms and topics of interest. At the simplest level, such divergence might indicate that rugby and ice hockey are not shared aspects of experience. In this example, speech divergence is less an emotional statement of defiance than a means of facilitating the process of social categorization. In similar vein, Ellen B. Ryan (personal communication) has talked of the "social utility" of certain speech forms, noting that an accentuation of, say, an accent, the slowing down of speech rate, and even a self-disclosure can signal in certain, often intercultural or interrole, contexts that the speaker is not a member of the host community or a regular role occupant, and thereby any norms inadvertently broken are attributed externally with the possibility that the speaker will be allowed a greater latitude of tolerable behaviors. Finally, speech divergence in other contexts can function as a strategic move to bring another's behavior to an acceptable level as well as to facilitate the coordination of speech patterns. Two studies cited earlier (Matarazzo et al., 1968, Street et al., 1981) indicated that some interactants (therapists and adults) may diverge on amount of talk to encourage other interactants (patients and children) to talk more. Divergence as compensation (that is, used for cognitively instrumental purposes) is likely to be markedly different from its more affective dissociative counterpart. For instance, the former is probably not maintained for an extended period of time, as would be the latter, since divergence for compensation entails a momentary adjustment to bring another's behavior into the acceptable zone, whereas divergence for dissociation implies continued efforts toward differentiation. Moreover, with compensation we would expect divergence only for offending behaviors, whereas with dissociation divergence would occur among several noncontent speech behaviors.

Finally, some situations allow dissimilarity between partners' speech behaviors to be acceptable (see Grush et al., 1975). Certain contexts (such as interviews) call for differential speech performances (Miller and Steinberg, 1975; Watzlawick et al., 1967). Interactants, then, do not create similar speech but do maintain a similar *pattern* of speech. Matarazzo and Wiens (1972) review several types of interview data (from psychotherapy, presidential news conferences, interviews with nurses, and the like) and note utterance and response latency convergence in terms of moves in similar directions. That is, though their speech behaviors differed, interviewers and interviewees adjusted speech to maintain particular speech patterns. Giles (1977, 1980) calls speech shifts in these types of communication settings examples of "speech complementarity"—that is, diverging or maintaining dissimilar speech patterns in dyads in which a role or power discrepancy exists between participants. Such speech differences may index optimal sociolinguistic distance and are psychologically acceptable to both participants. Interactions susceptible to speech complementarity include male-female, employer-employee, interviewer-interviewee, and doctor-patient.

One important feature of SAT, however, is that it is the individual's perception of another's speech that will determine his or her behavioral and evaluative response. We have already made mention of this early in our citation of the Thakerar et al. study, in which high- and low-status interactants were judged to be diverging objectively from each other.

Nevertheless, data were obtained which suggested that they were actually converging toward what they believed to be the other's speech stereotype. Independently, Beebe (forthcoming) has found a similar finding with regard to her study on ten-year Chinese-Thai bilinguals who were interviewed in Thai by two different people. One of these interviewers was actually Thai; the other was ethnically Chinese but spoke Thai as a native and no differently from the former person. Nevertheless, the children introduced significantly more Chinese phonological variants into their speech when talking to the latter. Beebe claims that they were converging to the ethnic speech stereotype of what they expected and ultimately believed her to sound like.

Finally, we should note that SAT does not consider speech strategies to be all-or-none. It is conceivable that convergence, complementarity, dissociation, and compensation can occur similtaneously, albeit with regard to different speech features. As with other theories discussed, a host of situational and personal factors may influence the degree of convergence predicted besides the social affective variables discussed above. These would include age (Garvey and BenDebba, 1974; Street et al., 1981; Welkowitz et al., 1976), field independence, cognitive complexity (O'Keefe and Delia, forthcoming), self- and public consciousness, and self-monitoring (see Roloff and Berger, this volume).

Evaluations of Speech Adjustments

That convergence functions to establish optimal speech patterns represents a basic tenet of SAT and apparently discrepancy-arousal and communication models as well. Convergence contributes to similarity among speech styles and thus should enhance perceived intelligibility (Traindis, 1960), supportiveness and predictability (Berger and Calabrese, 1975; Berger, 1980), intersubjectivity (Rommetveit, 1979; Bishop, 1979; Sebastian et al., forthcoming), smoothness of interaction (Knapp et al., 1980) and perhaps metacommunicatively signal positive affect and attitudes toward interlocuters (Feldstein and Welkowitz, 1978). Indeed, an impressive array of studies confirm the notion that listeners perceive convergence positively across a range of evaluative dimensions, including warmth (Welkowitz and Kuc, 1973), competence (Giles and Smith, 1979), attraction (Giles and Smith, 1979; Street, 1982; Putman and Street, forthcoming), and cooperativeness (Feldman, 1968; Harris and Baudin, 1973). Behaviors accommodated in these studies included accent, language choice, speech rate, response latency, turn duration, and content.

Moreover, convergence is likely to mean that the participant is going to need to make less cognitive effort in reply on many speech dimensions (Thakerar, 1981). This reduction of cognitive effort on the part of the recipient is likely to be pleasurable, as it may spread across other processes, such as understanding the message, making judgments about the message and person, conceiving a response, and self-evaluating the response after it has been uttered. But such a reduction of cognitive effort may not be manifest in certain bilingual code-switching situations in which use of another's language or dialect may be cognitively strenuous (see Giles et al., 1973).

For convergence to be perceived favorably, however, it must be assumed or attributed to positive intent. For instance, when convergence is attributed externally to situational pressures pointing to the use of particular speech patterns, as in a commercial setting (Bourhis and Genesee, 1980) or a job interview (Ball et al., forthcoming), or if the person is known to have been forced to converge by, for example, an experimenter (Simard et al., 1976), then such modifications will not be so positively received.

Though the favorableness of similar speech styles is emphasized in SAT, it does not hold that the relationship between degree of convergence and positive evaluation is necessarily linear. Listeners may have tolerance or preference levels for various magnitudes and rates of speech discrepancies and adjustments. For example, conversants may converge too much (say, on accent), and this shift is perceived as inappropriate, ingratiating, condescending, and so on. Giles and Smith (1979), observing a speaker modifying speech rate, accent, and content, found the most positively received combination was convergence not on all three, but on speech rate and content with accent maintenance. Also, listeners appear to respond to one another's speech in terms of a "zone" of acceptable or preferred behavioral levels (Giles, 1980; Cappella and Greene, 1982). For example, Street (1982) reported that observers tolerated differences between an interviewer's and an interviewee's speech rate (up to 50 words per minute) and response latency (up to one second). However, when the interviewee diverged rate and latency beyond these discrepancy levels, he was subsequently downgraded. In a study seeking to identify parameters of preference regions, Street and Brady (forthcoming) noted that listeners' evaluations of speakers were apparently regulated by preferences for moderate and faster rates. However, these judgments of speakers with varying rates were also mediated by degree of similarity to the listeners' *own* typical speech rates. Faster-talking listeners tended to view faster speakers more favorably and slower speakers less favorably than did slower-talking listeners. Street and Brady's research also suggests the existence of a range of acceptance, as the listener-rate-by-speaker-rate interaction was attributable to the fast and slow rate extremes; all groups of listeners evaluated moderate speaker rate levels relatively similarly.

Conceptualizing an acceptance *region*, consisting of latitudes of acceptable speech responses, is warranted given the apparently flexible and negotiative nature of noncontent speech adjustments. Indeed, the greater the perceived overlap between acceptance regions of both participants, the wider is the range of acceptable noncontent speech performances (Cappella and Greene, 1982).

Whatever the cognitive dynamics underlying the motivation, maintenance and divergence are denigrated evaluatively by their recipients (see Giles et al., 1973; Simard et al., 1976; Giles and Smith, 1979; Street, 1982; Sandilands and Fleury, 1979), although sympathetic confederates of the diverging speaker may find it laudable on some dimensions (Bourhis et al., 1975; Doise et al., 1976). The negative interpersonal consequences of divergence usually operate, of course, only when the speech is processed, consciously or nonconsciously, as psychologically dissociative and attributed internally to a lack of interest and effort and/or to personal disdain on the part of the speaker. If maintenance, for example, is attributed externally to prevalent social norms or to a lack of repertoire flexibility for which the speaker is not held responsible, then such unfavorable reactions would be attenuated (Simard et al., 1976). Indeed, the whole area of misattribution (see Sillars, this volume) of accommodative strategies is one well worthy of empirical and theoretical pursuit in the future (Platt and Weber, forthcoming). The negative evaluation of maintenance and divergence can be mediated by a number of possible cognitive mechanisms, including (1) the reduction of dissonance in the face of divergence which signals to the recipient the speaker's apparent and debilitating lack of concern for gaining his or her respect and approval, and (2) the increase in perceived unpredictability (Berger and Calabrese, 1975) underscoring the *lack* of intersubjectivity between speaker and listener, which leads to cognitive discomfort through uncertainty in shaping an appropriate behavioral response.

Propositions

In summary, SAT can be presented in proposition form (slightly revised after Thakerar et al., 1982):

(1) People will attempt to converge linguistically toward the speech patterns believed to be characteristic of their recipients when they (a) desire their social approval and the perceived costs of so acting are proportionally lower than the rewards anticipated; and/or (b) desire a high level of communicational efficiency, and (c) social norms are not perceived to dictate alternative speech strategies.

(2) The magnitude of such linguistic convergence will be a function of (a) the extent of the speakers' repertoires, and (b) factors (individual dif-

ference and environmental) that may increase the need for social approval and/or high communicational efficiency.

(3) Speech convergence will be positively evaluated by recipients when the resultant behavior is (a) perceived as such psychologically, (b) perceived to be at an optimal sociolinguistic distance from them, and (c) attributed internally with positive intent.

(4) People will attempt to maintain their speech patterns or even diverge linguistically from those believed characteristic of their recipients when they (a) define the encounter in intergroup terms and desire a positive ingroup identity, or (b) wish to dissociate personally from another in an interindividual encounter, or (c) wish to bring another's speech behaviors to a personally acceptable level.

(5) The magnitude of such divergence will be a function of (a) the extent of speakers' repertoires, and (b) individual differences and contextual factors increasing the salience of the cognitive or affective functions in proposition 4.

(6) Speech maintenance and divergence will be negatively evaluated by recipients when the acts are perceived as psychologically diverging, but favorably reacted to by observers of the encounter who define the interaction in intergroup terms and who share a common, positively valued group membership with the speaker.

The Need for a Social Cognitive Approach

By recourse to a wide variety of data, we have attempted to demonstrate that language and noncontent speech adjustments stem from interactants' motivations, which include attempts to socially integrate, identify, dissociate, or respond appropriately to situational constraints. In addition, we have reviewed research indicating that optimal levels of sociolinguistic distance can be identified and that behaviors falling within these preference regions are favorably received while those outside elicit negative sanctions. Though SAT tenets regarding language choice and dialect remain relatively unchallenged, Cappella (1981; Cappella and Planalp, 1981; Cappella and Greene, 1982) has criticized SAT as being too cognitively "top-heavy" to account for the fast moment-by-moment adjustments typical of noncontent speech. To assume that speakers assess their intentions, make judgments of similarity, monitor another's speech behavior on multiple levels, and then decide to modify noncontent speech on a variety of dimensions to meet interaction goals is indeed an unrealistic expectation in most cases. It is also true that interactants are often very unaware of the nature of their speech modifications (Thakerar et al., 1982). However, Giles (1977, 1980; Giles and Powesland, 1975) has described noncontent speech moves as "covert accommodation," since they are nonconscious processes generated by goals and purposes. Admittedly, a conceptual concern among SAT researchers is describing the cognitive processes linking nonconscious behavior to actors' intention. Several theorists have offered insights.

Based on the work of Langer (1978), Berger (1980; Berger and Roloff, 1980; this volume) contends that much everyday communication is received and produced at low levels of awareness. This claim centers on three observations. First, in some situations, interactants may not be aware of specific goals or intentions (Turk, 1974). Berger states this may be particularly true of smooth-flowing, informal social interaction among friends and family. Second, actors are often not aware of the basis for certain attributional and evaluative judgements. That is, interactants may be cognizant of the judgments themselves but cannot accurately specify how they arrived at those judgments (see Nisbett and Wilson, 1977b). Third, many aspects of communication behavior are probably scripted. Given the unrealistic assumption that interactants consciously monitor all aspects of their behavior and environment, they have probably learned cognitive scripts of automated routines that constantly facilitate interaction and that are subconsciously enacted (see also von Raffler-Engel, 1980); that is, their perception and production processes are generally not noticed but indeed are operating. Berger and Roloff have suggested that covert or noncontent speech accommodation may be scripted behavior. Since convergence facilitates interaction maintenance and goals, actors may automatically apply a "convergence script" to move toward similar speech. This notion is akin to what Giles and Natale have respectively labeled response and perceptual sets.

As Langer (1978) points out, factors may intervene in the production and perception of mindless behavior and bring it to a state of mindfulness —for example, when one encounters a novel situation or information, or when consequences of a behavioral sequence are discrepant from expectations. (For a discussion of such issues regarding perceptual biases and implicit theories, see Hewes and Planalp, this volume.) If smooth-flowing interaction is characterized by automatic and subconscious employment of noncontent speech convergence, one would expect congruent speech patterns to occur relatively unnoticed and incongruent patterns to be recognized and subsequently downgraded. In Street's (1982) study, listeners were indeed unaware of response latency and speech rate convergence but were highly aware of divergence of these behaviors. Additionally, interactants converging speech were viewed significantly more socially attractive than those diverging speech. Interpreting these results, Street argued that, because of its pervasive and facilitatory nature within social discourse, noncontent speech convergence generally occurs unnoticed and may even be taken for granted. But divergent moves disrupt cooperative patterns and are brought to con-

sciousness. As mentioned above, the novelty and salience of social interaction also influence awareness. The more novel the situation, the more
likely interactants will monitor and be aware of situational events (see,
for example, Berger and Roloff, 1980). Thus, within intergroup encounters, participants often more readily attend to and are cognizant of
interlocutors' noncontent speech (Giles and Smith, 1979) than within
intracultural-interpersonal encounters (see Thakerar et al., 1982; Street,
1982). By the same token, scripts may also apply to certain speech-diver-
gent moves as well. As von Raffler-Engel (1980) noted, divergence may
be automatic and nonconscious as interactants unknowingly reveal
negative attitudes or seek dissociation from partners.

In short, our literature review indicates explicit and implicit links
between noncontent speech accommodation and communicators' goals
and intentions. The notion of scripts and automated routines suggests
that some forms of purposive behavior, including noncontent speech
adjustments, can be performed mindlessly and subconsciously. As Jesse
Delia (personal communication) has noted, a bias exists in the social
science literature associating terms like "intention," "strategies," and
"goals" to "planfulness," "consciousness," and "thoughtfulness." Obviously, behavior is organized at multiple levels by cognitive processes
(see Delia and O'Keefe, this volume); for example, conversants
similtaneously create nonverbal gestures, adjust noncontent speech to
appropriate levels, formulate grammatical constructions, make lexical
choices, monitor situational events, and so on. Given the apparent
infeasibility of consciously attending to all these processes, communicators must rely on production mechanisms that elicit rather
automatic deployment of behavioral routines. Thus, a major theoretical
challenge for SAT researchers concerns depicting the cognitive framework that allows for purposive, conscious, and nonconscious speech
behavior. The work of Norman (1981; Norman and Shallice, 1980)
provides a promising beginning.

Norman has proposed the activation-trigger-schema system (ATS)
model to account for the manner in which cognitive structures
hierarchically organize and regulate action (behavior) sequences at
multiple levels. Norman utilizes the popular notion of *schema* to refer to
those sensory-motor knowledge structures that control action sequences. Schemas are of two types: *parent* and *child* schemas. The
highest-level schema is the parent, which, when activated, enacts a series
of subschemas (or child schemas) that coordinate the component parts
of the action sequence. Given the hierarchical nature of the cognitive
machinery, child schemas may, in turn, serve as parent schemas for
other subschemas. Norman states that the highest order of parent
schema is intention. The resulting action sequence will be a function of
intention, perceptual assessment of contextual conditions, and the

connectedness of component schemas. Consider one of Norman's examples. One may intend to drive home from work (parent schema), which activates a series of component schemas (child schemas): getting into the car, using turn signals, steering, braking, and so forth. The manner in which these schemas are applied will also be a function of the situation, such as the route taken, any stops along the way or braking suddenly for a dog. Likewise, each child schema may also serve as a parent schema of constituent processes; for example, the braking schema, in turn, coordinates the motor skills necessary to fulfill the braking action. All the behaviors described, though many are performed subconsciously, contribute to achieving the intention of driving home.

Norman's model, though general, should be appealing to those investigators concerned with the role of consciousness and communication and with the multifaceted nature of purposive behavior. By focusing on the cognitive organization of communication behavior, we can surely justify examination of a wide array of speech dimensions within a single theoretical framework such as SAT. Consider the example of an employment interview. The applicant goes into the interview with the intention of getting the job (parent schema). This intention may invoke certain strategies, such as trying to appear competent without pretense, to appear ambitious, and to appear sociable. These strategies are perhaps child schemas to the overall get-the-job intention, but they also serve as parent schemas for particular behaviors. For the competence impression, the applicant may elaborate on topics about which he or she is knowledgable, standardize accent, and talk at a relatively fast clip. For the strategy of sociability, the applicant may smile a lot, express social interests similar to the interviewer's reciprocate self-disclosures, and (as we contend) converge toward the interviewer's noncontent speech behaviors. Of course, the applicant's strategies and subsequent behaviors may be adapted as needed during the course of the interview upon receiving perceptual cues; for example, the interviewer may be colder and more formal than expected, may be a talent scout rather than someone who has hiring capacities, or may be exhausted after a long day of interviewing. In brief, one can have intentions and low cognitive processing simultaneously.

At the same time, of course, we should not downplay the more "overt accommodations" (Giles and Powesland, 1975), in which speech adjustments are deliberatly produced by speakers. Such may often, though not always, be the case regarding self-disclosures (Berger, 1979) and language switching (Bourhis et al., 1979). With regard to the latter phenomenon, Bourhis (forthcoming) has shown by means of a sociolinguistic survey among English and French Canadians in Quebec

(ECs and FCs, respectively) that speakers can be consciously aware of convergences and divergences among language switches as well as the supposed reasons for them (see also Taylor and Royer, 1980). Thus, for instance, FC respondents reported being more likely to converge to speaking French in Montreal today than in the past. ECs also reported that currently FCs were less likely to converge to English than in the past. Correspondingly, FC respondents reckoned that they were more likely to use French in Montreal than ECs were to use English, and they also reported that currently ECs were more likely to converge to them by speaking French than in the past. However, in a field study designed to discover whether such cognitions matched actual accommodative behaviors, Bourhis (forthcoming) found that the overlap was far from strong in every instance. For example, in contrast to their expressed attitudes, FCs tended to reciprocate convergence more than ECs in intergroup encounters, whereas the latter were more likely to maintain their in-group language. Interestingly enough in the context of the foregoing discussion on scripts and schemas, Bourhis states that in spite of sociopolitical changes favoring the ethnolinguistic ideals of franco-phones in Montreal, ECs are still in the habit of maintaining English when interacting with FC interlocuters. Likewise, FCs still appear in the habit of converging English when interacting with EC interlocuters.

In sum, in addition to consciously generated behaviors such as self-disclosures, language choice, and certain lexical choices, communicators' purposes, intentions, and affective orientations to others may also be actualized through noncontent speech modifications which, either by scripts, schemas, or response sets, are generally produced at low awareness levels. Indeed, arousal may be a factor. For instance, extreme noncontent speech levels (such as very fast speech rates or long response latencies) may be overarousing and elicit divergent responses. However, the prominence of an affective and cognitive role is necessitated given evidence that noncontent speech shifts are related to speaker goals, need not be "noticed" to fulfill communication functions, are of evaluative import, and reflect sensitivity to situational differences. Future theoretical work needs to describe more thoroughly the cognitive machinery generating noncontent speech adjustments as well as other overt forms of speech behavior. Norman's activation-trigger-schema system (ATS) model is a promising theoretical perspective. In particular, the model posits a hierarchy of cognitive organization in which habitual, overlearned, and subconscious behaviors can be tied to more thoughtful action as a function of intention.

Conclusions

We believe that, given the complexity of data concerning the determinants and consequences of speech modifications, SAT is better able than its competitors to do justice to the phenomena and underlying processes mainly because it is part of a social cognitive approach to the communicative issues at hand in this volume. Future attention ought to be directed to the roles of arousal, awareness, cognitive scripting, and acquaintanceship in the accommodative process as well as to mapping out the nature of and variables influencing interlocutors' latitudes of acceptable speech behaviors. Indeed, the questions of which speech features are accommodated, when, and why, and which are reacted to, how, when, and why, require far greater exploration. Needless to say, the possibilities are endless, particularly when one contemplates specific applications of social cognitive principles in terms of categorization effects, attributional principles, cognitive complexity, perceived base rates and goal structures, inference principles, social identification, interactional definitions, unitizations, and so on (see Ryan and Giles, 1982). Nevertheless, an obvious priority for the immediate future will be not only an extensive research program aimed at testing specifically SAT propositions, but also to investigate empirically the relative merits of discrepancy-arousal and SAT predictions. The latter venture is, in fact, already under way.

While we believe that SAT is a social cognitive approach and that current thinking on social cognition can only enhance it, we do believe that SAT also has something to say for the future development of communication and social cognition itself. If we are not wary, we are likely to embrace all too uncritically the underlying tenets of the social cognition zeitgeist and its implicit ideology for the study of particularly interpersonal communication. Throughout the 1970s there has been an attempt in social psychology to explain social behavior in terms of the functioning of individual cognitive processes (Israel and Tajfel, 1982); such a view bids fair to flourish in the 1980s. However, social cognition can be criticized for its inherent "individualism" (Turner and Giles, 1981a; Sampson, 1981). Individualism is the thesis that the individual is the sole psychological reality and that reality does not include a distinct component corresponding to group behavior. It is theoretically objectionable because it (1) denies the psychological reality of the group, (2) misconstrues group processes as in opposition to individual rationality, and (3) disconnects the individual from social reality and produces theories difficult to contextualize in society. We would wish to proffer a truly *social* cognitive approach to communication which, as SAT does, makes a distinction between interpersonal and intergroup interactions, considers social identity and the functional interaction between psychological and social processes in group behavior, and acknowledges the influential role of cognitive representations of sociostructural forces. Unless communication explicitly attends to the more or less unique processes of intergroup behavior in face-to-face encounters and recognizes when they are operative, the area will develop assuredly yet regrettably in a blinkered and sterile fashion through an *asocial*, cognitive *intra*individual vacuum.

References

Aboud, F. E. Social development aspects of language. *Papers in Linguistics,* 1976, *9,* 15-37.

Argyle, M. Social interaction. London: Methuen, 1969.

Ball, P., Giles, H., Byrne, J., and Berechree, P. Situational constraints on accommodation theory: Some Australian data. *International Journal of the Sociology of Language,* forthcoming.

Beebe, L. Social and situational factors affecting the communicative strategy of dialect code-switching. *International Journal of the Sociology of Language,* forthcoming.

Beebe, L. and Zuengler, J. Accommodation theory: An explanation for style shifting in second language dialects. In N. Wolfson and E. Judd (Eds.) *TESOL and sociolinguistic research.* Rowley, MA: Newbury House, forthcoming.

Bender, L., and Brister, D. M. *Sex, synchrony, and sentence completion.* Unpublished manuscript, 1968.

Berger, C. R. Beyond initial interaction: Uncertainty, understanding, and the development of interpersonal relationships. In H. Giles and R. St. Clair (Eds.), *Introducing language and social psychology.* Oxford: Blackwell, 1979.

Berger, C. R. Self-consciousness and the study of interpersonal attraction: Approaches and issues. In H. Giles, P. W. Robinson, and P. M. Smith (Eds.), *Language: Social psychological perspectives.* Oxford: Pergamon, 1980.

Berger, C. R., and Calabrese, R. J. Some explorations in initial interaction and beyond: Toward a developmental theory of interpersonal communication. *Human Communication Research,* 1975, *1,* 99-112.

Berger, C. R., and Roloff, M. E. Social cognition, self-awareness, and interpersonal communication. In B. Dervin and M. J. Voight (Eds.), *Progress in communication sciences* (Vol. 2). Norwood, NJ: Ablex, 1980.

Bishop, G. D. Perceived similarity in interracial attitudes and behaviors: The effects of belief and dialect style. *Journal of Applied Social Psychology,* 1979, *9,* 446-465.

Black, J. W. Loudness of speaking: The effect of heard stimuli on spoken responses. *Journal of Experimental Psychology,* 1949, *39,* 311-315.

Bond, M. H., and Yang, K. Ethnic affirmation vs. cross-cultural accommodation: The variable impact of questionnaire language. *Journal of Cross-cultural Psychology,* forthcoming.

Bourhis, R. Y. Language in ethnic interaction: A social psychological approach. In H. Giles and B. St. Jacques (Eds.), *Language and ethnic relations.* Oxford: Pergamon, 1979.

Bourhis, R. Y. Cross-cultural communication in Montreal: Some survey data after Bill 101. *Journal of Multicultural and Multilingual Development,* forthcoming. (a)

Bourhis, R. Y. Cross-cultural communication in Montreal: Two field studies since Bill 101. *International Journal of the Sociology of Language,* forthcoming. (b)

Bourhis, R. Y. and Genesee, F. Evaluative reactions to code switching strategies in Montreal. In H. Giles, P. W. Robinson, and P. M. Smith (Eds.), *Language: Social psychological perspectives.* Oxford: Pergamon, 1980.

Bourhis, R. Y. and Giles, H. The language of intergroup distinctiveness. In H. Giles (Ed.), *Language, ethnicity, and intergroup relations.* London: Academic Press, 1977.

Bourhis, R. Y., Giles, H., and Lambert, W. E. Social consequences of accommodating one's style of speech: A cross-national investigation. *International Journal of the Sociology of Language,* 1975, *6,* 53-71.

Bourhis, R. Y., Giles, H., Leyens, J-P., and Tajfel, H. Psycholinguistic distinctiveness: Language divergence in Belgium. In H. Giles and R. St. Clair (Eds.), *Language and social psychology*. Oxford: Blackwell, 1979.

Bourhis, R. Y., Giles, H., and Rosenthal, D. Notes on the construction of "subjective vitality" questionnaire for ethnolinguistic groups. *Journal of Multicultural and Multilingual Development*, 1981, *2*, 145-155.

Bradac, J. A rose by another name: Attitudinal consequences of lexical variation. In E. B. Ryan and H. Giles (Eds.), *Attitudes toward language variation: Social and applied contexts*. London: Edward Arnold, 1982.

Brehm, J. W. *Responses to loss of freedom: A theory of psychological reactance*. Morristown, NJ: General Learning, 1972.

Brister, D. M. *The effects of music on verbal rate in an interview situation*. Unpublished manuscript, 1968.

Brown, B. L. Effects of speech rate on personality attributions and competency ratings. In H. Giles, P. W. Robinson, and P. M. Smith (Eds.), *Language: Social psychological perspectives*. Oxford: Pergamon, 1980.

Brown, R. J., and Turner, J. C. Interpersonal and intergroup behavior. In J. C. Turner and H. Giles (Eds.), *Intergroup behavior*. Chicago: University of Chicago Press, 1981.

Cacioppo, J. T., and Petty, R. E. Language variables, attitudes, and persuasion. In E. B. Ryan and H. Giles (Eds.), *Attitudes toward language variation: Social and applied contexts*. London: Edward Arnold, 1982.

Cappella, J. N. Mutual influence in expressive behavior: Adult-adult and infant-adult dyadic interaction. *Psychological Bulletin*, 1981, *89*, 101-132.

Cappella, J. N., and Greene, J. O. A discrepancy-arousal explanation of mutual influence in expressive behavior for adult and infant-adult interaction. *Communication Monographs*, 1982, *49*, 89-114.

Cappella, J. N., and Planalp, S. Talk and silence sequences in informal conversations III: Interspeaker influence. *Human Communication Research*, 1981, *7*, 117-132.

Cassotta, L., Feldstein, S., and Jaffe, J. The stability and modifiability of individual vocal characteristics in stress and nonstress interviews. Research Bulletin No. 2. New York: William Alanson White Institute, 1967.

Chapple, E. D. "Personality" differences as described by invariant properties of individuals in interaction. *Proceedings of the National Academy of Sciences*, 1940, *25*, 58-67.

Cialdini, R. B., Levy, A., Herman, C. P., Kozlowski, L. T. and Petty, R. E. Elastic shifts of opinion: Determinants of direction and durability. *Journal of Personality and Social Psychology*, 1976, *34*, 663-672.

Coupland, N. Linguistic variation and interpersonal accommodation theory: Some phonological data and their implications. *International Journal of the Sociology of Language*, forthcoming.

Crystal, D. *The English tone of voice: Essays in intonation, prosody, and paralanguage*. London: St. Martin's, 1975.

Day, R. R. Children's attitudes toward language. In E. B. Ryan and H. Giles (Eds.), *Attitudes toward language variation: Social and applied contexts*. London: Edward Arnold, 1982.

Doise, W., Sinclair, A., and Bourhis, R. Y. Evaluation of accent convergence and divergence in cooperative and competitive intergroup situations. *British Journal of Social and Clinical Psychology*, 1976, *14*, 247-252.

Drake, G. F. The social function of slang. In H. Giles, P. W. Robinson, and P. M. Smith (Eds.), *Language: Social psychological perspectives*. Oxford: Pergamon, 1980.

Edwards, J. R., and Giles, H. A social psychological perspective on language and education. In P. Trudgill (Ed.), *Applied sociolinguistics*. Cambridge: Cambridge University Press, forthcoming.

Feldman, R. E. Response to compatriots and foreigners who seek assistance. *Journal of Personality and Social Psychology,* 1968, 10, 202-214.

Feldstein, S. Temporal patterns of dialogue: Basic research and reconsiderations. In A. W. Siegman and B. Pope (Eds.), *Studies in dyadic communication.* New York: Pergamon, 1972.

Feldstein, S. and Welkowitz, J. A chronography of conversation: In defense of an objective approach. In A. W. Siegman and S. Feldstein (Eds.), *Nonverbal behavior and communication.* Hillsdale, NJ: Erlbaum, 1978.

Fishman, J. A. Language loyalty in the United States. The Hague: Mouton, 1966.

Fiske, D. W., and Maddi, S. R. A conceptual framework. In D. W. Fiske and S. R. Maddi (Eds.), *Functions of varied experience.* Homewood, IL: Dorsey, 1961.

Gardner, M. B. Effect of noise, system gain, and assigned task on talking level in loudspeaker communication. *Journal of the Acoustical Society of America,* 1966, *40,* 955-965.

Garvey, C., and BenDebba, M. Effects of age, sex, and partner on children's dyadic speech. *Child Development,* 1974, *45,* 1159-1161.

Giles, H. Accent mobility: A model and some data. *Anthropological Linguistics,* 1973, *15,* 87-105.

Giles, H. Social psychology and applied linguistics: Towards an integrative approach. *ITL: Review of Applied Linguistics,* 1977, *33,* 27-42.

Giles, H. Linguistic differentiation between ethnic groups. In H. Tajfel (Ed.), *Differentiation between social groups: Studies in the social psychology of intergroup relations.* London: Academic Press, 1978.

Giles, H. Ethnicity markers in speech. In K. R. Scherer and H. Giles (Eds.), *Social markers in speech.* Cambridge: Cambridge University Press, 1979.

Giles, H. Accommodation theory: Some new directions. In S. de Silva (Ed.), *Aspects of linguistic behavior.* York: University of York Press, 1980.

Giles, H., Bourhis, R. Y., and Taylor, D. M. Towards a theory of language in ethnic group relations. In H. Giles (Ed.), *Language, ethnicity, and intergroup relations.* London: Academic Press, 1977.

Giles, H., Brown, B. L., and Thakerar, J. N. *The effects of speech rate, accent and context on the attribution of a speaker's personality characteristics.* Unpublished manuscript, 1981.

Giles, H., and Byrne, J. L. An intergroup model of second language learning. *Journal of Multicultural and Multilingual Development,* forthcoming.

Giles, H., Hewstone, M., and St. Clair, R. N. Cognitive structures and a social psychology of language: New theoretical models and an overview. In H. Giles and R. N. St. Clair (Eds.), *Recent advances in language, communication and social psychology.* Hillsdale, NJ: Erlbaum, forthcoming.

Giles, H., and Johnson, P. The role of language in ethnic group relations. In J. C. Turner and H. Giles (Eds.), *Intergroup behavior.* Chicago: University of Chicago Press, 1981.

Giles, H., and Powesland, P. F. *Speech style and social evaluation.* London: Academic Press, 1975.

Giles, H., Scherer, K. R., and Taylor, D. M. Speech markers in social interaction. In K. R. Scherer and H. Giles (Eds.), *Social markers in speech.* Cambridge University Press, 1979.

Giles, H., and Smith, P. M. Accommodation theory: Optimal levels of convergence. In H. Giles and R. N. St. Clair (Eds.), *Language and social psychology.* Oxford: Blackwell, 1979.

Giles, H., Taylor, D. M., and Bourhis, R. Y. Towards a theory of interpersonal accommodation through language: Some Canadian data. *Language in Society,* 1973, *2,* 177-192.

Grush, J. E., Clore, G. L., and Costin, F. Dissimilarity and attraction: When differences make a difference. *Journal of Personality and Social Psychology,* 1975, *32,* 783-789.

Hamilton, D. L. A cognitive-attributional analysis of stereotyping. In L. Berkowitz (Ed.), *Advances in experimental social psychology* (Vol. 12). New York: Academic Press, 1979.

Harris, M. B., and Baudin, H. The language of altruism: The effects of language, dress, and ethnic group. *Journal of Social Psychology,* 1973, *97,* 37-41.

Harrison, G. and Piette, A. B. Young bilingual children's language selection. *Journal of Multicultural and Multilingual Development,* 1980, *1,* 217-230.

Heckel, R. V., Wiggins, S. L., and Salzberg, H. C. The effect of musical tempo in varying operant speech levels in group psychotherapy. *Journal of Clinical Psychology,* 1963, *19,* 129.

Heider, F. *The psychology of interpersonal relations.* New York: John Wiley, 1958.

Helfrich, H. Age markers in speech. In K. R. Scherer and H. Giles (Eds.), *Social markers in speech.* Cambridge: Cambridge University Press, 1979.

Hewes, D. E. The sequential analysis of social interaction. *Quarterly Journal of Speech,* 1979, *65,* 56-73.

Higgins, E. T. The "communication game": Implications for social cognition and persuasion. In E. T. Higgins, C. P. Herman, and M. P. Zanna (Eds.), *Social cognition: The Ontario Symposium.* Hillsdale, NJ: Erlbaum, 1980.

Hildebrandt, N., and Giles, H. The English language in Japan: A social psychological approach. *Journal of the Japanese Association of Language Teachers,* 1980, *2,* 63-88.

Israel, J., and Tajfel, H. *The context of social psychology: A critical assessment.* London: Academic Press, 1972.

Jaffe, J., and Feldstein, S. *Rhythms of dialogue.* London: Academic Press, 1970.

Jakobson, R. *Child, language, aphasia, and phonological universals.* The Hague: Mouton, 1968.

Kiesler, C. A., and Jones, J. M. The interactive effects of commitment and forewarning: Three experiments. In C. A. Kiesler (Ed.), *The psychology of commitment.* New York: Academic Press, 1971.

Knapp, M. L., Ellis, D. G., and Williams, B. A. Perceptions of communication behavior associated with relationship terms. *Communication Monographs,* 1980, *47,* 262-278.

Kramarae, C. Women and men speaking. Rowley, MA: Newbury House, 1981.

Labov, W. *The social stratification of English in New York City.* Washington, DC: Center for Applied Linguistics, 1966.

Lambert, W. E., and Lambert, W. W. *Social psychology.* Englewood Cliffs, NJ: Prentice-Hall, 1972.

Lane, H. L., and Tranel, B. The Lombard reflex and the role of hearing in speech. *Journal of Speech and Hearing Research,* 1971, *14,* 677-709.

Langer, E. J. Rethinking the role of thought in social interaction. In J. H. Harvey, W. J. Ickes, and R. F. Kidd (Eds.), *New directions in attribution research* (Vol. 2). Hillsdale, NJ: Erlbaum, 1978.

Larsen, K., Martin, H., and Giles, H. Anticipated social cost and interpersonal accommodation. *Human Communication Research,* 1977, *3,* 303-308.

Lauver, P. J., Kelley, J. D., and Froehle, T. C. Client reaction time and counselor verbal behavior in an interview setting. *Journal of Consulting Psychology,* 1971, *18,* 26-30.

Matarazzo, J. D. A speech interaction system. In D. J. Kiesler (Ed.), *The process of psychotherapy.* Chicago: Aldine, 1973.

Matarazzo, J. D., and Wiens, A. N. *The interview: Research on its anatomy and structure.* Chicago: Aldine, 1973.

Matarazzo, J. D., Wiens, A. N., Matarazzo, R. G., and Saslow, W. G. Speech and silence behavior in clinical psychotherapy and its laboratory correlates. In J. Schlier, H. Hunt,

J. D. Matarazzo, and C. Savage (Eds.), *Research in psychotherapy* (Vol. 3). Washington, DC: American Psychological Association, 1968.

Meltzer, L., Morris, W., and Hayes, D. Interruption outcomes and vocal amplitude: Explorations in social psychophysics. *Journal of Personality and Social Psychology*, 1971, *18*, 392-402.

Miller, G. R., and Steinberg, M. *Between people: A new analysis of interpersonal communication.* Chicago: Science Research Associates, 1971.

Murray, D. C. Talk, silence and anxiety. *Psychological Bulletin*, 1971, *75*, 224-260.

Myers, D. G., and Lamm, H. The group polarization phenomen. *Psychological Bulletin*, 1976, *83*, 602-627.

Natale, M. Convergence of mean vocal intensity in dyadic communication as a function of social desirability. *Journal of Personality and Social Psychology*, 1975, *32*, 790-804. (a)

Natale, M. Social desirability as related to convergence of temporal speech patterns. *Perceptual and Motor Skills*, 1975, *40*, 827-830. (b)

Nisbett, R. E., and Wilson, T. D. The halo effect: Evidence for the unconscious alteration of judgments. *Journal of Personality and Social Psychology*, 1977, *35*, 250-256. (a)

Nisbett, R. E., and Wilson, T. D. Telling more than we can know: Verbal reports on mental processes. *Psychological Review*, 1977, *84*, 231-259. (b)

Norman, D. A. Categorization of action slips. *Psychological Review*, 1981, *88*, 1-15.

Norman, D. A., and Shallice, T. *Attention to action: Willed and automatic control of behavior.* Unpublished manuscript, Center for Human Processing, University of California—San Diego, La Jolla, 1980.

O'Keefe, B. J., and Delia, J. G. Psychological and interactional dimensions of communicative development. In H. Giles and and R. N. St. Clair (Eds.), *Recent advances in language, communication and social psychology.* Hillsdale, NJ: Erlbaum, forthcoming.

Parkin, D. Emergent and stabilized multilingualism: Poly-ethnic peer groups in Urban Kenya. In H. Giles (Ed.), *Language, ethnicity, and intergroup relations.* London: Academic Press, 1977.

Platt, J. Review of H. Giles and P. F. Powesland, *Speech style and social evaluation.* *Lingua,* 1977, *28*, 98-100.

Platt, J. and Weber, H. Speech accommodation miscarried: An investigation into inappropriate accommodation strategies. *International Journal of the Sociology of Language,* forthcoming.

Powesland, P. F., and Giles, H. Persuasiveness and accent-message incompatibility. *Human Relations*, 1975, *28*, 85-93.

Putman, W., and Street, R. L., Jr. The conception and perception of noncontent speech performance: Implications for speech accommodation theory. *International Journal of the Sociology of Language,* forthcoming.

Robinson, W. P. Speech markers and social class. In K. R. Scherer and H. Giles (Eds.), *Social markers in speech.* Cambridge: Cambridge University Press, 1979.

Rommetveit, R. On the architectures of intersubjectivity. In R. Rommetveit and R. M. Blaker (Eds.), *Studies of language thought and verbal communication.* London: Academic Press, 1979.

Ryan, E. B. Why do low prestige language varieties persist? In H. Giles and R. N. St. Clair (Eds.), *Language and social psychology.* Baltimore: University Park Press, 1979.

Ryan, E. B., and Giles, H. *Attitudes toward language variation: Social and applied contexts.* London: Edward Arnold, 1982.

Sampson, E. E. Cognitive psychology as ideology. *American Psychologist*, 1981, *36*, 730-743.

Sandilands, M. L., and Fleury, N. C. Unilinguals in des milieux bilingues: one analyse of attributions. *Canadian Journal of Behavioral Science*, 1979, *11*, 164-168.

Scherer, K. R. Personality markers in speech. In K. R. Scherer and H. Giles (Eds.), *Social markers in speech*. Cambridge: Cambridge Unviersity Press, 1979.

Scherer, K. R., and Giles, H. *Social markers in speech*. Cambridge: Cambridge University Press, 1979.

Scotton, C. M., and Ury, W. Bilingual strategies: The social functions of code switching. *International Journal of the Sociology of Language*, 1977, *13*, 5-20.

Sebastian, R. J., Ryan, E. B., and Corso, L. Social judgments of speakers with differing degrees of accent. *Social Behavior and Personality*, forthcoming.

Segalowitz, N., and Gatbonton, E. Studies of the non-fluent bilingual. In P. Hornby (Ed.), *Bilingualism: Psychological and social implications*. New York: Academic Press, 1977.

Simard, L., Taylor, D. M., and Giles, H. Attribution processes and interpersonal accommodation in a bilingual setting. *Language and Speech*, 1976, *19*, 374-387.

Smith, B. L., Brown, B. L., Strong, W. J., and Rencher, A. G. Effects of speech rate on personality perception. *Language and Speech*, 1975, *18*, 145-152.

Smith, P. M., Giles, H., and Hewstone, M. New horizons in study of speech and social situations. In B. Bain (Ed.), *The sociogenesis of language*. New York: Plenum, 1982.

Stephenson, G. M. Intergroup bargaining and negotiation. In J. C. Turner and H. Giles (Eds.), *Intergroup behavior*. Chicago: Unviersity of Chicago Press, 1981.

Stern, D. M. Mother and infant at play: The dyadic interaction involving facial, vocal and gaze behavior. In M. Lewis and L. A. Rosenblum (Eds.), *The effect on the infant of its caregiver*. New York: John Wiley, 1974.

Street, R. L., Jr. Evaluation on noncontent speech accommodation. *Language and Communication*, 1982, *2*, 13-31.

Street, R. L., Jr., and Brady, R. M. Speech rate acceptance ranges as a function of evaluative domain, listener speech rate, and communication context. *Communication Monographs*, forthcoming.

Street, R. L., Jr., and Hopper, R. A model of speech style evaluation. In E. B. Ryan and H. Giles (Eds.), *Attitudes toward language variation: Social and applied contexts*. London: Edward Arnold, 1982.

Street, R. L., Jr., Street, N. J., and Van Kleeck, A. *Noncontent speech convergence among talkative and reticent three-year-olds*. Unpublished manuscript, 1981.

Tajfel, H. *Differentiation between social groups: Studies in intergroup behavior*. London: Academic Press, 1978.

Tajfel, H. *Social identity and intergroup relations*. Cambridge: Cambridge University Press, 1982.

Tajfel, H., and Turner, J. C. An integrative theory of intergroup conflict. In W. G. Austin and S. Worchel (Eds.), *The social psychology of intergroup relations*. Monterey, CA: Brooks/Cole, 1979.

Tajfel, H., and Wilkes, A. L. Classification and quantitative judgment. *British Journal of Psychology*, 1963, *54*, 101-114.

Tannen, D. New York Jewish conversational style. *International Journal of the Sociology of Language*, 1981, *30*, 133-149.

Taylor, D. M., and Giles, H. At the cross-road of research in language and ethnicity. In H. Giles and B. St.-Jacques (Eds.), *Language and ethnic relations*. Oxford: Pergamon, 1979.

Taylor, D. M., and Royer, S. Group processes affecting anticipated language choice in intergroup relations. In H. Giles, P. W. Robinson, and P. M. Smith (Eds.), *Language: Social psychological perspectives*. Oxford: Pergamon, 1980.

Taylor, D. M., Simard, L. M., and Papineau, D. Perceptions of cultural differences and language use: A field study in a bilingual environment. *Canadian Journal of Behavioral Science*, 1978, *10*, 181-191.

Thakerar, J. N. *Speech accommodation: Some psychological and linguistic parameters.* Unpublished doctoral dissertation, University of Bristol, 1981.

Thakerar, J. N., and Giles, H. They are—so they spoke: Noncontent speech stereotypes. *Language and Communication,* 1981, *1,* 255-262.

Thakerar, J. N., Giles, H., and Cheshire, J. Psychological and linguistic parameters of speech accommodation theory. In C. Fraser and K. R. Scherer (Eds.), *Advances in the social psychology of language.* Cambridge: Cambridge University Press, 1982.

Triandis, H. C. Some determinants of interpersonal communication. *Human Relations,* 1960, *13,* 279-287.

Trudgill, P. Sociolinguistics. Harmondsworth, England: Penguin, 1974.

Trudgill, P. Linguistic accommodation: Sociolinguistic observations on a sociopsychological theory. *Proceedings of Chicago Linguistics Circle,* forthcoming.

Turk, J. L. Power as the achievement of ends: A problematic approach in family and small group research. *Family Processes,* 1974, *13,* 39-52.

Turner, J. C. The experimental social psychology of intergroup behavior. In J. C. Turner and H. Giles (Eds.), *Intergroup behavior.* Chicago: University of Chicago Press, 1981.

Turner, J. C., and Giles, H. Introduction: The social psychology of intergroup behavior. J. C. Turner and H. Giles (Eds.), *Intergroup Behavior.* Chicago: University of Chicago Press, 1981. (a)

Turner, J. C., and Giles, H. *Intergroup behavior.* Chicago: University of Chicago Press, 1981. (b)

Valdes-Fallis, G. Code switching among bilingual Mexican-American women: Towards an understanding of sex-related language alternation. *International Journal of the Sociology of Language,* 1977, *17,* 65-72.

von Raffler-Engel, W. The unconscious element in intercultural communication. In R. N. St. Clair and H. Giles (Eds.), *The social and psychological contexts of language.* Hillsdale, NJ: Erlbaum, 1980.

Watzlawick, P., Beavin, J. H., and Jackson, D. D. *Pragmatics of human communication.* New York: Norton, 1967.

Webb, J. T. Interview synchrony. In A. W. Siegman and B. Pope (Eds.), *Studies in dyadic communication.* Oxford: Pergamon, 1972.

Welkowitz, J., Cariffe, G., and Feldstein, S. Conversational congruence as a criterion for socialization in children. *Child Development,* 1976, *47,* 269-272.

Welkowitz, J., and Feldstein, S. Dyadic interaction and induced differences in perceived similarity. *Proceeding of the 77th Annual Convention of the American Psychological Association,* 1969, *4,* 343-344.

Welkowitz, J., and Feldstein, S. Relation of experimentally manipulated interpersonal perception and psychological differentiation to the temporal patterning of conversation. *Proceedings of the 78th Annual Convention of the American Psychological Association,* 1970, *5,* 387-388.

Welkowitz, J., Feldstein, S., Finkelstein, M., and Aylesworth, L. Changes in vocal intensity as a function of interspeaker influence. *Perceptual and Motor Skills,* 1972, *35,* 715-718.

Welkowitz, J., and Kuc, M. Interrelationships among warmth, genuineness, empathy, and temporal speech patterns in interpersonal attraction. *Journal of Consulting and Clinical Psychology,* 1973, *41,* 472-473.

Williams, F. *Explorations in the linguistic attitudes of teachers.* Rowley, MA: Newbury House, 1976.

Williams, F., Whitehead, J. L., and Miller, L. Relations between attitudes and teacher expectancy. *American Education Research Journal,* 1972, *9,* 263-277.

Wolff, H. Intelligiblity and inter-ethnic attitudes. *Anthropological Linguistics,* 1959, *1,* 34-41.

7

Social Cognition

THE UNWANTED JUROR?

Gerald R. Miller

*It is . . . interesting to note that the symbol of justice stands
with a sword in her right hand, a pair of balance
scales in her left, and a blindfold over her
eyes—she can only hear!*

Maier and Thurber (1968: 30)

Despite the metaphorical appeal of a blind Lady Justice, the fact remains that participants in the legal process usually can see. Furthermore, as Maier and Thurber grant, these legal actors do not share the wise monkey's ability to "hear no evil." Trials and other legal hearings are highly rule-governed communication events (Miller and Fontes, 1979), and as a result, issues regarding the influence of social cognition —"how people think about people" (Wegner and Vallacher, 1977: Ch. 1)—are important to both legal processes and legal outcomes.

These issues become particularly crucial if one subscribes to an image of the trial as a test of credibility (Miller and Boster, 1977). Notwithstanding the ideological power of alternative visions such as "the search for truth," realism dictates at least tentative acceptance of the test-of-credibility image. Legal decisions are almost always grounded in probability rather than certainty; seldom can the guilt or innocence, the liability or nonliability of a defendant be unambiguously verified. Even in those infrequent instances when a confession has been obtained, questions regarding possible coercive tactics are almost certain to arise: Was the confession given freely by the defendant—*internally* motivated, caused, or controlled—or extracted by blatant or subtle environmental pressures—*externally* motivated, caused, or controlled? Because of the element of contingency that accompanies most legal decision making, social cognition is a powerful determinant of outcomes. Boster and I summarize the situation thusly:

> Since factual information and evidence are necessarily incomplete and biased, those charged with decision-making, whether they be judges or jurors, must not only weigh the information and evidence, but must also evaluate the veracity of the opposing evidential and informational sources. Making these judgments of credibility demands attention not only to the factual information presented, but also to the way in which it is presented, the apparent qualifications of witnesses, and numerous other relevant factors. In short, the judge or jurors must survey the rich field of stimuli that constitutes the trial setting and select cues which permit judgments about the probable trustworthiness and/or competence of particular witnesses [Miller and Boster, 1977: 28-29].

Indeed, by emphasizing the trial setting per se and by focusing on assessments of witnesses, the preceding quotation unduly restricts the role of social cognition in the legal process. Person perception and attributional processes that occur during the trial are markedly affected by pretrial happenings, most of which involve communication. Social cognition is not limited to witnesses; it extends to litigants, attorneys, judges, and all other trial participants. When verdicts are rendered by juries, social cognition invades the jury room and influences the outcome of deliberative processes. In short, from the time a forthcoming trial becomes public knowledge until the moment a verdict is delivered and a sentence passed, social cognition is a key psychic and communicative arbiter. While space does not permit a thorough examination of all facets of this arbitration process, the major sections of this chapter seek to provide a flavor of it.

Though not central to this chapter, it should be noted that the basic foundations of American jurisprudence, including its prevailing conception of justice, are rooted in an attributional distinction. To be guilty or legally liable, a defendant must be judged to be *personally responsible* for an action; if the action can be attributed reasonably to environmental factors over which the defendant has little control, she or he is absolved of guilt or liability. Thus, if I am involved in an automobile accident that results in death or injury to an occupant of another vehicle, I am likely to be seen as personally responsible—hence, criminally negligent or civilly liable—if it can be shown that I drove recklessly or overimbibed before taking the wheel. Conversely, if the accident stemmed from an unexpected failure of my brakes, I am likely to be exonerated, assuming, of course, that I have shown a prudent concern for having the car serviced and repaired.

Usually, the question of whether actions should be viewed as personally or environmentally caused cannot itself be resolved definitively, thereby bringing into play differing perceptions of the relative hegemony of personal volition as opposed to environmental causation. Legal liberals lean toward environmental factors as causal explanations of behavior, while legal conservatives tend to place the onus of responsibility on the actor and to interpret events in terms of personal causation. Thus, on the very day these words were written, President Reagan delivered a speech to an audience of law enforcement officials stressing the need to impose greater personal responsibility on individuals who commit criminal acts. In a similar vein, concern over *what* president will appoint replacements for retiring U.S. Supreme Court justices often centers on whether personal or environmental causes should be assigned priority when interpreting legal statutes.

Interesting as these global issues of social cognition may be, this chapter examines possible influences of social cognition on legal communication with a more modest objective in mind. Specifically, it discusses some ways social cognition may impact both pretrial and trial processes, emphasizing the role of communication in shaping the perceptions of triers-of-fact, especially jurors. Stated differently, it assumes that verbal and nonverbal messages influence the ways legal decision makers think about trial participants and, in turn, that these influences affect juridic decisions. I hope not only to identify areas in which social cognition fails to serve abstract legal principles of due process and justice, but also to suggest fruitful avenues for future research in legal communication.

Pretrial Communication and Social Cognition

During one of the most notorious trials of the past several decades, the Charles Manson murder trial, defense attorneys moved unsuccessfully on three occasions to have the trial terminated because Manson could not possible receive a fair hearing in a locale saturated with prejudicial pretrial communication. Even co-prosecutor Vincent Bugliosi (1970), who would eventually author the best-selling account of the crimes and their judicial aftermath, granted that the Manson case would be "one of the biggest cases in history regarding prejudicial publicity."

Clearly, publicity preceding the trial was of the kind calculated to influence perceptions and attributions about Manson and his "family." Habitual use of drugs, communal sex orgies, and preoccupation with death and violence—all practices and attitudes linked to Manson and his followers—can be expected to trigger intensely negative interpersonal evaluations. Most biasing, perhaps, were the repeated references to Manson's hypnotic, almost satanic power over other members of his "cult," a term itself certain to engender anxiety on the part of most middle-class, at least somewhat God-fearing citizens of Southern California. Buttressing these messages about perverse practices and unhealthy interpersonal control were the numerous striking descriptions of Manson's physical appearance: his piercing, menacing eyes, his baleful glances at his followers and other persons in the courtroom, and so on. If ever words were ideally chosen to encourage attributions such as "immoral," "fiendish," and "evil," the media accounts of the Manson case qualify as a prototypical case study.

It can be argued, of course, that the preceding example itself smacks of bias—that communicative circumstances are seldom as extreme as in the Tate and LaBianca murders. While undoubtedly correct, this contention is open to at least two lines of refutation. From the standpoint of legal values, guarantees of justice and due process are to be extended to *all* defendants, no matter how personally repugnant or socially deviant. In the case in question, the central legal issue is whether or not Manson and his followers murdered Sharon Tate and the LaBiancas, not whether they used drugs indiscriminately, engaged in wanton sexual excesses, or promulgated a violent social ideology. To the extent that pretrial communication stressing these latter activities created a cognitive climate that made reasonably dispassionate resolution of the central legal issue impossible, Manson and his clan, *regardless of their actual guilt or innocence*, did not receive a fair trial, and the abstract ends of justice were thus subverted.

Since many would deem it naive to anticipate that any value can be realized universally and without exception, a second line of refutation holds that pretrial messages need not be as connotatively extreme as those relating to the Manson family in order to trigger negatively or positively prejudicial perceptions of trial participants. Indeed, in terms of the social cognition processes central to this volume, the following relationship can be posited as a useful working hypothesis: Any personal information about trial participants communicated to triers-of-fact has the potential for activating social cognition processes that interfere with due process and undermine the ultimate judicial objective of fair and just proceedings.

Although the hypothesis is phrased so broadly as to render its convincing verification an impossibility at most, or a laborious undertaking at least, the scant research evidence available generally seems to support it, though not without exception. Studies by Kline and Jess (1966) and Tans and Chaffee (1966) suggest that jurors face difficulties when attempting to eliminate prejudicial pretrial publicity from their decisional equations. For instance, all four role-playing juries exposed to prejudicial pretrial communication by Kline and Jess mentioned the information during deliberation, and although in three instances a member of the jury reminded other members of the judge's admonition to disregard the information, the researchers report that the fourth jury actively used the information in reaching a verdict. By contrast, Simon (1966) found that when explicitly told to disregard prejudicial information appearing in sensational newspaper stories, jurors who read such accounts returned no more guilty verdicts than jurors who read less sensational stories, a result that argues against undue emphasis on the role of pretrial communication as a cognitive mediator of judicial decisions.

Because of procedural limitations associated with the previous studies, generalizations to actual legal settings must be offered cautiously at best. The small number of juries used in several investigations mandates against confident interpretation, as do the juror samples used and the simulation procedures employed. Role-playing college students depart markedly from the demographic characteristics of actual venirepersons; to mention but a few potentially important differences, they are younger, better educated, and usually more intimately acquainted with the mysteries of social science research. Severely truncated simulations—typically, brief, written synopses of the case—screen out much of the communication occurring during actual pretrial and trial stages and may often result in unrealistic "highlighting" or emphasis of independent variables (Colasanto and Sanders, 1976; Miller et al., 1981). Finally, the "let's pretend" aura of such role-playing simulations may culminate in information-processing and decision-making behaviors deviating markedly from those of jurors charged with the responsibility of reaching verdicts that have profound effects on the lives of the involved parties.

As yet, the most realistic studies dealing with possible relationships between pretrial publicity and judicial decision making have been conducted by Padawer-Singer and Barton (1975). Using audiotaped and videotaped reenactments of a murder trial, these investigators formed juries consisting of randomly selected actual jurors from Mineola, New York, and Brooklyn, New York. *Exposed* juries were given newspaper clippings describing the defendant's prior criminal record and his retraction of a confession to the murder, and *nonexposed* juries read neutral clippings with the prejudicial information omitted. In each of two studies, a greater percentage of jurors who read the prejudiced information said they believed the defendant to be guilty, and in one of the studies, the exposed juries returned more guilty verdicts than did the nonexposed juries. Comparison of jury verdicts was impossible in the other study because the relatively short, six-hour deliberation time resulted in a preponderance of hung juries. Padawer-Singer and Barton report that when the Mineola and Brooklyn data are combined, the prejudicial materials they used approximately doubled the rate of guilty verdicts.

The legal system offers three remedies for the possible biasing effects of pretrial communication. The first remedy, mentioned earlier, is the admonition to jurors to disregard such information. As previously noted, and as research on inadmissible materials briefly discussed later in this chapter also indicates, the ability of jurors to obey this admonition is open to serious question. Once social cognition processes have been activated by incoming messages, it seems unlikely that the effects can be magically erased by a command to ignore the information. This is not to suggest that such admonitions are invariably ineffective; indeed, one promising direction for research lies in identifying the kinds of message inputs that can and cannot be disregarded, as well as examining individual difference variables that may affect a decision maker's ability to disregard prejudicial information. These kinds of questions have been largely ignored in prior research, with investigators being content to demonstrate that prejudicial information can exert an impact on verdict preferences.

A second way of dealing with potentially prejudicial pretrial information involves the change of venue. If it is determined that the place of original jurisdiction has been contaminated by pretrial messages, the proceedings are moved to another site. As long as a case is considered only locally newsworthy, this remedy may prove effective. But given the saturation potential of the media, the quest for an unbiased site for some cases is almost certain to prove futile. Is it possible for a John Gacy, an Angela Davis, a David Berkowitz, or a John Hinckley to receive a fair trial anywhere in the United States? Upon considering the amount and type of information disseminated by the media about these defendants' cases, a skeptical response to this question seems warranted.

Finally, *voir dire* may sometimes permit attorneys to discharge potential jurors who have been exposed to biasing pretrial information. Here, however, the same question arises as occurred for the change of venue remedy: What if all members of the jury pool have been privy to this information? Under such circumstances, an attorney could exhaust all peremptory challenges and all challenges for cause and still end up with a jury stacked against his or her client. Thus, in some jurisdictions, it may be impossible to impanel even a relatively impartial jury, a situation encountered by Richard Christie and his colleagues in some of their research dealing with jury selection (Christie, 1976).

Reference to the power of the media in shaping social cognitions underscores a complex dilemma faced by those who might seek to limit the availability of pretrial information: *the inherent conflict between the values of fair trial and free press.* On the one hand, permitting the media unlimited access to and communication of trial-related information is certain to endanger some people's rights to due process; on the other, unduly restrictive censorship of information impinges on freedom of the press and could eventually constitute a threat to democratic judicial processes. The ideal situation would be for researchers to discover techniques of communicating pretrial information so as to minimize its prejudicial effects, thereby establishing a balance between these two crucial societal values. Unfortunately, research to date has not even scratched the surface of this important problem.

In concluding this section, it seems prudent to stress that efforts to reduce the effects of pretrial information on the social cognition processes of judicial decision makers are, of necessity, restricted to tightly defined spheres of information. Frequently, adversaries in a legal hearing bring to the courtroom backgrounds and images that are bound to influence the perceptions and attributions of jurors, and it would be impossible to purge this information from jurors' psyches. No doubt the *National Enquirer* and Carol Burnett are perceived quite differently by most potential jurors, and these differing perceptions are likely to come into play if jurors are asked to decide whether Burnett has been libeled by the *Enquirer*. But although the *Enquirer* may have to bear the cross of its questionable general reputation, it should not have to contend with the angry outbursts of Johnny Carson on his *Tonight* show while the trial is in progress, a judgment concurred with by the presiding judge, who dismissed several jurors who had viewed Carson's program. There are enough potentially biasing communication factors during the trial proper without creating situations in which decision makers enter the courtroom with their verdicts already cast. We now turn to a discussion of certain communication processes within the trial itself and consider their possible influence on the social cognition of jurors.

Trial Communication and Social Cognition

Social cognition processes enter into the communicative give-and-take of the trial itself in numerous ways. This section considers four trial-related areas in which social cognition may exert a strong influence on eventual judicial decision making: the *voir dire* process, personal characteristics of trial defendants, assessments of witness demeanor, and the presentation of inadmissible materials. Though these four certainly do not exhaust the available possibilities, examination of them should underscore the potential import of such cognitive activities as person perception and attributional judgments for trial processes and outcomes.

The *Voir Dire* Process

An idealistic vision of *voir dire* paints it as a process in which potential jurors who harbor biases about the case are purged from the jury box, thereby ensuring an unprejudiced tribunal of peers to arrive at a verdict. Actually, *voir dire* is a rough-and-tumble interrogative and persuasive event, with both attorneys not only seeking to screen out individuals who will be biased against their clients but also striving to seat jurors who will respond favorably to their cases. Judgments about the direction of potential jurors' biases inevitably involve assessments of how they they think about other people, with inferences about their probable attitudes and potential prejudices based largely on relevant demographic and personality characteristics. These characteristics may be apparent at the beginning or may be teased out during *voir dire* questioning.

In some areas, the courts have held that certain kinds of jury composition constitute prima facie grounds for probable violation of due process. For example, trying black defendants before a jury composed entirely of whites—until recently, a common practice in certain jurisdictions where blacks were largely excluded from jury duty—has resulted in appellate reversals based on failure to ensure due process. This ruling rests largely on the belief that the social cognition processes of white jurors asked to pass judgments on black defendants will be colored by the numerous negative attributions associated with the process of racial stereotyping. As will be explored more fully in the discussion of defendant characteristics, there is empirical support for this belief, as well as for the related view that black jurors are likely to possess more negative attitudes toward white defendants.

A similar argument can be leveled regarding the sexual makeup of juries, particularly when the case involves certain types of alleged victimizations of one sex. Thus, the prosecutor in a sexual assault case is not likely to feel sanguine about an all-male jury, nor is the defense attorney likely to be pleased with a jury composed entirely of women. Once again, social cognition processes are inextricably bound up in these varying preferences: The prosecutor assumes that an all-male jury may bring with it negative attributions and perceptions regarding the kind of woman who levels sexual assault charges, and realizes the defense attorney's arguments and questions during the trial will probably aim at triggering the salience of these negative social cognitions. Conversely, the defense attorney assumes that a jury made up solely of women is likely to sympathize excessively with the alleged victim and to perceive the defendant as an exceedingly unsavory person. Although sexual assault, with its attendant social taboos and strongly sexist overtones, provides the most dramatic example of the type of case that may produce gender bias in jurors, other areas of litigation are also fair game for juror sex differences. For example, the widely publicized "palimony" civil case, *Marvin* v. *Marvin*, dealt with issues that might be expected to excite sympathy for the litigants on the part of same-sex jurors. It should be stressed, however, that the preceding discussion about the possible impact of juror sex on social cognition is largely speculative and as yet unsupported by research. In fact, as far as women jurors are concerned, some persuasion research indicates that women evaluate other women less favorably than do men (Burgoon and Miller, forthcoming; Miller and McReynolds, 1973).

Characteristics such as racial or ethnic origin and sex can almost always be determined by casual scrutiny of potential jurors. Ideological biases and personality traits, on the other hand, are not as easily identified. As a consequence, inferences about these juror characteristics are usually arrived at through *voir dire* questioning or by systematic assessments of venire panels carried out by social scientists (Berk, 1976; Christie, 1976; Kairys et al., 1975; Schulman et al., 1973). These assessments typically seek to identify jurors whose psychological profiles suggest they will be minimally prejudiced against, or even somewhat biased in favor of, one of the trial principals, most frequently the defendant.

One trait that can be expected to influence cognitive processing and subsequent decision making is the relative dogmatism or authoritarianism of jurors. Several studies have shown that highly dogmatic and authoritarian jurors return more guilty verdicts and are more punitive in their sentencing recommendations (Boehm, 1968; Mitchell and Byrne, 1972, 1973). In a related vein, Nemeth and Sosis (1973) found that liberal jurors gave more lenient sentences than conservative jurors to a white defendant convicted of negligent automobile homicide, but that the two groups did not differ in severity of sentencing when the defendant was Black. This finding underscores the importance of examining possible conjunctive relationships between juror and defendant characteristics when attempting to weigh the impact of social cognition on judicial decision making.

Christie (1976) offers an interesting comparison of the methods used by lawyers and social scientists in jury selection. Underlying the interest of both groups in identifying optimally desirable jurors is the belief that differences in characteristics such as civil libertarianism and liberalism-conservatism will strongly influence the ways jurors perceive trial participants and will predispose them toward one of the litigants. Although attorneys are less concerned than social scientists with systematic sampling and intersubjective reliability, the attorney still operates as a naive yet astute social scientist who makes attributions about jurors on the basis of their responses to questions, their nonverbal demeanor, their social and occupational status, and other supposedly relevant indicators. When engaged in *voir dire* questioning, skilled attorneys also try to plant information and observations that bias the social cognitions of jurors (Blunk and Sales, 1977); in a real sense, persuasion during the *voir dire* aims at influencing the ways jurors perceive trial participants.

Characteristics of Trial Defendants

The widely held value that all persons are equal before the law prescribes how social cognition ought to operate in the courtroom: as a neutral, disinterested psychological spectator. Nevertheless, a large body of social science research speaks to the difficulty of achieving this unbiased state of affairs. Numerous characteristics of legal adversaries are capable of triggering cognitive processes that culminate in prejudicial judgments and decisions. Indeed, a number of potentially relevant cues reside in the verbal and nonverbal behavior of litigants; for example, physical appearance or speech dialect may cause legal decision makers to assign attributions or to arrive at personal judgments that markedly influence trial outcomes. This section examines how some of these cues influence perception of one trial principal, the defendant.

The possible biasing effects of racial cues were mentioned briefly in the earlier discussion of *voir dire*. Does a defendant's race influence verdicts and sentencing recommendations? A partial answer to this question emerges from a study by Bullock (1961) that summarizes sentencing patterns for black and white inmates confined to a Texas prison for murder, rape, or burglary. Bullock found that blacks received longer sentences than whites for burglaries, regardless of the race of the victim. In cases of rape and murder, whites received longer sentences when the crime involved a victim of the same race, but blacks received longer sentences when the rape or murder was committed against an opposite-race victim.

This latter result points to the potential complexity of generalizations linking the defendant's race with the social cognition processes of jurors and, subsequently, with their verdict and sentencing patterns. At a minimum, it is often necessary to consider both the defendant's and the victim's race. According to former Attorney General Ramsey Clark, only 455 defendants have received capital sentences for rape since 1931 (Miller and Fontes, 1979). In 405 of these cases, the defendants were black, and in every instance the victim was a white woman. Apparently, legal decision makers have typically perceived rapes inflicted on white women by black males very differently from rapes involving same-race assailants and victims or rapes involving white assailants and black victims.

The preceding generalization is further complicated by a third potentially relevant factor, the race of the juror. In a study dealing with the possible impact of several racial and evidential variables on mock jurors' judgments of defendant culpability in a rape case, Ugwuegbu (1979) found that both black and white jurors judged a dissimilar-race defendant more harshly than a similar-race defendant, particularly when the evidence was marginal. Since such cases are more likely to be tried than those in which evidence for conviction or acquittal is overwhelming, Ugwuegbu contends his results are of considerable legal significance.

In attempting to assess the overall import of the preceding findings concerning the impact of the defendant's race on verdicts and sentencing, two potential limitations should be noted. First, Bullock's (1961) statistics relating to sentencing of black and white inmates were compiled entirely in a single Texas prison. To the extent that legal decision makers in that area of the country may perceive black defendants, and, for that matter, blacks in general, differently from decision makers in other parts of the United States, it can be argued that Bullock's findings may either exaggerate or understate the influence of racial cues on sentencing judgments. Second, the descriptive and experimental studies described above have centered almost exclusively on rape trials. Because of the particularly repugnant nature of this crime, as well as the social taboos still associated with interracial sexual contacts, cognitive processes calculated to trigger more punitive judgments against racially dissimilar defendants may be particular apt to occur. In other words, rape may be an emotionally charged, atypical crime that maximizes the role of social cognition in judicial decision making.

A study by Sunnafrank and Fontes (1979), conducted with college-age respondents in Michigan, indicates that the biasing effects of racial cues probably transcend both the region of the country in which a trial is held and the particular crime being tried. Respondents were supplied with a list of 10 crimes along with pictures of 10 ostensible male offenders, five of whom were black and five of whom were white. When asked to pair each male offender with the crime he had committed, the respondents overassigned the black males to crimes such as assaulting a police officer, grand theft auto, and mugging. By contrast, white offenders were overassigned to crimes such as fraud, counterfeiting, and embezzlement. Thus, given only the nonverbal information communicated by the pictures, crime-specific racial stereotypes emerged; blacks were associated with violent crimes requiring relatively little cognitive ability, and whites were linked to nonviolent crimes requiring more intricate planning. Such stereotypes suggest that jurors may be predisposed to think differently about the criminal potentialities and preferences of various racial groups, a predisposition capable of interjecting strong negative or positive bias in the decision-making process.

Though little research has explored the possibility, certain types of jurors may be more influenced than others by nonverbal cues denoting racial or ethnic origin. The earlier-mentioned finding of Nemeth and Sosis (1973)—that liberal jurors gave more lenient sentences than conservative jurors to a white defendant convicted of negligent automobile homocide, but that sentencing severity did not differ for the two types of jurors when the defendant was black—relates to this possibility but does not support juror differences for the dissimilar-race defendant. In a similar vein, several studies reveal that highly dogmatic or highly authoritarian jurors return more guilty verdicts and recommend harsher sentences than their low-dogmatic or low-authoritarian counterparts (Boehm, 1968; Crosson, 1967; Jurow, 1971; Mitchell and Byrne, 1972, 1973). Unfortunately, none of these studies has varied the race of the defendant. Since dogmatic, authoritarian persons are often intolerant of racial and ethnic outgroups, cues denoting racially or ethnically dissimilar defendants could be expected to have a particularly strong prejudicial effect on their verdicts and sentencing recommendations.

Though the studies described above illustrate the probable complexity of relationships linking the racial or ethnic origins of defendants with the verdicts rendered and the sentences recommended by juries, the evidence suggests that legal decision makers do not respond rationally and dispassionately to the information communicated by nonverbal racial and ethnic cues. Indeed, by activating cognitive processes that culminate in biased judgments, it is likely that such cues frequently produce violations of due process and effectively impede courtroom justice. Thus while Lady Justice is symbolically blind, justice as practiced and dispensed is probably neither blind nor color-blind.

Physical attractiveness is a second defendant characteristic that has potential for triggering biasing social cognitions on the part of legal decision makers. Though beauty may, indeed, be only "skin deep," the question remains: Can legal decision makers ignore the physical appearance of defendants when attempting to assess their criminal or civil culpability? Most persons accept the idea, albeit grudgingly, that physical attractiveness confers social advantages. Furthermore, in the past dozen years these advantages have been systematically documented by a number of behavioral scientists (Berscheid and Walster, 1974; Byrne et al., 1968; Miller, 1970); with few exceptions, these investigations reveal that comeliness is an advantageous social commodity. Is the courtroom emphasis on justice and due process sufficient to dispel the psychological impact of a handsome countenance or a well-proportioned figure?

A study by Dion (1972), while not dealing directly with courtroom judgments, indicates that attractive wrongdoers are judged more leniently than unattractive offenders. Adult respondents read accounts of several offenses of differing severity committed by children of varying physical attractiveness. Severe offenses were perceived less negatively when committed by attractive children. Of particular import to the central concern of this chapter is the finding that respondents were more likely to interpret offenses committed by unattractive children as symptomatic of some enduring dispositional quality. Thus, couched in the parlance of attribution theory (Jones and Davis, 1965; Kelley, 1967; Sillars, 1982), respondents were more confident that offenses committed by unattractive transgressors provided valid evidence of a consistent, underlying personal characteristic. Moreover, they believed unattractive children were more likely to be involved in future transgressions; in the language of the legal system, they perceived the unattractive children as more likely candidates for the label, "habitual offender." Since severe sentences are sometimes justified by the probable recidivistic tendencies of defendants (the "menace to society" justification), this result underscores the possibility that attractive defendants might be sentenced to confinement less frequently or be given shorter sentences than unattractive defendants convicted of the same crime.

It should be noted that this possibility was not supported by Dion's findings, since the severity of recommended punishment did not differ significantly for attractive and unattractive children. Other studies do reveal, however, that attractive persons are likely to be punished less severely than unattractive individuals. Monahan (1941) reports that beautiful women are convicted of crimes less frequently than other defendants, and Efran (1974) indicates that respondents assigned more lenient punishments to attractive transgressors than to unattractive ones. On the whole, these studies emphasize the likelihood that nonverbal cues highlighting differences in attractiveness sometimes activate social cognition processes that influence jurors' verdicts and the severity of their recommended sentences.

As is true for nonverbal cues denoting racial and ethnic origin, the communicative impact of physical attractiveness cues on legal decision makers is probably affected by other situational or personal factors. Hocking et al. (1982) chose to vary both physical attractiveness and duration of the relationship to determine their joint effects on assessments of morality. Groups of respondents were given a scenario describing a situation in which a woman met a man in a restaurant, dined with him, and then went to his apartment and engaged in sexual intercourse. Half of the respondents were told the woman was quite attractive and the other half were told she was rather homely. In addition, half of those who were told the woman was attractive and half who were told she was unattractive were led to believe this was her first date with the man, while the remaining half were led to believe the two had been dating six months. On the basis of one of these four sets of information, respondents were asked to assess the woman's morality.

Not surprisingly, relational duration produced a significant effect such that the woman was judged less moral after engaging in sexual intercourse with a companion of one night than after engaging in intercourse with a companion she had been dating for six months. Of particular interest is the finding that the most unfavorable morality ratings were assigned to the attractive woman paired with a first-night companion. Hocking et al. tentatively invoke an attributional explanation of this result, suggesting that homely women are perceived as having little choice about their sexual activities, whereas beautiful women are perceived as having considerable personal control. Thus, the unattractive woman's behavior is largely at the mercy of the environment, while the attractive woman's actions are primarily dictated by personal moral values, a difference in perceived behavioral causality that produces harsher judgments of the attractive woman's morality when she elects to engage in sex with a relative stranger. Unfortunately, this interpretation is called into question by the finding that respondents did not differ in their ratings of degree of choice available to the attractive and unattractive woman.

Both the Hocking et al. results and their tentative interpretation differ from the earlier-mentioned findings of Dion (1972). Whereas Dion's respondents were more likely to link personal attributions to the socially unacceptable behaviors of unattractive persons, the Hocking et al. findings suggest an opposite relationship. At first glance, their results also appear to be at odds with a recent study by Jacobson (1981), which required mock jurors to make a number of judgments about a rape case. Jurors read an account describing the circumstances surrounding a rape charge leveled by a female victim against a male assailant. When the assailant was arrested, he denied the charge, asserting that he was merely out for a walk and that his presence in the vicinity and his apparent resemblance to the assailant were entirely coincidental. Accompanying the written scenario were four pairs of photographs: an attractive defendant with an attractive victim, an attractive defendant with an unattractive victim, an unattractive defendant with an attractive victim, and an unattractive defendant with an unattractive victim. After reading the scenario and examining the appropriate set of pictures, jurors indicated whether they believed the defendant's alibi, how much sympathy they had for both the defendant and the victim, whether or not they believed the defendant was guilty, and, if so, what sentence they would recommend for him.

Although women jurors were less inclined than men to believe the testimony of either alleged assailant, men and women alike placed greater credence in the alibi when it was offered by the attractive defendant. Both the attractive defendant and the attractive victim were viewed more sympathetically than their unattractive counterparts. Jurors found the attractive defendant guilty less frequently than the unattractive defendant, and those who returned guilty verdicts recommended a short sentence for the attractive defendant. Finally, both defendants were more likely to be found guilty when paired with the attractive victim.

When compared with the findings of Hocking and his associates, Jacobson's results point to the difficulties involved in attempting to identify the precise mediating cognitive processes that give rise to a particular set of judgments. Borrowing a page from the Hocking et al. study, it could be argued that jurors should evaluate attractive rape defendants more harshly. Because attractive males presumably have greater opportunity for normatively acceptable sexual contacts, recourse to an odious crime such as rape should more readily be taken as evidence of a depraved, immoral character. By contrast, unattractive males, largely deprived of conventional sexual outlets, may be driven to seek gratification forcibly. Thus, while rape will certainly not be condoned under any circumstances, jurors might be expected to deal with unattractive defendants somewhat more leniently by virtue of the fact that their behavior can more readily be perceived as resulting at least partially from environmental, rather than personal, causes.

There is, however, a key difference between the scenarios used in the two studies. Respondents in the Hocking et al. study were told unequivocally that the two parties had engaged in sexual relations; consequently, they were not required to decide whether the events had actually occurred. By contrast, respondents in the Jacobson study had to determine the likelihood that the defendant had actually raped the victim, a judgment more closely akin to the task faced by jurors in a trial setting. These latter respondents may have reasoned that an attractive male would be less likely to resort to rape, since he should be capable of finding other outlets for satisfying sexual needs. Such reasoning would explain both the greater credence placed in the attractive defendant's alibi and the tendency to accord him greater sympathy for his plight. Currently, several of us are conducting an extended replication of Jacobson's investigation, with half of the respondents being asked to assess the alleged assailant's probable culpability and the remaining half being told that his commission of the rape is an established fact. We have hypothesized that respondents asked to determine culpability will treat the attractive defendant more leniently, as was true in the Jacobson study, while those told that the defendant's participation in the rape is an established fact will evaluate the attractive defendant more harshly, as was true in the Hocking et al. study.

The preceding discussion emphasizes the probable conjunctive relationship between defendant attractiveness and the type of crime supposedly perpetrated. More specifically, Sigall and Ostrove (1975) have hypothesized that if physical attractiveness seems unrelated to successful commission of a crime—that is, if the crime is attractiveness-unrelated, as in the case of burglary or automobile theft—unattractive defendants will be judged more severely than attractive ones, but if physical attraction appears to facilitate successful commission of a crime—if the crime is attractiveness-related, as in the case of a swindle or confidence game—more punitive judgments will be directed at the attractive defendant. Results of Sigall and Ostrove's study substantiated this predicted interaction: An unattractive female defendant received a more severe sentence for the attractiveness-unrelated crime of burglary, while an attractive female defendant was sentenced more harshly for the attractiveness-related crime of a swindle.

This discussion of prior research dealing with the influence of physical attraction on judgments of wrongdoing has sought to illustrate how certain nonverbal characteristics of defendants may influence the cognitive processes of legal decision makers. Perhaps the present situation can best be summarized as follows:

> From a communication perspective . . . findings indicate that nonverbal cues denoting varying levels of physical attraction will be interpreted

differently by jurors depending upon other relevant features of the case. Thus, as with cues denoting racial or ethnic origin, we are left with the conclusion that considerable research examining potentially important variables must be conducted before it will be possible to specify the precise effects of these defendant nonverbal characteristics across a variety of trial circumstances and contexts. Although this conclusion is scientifically appropriate, it leaves open the possibility of miscarriages of justice resulting from unspecifiable effects on the responses of jurors produced by the nonverbal demeanor of defendants. That some of these miscarriages may operate in the defendant's favor and others to his or her detriment does not lessen the severity of the legal problem a whit [Miller and Bundens, 1982: 135].

Whatever the eventual outcome of such research, it seems clear that social cognition acts as a filter to influence jurors' perceptions of defendants and ultimately to affect the judgments rendered for or against them.

Assessing Witness Demeanor

The role of social cognition in legal decision making is also apparent upon considering the challenge of assessing the demeanor, or credibility, of witnesses. As emphasized earlier, the contingent nature of legal judgments often requires jurors to evaluate the accuracy and/or veracity of conflicting testimonial accounts. Such witness evaluations may or may not involve the issue of deliberate deceit. In some instances, jurors absolve the witness of any deliberate duplicity, reasoning that he or she is trying to testify honestly but is uncertain about the events that transpired. Often, however, perceptions of deceptive behavior emerge, and jurors "mentally indict the witness for lying," concluding "'I believe this witness is a perjurer'" (Miller and Burgoon, 1982: 170).

Since such judgments of veracity are frequently central to the decision-making process, it seems reasonable to ask how successful jurors are likely to be when attempting to assess the truthfulness of relative strangers. There is an abundant supply of folklore and conventional wisdom regarding the ways liars behave, particularly nonverbally, and most individuals probably believe they know what "clues" to look for in order to determine whether another person is seeking to deceive them. Nevertheless, the question remains: To what extent do these stereotypical conceptions of the behaviors of liars actually assist persons in detecting deception?

Based on the results of available research, the answer to this query is far from reassuring for those parties whose personal or financial futures may depend on the ability of jurors to make accurate assessments of witness veracity. After reviewing the results of a number of studies dealing with detecting deception, Miller and Burgoon (1982) assert that three conclusions are at least tentatively warranted.

(1) *People are not notably successful at detecting deception perpetrated by relative strangers.* In most cases, observers are accurate about half the time, with overall accuracy ranging from 40 to 60 percent. Since many of the studies relied on situations that required communicators to lie and tell the truth with equal frequency, this conclusion suggests that observers charged with detecting deception were functioning at a level of accuracy that closely paralleled chance guessing; that is to say, they could have done about as well by flipping a coin to determine whether or not the communicator was lying.

(2) *Despite relatively low accuracy rates, observers report considerable confidence in their judgments.* Stated differently, people apparently believe they have successfully unmasked deceptive communicators, even though objective measures of accuracy point to the opposite conclusion. This disparity between accuracy and confidence has particularly disquieting implications for trial outcomes, since it underscores the possibility of jurors making erroneous judgments concerning the truthfulness of testimony while at the same time harboring great confidence in these mistaken assessments.

(3) *Success in detecting deception is not positively related to the amount of nonverbal information available in the message; if anything, observers are somewhat more successful when nonverbal information is minimized.* This conclusion, of course, casts doubt on the widely shared assumption that liars reveal themselves by their nonverbal behaviors. Quite to the contrary, Maier and Thurber (1968) report that detection accuracy was higher when observers listened to or read an interview containing deceptive responses, rather than watching it live; and both Bauchner et al. (1977) and Hocking et al. (1979) found no indication that amount of available nonverbal information affected the accuracy of observers who were exposed to truthful and untruthful responses via different presentational modes. Specifically, observers who viewed the communicators live or on videotape were no more accurate than observers who heard the communicators on audiotape or read typed transcripts of their lying and candid responses. For both of these latter studies, the power associated with all tests exceeded .80, indicating that the likelihood of Type II error was low. Miller and Burgoon (1982: 190) conclude that "it appears the greater access to nonverbal cues afforded by some presentational modes does not enhance detection accuracy; in fact, some evidence suggests that elimination of such cues actually leads to greater accuracy."

One possible explanation for this relative lack of success at detecting deception perpetrated by relative strangers, as well as the apparent failure of nonverbal cues to contribute positively to judgmental accuracy, is closely related to the social cognition processes of prospective jurors. It is generally assumed that a communicator's awareness of his or her intent to deceive results in heightened arousal, or drive, and, in turn, that this heightened arousal is manifested by certain nonverbal and paralinguistic behaviors. Although this assumption undoubtedly has merit—indeed, polygraph examinations rely on physiological indicators of increased arousal that accompany untruthful responses—the fact remains that antecedent conditions other than awareness of intent to deceive can also culminate in the kinds of nonverbal behaviors characteristically associated with lying. For instance, communicatively apprehensive persons (McCroskey, 1977) typically approach any communicative transaction in a highly aroused, anxious state. As a result, they are likely to engage in nervous adaptor behaviors, avoid sustained eye contact, show a high incidence of nonfluency, and engage in other nonverbal behaviors that are thought to be symptomatic of lying.

In addition, certain kinds of situational factors can also result in increased arousal and subsequent disruptions of paralinguistic and nonverbal responses. Indeed, the stress associated with testifying in an open courtroom could be sufficient to trigger the kinds of behavioral displays associated with lying, even though the witness is responding candidly. Seasoned trial attorneys are aware of this fact and sometimes rely on an examination strategy known as "white knuckling" the witness. This strategy gains its name from the occasional courtroom sight of a highly aroused, anxious witness gripping the arms of the witness-box chair ever more tightly, thus reducing circulation to the hands and causing the knuckles to become white. To heighten stress, the attorney questions the witness in a hostile, threatening manner, asking questions calculated to produce extreme embarrassment or personal distress. A classic example of white knuckling often occurs in rape trials when the defense attorney seeks to discredit the testimony of the alleged victim by raising questions about her prior sexual activities and demanding answers to extremely specific questions about the sexual assault. This line of questioning assumes that the witness will become increasingly anxious and that her anxiety will result in nonverbal behaviors that, at best, lead jurors to question the accuracy of her testimony and, at worst, cause them to brand her a liar.

The preceding example pinpoints the inferential problem faced by jurors striving to assess the credibility of courtroom testimony, a problem that provides a possible explanation for the frequent judgmental errors observed in prior research. When faced with a witness whose nonverbal behavior is hesitant and evasive, jurors must hazard a guess as to the cause of the behavioral display they are observing. Because it is common to link such displays with deceit and because the legal system places great emphasis on the importance of truth telling (consider the oath that all witnesses must swear upon taking the stand), the immediate inclination may be to doubt the veracity of the witness. Often, however, this inference may be erroneous; the witness may simply be a chronically anxious person who consistently communicates in a nervous, hesitant, uncertain manner; or certain features of the courtroom environment may have acted to produce heightened arousal and subsequent nonverbal and paralinguistic disruptions. In any event, it is likely that many communicative displays that are taken as valid evidence of intent to deceive are actually triggered by other causes.

The potential importance of social cognition to this inference-drawing process is further illustrated by the likelihood that a juror's perceptions of other aspects of the trial and its principals will influence her or his judgment of whether or not the nonverbal displays of a particular witness are evidence of prevarication. Thus, if a juror clings to the male-chauvinistic conception that "any woman who gets raped is asking for it," hesitant, evasive nonverbal behavior by an alleged rape victim is likely to be taken as a sign of deceit. Conversely, a juror who appreciates the psychological and social trauma experienced by a rape victim is more likely to infer that her uncertain communicative behaviors while on the witness stand result from the debilitating effects of extreme stress and anxiety. In either instance, the inference drawn may be correct or incorrect; the important point remains that social cognition is a crucial determinant of how the juror interprets the nonverbal behaviors of the witness.

Before leaving the issue of assessing witness demeanor, it seems prudent to note that prior research on deception detection does not closely approximate the situation faced by jurors attempting to evaluate the veracity of witnesses. None of the studies discussed above used either a real or simulated trial situation. In a number of investigations, communicators lied and told the truth about their own feelings and emotions, a procedure that departs from courtroom testimony, in which witnesses typically are responding to questions relating to past facts and events. Even when communicators were required to respond untruthfully about matters of fact—for example, when they were induced to collaborate in a cheating incident and then quizzed about their strategy for completing the task (Bauchner et al., 1977)—their answers to the questions did not reflect the continuity that usually exists in ongoing testimony elicited by an attorney. Finally, lying in these studies usually occurred spontaneously, with little opportunity to rehearse, while in an actual trial, it seems reasonable to assume that witnesses would plan and rehearse deceitful testimony. Because of these limitations, further research conducted under conditions more closely corresponding to the courtroom setting is necessary before generalizations about the precise role of social cognition in assessing witness demeanor can be offered with confidence.

Inadmissible Materials

If attorneys did not subscribe to the notion that social cognition processes intrude on the judgments of legal decision makers, the introduction of rule-violating, inadmissible materials during trials would rarely happen. Occasionally, such material may be introduced because of ignorance or honest error; but in most instances, the offending attorney probably believes that the rule-violating material will cause jurors to be favorably influenced toward his or her client's case, even if the judge admonishes jurors to disregard it. In other words, the strategy of introducing inadmissible materials—whether they be in the form of improper questioning, inappropriate testimony, or inadmissible evidence—rests on the assumption that jurors cannot erase such messages from their psyches, despite the judge's instructions to do so.

Most students of communication would undoubtedly endorse this assumption or at least some modified version of it. Such a modified version would grant the possibility that inadmissible material is sometimes relatively unimportant in the decision-making process, while at the same time holding that it can often exert a powerful effect on the social cognition of jurors. When the latter circumstance prevails, the right of due process is severely threatened because of the likelihood that jurors' decisions will be biased by information that should never have been introduced in the proceedings.

Not only may the rules of admissibility sometimes fail to blunt the cognitive impact of inadmissible materials; their implementation may, in some cases, actually heighten the effect of the offending material. This intriguing yet disquieting possibility has been probed in at least two studies. Broeder (1959) prepared three versions of an automobile liability case, each of which were presented to 10 mock juries. In the first version, where the defendant disclosed he had no liability insurance, the average award of the 10 mock juries was $33,000. In the second version, the defendant's disclosure that he had liability insurance resulted in an average award of $37,000. In the third, key version, the defendant's disclosure that he had liability insurance was ruled inadmissible, and the judge instructed jurors to disregard the information. Despite these instructions, the average award increased to $46,000, suggesting that the objection and subsequent instruction to disregard actually increased the impact of the inadmissible testimony. This conclusion is tempered by the fact that Broeder reports no tests of significance for differences among the three versions of the trial.

Reasoning from a reactance theory perspective, Wolf and Montgomery (1977) posited that if jurors are instructed to disregard inadmissible material, the material will exert a greater impact on their verdicts than if the inadmissibility is merely pointed out to them. Since reactance theory holds that threatening a previously held free behavior triggers a state of arousal directed at restoring the threatened option, jurors should see the judge's admonishment as impinging on their freedom to consider anything presented during the trial and, as a consequence, should weigh the rule-violating material more heavily in reaching their verdicts. By contrast, mere assertion that the material is inadmissible does not constitute an explicit threat to jurors' freedom to consider it but does clearly identify the illicit nature of the material, thereby increasing the likelihood of jurors disregarding it.

Role-playing jurors heard the same testimony presented under one of three conditions: a condition in which it was ruled admissible, a condition in which it was ruled inadmissible with no additional comments, and a condition in which it was ruled inadmissible and the jurors were further instructed to disregard it. As expected, when jurors were explicitly charged to disregard the inadmissible material, their verdicts were influenced in the direction of the testimony. On the other hand, when they were simply told the material was inadmissible, it had no appreciable effect on their judgments. The findings were thus consistent with reactance theory predictions. Moreover, they illustrate that full exercise of the procedures for ruling material inadmissible is sometimes not only ineffective, but actually counterproductive to achieving due process.

Veteran trial attorneys are aware that even sustained objections often have a harmful potential for their cases, and they may counter by using a tactic that Bundens and I (Miller and Bundens, 1982) label *failure to take the bait*. Rather than objecting to potentially inadmissible material, the attorney allows it to be introduced without challenge, a course of action which assumes that even a sustained objection will enhance the persuasiveness of the inadmissible material rather than purge it from the minds of the jurors. Use of this tactic implicitly endorses the view that the social cognition processes activated by inadmissible material may often exercise greater impact on judicial decision makers than the procedural and substantive rules imposed by the legal system. To counter this potential threat to due process, a number of legal professionals have advocated increased use of videotaped trials and depositions on the grounds that inadmissible material can be expunged before it intrudes on the minds of jurors (Miller and Fontes, 1979).

Before concluding unalterably that inadmissible material inevitably affects the social cognitions of jurors, thereby producing biased decision making, I should emphasize that most of the research discussed above used simulations that departed markedly from actual courtroom conditions. In most instances, the "trials" employed consisted of brief, written synopses; as noted earlier, reliance on such truncated messages may exaggerate the importance of the independent variable—in this case, the introduction of inadmissible material. Furthermore, all of the studies relied on role-playing jurors, a circumstance that could well reduce the feeling of responsibility associated with decision making and cause jurors to be less constrained by judicial instructions. The question thus remains: Is the impact of inadmissible material on juror decision making as pronounced when violations happen under more realistic trial conditions?

Several studies conducted in the context of a larger research program dealing with the effects of videotaped trials and depositions on juror responses constitute a beginning step in answering this question (Miller, 1976; Miller and Fontes, 1979). The stimulus for the first two studies was a taped, 3½-hour, reenacted trial of an actual civil case involving an automobile injury claim. One hundred and twenty jurors of the Wayne County Circuit Court (Detroit) panel participated in the first study. After being led to believe they were hearing an actual case and that their verdicts would be binding, jurors were randomly assigned to hear one of seven versions of the trial. The seven versions differed in the number of instances of inadmissible material they contained. Specifically, the number of instances of inadmissible material ranged from zero to six, with all items introduced by the plaintiff's attorney and aimed at weakening the defendant's case. Following their viewing of the trial, the jurors individually reported their verdicts, and those who found for the plaintiff also recommended a dollar amount for settlement.

There was no indication that the amount of inadmissible material contained in the trial influenced the verdicts of jurors or the amount of money recommended by those jurors finding for the plaintiff. Although there was a higher proportion of verdicts for the plaintiff in all seven trials, verdicts did not differ significantly with the amount of inadmissible material introduced. Apparently, jurors were generally able to disregard the rule-violating information in reaching their decisions.

In a second study, only three versions of the trial were used: the trials containing zero instances, three instances, and six instances of inadmissible material. This modification was occasioned by the possibility that failure to detect differences in the first study conceivably could have resulted from an overly subtle manipulation of the independent variable, that is, variations of a single instance of inadmissible testimony in a 3½-hour trial may have been insufficient to produce systematic differences in decision making. Nevertheless, as in the earlier study, the amount of inadmissible material did not affect the verdicts of individual jurors or the magnitude of their recommended awards.

Since the two previous studies relied on individual, predeliberation measures, a third study centering on postdeliberation jury verdicts was conducted to examine the possibility that discussion of inadmissible material during deliberation might subsequently influence the collective decision of the group. Two videotaped versions of a civil case involving a charge of conversion of funds by a bank were prepared, one containing no instances of inadmissible material and one containing six instances, all damaging to the defendant's case. Fifteen role-playing juries of Lansing, Michigan, adults heard each of the versions and deliberated until they reached a verdict.

Of the 15 juries exposed to the inadmissible material, 8 discussed it during deliberation. There was no evidence, however, that these discussions influenced the eventual verdict. Juries hearing the two versions of the trial did not differ in their frequency of deciding for the plaintiff, a finding consistent with the results of an earlier study by Hoffman and Brodley (1952). Consequently, though jurors were cognizant of the material and frequently alluded to it during deliberation, it did not appear to trigger biasing social cognition processes. Miller and Bundens (1982: 145) summarize the implications of the preceding three studies thusly:

Taken together, these three studies indicate that the effects of typical instances of inadmissible material on juror decision-making may not be as marked as some social scientists and legal experts have assumed. In some circumstances, jurors are not persuaded by the content of rule-violating material, even when it is discussed during deliberation. Still, since such illicit information is sometimes biasing, it seems prudent to expunge it from trial proceedings whenever possible. Furthermore, future research should determine how variations in the substance or quantity of inadmissible material affect juror behavior and examine other potentially relevant independent and dependent variables that may figure in this complex communicative process.

Commonplace as it may be, this plea for expanded research activity provides an appropriate, convenient stopping place for my discussion of the impact of inadmissible materials on the social cognition processes of jurors.

A Summation

This chapter has sought to demonstrate that certain kinds of verbal and nonverbal communication occurring before and during trial proceedings can activate social cognition processes on the part of jurors that lead to denial of due process and subvert the ends of justice. That such a demonstration is possible is not likely to come as a surprise to either social scientists or legal professionals, both of whom have long realized that the trial system in this country, while undoubtedly as good or better than the systems found in most other countries, is not without fault. Cooperative efforts on the part of both groups are necessary if these faults are to be precisely identified and remedies discovered.

How is the question posed in this chapter's title to be answered? On the basis of prior research, it appears that social cognition is sometimes an unwanted juror and sometimes a relatively impartial bystander. Much more research is required if we are to identify the communication processes that result in judgmental bias, as opposed to those which produce the relatively unprejudiced decision making that is one of the cornerstones of our judicial institutions.

References

Bauchner, J. E., Brandt, D. R., and Miller, G. R. The truth deception attribution: Effects of varying levels of information availability. In B. D. Ruben (Ed.), *Communication Yearbook 1*. New Brunswick, NJ: Transaction, 1977.

Berk, R. A. Social science and jury selection: A case study of a civil suit. In G. Bermant, C. Nemeth, and N. Vidmar (Eds.), *Psychology and the law: Research frontiers*. Lexington, MA: D. C. Heath, 1976.

Berscheid, E., and Walster, E. Physical attractiveness. In L. Berkowitz (Ed.), *Advances in experimental social psychology* (Vol. 7). New York: Academic Press, 1974.

Blunk, R. A., and Sales, B. D. Persuasion during the voir dire. In B. D. Sales (Ed.), *Psychology in the legal process*. Jamaica, NY: Spectrum, 1977.

Boehm, V. Mr. Prejudice, Miss Sympathy, and the authoritarian personality: An application of psychological measuring techniques to the problem of juror bias. *Wisconsin Law Review, 1968, 1968,* 734-750.

Broeder, D. W. The University of Chicago jury project. *Nebraska Law Review,* 1959, *38,* 744-760.

Bugliosi, V. Associated Press report from Los Angeles, California, August 6, 1970.

Bullock, H. A., Significance of the racial factor in the length of prison sentences. *Journal of Criminal Law, Criminology, and Political Science,* 1961, *52,* 411-417.

Burgoon, M., and Miller, G. R. An expectancy interpretation of language and persuasion. In H. Giles and R. N. St. Clair (Eds.), *The social and psychological contexts of language.* Hillsdale, NJ: Erlbaum, forthcoming.

Byrne, D., London, D., and Reeves, K. The effects of physical attractiveness, sex and atittude similarity on interpersonal attraction. *Journal of Personality,* 1968, *36,* 259-271.

Christie, R. Probability v. precedence: The social psychology of jury selection. In G. Bermant, C. Nemeth, and N. Vidmar (Eds.), *Psychology and the law: Research frontiers.* Lexington, MA: D. C. Heath, 1976.

Colasanto, D., and Sanders, J. From laboratory to juryroom: A review of experiments on jury decision-making. Center for Research on Social Organization Working Paper No. 136, July 1976.

Crosson, R. F. An investigation into certain personality variables among capital trial jurors. *Dissertation Abstracts,* 1967, *27,* 3668B-3669B.

Dion, K. Physical attractiveness and evaluation of children's transgressions. *Journal of Personality and Social Psychology,* 1972, *24,* 207-213.

Efran, M. E. The effect of physical appearance on the judgment of guilt, interpersonal attraction, and severity of recommended punishment in a simulated jury task. *Journal of Research in Personality,* 1974, *8,* 45-54.

Hocking, J. E., Bauchner, J. E., Kaminski, E. P., and Miller, G. R. Detecting deceptive communication from verbal, visual, and paralinguistic cues. *Human Communication Research,* 1979, *6,* 33-46.

Hocking, J. E., Walker, B. A., and Fink, E. L. Physical attractiveness and judgments of morality following an "immoral" act. *Psychological Reports, 1982, 51,* 111-116.

Hoffman, H. M., and Brodley, J. Jurors on trial. *Missouri Law Review,* 1952, *17,* 235-251.

Jacobson, M. B. Effects of victim's and defendant's physical attractiveness on subjects' judgments in a rape case. *Sex Roles,* 1981, *7,* 247-255.

Jones, E. E., and Davis, K. E. From acts to dispositions: The attribution process in person perception. In L. Berkowitz (Ed.), *Advances in experimental social psychology* (Vol. 2). New York: Academic Press, 1965.

Jurow, G. L. New data on the effect of a "death qualified" jury on the guilt determination process. *Harvard Law Review,* 1971, *84,* 567-611.

Kairys, D., Schulman, J., and Christie, R., Eds. *The jury system: New methods for reducing prejudice.* Philadelphia: Philadelphia Resistance Print Shop, 1975.

Kelley, H. H. Attribution theory in social psychology. In D. Levine (Ed.), *Nebraska Symposium on Motivation* (Vol. 15). Lincoln: University of Nebraska Press, 1967.

Kline, F. G., and Jess, P. H. Prejudicial publicity: Its effect on law school mock juries. *Journalism Quarterly,* 1966, *43,* 113-166.

Maier, N.R.F., and Thurber, J. A. Accuracy of judgments of deception when an interview is watched, heard, and read. *Personnel Psychology,* 1968, *21,* 23-30.

McCroskey, J. C. Oral communication apprehension. *Human Communication Research*, 1977, *4*, 78-96.

Miller, A. G. Role of physical attractiveness in impression formation. *Psychonomic Science*, 1970, *19*, 241-243.

Miller, G. R. The effects of videotaped trial materials on juror response. In G. Bermant, C. Nemeth, and N. Vidmar (Eds.), *Psychology and the law: Research frontiers.* Lexington, MA: D. C. Heath, 1976.

Miller, G. R., and Boster, F. J. Three images of the trial: Their implications for psychological research. In B. D. Sales (Ed.), *Psychology in the legal process.* Jamaica, NY: Spectrum, 1977.

Miller, G. R., and Bundens, R. W. Juries and communication. In B. Dervin and M. Voigt (Eds.), *Progress in communication sciences* (Vol. 3). Norwood, NJ: Ablex, 1982.

Miller, G. R., and Burgoon, J. K. Factors affecting assessments of witness credibility. In R. Bray and N. Kerr (Eds.), *The psychology of the courtroom.* New York: Academic Press, 1982.

Miller, G. R., and Fontes, N. E. *Videotape on trial: A view from the jury box.* Beverly Hills, CA: Sage, 1979.

Miller, G. R., Fontes, N. E., Boster, F. J., and Sunnafrank, M. J. *Methodological issues in jury research: Some recommendations on trial simulations.* Unpublished manuscript, Department of Communication, Michigan State University, 1981.

Miller, G. R. and McReynolds, M. Male chauvinism and source competence: A research note. *Speech Monographs*, 1973, *40*, 154-155.

Mitchell, H. E., and Byrne, D. *Minimizing the influence of irrelevant factors in the courtroom: The defendant's character, judges' instructions, and authoritarianism.* Presented at the annual convention of the Midwestern Psychological Association, Chicago, 1972.

Mitchell, H. E., and Byrne, D. The defendant's dilemma: Effects of jurors' attributions and authoritarianism on judicial decisions. *Journal of Personality and Social Psychology*, 1973, *25*, 123-129.

Monahan, F. *Women in Crime.* New York: Washburn, 1941.

Nemeth, C., and Sosis, R. H. A simulated jury study: Characteristics of the defendant and the jurors. *Journal of Social Psychology*, 1973, *90*, 221-229.

Padawer-Singer, A. M., and Barton, A. H. The impact of pretrial publicity on jurors' verdicts. In R. J. Simon (Ed.), *The jury system in America: A critical overview.* Beverly Hills, CA: Sage, 1975.

Schulman, J., Shaver, P., Colman, R., Emrick, B., and Christie, R. Recipe for a jury. *Psychology Today*, May 1973, pp. 37-44; 77; 79-84.

Sigall, H., and Ostrove, N. Beautiful but dangerous: Effects of offender attractiveness and nature of the crime on juridic judgments. *Journal of Personality and Social Psychology*, 1975, *31*, 410-414.

Sillars, A. L. Perspectives on attribution and communication: Are people "naive scientists" or are they just naive? In M. E. Roloff and C. R. Berger (Eds.), *Social cognition and communication.* Beverly Hills, CA: Sage, 1982.

Simon, R. J. Murder, juries and the press: Does sensational reporting lead to verdicts of guilty? *Transaction*, 1966, *3,*40-42.

Sunnafrank, M. J. and Fontes, N. E. *The effects of ethnic affiliation on juror responses: General and crime-specific ethnic stereotypes.* Presented at the annual convention of the Western Speech Communication Association, Los Angeles, 1979.

Tans, M. D., and Chaffee, S. H. Pretrial publicity and juror prejudice. *Journalism Quarterly*, 1966, *43*, 647-654.

Ugwuegbu, D.C.E. Racial and evidential factors in juror attribution of legal responsibility. *Journal of Experimental Social Psychology*, 1979, *15*, 133-146.

Wegner, D., and Vallacher, R. *Implicit psychology: An introduction to social cognition.* New York: Oxford University Press, 1977.

Wolf, S., and Montgomery, D. A. Effects of inadmissible evidence and level of judicial admonishment on the judgments of mock jurors. *Journal of Applied Social Psychology*, 1977, *7*, 205-219.

8

Organizational Communication

AN ASSIMILATION APPROACH

Fredric M. Jablin

Despite the fact that most organizational communication/behavior researchers accept the position that organizations can be characterized as cognitive systems ("An organization is a body of thought thought by thinking thinkers"; Weick, 1979: 42), few investigations have been directed at exploring *how* social cognition affects and is affected by organizational communication. Rather, the focus of most extant cognition-oriented research about communication in organizations has revolved around describing psychological organizational communication climates (see Jablin, 1980). As a result, we have developed techniques for measuring various cognitive and affective states of perception about organizational communication but know little about the individual cognitive processes that cause and/or facilitate the emergence of these levels of perception.

Given the limited amount of study that has been devoted to date to understanding cognitive processes and organizational communication, the present essay proposes to provide a framework for exploring such processes as well as to attempt to integrate the existing literature related to these issues. In other words, this chapter attempts to integrate relevant research from a number of disciplines (including psychology, organizational behavior, administrative science, and communication) into a coherent and heuristic model from which to explore social cognition and organizational communication.

The following discussion is organized into two major sections. The first section outlines an organizational assimilation approach to the study of organizational behavior. The latter portion of the chapter reviews existing research on communication and cognition in organizations via the assimilation paradigm. Where applicable, recommendations for future research are offered.

Organizational Assimilation: A Theoretical View

Organizational assimilation refers to the process by which organizational members become a part of, or are absorbed into, the culture of an organization. This process is perhaps better known of as organizational "role taking" (Katz and Kahn, 1966) or "role making" (Graen, 1976). The role-taking/making process can, in turn, be subdivided into two basic dimensions: (1) the organization's attempts at "socializing" the new employee to acceptable organizational behaviors and attitudes (dominant schemas), and (2) the recruit's efforts to negotiate or "individualize" his or her role in the organization.

Organizational Socialization

Van Maanen (1975: 67) suggests the following definition of organizational socialization: "the process by which a person learns the values and norms and required behaviors which permit him to participate as a member of the organization." Schein (1968: 2) adds that it is also the "process of 'learning the ropes,' the process of being indoctrinated and trained, the process of being taught what is important in an organization." Moreover, it should be noted that organizational socialization is *not* a temporary process that concludes after the first few months a new employee is on the job, but rather is a continuous one that will "change and evolve as the individual remains longer with the organization" (Porter et al., 1975: 161).

Typically, the organizational socialization process is described as involving a number of phases or stages. The initial stage in the process has been labeled the "pre-arrival" (Porter et al., 1975) or "anticipatory socialization" (Van Maanen, 1975) stage. Feldman (1976: 434) suggests that the "the main activities the individual engages in at this stage are forming expectations about jobs—transmitting, receiving, and evaluating information with prospective employers—and making decisions about employment." In other words, as a result of the potential recruit's education, previous work experience and sociocultural background, the organization's recruitment procedures, and so on, the prospective employee acquires a set of expectations about what life will be like in the organization. Hence, if the prospective employee does become a member of the organization, the "organization's socialization process does not construct a brand-new individual, so to speak, but rather attempts to reconstruct him" (Porter et al., 1975: 164).

When an individual enters into the organization, he or she begins the "encounter" phase of socialization (Van Maanen, 1975; Porter et al., 1975). Sometimes this encounter can be a "reality" (Hughes, 1958) or "role shock" (Minkler and Biller, 1979), but more often than not it "involves a pattern of day-to-day experiences in which the individual is subjected to the reinforcement policies and practices of the organization and its members" (Porter et al., 1975: 164). Essentially, if the recruit's expectations resulting from anticipatory socialization conform with the reality of organizational life, the encounter stage is one of reaffirmation, reinforcement, and confirmation. However, if the recruit has not accurately anticipated his or her role in the organization, the "role shock" can be intense and involve a "destructive phase (analytically similar to the Lewinian concept of unfreezing) which serves to detach the individual from his former expectations" (Van Maanen, 1975: 84).

The final major stage in the organizational socialization process has been termed the "metamorphosis" (Van Maanen, 1975) or "change and acquisition" (Porter et al., 1975) phase. During this stage, as a result of the recruit's various "encounters," he or she attempts to become an accepted, participating member of the organization by learning new attitudes and behaviors and/or modifying existing ones to be consistent with the organization's expectations. Caplow (1964) suggests four acquisition requirements that occur during this period: (1) developing a new self-image, (2) establishing new interpersonal relationships, (3) acquiring new values, and (4) learning a new set of behaviors. With respect to the acquisition of role behaviors, Schein (1968) argues that the recruit must learn to distinguish between three kinds of behaviors: (1) pivotal behaviors—those that the organization considers essential and must be adopted, (2) relevant behaviors—those that the organization considers highly desirable but are not an absolute necessity, and (3) peripheral behaviors—those that are not required or desirable but are permitted (often over time these become relevant behaviors).

It is essential to observe that the encounter and metamorphosis stages of socialization are to some degree a constant feature of all employees' lives (regardless of tenure in the organization). Assuming that organizations are "open systems" (see Katz and Kahn, 1966), they and their component subsystems (including personnel) are in continual flux and change. Thus, for example, when an employee who has worked in an organization for ten years is introduced to a new method of performing his or her job, the worker is experiencing an encounter stage; the period in which the employee begins to accept the new work methods could be considered the metamorphosis phase.

Individualization

While most organizational assimilation research has focused on the process from the organization's perspective, there is an equally important reciprocal process occurring from the employee's perspective: "individualization" (Porter et al., 1975) or "innovation" (Schein, 1968). As Porter et al. (1975: 170) observe, "at the same time that an organization is attempting to put its distinctive stamp on an individual, he in turn is striving to influence the organization so that it can better satisfy his own needs and his own ideas about how it can best be operated." Thus, the organizational socialization process and employee individualization process are closely linked and are probably equally important to the survival of the organization. For example, there would be very little organizational renewal without the individualization efforts of employees.

Schein (1968) and Van Maanen (1975) suggest a number of individualization strategies utilized by employees. However, prior to discussing these individualization strategies it is important to note that (1) the intensity of an employee's individualization efforts is often determined by the magnitude of the organization's socialization attempts, and (2) individualization initiatives occur along a continuum from high to low in intensity, which are presented below as "types" only for discussion purposes.

Schein (1968) has classified individualization-type behaviors into three major categories—rebellion, creative individualism, and conformity—and suggests that creative individualism is the most desirable response. A rebellion response is essentially the rejection of all organizational values and norms by the recruit. On the other hand, creative individualism refers to an employee's acceptance of pivotal values and behaviors but rejection of relevant and peripheral ones. Schein argues that this type of response is functional for the organization, since the recruit's individualization efforts infuse new and possibly more effective ideas into the system. Finally, conformity is essentially the opposite of a rebellious response; the recruit accepts all the organization's values and behaviors. Van Maanen (1975) provides a slightly different typology of individualization approaches, one that focuses on employee adjustments to relevant group and organizational socialization attempts. This schema categorizes employees as either assuming "teamplayer," "isolate," "warrior," or "outsider" individualization roles. A teamplayer is a recruit who accepts both group and organizational expectations (for example, meets organizational performance levels without "ratebusting" his or her unit's informal restrictions). An isolate is an individual who does not meet the expectations of his or her workgroup but does satisfy organizational demands (for example, a ratebuster). In contrast, a warrior is a recruit who fulfills the expectations of the workgroup (and receives support from it) but is constantly engaged in a struggle against the organization's rules, policies, and management. Finally, an outsider is a person who deviates from both the norms of the group and organization.

Role Taking/Making

Taken together, the organizational socialization and employee individualization processes describe the basic attributes of organizational role taking/making. Katz and Kahn (1966) probably provide the most parsimonious and theoretically useful model of the role-taking process. For these researchers the concept of a role "is at once the building block of social systems and the summation of the requirements with which the system confronts the individual member" (1966: 171). Defining organizations as role systems, they suggest that within an organization each "office" has a particular set of duties, rights, and privileges associated with it—that is, a role. These roles have content, are learned, have formal and informal properties, and are capable of being understood by examining the communication of expectations by relevant others. This group of relevant others is termed an office's "role set." Katz and Kahn (1966: 189) propose that an organizational member's role set generally includes those persons with whom the individual's office is directly related and who are "defined into the member's role set by virtue of the workflow, technology, and authority structure of the organization"—for example, the worker's immediate supervisor, subordinates, and co-workers in the department. Thus, in essence, it is as a result of the communication of expectations by members of the role set that the new employee "encounters" his or her organizational role and learns the values, behaviors, and patterns of interaction and thinking that are considered acceptable to the organizational system.

Several points about Katz and Kahn's model require elaboration. First, it should be noted that the expectations of role senders and the actual messages these individuals transmit to the focal person (the new employee) are not necessarily isomorphic. Specifically, because of encoding difficulties, the messages role senders intend to transmit to the focal person and the messages actually communicated are often quite disparate. Similarly, it is evident that the messages that are received by the focal person and the messages sent by role senders are not necessarily equivalent (as a result of selective perception, psychological filtering, closure, and the like on the part of the focal person). Second, inspection of the Katz and Kahn model reveals that moderating the entire role-taking process are three exogenous variables: (1) organizational factors (such as technology, authority structure, rewards and punishments, organizational policies and rules), (2) enduring attributes of the role sender(s) and the focal person (such as knowledge, ability, values, motives), and (3) interpersonal factors that define the quality of the relationship(s) between the role sender(s) and the focal person. Finally, one should be cognizant that the role-taking model suggests that initiation of role sending is a unilateral process; that is, the focal person is represented as a responder as opposed to an initiator of role sendings and thus is depicted as somewhat of a passive element of the model.

Given the failure of Katz and Kahn's (1966) role-taking model to take into consideration that recruits may "negotiate" their roles as well as respond to role sendings, Graen (1976) has recently proposed a revised role-taking model, which he terms "role making." In contrast to role taking, in role making an individual may help to mold his or her role directly by attempting to modify the expectations of members of his or her role set. Moreover, in Graen's model the recruit's superior is of central importance. As Graen (1976: 1206) argues,

> One of the crucial mechanisms that is assumed to modify the role during the process of assimilating a new member into the organization . . . is the interpersonal exchange relationship between the new role incumbent (member) and his immediate superior (leader). Although other members of the new person's role set can enter the negotiation of the definition of the new person's role, their bargaining tools are limited to informal sanctions. Only the leader is granted the authority to impose formal sanctions to back up his negotiations.

It is also important to note that the role-making approach maintains that the early dyadic relationship between superior and subordinate is crucial to the role-making process. Specifically, Graen and his colleagues have found that it is during the initial employment period that the leader and recruit develop a negotiating pattern that will eventually lead to either a "leadership" or "supervision" exchange mode of interpersonal interaction. They further contend that the type of working relationship associated with the most productive outcomes is one characterized by support, sensitivity, and trust between the interactants (see Dansereau et al., 1975).

Summary

The preceding sections have attempted to provide a theoretical perspective from which to view the role-making/assimilation process in organizations. This process has been presented as an ongoing sequence of learning and adapting to the norms, expectations, and perspectives of the organization and its members. As Schein (1968) observes, this adaption is "defined as the price of membership" in the organization.

However, it has also been proposed that new organizational members can take an active part in defining their organizational roles and that the primary individual that negotiates this set of expectations with the recruit is his or her supervisor. Furthermore, evidence has been presented which indicates that the first few months of a recruit's employment are critical to his or her development of "healthy" attitudes and behaviors within the organization. In summary, organizational assimilation has been viewed as an organizational role-taking/making process.

Organizational Assimilation, Communication, and Cognition

The assimilation approach to organizational behavior outlined above not only provides an effective framework for summarizing and integrating existing research concerned with organizational communication and cognition, but also can serve as a vehicle for proposing other potential relationships between variables related to these constructs. Specifically, an assimilation approach allows one simultaneously to explore individual cognitive and communication processes, as well as organizational processes, in dynamic rather than static terms; that is, individual behavior and organizational processes are viewed as interactive, reciprocal (although not necessarily always of equal magnitude), and occurring over time. Furthermore, this framework assumes that cognition and communication behaviors in organizations are developmental and historical in nature and, as a result, may have some degree of predictability.

The following discussion of organizational assimilation, communication, and cognition is divided into four major sections. The first three of these divisions correspond to the three major phases of the organizational socialization-individualization process: anticipatory socialization, encounter, and metamorphosis. The fourth section is concerned with a number of communication-related outcomes associated with the organizational assimilation process. Within these sections various theories of social cognition are related to organizational assimilation and communication. Existing research, where available, is reviewed and/or potential relationships between organizational assimilation, communication, and cognition are proposed.

Anticipatory Socialization

As noted earlier, the anticipatory socialization phase of organizational assimilation occurs prior to a recruit's entry into an organization. Anticipatory socialization, in turn, can be separated into two related phases: (1) anticipatory vocational (or occupational) socialization and (2) anticipatory organizational socialization.

Anticipatory Vocational Socialization. This phase has been described as a developmental exclusionary process by which the individual reduces an initially limitless number of career possibilities to a few realistic choices (see Crites, 1969). Probably the most influential contemporary theory of vocational choice is that of Super and his colleagues (1963). A basic premise of their approach is the contention that an individual's occupational preferences are an attempt to enact desired self-concepts. Essentially, Super maintains that a "person selects vocations whose requirements will provide a role which is consistent with his picture of himself" (Holland, 1976: 535). Moreover, like most contemporary theories of vocational choice, Super's theory emphasizes the individual's conscious process of testing potential self-concepts against his or her environment, evaluating their efficacy, discriminating among alternatives, and finally making a conscious decision about career direction (see Van Maanen, 1975). Interestingly, studies suggest that the process of vocational choice begins as early as the preschool years (see Vondracek and Kirchner, 1974).

To date, little research has been conducted exploring potential relationships between anticipatory vocational socialization and organizational communication. However, in one of my own studies (Jablin, 1982), I have found that children (as reported by their teachers) do learn about the communication styles of different occupations during their growth from childhood to adolescence, develop unique expectations of the communicator styles of different occupations, and probably develop these expectations to a large extent from class discussions and readings in course texts. Furthermore, my results suggest that it is probably during the process of vocational organizational communication socialization (VOCS) that people learn the initial (and often dysfunctional) communication styles they will use in the work world.

Since VOCS is essentially cognitive in nature, it seems that our understanding of the process would greatly benefit from research extrapolated from theories of social cognition. For example, implicit-self theory (see Wylie, 1973) and schema theory (Markus, 1977; Cantor and Mischel, 1977) appear appropriate to the analysis of VOCS. Specifically, these theories could be used to determine how one goes about the process of testing his or her own communication self-concept against the communication self-concepts one associates with persons in various occupations. Similarly, it would be interesting to ascertain the types of person prototypes children develop with regard to the communication styles of various occupations, and how these change over time. Moreover, one might explore how an individual's self-schemata about communication and the person prototypes he or she associates with the communication styles of various occupations are related.

Analysis of VOCS from the perspective of script theory (such as Abelson, 1976) would also seem quite useful. For example, script theory could be employed to determine how children's perceptions of the communication behaviors of persons in various occupations vary across different classes of situations, and how scripts vary between the occupations one has excluded or included as potential career avenues. Such studies might require children at various age levels to write stories (or role-play situations) describing how they believe people in the occupations they wish to enter communicate in various work contexts (for example reprimanding a subordinate, motivating workers, providing work instructions, or leading a production meeting). In turn, these stories (or videotapes) could be content analyzed to determine the types of scripts children associate with how role occupants communicate in a wide variety of everyday work situations. Cross-sectional research could focus on building a typology of communication scripts that children perceive as prevalent in work settings, while longitudinal investigations might explore how these scripts evolve over time and vary from one occupation to another.

In summary, the preceding paragraphs have attempted to outline only a few of the possible ways that theories of social cognition could be applied to the analysis of vocational organizational communication socialization. It is hoped that this discussion has demonstrated that the exploration of VOCS via theories of social cognition presents some exciting research and theory-building possibilities.

Anticipatory Organizational Socialization. This phase of socialization is concerned with the process by which the individual forms expectations of his or her job and organization prior to actually entering that organization. The information-sharing that takes place between the recruit and organization during the selection-recruitment process is considered to be a key part of this stage, particularly in terms of how it affects employment decisions. One of the primary vehicles for information exchange between applicant and organization is the selection interview.

Prior to discussing the role of the interview in anticipatory socialization, it is important to note that regardless of method of information exchange between applicant and employer, recent research suggests that the typical outcome of this process is the emergence of inflated expectations by the recruit of what his or her potential job and organization will be like (Wanous, 1977, 1980). Furthermore, a number of studies have found that the more inflated the recruit's expectations, the lower will be his or her subsequent level of job satisfaction and the higher the probability of job turnover (Wanous, 1977). Moreover, there is evidence suggesting that, upon entering organizations, recruits have inflated expectations about the communication climates of their jobs and organizations and that those who later quit their jobs tend to have more inflated initial communication expectations than those who stay (Jablin, 1979a, 1981).

Relationships between recruits' initial job expectations and their later attitudes and turnover propensities are typically explained by some form of the "met expectations hypothesis" (see Porter and Steers, 1973). As relates to communication, this hypothesis would predict that "recruits who possess inflated expectations of their organizations' communication climates will have greater difficulty meeting those 'unrealistic' expectations once on the job than recruits with less inflated expectations. . . . As a result of large discrepancies between expectations and reality, recruits with inflated communication climate expectations may have a higher probability of job turnover and/or less job satisfaction" (Jablin, 1981: 2). In other words, large discrepancies between the interpretive schemes recruits construct as a result of anticipatory socialization and what they find their organizations and jobs actually to be like often lead to negative job outcomes.

In part, recruits create unrealistic schemas of what life will be like in prospective organizations because of the manner in which they make employment decisions. Several models have been developed to explain how applicants choose an organization to work for from among their employment alternatives. Two decision-making models are predominant in the literature (Wanous, 1980). The first approach is an expectancy model, while the second is founded on implicit decision-making theory. The former process postulates that an applicant is a rational decision maker whose motivation to join an organization is a multiplicative function of his or her expectancy of being admitted to the organization and his or her attraction to the organization (Lawler, 1973). Ultimately, it is the individual's attraction to the organization that will determine if he or she will join it. In contrast, the implicit theory posits that the recruit makes an implicit and unconscious decision about job-choice criteria, makes an organizational choice, and subsequently attempts to justify the choice (Soelberg, 1967). Research findings suggest that expectancy theory is fairly accurate in predicting organizational choice, while insufficient evidence exists to evaluate the efficacy of the implicit decision-making model.

An applicant's attraction to and eventual decision to join an organization is also affected by his or her perceptions of the recruiter, the recruitment situation (typically an interview), and characteristics of the applicant himself or herself (Rynes et al., 1978). For example, a number of studies have demonstrated that characteristics of the recruiter/interviewer are often the major reason an applicant chooses to work for a particular organization (Glueck, 1973; Alderfer and McCord, 1970; Schmitt and Coyle, 1976). More specifically, research has shown that an applicant's perceptions of an interviewer are affected by the interviewer's (1) interview preparation and knowledge about the job and organization (Hilgert and Eason, 1968; Downs, 1969; Schmitt and Coyle, 1976), (2) verbal fluency and personality (Rogers and Sincoff, 1978; Sutton and Carleton, 1962; Schmitt and Coyle, 1976), and (3) age, sex and job title (Rogers and Sincoff, 1978; Wyse, 1972). However, at present we know little about how applicants cognitively organize these perceptions of their interviewers and use these data to construct interpretive schemes of what working in each organization would be like.

Focusing on the employment interview from the perspective of the recruiter, we find a considerable amount of study exploring the relationships between interviewer information-processing behavior and decisions about the employability of applicants (Mayfield, 1964; Wright, 1969; Daly, 1978). However, these studies have been more concerned with ascertaining the effects of information cues on recruiter decision-making behavior than with discovering *how* such information is being processed. For example, research in this tradition has examined the effects of information valence (Carlson and Mayfield, 1967), mode of information presentation (Peters and Toerborg, 1975), and contrast and assimilation effects of information (Hakel et al., 1970) on recruiters' employment decisions. However, it should be noted that more recent studies have begun to explore how interviewers use verbal cues from applicants and implicit personality theories in making judgments about applicants (for example, Jackson et al., 1980).

Finally, recent research utilizing attribution theory to explore interviewer information-processing and decision-making behavior warrants attention. Specifically, Tucker and Rowe (1979) suggest that since interviewer questions typically are directed at understanding the causes of an applicant's past and present behaviors, the interview essentially functions as a medium for the interviewer to make causal attributions about the applicant. By experimentally manipulating subjects' expectancies prior to reading an interview transcript, these researchers have found that a recruiter who begins an interview with a favorable applicant expectancy makes more "internal attributions about the applicant's past successes and fewer internal attributions about past failures" (Tucker and Rowe, 1979: 32) than do interviewers who begin with unfavorable applicant expectancies. Moreover, their results show that the more internal attributions the interviewer makes, the greater the probability that he or she will hire the applicant. However, the question still remains whether or not the presentation of positive or negative information about the applicant during the interview itself produces similar attributional effects. As the results of Tucker and Rowe's study suggest, examination of the employment interview from an attributional perspective presents some intriguing research possibilities. In particular, it is suggested that future investigations be directed at exploring the attributions applicants make about interviewers during the selection process, as well as how applicant and recruiter attributions interact to affect employment decisions.

Organizational Encounter

The encounter or "breaking-in" period of organizational assimilation is often a traumatic one for the new employee. During this phase the recruit's assumptions about work developed from past job experiences are often brought into question, and old attitudinal and behavioral work patterns may require reformulation. In other words, the new employee's cognitive scripts and schemas must be redefined or recalibrated and attributional models created to explain why people behave and think as they do in the new work environment. As Louis (1980) suggests, upon entering the unfamiliar organizational setting, the recruit experiences "surprises" (discrepancies), which in turn stimulate cognitive "sense-making" processes (attributing meaning to surprises) within the individual. Essentially, in order for the recruit to locate himself or herself in the time and space of the organization he or she must "normalize the setting" (Van Maanen, 1975), that is, discover what are normal and abnormal behaviors and thinking patterns in the organization. Thus, during the encounter phase of organizational assimilation the recruit is attempting to cope with the initial agitated state of "mindfulness" by beginning the process of normalizing the work setting (with the eventual goal of moving to a more adjusted state of "mindlessness"; see Langer, 1978).

The normalizing or sense-making process is essentially communicative in nature. The recruit develops initial interpretation schemes for his or her new work environment primarily from formal and informal communication received from others. Formal role requirements are transmitted primarily by the new employee's supervisor and via "official" (typically, written) downward communication sources, whereas informal or unofficial expectations are learned primarily through interactions with members of the workgroup. However, as has been noted by several researchers (for example, Graen, 1976; Weiss, 1977; Van Maanen, 1977), the creation of a particular reality may be "supported by a chorus of co-workers and subordinates, but it is usually defined for one by those in authority" (Van Maanen, 1977: 27), since those sources have the sanctions, more so than others, to upset reality.

It should also be noted that an individual's personality predispositions are also likely to affect the initial type of interpretation schemes he or she develops to explain the new work environment. As Louis (1980) observes, one's predispositions toward locus of control (Rotter, 1966) and anomie (McClosky and Schaar, 1963) probably mediate sense-making processes. Furthermore, it is likely that a recruit's cognitive complexity will affect his or her ability to conduct information searches to reduce the uncertainty of the new work setting (Herman, 1977; Stabell, 1978). Similarly, predispositions toward high or low self-monitoring, and self- versus public consciousness may affect the direction of information searches and the interpretation of information that is gathered. And obviously, a recruit's past job experiences (expectations) will interact with his or her personality predispositions and information acquired from others about the new work setting to affect the sense-making process.

In summary, the encounter stage of organizational assimilation is a time when the recruit begins to define, label, and socially map the new work environment. During this juncture the employee begins to realign existing scripts and schemas he or she has built to explain organizational life so that they are more congruent with the "reality" of the new organization. The recruit's construction of organizational "reality" is a by-product of his or her personality, past job experiences, and information derived from superiors, fellow workers, and "official" (typically, media-related) organizational sources. The effects of each of these information sources on the recruit's assimilation into the organization during encounter and metamorphosis are discussed below.

Organizational Metamorphosis

As suggested above, it is during the encounter stage of organizational assimilation that the recruit (1) becomes aware of the discrepancies between his or her attitudes, values, and behaviors and those prevailing in the organization, and (2) begins to make shifts to adapt to these incongruencies. Subsequently, during the metamorphosis or "change and acquisition" stage, the employee completes the process of building the interpretive schemes that he or she will use to understand the work environment. The manner in which the recruit changes his or her previous attitudes and behaviors during metamorphosis has often been explained by consistency or balance theories (Festinger, 1957; Newcomb, 1958; Heider, 1953), since it is expected that the recruit changes his or her views to be consistent with those of persons who are already a part of the organization's culture.

As noted in the previous section, the recruit obtains role-related information during encounter and metamorphosis from three primary sources: (1) "official" downward, media-related management sources, (2) his or her superior, and (3) members of the workgroup. Each of these sources is now discussed in terms of how it functions in the recruit's attempts to adapt to the organization's socialization efforts as well as to individualize his or her own role.

Official Downward Communication. The new recruit receives information relevant to his or her role, and why people around him or her think and behave as they do, from numerous media-related (typically, written) downward communication sources. For example, role- and organization-defining messages are communicated to employees via official house magazines and newspapers, handbooks, manuals, memos, bulletin boards, information racks, closed-circuit television, and the like (see Cutlip and Center, 1971).

Little research has been conducted exploring the role of media-related sources of downward communication in the organizational assimilation process. To date, about all we know is that recruits often have expectations that they will be receiving more information from official sources and channels of communication than they actually do (Jablin, 1979a). However, the questions of what cognitive processes lead to these expectations and what are the results of their violation still remain to be answered.

Future research exploring the effects of downward media-related communication and organizational assimilation from a social cognition perspective would seem useful. For example, extrapolating from nonassimilation research on media-related downward communication in organizations, one might hypothesize that such sources serve more to inform employees about "acceptable" interpretive schemes than to change existing ones (Weiss, 1968; Redding, 1972). Consequently, it may be that media-related communication sources play a more crucial function in the encounter stage than in the metamorphosis stage of assimilation. The work of Langer et al. (1978) on "mindlessness" and attentional processes would also appear relevant to research on media effects in organizations. Specifically, these researchers have found that the structural properties of memos can affect the degree to which recipients pay attention to the semantic communication contained within them. Assuming that organizations produce their internal media-related messages for employees not only to receive but to read and interpret, it would follow that the more often employees (and particularly recruits) consume these messages in "mindless" states, the less effective the communication. Thus, research exploring the properties of media-related organizational communiqués that result in "mindful" versus "mindless" messages might be initiated.

Superior-Subordinate Communication. As suggested earlier, most organizational socialization researchers posit that a recruiter's supervisor plays a key role in the new employee's assimilation into the organization. It is assumed that the immediate supervisor is crucial to effective assimilation because (1) the supervisor frequently interacts with the subordinate and thus may serve as a role model (Weiss, 1977), (2) the supervisor has the formal power to reward and punish the employee, (3) the supervisor mediates the formal flow of downward communication to the subordinate (for example, the supervisor serves as an interpreter/filter of management messages), and (4) the supervisor usually has a personal as well as a formal role relationship with the recruit.

Downward superior-to-subordinate communiation usually consists of five basic types of messages: job instructions, feedback about performance, job rationale (information designed to help the employee understand the relation of his or her task to tasks being performed by others), information about organizational practices and procedures, and messages designed to inculcate organizational goals (Katz and Kahn, 1966; Jablin, 1979b). In turn, upward communication from subordinate to superior usually relates information about the subordinate or his or her co-workers, feedback about organizational policies and practices, or information about tasks or work-related issues that require attention (Jablin, 1979b). Almost all cognition-oriented research on superior-subordinate communication has focused on superior-to-subordinate performance feedback and has examined this process through attributional models.

A considerable amount of research on the attribution processes of superiors in superior-subordinate interaction has been generated by

Mitchell and Green and their associates (see Mitchell et al., 1977; Green and Mitchell, 1979; Mitchell and Wood, 1980; Knowlton and Mitchell, 1980; Mitchell and Kalb, 1981). From their perspective, a superior is viewed as an information processor whose "naive causal attributions . . . mediate between the stimulus behaviors of subordinates and the behavior of the leader" (Green and Mitchell, 1979: 430). In other words, they suggest that subordinate behavior → leader attributions → leader behavior.

Many of the propositions that Green and Mitchell (1979) present relate directly to organizational assimilation and communication between superiors and subordinates. For example, they propose that whether or not a recruit's work "success or failure is ascribed to ability, effort, task, difficulty, or luck will have clear implications for the type of exchange . . . which will develop between a leader and a member" (Green and Mitchell, 1979: 435). Furthermore, they suggest that because of observer errors (Jones and Nisbett, 1972) superiors are more likely to perceive subordinate performance as resulting from internal versus external causes. Since these performance attributions may frequently be incorrect, Green and Mitchell (1979) argue that they are probably often the cause of superior-subordinate "miscommunication." Thus, it is possible that the frequent phenomenon of superior-subordinate semantic-information distance (see Jablin, 1979b) is often the result of observer errors on the part of both superiors and subordinates.

Empirical investigations of superior-subordinate interaction employing attributional analyses have supported its value as a tool for understanding leader-member behavior. Among numerous findings, results of studies have shown the following: (1) When subordinates perform poorly, superiors attribute performance more to internal factors than to external ones, and the more internal the attribution the more the supervisors' responses are directed at the subordinates (through such methods as verbal reprimand or counseling) than to the situations (for example, work schedule, staff support; see Mitchell and Wood, 1980; Kipnis et al., 1981). (2) "Effort and ability cues result in differences in performance evaluations under conditions of high and low performance" (Knowlton and Mitchell, 1980: 464). (3) Subordinate "success perceived as externally caused (e.g., task) is unlikely to result in rewards, whereas failure externally caused is more likely to produce 'sympathy and support'" from superiors (Hargrett, 1981: 67). (4) Supervisors appear to have difficulty giving "appropriate" (congruent) feedback when subordinate performance is attributed to ability versus effort (Ilgen and Knowlton, 1980). (5) While superiors generally positively distort negative feedback to low performers, this effect is more pronounced for subordinates who are believed to be poor performers because of lack of ability (Ilgen and Knowlton, 1980).

As is obvious from the above discussion, research utilizing attribution theory to understand superior-subordinate interaction has focused primarily on how superiors process information, make attributions, and provide performance feedback to subordinates. However, since superior-subordinate communication is a dynamic *reciprocal* process, it is strongly suggested that future research needs to explore how subordinates make attributions about their superiors' behaviors, and how subordinates' and superiors' attributions interact to effect communication processes. Also, it is apparent that attribution research in this area has concentrated almost solely on the performance feedback process, without consideration of how attributional processes operate when superiors and subordinates exchange other types of messages (see the earlier discussion of message types). In addition, since there is evidence that stereotypes of personal characteristics (such as sex and race) affect an individual's causal attributions (see Garland and Price, 1977; Heilman and Guzzo, 1978), research exploring their impact on communication and attribution processes in organizations should be initiated.

It is also recommended that future investigations of superior-subordinate communication be directed at exploring the cognitive processes of interactants from perspectives other than attribution theory. For example, it would be interesting to determine the degree to which a recruit's level of cognitive complexity interacts with the schemas he or she develops to explain the communicative behavior of his or her superior. Moreover, longitudinal research exploring how these communication-oriented schemas evolve over time and affect the nature of the exchange relationship between superior and subordinate is warranted (see Graen, 1976). Finally, the process of how a superior and subordinate negotiate the subordinate's individualization efforts would profit from analysis via theories of social cognition.

Workgroup and Co-Worker Communication. Through informal communication from his or her workgroup and co-workers, the recruit receives information that he or she can use to develop normative referents for "acceptable" types of behaviors and attitudes, as well as information that may help him or her to solve work-related problems (Van Maanen, 1975; Feldman, 1981). In addition, in organizations that assimilate a number of new recruits simultaneously, the members of the workgroup can serve as a buffer or "mutual defense" (Burns, 1955) against the forces of the organization's socialization efforts. In other words, the workgroup can help the new employee decode and interpret the scripts and schemas that prevail in the organization as well as cushion the impact of the recruit's organizational encounter. However, the workgroup typically will serve these functions only after the recruit has been initiated into the group and accepted by his or her fellow workers (Roy, 1952, 1955). Thus, along with the recruit's supervisor, the workgroup helps the new employee locate and define his or her place in the organization's time and space. However, it is important to keep in mind that within the organization the recruit may have many reference groups and/or be part of a number of communication networks, which may affect the development of his or her interpretive schemes (see Van Maanen, 1975).

Through ambient and discretionary stimuli (Hackman, 1976), the workgroup supplies the recruit with information relevant to the formation of interpretive schemes. Ambient stimuli are stimuli that pervade the group setting (for example, the other people in the group, the physical environment of the group's workplace, materials used in doing the task), whereas discretionary stimuli are "transmitted to individual group members at the discretion of their peers" (Hackman, 1976: 1458). In essence, ambient stimuli are unavoidable, noncontingent, and amorphous, while discretionary stimuli are intentional, controlled, and selective. Thus, discretionary stimuli from workgroups to recruits probably account for a large portion of the variation in the interpretive schemes recruits ultimately develop to explain and understand their work environments.

Communication-oriented cognition research exploring the role of workgroups in the organizational assimilation process is scarce. However, at a theoretical level, Hackman (1976) has indirectly advanced a number of propositions relevant to these processes that beg empirical investigation. For example, he suggests that ambient and discretionary stimuli serve a cueing function, in that they can inform an employee about behavior-outcome expectancies relevant to the group and organization. In respect to just discretionary stimuli, Hackman proposes that new employees often seek out stimuli (indicative of individualization efforts) in order to obtain information or group-controlled rewards. Information solicited from the group can help the recruit master his or her environment, test his or her ability level, assist in the social mapping process, and provide data on behavior-reward contingencies. And obviously, the discretionary information the group sends to the recruit may affect his or her perceptions about the group and organization, self-concept, and assessment of job knowledge and skill. Cognitive theories that have been applied mostly in nonorganizational settings to explain group initiation rites and members' subsequent attitude and behavior changes would appear appropriate to the study of the above issues—for example, dissonance theory (Festinger, 1957), self-attribution theory (Bem, 1965), expectancy theory, (Fishbein, 1967), and social comparison theory (Festinger, 1954).

Additional empirical research exploring the interaction of work-group communication, employee cognition, and organizational assimilation is sorely needed. A wide avenue of theoretical and methodological approaches to the investigation of these issues are available. For example, studies might be undertaken examining how recruits integrate their existing implicit theories of work with those that members of their workgroups communicate to them as "appropriate" models. At present, we know little about how recruits change (if at all) the manner in which they process information from their workgroups as their longevity in these groups increases. One might hypothesize that once a recruit obtains a basic perspective for interpreting the work environment, he or she may become less reliant on the group (an external source) for the construction of events and shift to more personal (internal) explanations. Since the recruit is likely to be a part of a network of embedded groups within the organization, it is probable that he or she often receives conflicting messages about organizational reality from them. Research investigating how the recruit processes these messages and constructs composite interpretive schemes should be initiated. Similarly, research directed at determining how recruits resolve potential conflicts between the interpretive schemes their workgroups accept and those that their superiors maintain should be undertaken. Finally, the manner in which recruits cognitively distinguish (if at all) between ambient and discretionary communications from their groups and strategies they employ to solicit discretionary information warrant exploration.

Communication-Related Outcomes of Assimilation

A wide variety of outcomes can be expected to result from the organizational assimilation process (see Feldman, 1981). Several of those likely to be associated with organizational communication, assimilation, and social cognition are discussed below. These include the development of perceptions of organizational communication climate, integration of organizational decision-making approaches, and some degree of work motivation and job/communication satisfaction.

Communication Climate. As a recruit is assimilated into an organization, he or she develops an evolving set of perceptions about what the organization is like as a communication system (Jablin, 1979a). However, at present we know very little about the cognitive and behavioral processes that lead an employee to these perceptions. In part, this void in our knowledge is a result of the traditional focus of communication climate research, which has been exploring the construct in terms of a number of specific a priori dimensions of communication, such as an employee's perceptions of the timeliness, accuracy, and clarity of communication received/sent from/to superiors, subordinates, and peers. As a consequence, we can determine the degree to which an individual self-reports perceptions about the existence or sufficiency of certain aspects of organizational communication, but know little about the cognitive processes that caused those perceptions. Recent research on the development of perceptions of psychological organizational climate by James and his associates (1978, 1979), however, does offer a potential direction for the study of how employees develop perceptions of communication climate.

James et al. (1978) suggest that the emergence of perceptions of psychological climate can best be studied by combining theories of cognitive social learning (Mahoney, 1977) and interaction psychology (Endler and Magnusson, 1976). Specifically, these researchers propose that in organizations "individuals respond primarily to cognitive representations of situations rather than to situations per se" (James et al., 1978: 787). As a result, they maintain, people to some degree have dissimilar cognitive interpretations of the same situations. Furthermore, James et al. argue that an individual's psychological climate perceptions are analogous to a set of higher-order schemas, which vary between individuals because of disparities in their individual cognitive construction competencies, encoding strategies, behavior-outcome and stimulus-outcome expectancies, linguistic backgrounds, need states, self-imposed goals, and prior experiences and learning.

Extrapolating from the proposals of James et al. (1978), it would seem that one way to explore how people develop their communication climate perceptions is to trace over time the schemas they employ to explain the communication environments of their organizations. Obviously, such an approach would need to pay greater attention to individual differences in perceptions and not merely consider such differences as "error" variance. Moreover, as James et al. (1978, 1979) observe, this type of positio would require a historical versus ahistorical, static view of the emergence of climate perceptions. This latter point is important, since it suggests that climate perceptions should not necessarily be viewed, as has traditionally been the case, as "accommodative or functional, bending to the need to develop an adaptive (homeostatic) person-situation fit in each new situation" (James et al., 1978: 796). In other words, this perspective assumes that "individuals have capacities to construct subjective

environments that reflect assimilation toward learned cognitive dispositions and differential attention to selected aspects of situations" (James
et al., 1979: 584). Research methodologies employing data manipulation
techniques such as multidimensional scaling, confirmatory factor analysis, and causal modeling would appear suitable for exploring climate
perceptions given the above assumptions (see James et al. 1978; Albrecht,
1979).

Work Motivation. A by-product of effective organizational assimilation should be the emergence of intrinsic work motivation within the
new employee (Feldman, 1981). Generally speaking, an individual is
considered to be intrinsically motivated when his or her behavior does
not appear to be the result of external rewards. Although communication and, in particular, feedback play an important role in the
development of intrinsic motivation (Cusella, 1980), no research that
this author is aware of has explored the relationships between communication, intrinsic motivation, and organizational assimilation. While a
number of theoretical models are available from which to initiate such
studies, a cognitive approach to intrinsic motivation proposed by Deci
(1975) and termed cognitive evaluation theory (CET) probably provides
the most inviting perspective.

According to Deci, within organizations every reward contains both
a controlling and an information aspect. If the controlling dimension of
a reward is perceived as salient by a worker, it will decrease his or her
perceptions of control or causality over the task being performed (as a
result of self-attributional and expectancy processes) and will likely lead
to lower levels of intrinsic motivation. In contrast, if the information
dimension is more salient, the employee's feelings of competence and
self-determination will increase, resulting in higher levels of intrinsic
motivation. Thus, "Deci argues that extrinsic rewards, since they are
primarily 'controlling' in nature, reduce intrinsic motivation by causing
a change in perceived locus of causality from internal to external"
(Arnold, 1976: 279). On the other hand, CET proposes that an
individual's feelings of competence and self-determination (and con-
comitantly intrinsic motivation) should be increased by feedback on
task performance, since task feedback is informational in nature.

While CET has been the subject of some controversy and criticism
(see, for example, Scott, 1975), studies have consistently supported the
hypothesis that feedback on task performance does influence workers'
feelings of competence and intrinsic motivation (Deci, 1975). This
finding would appear to have direct relevance to the study of organizational assimilation, since during the first months of employment,

recruits, in their efforts to develop interpretive schemes of their work environments, are very sensitive to any information about their job performance (Feldman, 1981). Consequently, principles of CET could be used to explore how variations in performance feedback over time and from different sources affect recruits' perceptions of intrinsic motivation.

In conclusion, it should be noted that Cusella's (1980) review and interpretation of the feedback and intrinsic motivation literature present a series of excellent propositions concerning relationships between feedback message characteristics, feedback channels, feedback sources, recipients of feedback, and the emergence of intrinsic motivation. While these propositions were not originally designed to study organizational assimilation, most do appear relevant to the process and provide an excellent point from which to initiate investigations into the relationships between feedback, intrinsic motivation, and organizational assimilation.

Decision-Making Strategies. As a recruit is assimilated into an organization, he or she learns about the predominant methods/strategies that members of the organization use to process information relevant to decision making. Over time, it is expected that the new employee will integrate these patterns of thinking with his or her existing decision-making strategies. While to date no research has explicitly explored the relationships between organizational assimilation, communication and decision making in organizations, a considerable amount of cognition-oriented information-processing research relevant to organizational decision making has been conducted. The major directions and limitations of these studies are briefly reviewed below, followed by a discussion of their, as well as other approaches', applications to the organizational assimilation process.

Research on individual decision making in organizations and information processing has followed one of two major paths: (1) building normative decision models, or (2) creating descriptions of how people make decisions (Ungson et al., 1981). Normative approaches have focused on using Bayes's theorem (for example, Raiffa and Schlaifer, 1961) to build psychological theories of inference. However, these models have come under increasing criticism (see Tversky and Kahneman, 1974) because of evidence that decision makers have biases and use heuristics that often violate Bayesian principles.

On the other hand, descriptive approaches to the study of individual decision making have been dominated by model-fitting studies, process-tracing approaches, and investigations of cognitive decision-making style (Ungson et al., 1981). Model-fitting studies have focused on using mathematical models (such as regression) to determine the ways people weight, integrate, and trade off information during decision making (see Brunswick, 1952; Dawes, 1979). In contrast, process-tracing approaches have employed decision makers' verbal protocols to map "actual" cognitive decision-making processes (Payne et al., 1978; Svenson, 1979). Finally, the third approach has attempted to explain variations in decision making by delineating individual information-processing styles (Schroder et al., 1967).

While descriptive approaches to the study of decision making have been criticized on a number of fronts, probably the greatest weakness of this research tradition is its focus on relatively well-structured versus ill-structured decision problems (see Simon and Hayes, 1976). Since most organizational problems, particularly those facing managers, are ill-structured (containing incomplete and ambiguous data that often require restructuring) and may involve group rather than individual decision making, the applicability of much of this research to actual organizations is questionable (see Mintzberg, 1973; Connolly, 1977; Ungson et al., 1981). Moreover, since the information environments that exist for recruits are typically quite ill-structured, due to the fact that recruits are new to their organizations' information environments, research exploring organizational communication, assimilation, and decision making should probably focus more on how employees learn to make decisions in ill- versus well-structured problem situations.

Studies of organizational assimilation and decision making might also benefit from exploring how recruits integrate their own personal theories of information search (heuristics) with those existing within their organizations. Other investigations might examine the interactions between decision makers' levels of cognitive complexity, their use of information sources, and phases of the decision-making process (see Stabell, 1978). In addition, studies might be conducted examining how recruits' perceptions of the relationships between the number, abstractness, and redundancy of information cues involved in decision-making situations change as they are assimilated into their organizations. Finally, research exploring how people use causal models in decision making should be initiated (Ungson et al., 1981). For example, studies investigating recruits' preferences for certain types of relational algorithms or "operators" (Newell and Simon, 1972; Weick, 1979) might help us better understand how causal models bias decision making and/or lead to "mindless" decisions.

Communication/Job Satisfaction. As a result of the recruit's assimilation into the organization's communication system, it is expected that he or she will experience some degree of work and communication satisfaction (Feldman, 1981). Most existing approaches to the study of satisfaction in organizations are based on need satisfaction models (Alderfer, 1972; Maslow, 1943), expectancy theories (Ilgen, 1971), and operant conditioning principles (Skinner, 1953). Essentially, these approaches posit that to the extent an individual expects or finds the work environment can or does meet his or her a priori needs and values, that individual will be satisfied (Locke, 1976). The above assumptions are also typical of most approaches to the measurement of communication satisfaction in organizations (see Downs, 1977; Hecht, 1978).

Interestingly, most organizational assimilation research suggests that recruits have much higher expectations of communication, job, and organizational satisfaction when they first enter their organizations than they actually experience once on their jobs (Jablin, 1979a). As Wanous (1977: 615) observes, "Increasing experience in a new organization is associated with a less favorable view of it." Other research has shown that there is a significant correlation between a recruit's effectiveness in role making/negotiation and his or her general work satisfaction (see Dansereau et al., 1975; Feldman, 1976). Obviously, additional research exploring the role-making process and the emergence of levels of work and communication satisfaction within employees is needed. However, it is suggested that such studies consider the social information-processing approach to the development of job attitudes recently advanced by Salancik and Pfeffer (1978).

Salancik and Pfeffer (1978: 229) propose that job attitudes and levels of satisfaction result from three causes: "(1) the individual's perception and judgment of the affective components of the job or task environment; (2) the information the social context provides about what attitudes are appropriate; and (3) the individual's self-perception, mediated by processes of causal attribution, of the reasons for his past behavior." This approach to job attitudes and satisfaction is somewhat different from the theories outlined above, in that it suggests that a worker's job attitudes are to a large extent a result of evaluations of the work environment communicated to him or her by others (particularly co-workers) in the work context. In other words, Salancik and Pfeffer maintain that an individual's attentional processes become focused on certain aspects of the work setting because others frequently talk about and construct meanings for those elements of the environment. As a result, to some extent a recruit learns what his or her needs at work ought to be (versus possess them a priori) from interactions with others in the work setting. For example, if a recruit's co-workers constantly call attention to the fact that their jobs do not give a person a chance to think, the implication is that "the presence or absence of that feature should be important to the person" (Salancik and Pfeffer, 1978: 230); hence, a need has developed that might not have otherwise, and it will eventually affect the recruit's level of work satisfaction.

A social information-processing approach to organizational assimilation and the emergence of recruits' perceptions of organizational communication satisfaction presents some exciting research possibilities. Foremost, investigations are needed to explore the extent to which communication satisfaction at work is a result of individual dispositions or social interpretations. Studies might also be conducted aimed at determining what recruits identify as their communication needs on entering an organization, how these change and develop over time, and their relation to the existing communication needs expressed by members of the workgroup. The social information-processing approach would hypothesize that the recruit's needs (that is, criteria for satisfaction) would over time come to resemble those of the workgroup. Finally, research exploring how recruits rationalize and cognitively adapt to situations where their communication needs cannot be met should be initiated.

Concluding Statement

This chapter has attempted to accomplish two goals. First, an attempt has been made to integrate the rather diffuse literatures on organizational communication and social cognition by discussing them in terms of the organizational assimilation process. Second, this essay has endeavored to identify areas in which future research exploring organizational communication and social cognition might be fruitful.

Organizational communication and social cognition have been discussed throughout this chapter in terms of how they function in the role-making/assimilation process. While other approaches could have been employed to integrate the organizational communication and cognition literatures, the role-making/assimilation paradigm was utilized because that process, like communication and cognition, is social, dynamic, and continuous. Moreover, as is evident from the role-taking and role-making models discussed in the first part of this chapter, organizational assimilation itself is essentially a communication and cognition process; that is, it is through communication and cognition that a recruit is able to become a part of, and share, the dominant schemas that define an organization's reality.

Examination of the literature reviewed in this chapter suggests that a wide variety of theories of social cognition have been applied to the study of organizational communication. However, it should be noted that in no case have the relationships between organizational communication and a theory of social cognition been thoroughly explored. Of the various theories discussed in this essay, attribution theory has probably received the most research attention. In part, this is probably due to the fact that attribution theory is easier to operationalize in laboratory and field settings than are some of the other approaches. In addition, the organizational setting provides an ideal environment from which to explore attribution processes, since an observer's attributions are based on many observations of an actor's behavior (typically over a wide variety of situations). For example, a supervisor's attributions about a subordinate's performance are based on not just one incident of task behavior, but also the subordinate's performance on a wide variety of tasks over a period of time.

Inspection of the research reviewed in this essay also indicates that few investigations of social cognition and organizational communication have taken into consideration the effects of organizational and workgroup contexts on results. Such variables as organizational technologies, structures, and environments can affect organizational assimilation processes (see Katz, 1980), as well as communicative behaviors and attitudes (see Hage et al., 1971). Future research on the relationships between organizational communication and social cognition should delineate more carefully the possible effects of contextual variables on research results.

In addition, investigations exploring communication and social cognition in organizations might benefit from focusing more on how organizations, particularly managers, manipulate the "stuff" of thought—symbols, labels, and images—to create socially shared realities and facilitate organizationally desired outcomes. As Weick (1979: 42) observes, "The manager who controls labels that are meaningful to organizational members can segment and point to portions of their experience and label it in consequential ways so that employees take that segment more seriously and deal with it in a more organizationally appropriate manner." The study of cognitive responses (by both workers and management) to explicit and implicit persuasion within the organization obviously warrants more attention by organizational communication researchers (see Petty et al., 1981).

In conclusion, as should be evident to the reader by now, research exploring social cognition and organizational communication is still in its infancy. As a relatively new focus of organizational communication research, theories of social cognition present many exciting research possibilities. It is hoped that the literature and research suggestions presented in this chapter will be useful in guiding future investigations in this area.

References

Abelson, R. Script processing in attitude formation and decision making. Pp. 33-45 in J. Carroll and T. Payne (Eds.), *Cognition and social behavior*. Hillsdale, NJ: Erlbaum, 1976.

Albrecht, T. L. The role of communication in perceptions of organizational climate. Pp. 343-357 in D. Nimmo (Ed.), *Communication Yearbook 3*. New Brunswick, NJ: Transaction, 1979.

Alderfer, C. P. *Human needs in organizational settings*. New York: Free Press, 1972.

Alderfer, C. P., and McCord, C. G. Personal and situational factors in the recruitment interview. *Journal of Applied Psychology*, 1970, *54*, 377-385.

Arnold, H. G. Effects of performance feedback and extrinsic rewards upon high intrinsic motivation. *Organizational Behavior and Human Performance*, 1976, *17*, 275-288.

Bem, D. J. An experimental analysis of self-persuasion. *Journal of Experimental Social Psychology*, 1965, *1*, 199-218.

Brunswick, E. *Conceptual framework of psychology*. Chicago: University of Chicago Press, 1952.

Burns, T. The reference of conduct in small groups: Cliques and cabals in occupational milieux. *Human Relations*, 1952, *8*, 467-486.

Cantor, N., and Mischel, W. Traits as prototypes: Effects on recognition memory. *Journal of Personality and Social Psychology*, 1977, *35*, 38-48.

Caplow, T. *Principles of organization*. New York: Harcourt, Brace & World, 1964.

Carlson, R. E., and Mayfield, E. C. Evaluating interview and employment application forms. *Personnel Psychology*, 1967, *20*, 441-460.

Connolly, T. Information processing and decision making in organizations. Pp. 205-235 in B. M. Staw and G. R. Salancik (Eds.), *New directions in organizational behavior*. Chicago: St. Clair, 1977.

Crites, J. O. *Vocational psychology*. New York: McGraw-Hill, 1969.

Cusella, L. P. The effects of feedback on intrinsic motivation: A propositional extension of cognitive evaluation theory from an organizational communication perspective. Pp. 367-387 in D. Nimmo (Ed.), *Communication Yearbook 4*. New Brunswick, NJ: Transaction, 1980.

Cutlip, S. M., and Center, A. H. *Effective public relations* (4th ed.). Englewood Cliffs, NJ: Prentice-Hall, 1971.

Daly, J. A. *The personnel selection interview: A state-of-the-art review*. Presented at the annual meeting of the International Communication Association, Chicago, 1978.

Dansereau, F., Graen, G., and Haga, W. J. A vertical dyad linkage approach to leadership within formal organizations: A longitudinal investigation or the role-making process. *Organizational Behavior and Human Performance*, 1975, *13*, 46-78.

Dawes, R. M. The robust beauty of improper linear models in decision making. *American Psychologist*, 1979, *34*, 571-584.

Deci, E. L. *Intrinsic motivation*. New York: Plenum, 1975.

Downs, C. W. Perceptions of the selection interview. *Personnel Administration*, 1969, *32*, 8-23.

Downs, C. W. The relationship between communication and job satisfaction. Pp. 363-375 in R. C. Huseman, C. M. Logue, and D. L. Freshley (Eds.), *Readings in interpersonal and organizational communication* (3rd ed.). Boston: Holbrook Press, 1977.

Duval, S., and Wicklund, R. *A theory of objective self-awareness*. New York: Academic Press, 1972.

Endler, N. S., and Magnusson, D. Toward an interactional psychology of personality. *Psychological Bulletin*, 1976, *83*, 956-974.

Feldman, D. C. A contingency theory of socialization. *Administrative Science Quarterly*, 1976, *21*, 433-452.

Feldman, D. C. The multiple socialization of organization members. *Academy of Management Review*, 1981, *6*, 309-318.

Festinger, L. A theory of social comparison processes. *Human Relations*, 1954, *7*, 117-140.

Festinger, L. *A theory of cognitive dissonance*. Stanford, CA: Stanford University Press, 1957.

Fishbein, M. A behavior theory approach to the relations between beliefs about an object and the attitude toward the object. In M. Fishbein (Ed.), *Readings in attitude theory and measurement*. New York: John Wiley, 1967.

Fishbein, M., and Ajzen, I. *Belief, attitude, intention and behavior: An introduction to theory and research*. Reading, MA: Addison-Wesley, 1975.

Garland, H., and Price, K. H. Attitudes toward women in management and attributions for their success and failure in a managerial position. *Journal of Applied Psychology*, 1977, *62*, 29-33.

Glueck, W. Recruiters and executives: How do they affect job choice? *Journal of College Placement*, 1973, *34*, 77-78.

Graen, G. Role-making processes within complex organizations. Pp. 1201-1245 in M. D. Dunnette (Ed.), *Handbook of industrial and organizational psychology*. Chicago: Rand McNally, 1976.

Green, S. G., and Mitchell, T. R. Attributional processes of leaders in leader-member interactions. *Organizational Behavior and Human Performance*, 1979, *23*, 429-458.

Hackman, J. R. Group influences on individuals. Pp. 1455-1525 in M. D. Dunnette (Ed.), *Handbook of industrial and organizational psychology*. Chicago: Rand McNally, 1976.

Hage, J., Aiken, M., and Marrett, C. B. Organizational structure and communication. *American Sociological Review*, 1971, *36*, 860-871.

Hakel, M. D., Ohnesorge, J. P., and Dunnette, M. D. Interviewer evaluations of job applicants' resumes as a function of the qualifications of the immediately preceding applicants. *Journal of Applied Psychology*, 1970, *54*, 27-30.

Hargrett, N. T. Potential behavioral consequences of attributions of locus of control. *Journal of Applied Psychology*, 1981, *66*, 53-68.

Hecht, M. L. The conceptualization and measurement of interpersonal communication satisfaction. *Human Communication Research*, 1978, *3*, 253-264.

Heider, F. *The psychology of interpersonal behavior*. New York: John Wiley, 1953.

Heilman, M. E., and Guzzo, R. A. The perceived cause of work success as a mediator of sex discrimination in organizations. *Organizational Behavior and Human Performance*, 1978, *21*, 346-357.

Herman, J. B. Cognitive processing of persuasive communication. *Organizational Behavior and Human Performance*, 1974, *19*, 126-147.

Hilgert, R., and Eason, L. How students weigh recruiters. *Journal of College Placement*, 1968, *28*, 99-102.

Holland, J. L. Vocational preferences. Pp. 521-570 in M. D. Dunnette (Ed.), *Handbook of industrial and organizational psychology*. Chicago: Rand McNally, 1976.

Hughes, E. C. The study of occupations. In R. K. Merton, L. Broomand, and L. Cotrell (Eds.), *Sociology today*. New York: Basic Books, 1958.

Ilgen, D. R. Satisfaction with performance as a function of the initial level of expected performance and the deviation from expectations. *Organizational Behavior and Human Performance*, 1971, *6*, 345-361.

Ilgen, D. R., and Knowlton, W. A. Performance attributional effects on feedback from superiors. *Organizational Behavior and Human Performance*, 1980, *25*, 441-456.

Jablin, F. M. *A longitudinal study of employee organizational communication socialization.* Presented at the annual meeting of the International Communication Association, Philadelphia, 1979. (a)

Jablin, F. M. Superior-subordinate communication: The state of the art. *Psychological Bulletin,* 1979, *86,* 1201-1222. (b)

Jablin, F. M. Organizational communication theory and research: An overview of communication climate and network research. Pp. 327-347 in D. Nimmo (Ed.), *Communication Yearbook 4.* New Brunswick, NJ: Transaction, 1980.

Jablin, F. M. *Organizational entry and organizational communication: Job retrospections, expectations, and turnover.* Presented at the annual meting of the Academy of Management, San Diego, 1981.

Jablin, F. M. *Anticipatory socialization and organizational communication: Perceptions of the communication styles of role occupants.* Presented at the annual meeting of the International Communication Association, Boston, 1982.

Jackson, D. N., Peacock, A. C., and Smith, J. P. Impressions of personality in the employment interview. *Journal of Personality and Social Psychology*, 1980, *39*, 294-307.

James, L. R., Gent, M. J., Hater, J. J., and Coray, K. E. Correlates of psychological influence: An illustration of the psychological climate approach to work environment perceptions. *Personnel Psychology,* 1979, *32,* 563-588.

James, L. R., Hater, J. J., Gent, M. J., and Bruni, J. R. Psychological climate: Implications from cognitive social learning theory and interactional psychology. *Personnel Psychology*, 1978, *31*, 783-813.

Jones, E., and Davis, K. From acts to dispositions: The attribution process in person perception. Pp. 220-266 in L. Berkowitz (Ed.), *Advances in experimental social psychology* (Vol. 2). New York: Academic Press, 1965.

Jones, E., and Nisbett, R. The actor and the observer: Divergent perceptions of the causes of behavior. Pp. 79-94 in E. Jones et al. (Eds.), *Attribution: Perceiving the causes of behavior.* Morristown, NJ: General Learning, 1972.

Katz, R. Time and work: Toward an integrative perspective. Pp. 81-127 in B. M. Staw and L. L. Cummings (Eds.), *Research in organizational behavior* (Vol. 2). Greenwich, CT: JAI Press, 1980.

Katz, R. L., and Kahn, D. *The social psychology of organizations.* New York: John Wiley, 1966.

Kipnis, D., Schmidt, S., Price, K., and Stitt, C. Why do I like thee: Is it your performance or my orders? *Journal of Applied Psychology*, 1981, *66*, 324-328.

Knowlton, W. A., and Mitchell, T. R. Effects of causal attributions on a supervisor's evaluation of subordinate performance. *Journal of Applied Psychology*, 1980, *65*, 459-466.

Langer, E. Rethinking the role of thought in social interaction. Pp. 35-58 in J. H. Harvey, W. J. Ickes, and R. F. Kidd (Eds.), *New directions in attribution research* (Vol. 2). Hillsdale, NJ: Erlbaum, 1978.

Langer, E., Blank, A., and Chanowitz, B. The mindlessness of ostensibly thoughtful action: The role of placebic information in interpersonal interaction. *Journal of Personality and Social Psychology*, 1978, *36*, 635-642.

Lawler, E. E. Motivation in work organizations. Monterey, CA: Brooks/Cole, 1973.

Locke, E. A. The nature and causes of job satisfaction. Pp. 1297-1349 in M. D. Dunnette (Ed.), *Handbook of industrial and organizational psychology.* Chicago: Rand McNally, 1976.

Louis, M. R. Surprise and sensemaking: What newcomers experience in entering unfamiliar organizational settings. *Administrative Science Quarterly*, 1980, *25*, 226-251.

Mahoney, M. J. Reflections on the cognitive learning trend in psychotherapy. *American Psychologist*, 1977, *32*, 5-13.

Markus, H. Self-schemata and processing information about the self. *Journal of Personality and Social Psychology*, 1977, *35*, 63-78.

Maslow, A. H. A theory of human motivation. *Psychological Review*, 1943, *50*, 370-396.

Mayfield, E. C. The selection interview: A reevaluation of the published research. *Personnel Psychology*, 1964, *17*, 239-260.

McClosky, H., and Schaar, J. H. Psychological dimensions of anomie. *American Sociological Review*, 1963, *30*, 14-40.

Minkler, M., and Biller, R. P. Role shock: A tool for conceptualizing stresses accompanying disruptive role transitions. *Human Relations*, 1979, *32*, 125-140.

Mintzberg, H. *The nature of managerial work*. New York: Harper & Row, 1973.

Mitchell, T. R., and Kalb, L. S. Effects of outcome knowledge and outcome valence on supervisor's evaluations. *Journal of Applied Psychology*, 1981, *66*, 604-612.

Mitchell, T. R., Larson, J., and Green, S. G. Leader behavior, situational moderators, and group performance: An attributional analysis. *Organizational Behavior and Human Performance*, 1977, *18*, 254-268.

Mitchell, T. R., and Wood, R. E. Supervisors' responses to subordinate poor performance: A test of an attributional model. *Organizational Behavior and Human Performance*, 1980, *25*, 123-138.

Newcomb, T. M. Attitude development as a function of reference groups: The Bennington study. In E. E. Maccoby, T. M. Newcomb, and E. L. Hartley (Eds.), *Readings in social psychology* (3rd ed.). New York: Holt, Rinehart & Winston, 1958.

Newell, A., and Simon, H. A. *Human problem solving*. Englewood Cliffs, NJ: Prentice-Hall, 1972.

Payne, J. W., Braunstein, M. L., and Carroll, J. S. Exploring predecisional behavior: An alternative approach to decision behavior. *Organizational Behavior and Human Performance*, 1978, *22*, 17-44.

Peters, L. H., and Terborg, J. R. The effects of temporal placement of unfavorable information and attitude similarity on personnel selection. *Organizational Behavior and Human Performance*, 1975, *13*, 279-293.

Petty, R. E., Ostrom, T. M., and Brock, T. C. *Cognitive responses in persuasion*. Hillsdale, NJ: Erlbaum, 1981.

Porter, L. W., Lawler, E. E., and Hackman, J. R. *Behavior in organizations*. New York: McGraw-Hill, 1975.

Porter, L. W., and Steers, R. M. Organization, work, and personal factors in employee turnover and absenteeism. *Psychological Bulletin*, 1973, *80*, 151-176.

Raiffa, H., and Schlaifer, R. *Applied statistical decision theory*. Boston: Harvard Graduate School of Business Administration, 1961.

Redding, W. C. *Communication within the organization: An interpretive review of theory and research*. New York: Industrial Communication Council, 1972.

Rogers, D. P., and Sincoff, M. Z. Favorable impression characteristics of the recruitment interview. *Personnel Psychology*, 1978, *31*, 495-503.

Rotter, J. B. Generalized expectations for internal versus external control of reinforcement. *Psychological Monographs: General and Applied*, 1966, *80*, No. 1.

Roy, D. C. Quota restriction and goldbricking in a machine shop. *American Journal of Sociology*, 1952, *57*, 426-442.

Roy, D. C. Banana time: Job satisfaction and informal interaction. *Human Organization,* 1955, *18,* 158-168.

Rynes, S. L., Heneman, H. G., and Schwab, D. P. Individual reactions to organizational recruiting: A review. *Personnel Psychology,* 1978, *31,* 495-503.

Salancik, G. R., and Pfeffer, J. A social information processing approach to job attitudes and task design. *Administrative Science Quarterly,* 1978, *23,* 224-253.

Schein, E. H. Organizational socialization and the profession of management. *Industrial Management Review,* 1968, *9,* 1-16.

Schmitt, N., and Coyle, B. W. Applicant decisions in the employment interview. *Journal of Applied Psychology,* 1976, *61,* 184-192.

Schroder, H. M., Driver, M. H., and Streufert, S. *Human information processing.* New York: Holt, Rinehart & Winston, 1967.

Scott, W. E. The effect of extrinsic rewards on "intrinsic motivation": A critique. *Organizational Behavior and Human Performance,* 1975, *15,* 117-129.

Simon, H. A., and Hayes, J. R. Understanding complex task instructions. Pp. 269-285 in D. Klahr (Ed.), *Cognition and instruction.* Hillsdale, NJ: Erlbaum, 1976.

Skinner, B. F. *Science and human behavior.* New York: Crowell-Collier & MacMillan, 1953.

Synder, M. Self-monitoring processes. Pp. 85-128 in L. Berkowitz (Ed.), *Advances in experimental social psychology* (Vol. 12). New York: Academic Press, 1979.

Soelberg, B. M. Unprogrammed decision making. *Industrial Management Review,* 1967, *8,* 19-29.

Stabell, C. B. Integrative complexity of information environment perception and use. *Organizational Behavior and Human Performance,* 1978, *22,* 116-142.

Super, D. E., Starishevsky, R., Matlin, M., and Jordaan, J. P. *Career development: Self-concept theory.* New York: College Entrance Examination Board, 1963.

Sutton, D. E., and Carleton, F. P. Students rate the college recruiter. *Journal of College Placement,* 1962, *23,* 106-112.

Svenson, O. Process descriptions of decision making. *Organizational Behavior and Human Performance,* 1979, *23,* 86-112.

Tucker, D. H., and Rowe, P. M. Relationships between expectancy, causal attributions, and final hiring decisions in the employment interview. *Journal of Applied Psychology,* 1979, *64,* 27-34.

Tversky, A., and Kahneman, D. Judgment under uncertainty: Heuristics and biases. *Science,* 1974, *185,* 1124-1131.

Ungson, G. R., Braunstein, D. N., and Hall, P. D. Managerial information processing: A research review. *Administrative Science Quarterly,* 1981, *26,* 116-134.

Van Maanen, J. Breaking in: Socialization to work. Pp. 67-120 in R. Dubin (Ed.), *Handbook of work, organization and society.* Chicago: Rand McNally, 1975.

Van Maanen, J. Experiencing organization: Notes on the meaning of careers and socialization. Pp. 15-45 in J. Van Maanen (Ed.), *Organizational careers: Some new perspectives.* New York: John Wiley, 1977.

Vondracek, S., and Kirchner, E. Vocational development in early childhood: An examination of young children's expressions of vocational aspirations. *Journal of Vocational Behavior,* 1974, *5,* 261-270.

Wanous, J. P. Organizational entry: Newcomers moving from outside to inside. *Psychological Bulletin,* 1977, *84,* 601-618.

Wanous, J. P. *Organizational entry: Recruitment, selection and socialization of newcomers.* Reading, MA: Addison-Wesley, 1980.

Washburn, P. V., and Hakel, N. D. Visual cues and verbal content as influences in impressions found after simulated employment interviews. *Journal of Applied Psychology*, 1973, *58*, 137-141.

Weick, K. E. Cognitive processes in organizations. Pp. 41-74 in B. M. Staw (Ed.), *Research in organizational behavior* (Vol. 1). Greenwich, CT: JAI Press, 1979.

Weiss, H. M. Subordinate imitation of supervisor behavior: The role of modeling in organizational socialization. *Organizational Behavior and Human Performance*, 1977, *19*, 89-105.

Weiss, W. Effects of the mass media of communication. Pp. 77-195 in G. Lindzey and E. Aronson (Eds.), *Handbook of social psychology* (Vol. 5). Reading, MA: Addison-Wesley, 1968.

Wright, O. Summary of research on the selection interview since 1964. *Personnel Psychology*, 1969, *22*, 391-413.

Wylie, R. *The self-concept*. Lincoln: University of Nebraska Press, 1973.

Wyse, R. E. Attitudes of selected black and white college of business administration seniors toward recruiters and the recruiting process. (Doctoral dissertation, Ohio State University). *Dissertation Abstracts International*, 1972, *33*, 1269-1270A.

9

Social Cognition and Mass Communication Research

Byron Reeves
Steven H. Chaffee
Albert Tims

. . . the real environment is altogether too big, too complex and too fleeting for direct acquaintance. We are not equipped to deal with so much subtlety, so much variety, so many permutations and combinations. And although we have to act in that environment, we have to reconstruct it on a simpler model before we can manage with it.

Walter Lippmann (1922: 16)

We can only speculate on how the study of mass communication might have emerged if more attention had been paid to Walter Lippmann's notions about the "pictures in our heads" and less paid to Harold Lasswell's (1948) questions about "who, says what, in which channel, to whom, with what effect?" Lippmann, a journalist and social commentator by profession, argued that the individual does not respond directly to events in the environment but to a mentally constructed "pseudo-environment." A half-century later, Wilbur Schramm (1973: 194) echoed the same argument about the impact of communication. He maintained that "the main effect of communication on us is on the pictures in our heads . . . in other words, the translation of experiences we have stored in our central nervous system." Lippmann's influence on Schramm seems readily apparent. Not so apparent, however, is his influence on the dominant traditions in mass communication research. It is Lasswell's questions that most easily translate into the major analytic frameworks characterizing the history of empirical mass communication research. They are control analysis, content analysis, channel analysis, audience analysis, and effects analysis.

Only recently have mass communication researchers begun to question the sender orientation embodied in this set of questions and to propose new ones. The orientation we consider here is focused on the individual as an active participant in the mass communication process and is decidedly cognitive. The chapter will review assumptions and themes of past cognitive research in mass communication, current research areas in social cognition, and some of the ways each field might stimulate new kinds of inquiry in the other.

We have chosen to deal with both *social* cognition and social *cognition,* and with mass *communication* and *mass* communication. The first distinction has led us to comment on cognitive processes in general (social *cognition*) as well as cognition specifically related to people (*social* cognition). Perhaps more than other chapters in this volume, our emphasis will be on general cognitive processes and theoretical arguments that justify this more basic consideration. There are also two ways that the term "mass" will be used. Most of the chapter will consider mass-produced messages communicated to individuals (mass *communication*). This emphasis is consistent with the psychological basis of theory in social cognition. "Mass" can describe audiences as well as means of production, however, and we will briefly consider how media influence cognitive processing *across* individuals within a social system (*mass* communication).

Cognitive Themes in
Mass Communication Research

Although students of mass communication processes and effects are likely to find much of the terminology of social cognition research unfamiliar, they should recognize many of the working assumptions upon which the latter field is based. Many of the same beliefs about human behavior that underlie cognitive psychology have found their place, albeit not always a dominant one, in mass communication research. Sociobehavioral theory of mass communication, in particular, has been moving in directions that are quite compatible with the perspectives of social cognition.

At the most general level, the centrality of cognitive, as distinguished from affective and behavioral, concerns is a major feature of some of the most active areas of research on mass communication effects that have emerged in recent years. In political communication, for example, there has been a marked shift from the early focus on voting and stable attitudes to the role of mass media in informing the electorate (see Patterson and McClure, 1976; Chaffee, 1978) and setting the public agenda by making some issues more salient than others (see McCombs and Shaw, 1972; Becker et al., 1975; Weaver et al., 1981). In the study of children and television, Piagetian conceptions of stages of cognitive development have received most attention (Wackman and Wartella, 1977; Collins, forthcoming). Research programs have focused on such cognitive criterion variables as message discrimination (Clarke and Kline, 1974), perceptions of social reality (Gerbner et al., 1980; Hawkins and Pingree, 1981 and forthcoming), decision-making strategies (Bybee, 1981), and logical resolution of environmental issues (Grunig and Stamm, 1979), to note but a few. This represents a considerable shift from the research of two decades ago, which emphasized behavioral consequences of media (such as voting or violent behavior), selective exposure, dogmatism, cognitive dissonance (which in retrospect was a highly affective concept), attitudinal persuasion, and motivation. Even motivation research today has a strongly cognitive flavor; studies of the "gratifications sought" from mass media often find informational and rational purposes ranking high on people's self-reported lists (consult Blumler and Katz, 1974).

Social cognition theories generally assume that the person is mentally active, organizing and processing stimuli from the environment rather than simply responding directly to them. This has been a recurrent theme in mass communication studies, dating back at least to McGuire's work on syllogistic reasoning (Rosenberg et al., 1960) and Osgood's model of representational mediating processes (Osgood et al., 1957). More recent examples are studies on counterarguing in the face of a persuasive media message (Roberts and Maccoby, 1973) and information seeking (such as Donohew and Tipton, 1973).

There is also a common assumption about the unidirectionality of thinking. The cognitive processing of stimuli is presumed to consist of the reduction of complex perceptions into simplified structures, rather than the reverse. Stereotypes, long a focus of media content analyses because of their sometimes pernicious social consequences, are seen by cognitive psychologists to be the product of quite reasonable, ubiquitous, and on the whole unexceptionable thinking processes (Nisbett and Ross, 1980). In addition to the study of repetitive cognitive structures, which are communicated whole, communication theorists have also attempted to predict the cognitive structures that will result when objects that arouse different "meanings" are linked (Osgood and Tannenbaum, 1955).

Salience, or psychological availability, is a key factor in the psychology of cognitive heuristics (Tversky and Kahneman, 1973), and it has long been a prominent concept in mass communication research. Carter (1965) saw salience as a basic source of value produced by communication, and a series of subsequent experiments bore this out and explored its social implications (Chaffee et al., 1969). Issue salience is, of course, the main dependent variable in agenda-setting research (Becker et al., 1975), and some studies have gone on to examine its indirect effect as a heuristic in voter decisions (McLeod et al., 1974). The importance of salience in practical campaigns is clearly recognized by communication strategists who concentrate on "name recognition" of brands or candidates in their advertisements.

Two other themes of cognitive psychology are echoed in certain areas of mass communication research. One is the proposition that it is the total structure of a set of cognitions that determines what simplified structure will result. The second is the assumption that the sequence in which mental events occur determines their cognitive outcome. Neither of these is universally accepted in either area of study, but there are interesting bodies of evidence that support both. Familiar to mass communication researchers are such topics as primacy-recency and mental set in media effects (Hovland et al., 1957) and the differential stimulation of communication behaviors that result from different sequences of disconfirmation of expectations (Pearce and Stamm, 1973). Much research on such topics as verbal contact, cueing, and conclusion-drawing grows out of these assumptions and has had its impact on mass communication theory.

The foregoing assumptions have to do with cognition in general. There is less agreement among scholars as to whether *social* cognition is a distinct topic or simply a convenient way to study cognition in the real world. We will point out in the next section that relatively few theorists in either field see social cognition as different in character from cognitive processing that does not involve other people. Still, some provocative further assumptions can be noted among those who do take a distinctively social position. There is evidence, for example, that social factors are weighed more heavily than intrapersonal factors in motivating people to seek information via media (Chaffee and McLeod, 1973). This may mean that cognitions involving significant others are more salient and, consequently, more likely to guide one's thinking and subsequent behavior. Put another way, social relationships may constitute an additional cognitive heuristic, beyond those already identified by psychologists. The assumption that people think about and act upon what they believe other people think is central to the study of co-orientation (McLeod and Chaffee, 1973), a research model that has been applied in a variety of communication settings. Empathy, or the ability to imagine oneself in another person's role, has been stressed as a key contribution of mass media in the transition of traditional societies to modernity (Lerner, 1958). The social role one anticipates taking in subsequent communication situations can affect the way one processes a media message (Zajonc, 1960; Zimmerman and Bauer, 1956). Perhaps it is the social importance of social cognitions that suggests to some that they are also of greater theoretical importance than other kinds of cognitions. (The "representativeness heuristic" could account for this; see Nisbett and Ross, 1980.)

A final point of growing similarity between social cognition and mass communication is the low estate of personality, or individual differences variables. In the case of social cognition, this has been practically a matter of definition. To explain a person's behavior by inferring a consistent disposition on his or her part is considered the "fundamental attribution error" (Nisbett and Ross, 1980). The period 1945-1965 was a veritable heyday of individual differences research and theory regarding mass communication. The learning of attitudes led to selective exposure and cognition, it was thought, and this explained why the same media content had different "effects" on people of different backgrounds (DeFleur and Ball-Rokeach, 1975). This approach survives in empirical work, but at a theoretical level it requires an assumption that people's behavior is consistent across time and differing situations. Recent work demonstrates that this is not the case for either mass communication (Allen, 1981) or interpersonal communication (Hewes and Haight, 1979). Long before that, pessimistic images of audience members as "chronic know-nothings" (Hyman and Sheatsley, 1947) and "laggards" (Rogers, 1962) had given way to the demonstrated fact that almost everyone can be reached with information through a well-designed campaign (Douglas et al., 1970; Rice and Paisley, 1981). Even if a person is dogmatic, a laggard, chronically given to knowing nothing and selectively exposing him- or herself only to compatible messages, the mass communication field today is likely to assume that there is a way of getting an important message through—and to refrain from blaming the individual if it fails (Rogers, 1976). Dispositional explanations belong to a less optimistic era of mass communication research.

Overall, it is important to note that most treatments of cognition in mass communication research have referred to cognitive variables that are the results of cognitive processes. Thoughts that people have about or in relation to media messages are the most common concepts in the research reviewed (for example, information holding, information gain, issue agendas). The research in social cognition is not directed at single *cognitive consequences* of exposure to stimuli, but at the *cognitive processes* that cause these results. This level of theorizing is not common in mass communication research and represents a more detailed and specific treatment of *how* people think rather than *what* they think about. Many of the shared assumptions, however, at least suggest there is enough common ground for the two research areas to be fundamentally compatible. We will begin by looking at the implications of ideas about social cognition for mass communication research.

Social Cognition: Why Should Mass Communication Researchers Consider It?

Most major advances in social psychology have at some time made their way into the literature of mass communication, and it has even been argued that the history of social psychology in the United States is very much the history of media studies (McLeod and Reeves, 1980). Not all of the influences have been enduring, nor should they have been, which leads us initially to question the merits of a social cognitive perspective on mass communication processes. Quite simply, what is social cognition, and why should mass communication researchers consider it?

At the broadest level, social cognition is the study of how people think about people (Roloff and Berger, this volume). This definition implies an interest in individuals as the unit of analysis, in people as the objects of perception, and in how people actively process information. The definition also suggests that a useful psychological theory of mass communication will refer to unobservable mental links between media stimuli and response. The major research task becomes one of discovering empirical constraints on classes of cognitive models that are plausible and that adequately describe the interactions among messages, channels, information processing, and response. This task inevitably places cognition in a central role and implies a need for more than "black box" descriptions of intervening mental processes.

As our brief history of mass communication shows, we have not been exclusively hard-core behaviorists. Yet our cognitive concepts reflect more of a world view than a rigorous attempt to falsify different ideas about how individuals process media information. In this sense, we may be de facto behaviorists, even though our history shows frequent theoretical attention to cognitive variables. Much of the empiricism related to mass communication has attempted to catalog associations between media content and response (for example, public affairs content and voting, violent entertainment and aggressive behavior, advertising and consumer purchases) without much empirical or theoretical regard for the cognitive mechanisms involved. Even with the recent shift to cognitive variables noted in the first section of this chapter, few explanations have been proposed that describe the cognitive *processes* that might explain how mass media bring about these results.[1]

In considering the implications of social cognition for mass communication, two issues emerge: differences between social and nonsocial information, and the impact of mediated information on processing. The first issue is whether "social" refers to stimulus information that is processed differently from information in other domains. There appears to be a growing consensus that the perception and categorization of objects involve the same mental activities as do the perception and categorization of persons (Glucksberg, 1981). In commentary on the relationship between personality and cognitive psychology, Glucksberg (1981: 334) summarizes:

> Memory for events, memory for persons, and memory for people's actions share important structural and processing mechanisms. In short, we (cognitive and personality psychologists) have learned—or at least we all seem to agree—that the way we deal with the world of physical objects shares important characteristics with the way we deal with persons and with ourselves. At the level of conceptual knowledge, common mental processes are used irrespective of the specific domains.

Several examples of cross-domain theorizing exist in the recent personality literature. The concept of category prototypes (see Hewes and Planalp, this volume, for a review of definitions of prototypes and other similar concepts) has been drawn from work in cognitive psychology on the organization of information about common objects (Rosch, 1978; Tversky, 1977) and has been applied to the perception and categorization of personality types (Cantor and Mischel, 1977), psychiatric diagnoses (Cantor et al., 1980) and the concept "self" as a cognitive prototype (Kuiper and Derry, 1981). Other researchers have hypothesized not only that mental *structures* exist across domains, but also that *processes* are constant across domains. Cohen (1981) and Wyer and Srull (1980) have recently theorized that observers' goals may influence how information about people is processed. Their work relies on earlier cognitive research by Newtson (1973; Newston et al., 1977) on how people unitize or chunk information in relation to processing goals and the implications of unitization for memory. Similarly, Fiske and Kinder (1981) propose a cognitive explanation of how political involvement affects the availability, organization, and recall of political information, depending on the consistency of the information with prior schemata.

The important implication of this research for mass communication is that attention to the prescriptions of cognitive psychology may be more important than differentiating social from nonsocial media information. A great deal of research in mass communication has dealt with the presentation of people (such as women, minorities, members of different social classes and occupations, political candidates, and personality types), and these research areas can surely benefit from what the literature on social cognition has to say about person perception and categorization. Yet, if the cognitive structures and processing mechnisms are not domain-specific, the theories should be relevant across different types of media information. The term "social cognition" exists largely because personality psychologists were looking for plausible cognitive explanations of person perception and memory. They had rejected neobehaviorism and turned to the work of cognitive psychologists who had for the most part been operating independently of their personality and social psychology peers.[2] Since the interests of mass communication researchers obviously do not parallel the interests of personality psychologists, we should not be anxious to limit the application of cognitive models to social information.

A second issue concerns the fact that social information in mass communication sources is *mediated* information. An important question is whether this influences how media information is processed. Interestingly, most psychologists seem to ignore this question. Research in social cognition is heavily dependent on the economies of using mediated presentations of people (such as slides, videotapes, and film) in experimental manipulations. There are few considerations of the differences in information between live and mediated presentations as well as the possible influence that presentation modes have on aspects of processing, such as focusing, mental representation, or even differences in the physiological processing of information. Essentially, we must ask whether mass communication requires a different cognitive psychology. Are there characteristics of media presentations that trigger unique processing mechanisms, or do media just represent special data sets for more universal mental software?

The answer to this question cannot be final; the simplest alternative, however, would be to propose that media stimuli do not enable processing *mechanisms* that would otherwise be absent. It is entirely reasonable to expect that media information may cultivate certain processing *strategies* or be best matched with individuals who favor certain processing *styles,* but at this time no evidence would suggest that media—in their various forms—alone cause the existence of separate processing mechanisms. As we will discuss in the next section, we definitely feel that media deserve attention as unique carriers of information. Our point here is that, just as cognitive models are sufficiently general to account for processing of social and nonsocial information, they are also sufficiently general to deal with mediated and directly experienced information. At the least, we may reasonably assume these levels of generality until, and unless, evidence is produced to the contrary.

What Mass Communication Means
for Social Cognition

In the previous section we dealt with possible benefits of considering social cognition in mass communication research. The general question in this section is, What differences in processes of social cognition might be due to mass communication? We deal with this in two parts. First, we consider possible differences within mass communication between the major media, such as television versus the printed word. Then we consider mass communication as a general class of human activities and institutions, and discuss ways in which it controls and conditions social cognitive processes in contrast with direct, personal communication. The emphasis in the first section is psychological and is on social *cognition;* in the second section, the emphasis is sociological and is on *social* cognition.

Media Differences and Cognitive Processing

An important implication of mass communication research for social cognition is that differences in media, irrespective of content, may substantially affect cognitive processing. As previously mentioned, psychologists often assume that these differences are inconsequential, and, unfortunately, mass communication researchers themselves often ignore the interaction between communication channels and mental processing. We remind each other that the term "media" is plural, yet often we do not take this seriously in anything but a grammatical sense. When differences are acknowledged, it is mostly in terms of media organizations, occupations, regulations, and content, without attention to the characteristics of the technologies and communication symbols that might affect mental processes. We often assume that media are envelopes into which identical messages can be inserted, and we fail to acknowledge that channel characteristics are hopelessly confused with message content. To talk about a television news story and a newspaper article that report the same event is to talk about essentially two different messages. Salomon (1979) noted that although the medium may not be the message, as McLuhan suggested, it is certainly influential.

A focus on cognition may help determine the characteristics of media, other than content, that will influence mental processing. Cognition is most often defined by psychologists as a process that enables individuals to represent mentally and deal symbolically with the external world (Rosenthal and Zimmerman, 1978). Almost all information-processing models propose mental representation as a necessary component (Crowder, 1976; Hewes and Planalp, this volume), and several studies suggest that representation may take two or more forms. It follows, then, that the structure of media may influence the form of mental representation. Although some psychologists argue that all mental representation takes an identical propositional form (Pylyshyn, 1973; Rosenberg and Simon, 1977), most researchers now favor a dual or even multiple representational system (Kosslyn and Pomerantz, 1977; Anderson, 1978). The dual-modality conceptions of representation often postulate a verbal or propositional system and an analog or pictorial system (Szczepkowski, 1981).

These representational systems have direct ties to characteristics of media, suggesting that a medium may cultivate a preferred method of internal representation (for example, pictures versus words) or require an individual to store information in a form most consistent with the stimulus to minimize internal translation of messages into other forms (Salomon, 1979). Singer (1980) has suggested that pictorial information, stored in the right hemisphere of the brain, requires more active processing for efficient storage and that because television formats are fast-paced and crowded with information there is little time for the mental activity necessary for effective processing. In this way television viewing may actually *promote* passive processing. Thomas Mulholland (1978) has even suggested that television may become a conditioned stimulus for low levels of brain activity and visual attention.

This proposal contrasts with the process of reading, where more easily accessed representational forms may be used with ample time for cognitive rehearsal. Mental activity may also be increased because of the necessity to translate visually represented words into both verbal *and* pictorial mental images, a combination that maximizes learning (Hartman, 1961; Seamon, 1974). There are also physiological data about the mental activity associated with the processing of audiovisual versus print material which show that brain activity is greater for reading than watching television and that the increased activity is located in the left hemisphere (Weinstein et al., 1980). Previous research has shown that the increased brain activity is related to both recall (Weinstein et al., 1980) and interest in media content (Schafer, 1978).

Once again, the major implication of this discussion for studying cognition is that certain aspects of information processing may be affected by communication channels alone. In relation to *social* cognition, we should be reminded that television is not the only medium that transmits social information. In the area of political communication, for example, information about a political candidate would likely be available from all media and, if the candidate were local, even from direct observation. Even controlling for content to the fullest extent possible, those reliant on different media would have a good chance of acquiring and representing different information.

Social Implications of Mass Communication

The previous section dealt with the impact of different mass media on *intra*personal considerations of information processing. In addition to this psychological focus, much has been written by sociologists and political scientists about changes in the functioning of societies as they develop and disseminate media of mass communication. We will not attempt to review that vast literature here, but will focus instead on some characteristics of *mass* communication systems that might modify social cognition phenomena *across* individuals.

Transcendence of Time and Space. A central feature of mediated communication is that it alters the spatial and temporal relationships between people, between a person and a stimulus, and between the elements of complex stimuli. The capacity of media systems to store messages and of people to retrieve them at a later time and in a different place has been of marked historical importance (DeFleur and Ball-Rokeach, 1975). Media systems also control the flow of messages, determining which of the many messages available reach which of the many sectors of a society (Schramm, 1954). Media organizations package messages from different times and places, juxtaposing for their audiences cognitive stimuli that would not otherwise be found together. These capacities enable a society to work as a set of interacting parts, focusing on a commonly understood body of information. Lasswell (1948) has called this the "correlation function" of communication.

At the level of social cognition, these conditions have a number of implications. One is that people who are physically distant can be brought into contact. At the interpersonal level, the telephone enables us to think together without being together. Macroscopically, people of different cultural backgrounds or social strata can, through mass media, come to understand one another's worlds. The transcendence of time constraints is perhaps less obvious, mainly because we have become so accustomed to it. Written communication, and more recently the emerging technologies for storing messages, release us from the limitations of communicating in real time. Our minds are, of course, wondrous storage-and-retrieval systems too, but it is clear from research on such topics as memory and cognitive heuristics that reliance solely on mental processes leads to systematic patterns of error. Communication technologies provide us with, in effect, a parallel "backup" system on which we can often rely to do some of our thinking for us.

There is an understandable tendency to place more trust in information from media, which are professionally organized to validate and edit their content, than in messages we hear from other people or draw from our own memories (Roling et al., 1976; Banta, 1964; Edelstein and Tefft, 1974). But we would do well to bear in mind that, beyond the simple technical level, the media consist of people too. The processing of information by media people is no less subject to cognitive biases and errors, and no less reliant on culturally accepted schemata, than our own. Films and television programs are built on stereotypes and familiar scripts because that is the content of our culture. These media portrayals, which juxtapose characters and plot elements in highly predictable ways, serve to reinforce popular beliefs. (Characterizations that run counter to widely accepted schemata and scripts are unlikely to survive in the competitive world of mass communication, where so much depends on the audience size one can attract.)

Mass Production. Images of "mass society" and "communication to the masses" belong to an earlier age of social theory. The term "mass" in the phrase "mass communication" now refers more to the mass production of the same message materials. The audience that receives these messages is in fact quite heterogeneous and active, but mass communication does help a society to achieve a commonness of experience and meaning that would otherwise be absent. The mass production of messages is a matter of economies of scale. Once one has designed a message that can achieve a particular purpose in some people, the unit cost of additional copies declines rapidly. Consequently, mass-sales industries, such as recorded popular music, produce considerably more copies than will be consumed of the relatively few songs they choose for marketing.

People who have not previously met can nevertheless assume that they share a number of prior experiences to the extent that they have been part of the same mass market for media messages. This facilitates social interaction, but it also narrows its range to those few subjects that have been popularized by the media. Just as the media draw on popular scripts and stereotypes in selecting material for mass production and distribution, so, in turn, will the members of their audience tend to focus on the combinations of elements that have been juxtaposed for them by the media. Examples are the reflexive linking of "law and order" or "free press versus fair trial"; it is a common error to talk, and think, of the latter as being in opposition and the former as being practically synonymous.

Interpersonal interaction often involves subtle attempts at persuasion, and effective persuasion relies on anticipating the cognitions that will be salient and the linkages that will be made among cognitions in other people. Media content, then, is a pretty fair guide to what other people will be thinking about. A study of conversations overheard in public places found that references to mass media were more likely to occur when persuasion was attempted than when it was not, especially when the persuasion attempt was successful (Greenberg, 1975). The same general principle is followed in mass communication as well. Advertisements and political rhetoric are replete with allusions to widely shared schemata that are counted upon to set in motion a predictable sequence of cognitive linkages that would produce mass behavior desired by the communicator. During the Vietnam War years, for example, when mass media portrayed a rebellious younger generation, consumers were urged to join such entities as "the Dodge Rebellion" and "the Pepsi Generation," and the United States elected a president (Richard Nixon) who promised to "bring us together."

Because of mass communication, large social systems can be assumed to hold, in the aggregate, cognitive structures that are similar to those of individual members. These, in turn, channel organized social action in predictable ways (Lazarsfeld and Merton, 1948). Boorstin (1962) coined the term "pseudo-event" to describe the staging of image-building occurrences for purposes of media exposure. A successful example was "E-Day" in 1970, which was observed on campuses across the United States and indelibly stamped the term "environment" on the national consciousness (Chaffee and Petrick, 1975). Before that time the term (and its faithful companion, "ecology") had been technical or unfamiliar terms for most people. Since then, while political controversies have added affective meaning to these labels, they have become constant public concerns because of their cognitive pervasiveness.

Media-Society Transactions. Research on agenda setting demonstrates the reciprocal flow of salient cognitions via the news media. On the one hand, an issue emphasized in media reports can become more salient in people's minds. In their study of the 1968 presidential election campaign, McCombs and Shaw (1972) found a high correlation between the amount of press coverage given to different topics (welfare, civil rights, foreign policy, and the like) and the frequency with which people said each issue was important in forming their voting decisions. But the reverse can occur as well. A more detailed study of the 1976 Ford-Carter debates found evidence suggesting that issues people said were important (in Gallup polls) *prior to* the debates influenced the selection of debate topics by both the candidates and the reporters questioning them (Becker et al., 1979). There seems to be a spiraling transactional selection of cognitions: people absorb those few topic labels made highly available by media emphasis; then, those who produce media messages align their presentations with the images market research finds salient to the public.

A general effect of mass communication, then, is to narrow further the mental repertoire of cognitions people are likely to hold. This occurs at the same time that the media, by bringing ideas and information from distant times and places, are enlarging the store of *potential* cognitions may times over what it would be in the absence of mass media systems. These countervailing tendencies of the media do not necessarily neutralize one another. It is conceivable that for some social systems the dominant impact of media input is to expand the range of cognitions, while in others it is to contract it. Another possibility is that there is a relatively constant and narrow quantitative range of cognitions that a person can hold and process, so that the narrowing process in which the media are involved is a response to the constant impingement on people of new cognitions from the media, which must be mentally accommodated somehow.

A Model of Social Information Processing

In this section, we will look at a comprehensive model of social information processing that should help organize the current research related to social cognition and suggest new directions for future mass communication studies. There are enough different research areas in social cognition that a more general schematic of the area may be helpful, especially as specific applications of social cognition of mass communication are considered in the last section. We begin, however, with a criticism. Models of cognitive processing result from a research strategy aimed more at finding confirming evidence for positions that have consensual plausibility rather than specifying detailed hypotheses which, if rejected, would discriminate among theoretical alternatives (Glucksberg, 1981; Hastie and Carlston, 1980). The model we will review, and other similar models, likely suffer from being merely plausible rather than falsifiable, but they do demonstrate potential applications of cognitive psychology to studying the individual's processing of social information from the media.

A good example of a comprehensive model of social information processing is the one proposed by Wyer and Srull (1980). Their model allows for three major stages of processing—acquisition, retention, and retrieval—and is similar in this respect to other models in cognitive psychology (Newell and Simon, 1972; Shiffrin and Atkinson, 1969; Bower, 1975; Crowder, 1976; Hastie and Carlston, 1980; Hewes and Planalp, this volume).[3] Wyer and Srull (1980) comment, however, that while their model acknowledges that the means of processing social and nonsocial information share a similar mechanism, so far cognitive psychologists have not considered information that is as complex and heterogeneous as that available about people. Therefore, primary attention is given to the ways in which this diverse information is represented in memory and the effects of the representations on recall of stored information, interpretations of new information, and judgments based on stored information. It is still likely, however, that research suggested by the model would apply to many different kinds of media information.

This and other similar models borrow automata theory terms and discuss information processing using the analogy of an operating computer system. These terms will be new to many researchers in mass communication. We will retain them because of their widespread use in cognitive psychology, because they describe concepts not often considered in mass communication, and because they represent the important influence that the computer analogy has had on psychological theory. Some theorists also expect that the components of the models have physiological counterparts. We feel it is important, however, not to reify these terms in the absence of evidence that these functions actually exist in physical reality and to view the model more as a metaphor for cognitive processing.[4]

Information about persons and events may enter the system from any source—including media sources—and in different sense modalities. Several assumptions are made about incoming information: (1) The information may be about people or about the events and actions in which people are involved; (2) the information may vary with respect to specificity (specific behaviors in specific situations; general behaviors, traits, physical characteristics; social roles; or social groups); (3) the information may vary in the completeness with which it represents social reality, which may require individuals to supply missing information; and (4) much of the information that enters the systems may be generated by people themselves in the form of contextual thoughts or feelings. In this sense, individuals are seen as active participants capable of greatly supplementing perception with cognitive activity during the course of processing.

The system is divided into storage units and processing units. The four storage units are the sensory story, work space (or short-term memory), goal specification box, and permanent storage unit (or long-term memory). The sensory store holds all information impinging on any given sense organ. The information is held in veridical form and decays within seconds. The work space is a short-term store for information that is being processed by the system in pursuit of some objective. One part of the work space contains information from a preencoder (an initial filter). If the information is not encoded and organized with other information in permanent storage, the information is eventually lost. Other parts of the work space are taken by input and output information relevant to the functioning of the three main processing units. Information remains in the work space depending on whether processing objectives have been met or time delays in processing are likely.

The permanent information store is the most important storage unit. It contains not only the results of past processing, but also information relevant to current material to be processed. Determining the structure of social information in long-term storage is probably the most active area in social cognition research. The organization of information in memory has been conceptualized as an interconnected network of concept nodes (Wyer and Carlston, 1979); as mental images, likely in multiple codes (Kosslyn and Pomerantz, 1977); as multidimensional spatial representations or implicit personality theories (Rosenberg and Sedlack, 1972); as schemata (Cohen, 1981; Taylor et al., 1978); as scripts or story grammars (Schank and Abelson, 1977); and as prototypes (Cantor and Mischel, 1977).[5]

Certain of these concepts deal with the linkages between elements in memory (networks, spatial representations, story grammars, and implicit personality theories), and other concepts (schemata, scripts, and prototypes) refer to the actual structure of information. Of the terms referring to memory structure, "schema" is the most general. Cohen (1981: 49) defines schema as:

> an hypothetical cognitive structure that represents associations among lower-level units of information, resulting in a functional higher-level cohesive meaningful unit. Of interest . . . are schemata that represent portions of a perceiver's social world knowledge, that is, associations between behavioral and person-related elements that develop through experience and are stored in semantic memory. . . . Obviously, to represent social knowledge adequately, an individual must have an enormous number of schemata, which reflect diverse contents. . . .

Schemata may exist at varying levels of abstraction and complexity and may embody different kinds of associative relationships among their elements.

A script is defined as a special type of schema that is useful for representing social action as a sequence of events (Schank and Abelson, 1977). A prototype is an idealized schema that can be used to categorize more highly variant schemata into a smaller number of useful formulations.

Wyer and Srull (1980) propose that memory elements—single concepts, schemata, scripts, and/or prototypes—are stored in "storage bins" which are content-addressable and tagged according to the information they contain. There are semantic bins, which function as mental dictionaries that can interpret experience; person bins, which contain information about a single person or category of people (called person schemata); and goal bins (or goal schemata), which are used to identify and interpret processing objectives as well as to specify how they are to be achieved. Information is placed in these bins as it is acquired, the most recently used material being placed (or returned) to the top. Also, single units of information may vary considerably in type and complexity (for example, a single attribute of a person, event, or processing goal or an organized set of features).

Representations of processing objectives are contained in the goal specification box, the fourth storage unit. Processing goals are either transmitted from permanent storage or are the result of new information. This storage unit contains directions for achieving processing goals and directions identifying the bins in permanent storage that should be used in attaining the goals. This storage unit may contain information about more than one objective which would enable parallel processing of information about more than one goal. Because of limited capacity, however, as new goals are added, others are removed and cease to affect processing.

There are five processors in the system: a preencoder, an executive unit, an encoder/organizer, an integrator, and a response selector. Wyer and Srull (1980) place most emphasis on the executive unit and encoder/organizer in their discussion of person perception and memory; however, the preencoder may be just as important for mass communication researchers. The function of the preencoder is to act as an initial editing and selecting device that transmits appropriate material to other units. It may act as a series of filters, permitting the passage of some material and prohibiting the passage of other types, and in this sense is similar to the concept of selectivity in past mass communication research. One of the major functions of the preencoder is to distinguish between information relevant to processing objectives (sent to the goal specification box) and information to be sent to the work space for possible integration into permanent memory. If a processing goal has already been established, the preencoder will send only information relevant to that goal. If information is simple, then it may be transmitted in nearly its original form; however, if the information is complex (as is multiple-channel information), the preencoder may transmit only meaningful segments of the entire passage.

The executor is similar to executive routines on main-frame computers. The executor directs the flow of information between the various storage and processing units in accordance with processing goals. When a new goal enters the goal specification box, the executor may search permanent storage for a goal schema (that is, a set of actions that will help obtain a goal) and place the schema in the goal box. Other types of information may be sent to the encoder/organizer, such as previously acquired information about a person or event that will be integrated with new information and sent back to permanent storage by the executor. Information that is routed to other processors for the purpose of dealing with new information is not sent back to storage in its original form or to its original place. Information is always placed at the top of the bin and information that was operated on is sent to storage only in its new form.

The encoder/organizer matches new information in the work space with other relevant material acquired from permanent storage. In the first stage of this process, the encoder designates information as exemplars of concepts or schemata that exist in memory. This comparison process may take place in two stages. First, specific attributes of a person, for example, may be classified as belonging to a certain trait based on the comparison of new information with schemata contained in the bin for that trait. Once this is done for several attributes, the entire representation of the person may be placed in a person bin based on similarity to other prototypic schema. The calculus used for organizing encoded information may be of several different types. (See Hewes and Planalp, this volume, for a review of these deductive calculi.) Descriptive information may be organized spatially or temporally or on the basis of criteria that are not part of sensory experiences (that is, semantic, logical, or affective criteria). It is important for mass communication researchers to note that information being organized may originally come from different sources and at different points of time. Thus, person schemata, for example, may not be based totally on media information from one point in time or media information in isolation from other experiences.

Finally, the search for a relevant schema to encode and organize new information may proceed from the top of a storage bin down until a schema is determined to be applicable. Schemata that are drawn from a bin during the course of this search are not immediately replaced, but are temporarily sent to a dump until the encoding is complete. After encoding, the schemata in the dump are returned to the bin in the order they were deposited, followed by the schema used for encoding and organizing. In this way, schemata called up but not used are given a lower position than the schemata used.

The final two processors, the integrator and the response selector, translate the results of processing into a language that can ultimately be communicated to another. The integrator identifies the implications of newly processed information (left in the work space by the encoder/organized) for judgments or decisions relevant to the information. This result is then integrated with previous results transmitted from permanent storage by the executor to arrive at a single judgment or decision. Several algebraic descriptions of the processes involved in formulating judgments have been proposed (see Wyer and Carlston, 1979, for a review). The response selector then transforms the internally coded judgment into verbal or nonverbal codes. Interestingly, it is this final process that has received the least attention in cognitive explanations of information processing.

This model allows much of the work in social psychology to be explained in terms of the storage and organization of information in memory. The following hypothetical situation may help to illustrate the role of each component of the model in forming judgments about media information. Suppose that a politically involved person tunes in a television debate for the purpose of learning more about how the candidates stand on issues. Information from the broadcast enters the processing system through the sensory store (in this case, audio and visual information) and is sent by the preencoder to the first part of the work space and to the goal specification box of the executive unit.

The executor first searches permanent storage for a goal schema consistent with the goal of "learning about political candidates." This schema could contain directions for processing the broadcast and might focus processing on the audio channel and information chunks that correspond to prominent issues in the election. Other goal schemata—for example, the goal of impression formation—might focus processing on personality characteristics of the candidates, nonverbal features, and the visual channel. Based on rules defined in the goal schema, the executor would also identify appropriate attribute, behavior, or event bins (also in permanent storage) and send schemata from them to the encoder/

organizer in the order in which they are found. In this example, these schemata could be past representations of issues being discussed in the broadcast, script information about the procedures or rules for political debating, or agendas that identify the relative importance of issues. When the encoder finds a schema that is appropriate for interpreting part of the information in the work space, the information is then encoded. Once the schemata used for encoding are no longer needed, they are returned to permanent storage at the top of the storage bin from which they were taken. The encoded information remains in the work space for use in encoding additional information about the broadcast or for use in forming judgments or responses as specified by processing goals.

Several predictions could be made about how the broadcast information will be used that relate to previous research areas in social psychology and communication. The following are examples.

(1) The more recently the broadcast had been viewed, the more likely the information would be recalled and used again. Information not sent to permanent storage would eventually decay in the work space. Information that did make it to the long-term store would likely have other information placed on top of it in the storage bin as time elapsed.

(2) The goal of "learning about how the candidates stand on issues" will influence the types of subsequent situations in which recall will be most likely. Processing goals determine to which of several possible storage bins the information is sent, and retrieval will be more likely if the goals at the time of recall match those at the time of processing. For example, if information is stored in terms of "election issues," it would most likely be recalled when issue information is needed, rather than when "candidate image" judgments are required.

(3) The schemata used to interpret incoming information will determine the extent to which the stored information differs from the original information. For example, if the debate broadcast were interpreted in terms of an entertainment schema, the stored information might not resemble the political information originally contained in the broadcast.

(4) The processing goals and the schemata used to interpret the broadcast will determine where the information is stored. Identical information could be relevant to event bins, person bins, attribute bins, and/or behavioral bins. The location for storage will determine what other information in permanent storage will be linked implicitly with the new information.

(5) If one of the candidates was judged to be a member of a particular group (such as "candidates I support"), then a prototypic schema would

be applied to the incoming information. Information may be added or subtracted from the original information to make the candidate more consistent with the prototype.

(6) When a person tries to remember what he or she has viewed in the broadcast, recall will be better for schema-consistent information than for information inconsistent with the schema used in the original processing. This will be particularly true after some time has elapsed and the original information has been cleared from the work space.

(7) If several schemata are applicable to the interpretation of the information in the broadcast (such as schemata for "election issues," "personalities of the candidates," or "behaviors appropriate to political debates"), the schema that has been used most recently will be the one used.

(8) Once a representation of a candidate has been formed (as suggested by appropriate schemata), that information will be used for judgments about the candidate independent of the implications of the original information. It is representations of social information that affect judgments rather than the stimuli per se.

Despite this extensive review of a social information-processing model, we have likely not done justice to the literature the model helps organize. Our purpose, however, is to provide a framework for research on how people process media information. While it would be impossible (and inappropriate) to review our entire field in relation to models of cognitive processing, we will review research that either has directly applied these models to mass communication questions or is sufficiently applicable to cognitive models that future studies could benefit from theoretical explanations of cognitive processing. We will concentrate on mass communication research in the areas of media uses and gratifications, media socialization, and political communication.

Viewing Motivations and Cognitive Processing

One inescapable observation of social cognition research and recent mass communication research is the emphasis placed on individuals as active participants who can to a great extent determine the selection and representation of information *depending on processing goals*. This result is suggested by the model just presented (the goal specification box), by recent research on the cognitive unitization of ongoing behavior, and by attempts to use individuals' motivations to explain different effects of media messages. In political communication research, for example, McLeod et al. (1974) showed that audience members who were motivated to seek information from newspapers were less likely to form issue agendas that corresponded to the newspaper they read than were those people without such a motivation. This contingent role for processing goals persisted when exposure to news sources was first controlled (McLeod and Becker, 1974). For television news, Gantz (1976) found that people could recall more news items when viewing for the purpose of gaining information than when "casually viewing" or when seeking diversion. Similar results were found for those anticipating future communication about the content of media public affairs (Kline et al., 1974; Chaffee and McLeod, 1973). Other suggestions have been made that audience motivations and needs will determine effects of other categories of media content (Katz et al., 1973/1974; Weiss, 1969; Roberts and Bachen, 1981) as well as effects on special audiences such as children (Greenberg, 1974) and adolescents (Lometti et al., 1977). Despite this promise, however, McLeod and Becker (1981: 86) have recently concluded that "relatively little empirical work has actually addressed the question of *how* motives can assist in an understanding of the media's impact on audience members" (emphasis added).

It is interesting to contrast this last statement with a recent comment by Cohen (1981: 48) about the cognitive processing of social information: "Despite evidence in the person perception literature that an observer's goal or purpose may influence processing of information about an actor, . . . no previous theoretical treatment has suggested specific mechanisms that might underlie this process." Cohen goes on to propose a description of a process that is very similar to the rationale that Wyer and Srull (1980) derive from their processing model. Both are based on cognitive schemata and both may be generalizable to the purposeful processing of media information. A fundamental assumption of social cognition theories is that prior experience (that is, stored schemata) will affect how new information is processed. Cohen (1981: 50) summarizes that "schema-relevant information should be easier to process; the meaning extracted from a particular behavior should depend on the operative schemata; and memory should be best for, and err in the direction of, schema-relevant information."

Wyer and Srull (1980) propose that goal schemata reside in permanent storage and that, depending on individual needs at any given time, the executor will place an appropriate goal schema in the goal specification box. The goal schema will then influence the processing of new information by focusing the perceiver on those aspects of the new information that are most consistent with the schema. Cohen (1981) does not differentiate between goal schemata and other schemata but similarly suggests that observational goals will be instrumental in selecting the person or behavioral schema to be applied. It may be possible to conceive of motivation associated with media exposure as different goal schemata. For example, the need to gain information may consist of a series of directions about how to perceive important features of people, behaviors, or events (such as behavioral details, non-expressive features of people, or temporal order) in contrast to an entertainment goal schema that might focus attention on humorous people and situations, overall impressions of people, or specific incidents that are not connected with an overall story. The subsequent application of different schemata during processing could affect what information is stored and used, by focusing perception on schema-relevant parts of media messages.

One could ask how schemata structure information and memory, and in answer to this question most proposals have relied on the work of Newtson and others on cognitive unitizing (Newtson, 1973; Newtson et al., 1977; Massad et al., 1979). The basic premise of unitization research is that incoming information need not be stored in veridical form in order for a person to reconstruct later the information for the purposes of understanding, replication, or action based on the original stimulus. Only certain key "frames" or "chunks" need to be encoded and stored to enable a person to use the information effectively. The breakpoints between segments typically occur at transition points in an information stream, and it is information at these points that is encoded rather than the details that come between the breaks. Breakpoints are measured by having people press a button (attached to an event recorder) "when one meaningful action ends and another begins." People are more likely to notice that small parts of information are missing if the information comes from breakpoints, and they are better able to remember that particular information is part of the stimulus if it is a slide taken from a breakpoint than if the slide represents a random segment in a continuous stimulus (Newtson and Engquist, 1976).

Schemata then may influence the nature of information that is ultimately encoded by focusing perception on schema-relevant break-points. If this is the case, then people with different processing goals should unitize the stimulus differently, and at least three experiments find this result. Ebbesen (1980) reported that more breakpoints were identified when people unitized a videotape with instructions to remember details than when they were instructed to form an impression of the person in the tape. A similar experiment found only a 25 percent overlap in the breaks for people in the two different conditions (Cohen and Ebbesen, 1979). Different processing goals affected not only the number and placement of breaks, but also performance on dependent measures of recall and impression formation. In a repeated measures experiment using two instructional sets (learning versus impression formation) and two dependent measures (recall versus appropriateness of impressions formed), Cohen and Ebbesen (1979) showed that instructional set has an impact on the criterion measure that is consistent with the instructions. That is, learning instructions not only increased the number of facts that a person could remember, but also decreased the accuracy of impressions about people. The opposite was true for the impression formation instructions.

Cognitive schemata may have an analogous effect on people's processing of media. Different viewing motivations may activate specific goal schemata, which cause people to unitize media presentations in a format most consistent with a schema. Furthermore, a processing goal may influence attention to different channels in a multiple-channel message (for example, audiovisual) or the format of mental representation. Pretest evidence from a current study indicates that college students unitized a five-minute television political advertisement differently depending on the instructions they received (Reeves et al., forthcoming). The breakpoints for those asked to "learn as much as possible about the candidate" closely parallel the audio breaks in the tape (such as sentence ends and pauses by the narrator), whereas those told to "form an impression of what the candidate is like" have breakpoints that correspond more with the visual grammar of the tape (such as editing cuts and severe changes in camera angle).

Although few other mass communication studies have used specific proposals from the social cognition literature, one line of media research, begun even before Newtson's experiments, has suggested that cognitive switching, a concept similar to unitizing, is important in information processing (Carter, 1971; Carter et al., 1973). Carter proposed that people define meaningful units of information by mentally "stopping" the information flow. These stops (signaled with the press of a button) help organize and prioritize information that would otherwise be difficult to store effectively. Studies have shown that stopping behavior is most similar for people given the same processing instructions (Heffner, 1972), people with similar preconceptions about a message (Carter et al., 1973), and people in similar viewing situations, regardless of message content (McCain and Ross, 1979). These studies, in combination with the psychological research, suggest that people do chunk information, that the information chunks can affect how the information is used to make judgments and decisons, and that the number and boundaries of chunks are in large part the result of processing goals. Despite the fact that the two research areas have generated different taxonomies of processing motivations,[6] they might in the future share the task of defining the schemata associated with each goal and the effects of the schemata on how incoming information is formatted and stored. Most important, they offer an explanation of how cognitive processing might affect memory and behavior, and they begin to suggest how we might design research to test those ideas.

Developmental Research on Media and Youth

Our previous comment that communication research does not emphasize cognition is probably least applicable to research on media and youth. In general, the trend in the late 1950s away from mechanistic theories of learning and toward cognitive variables was for developmental psychology a *re*discovery of the cognitive developmental theory of much earlier writers such as Baldwin and Piaget (Cairns and Ornstein, 1979). Probably because the study of media and children fell so clearly into the domain of psychology (rather than experiencing competition from sociology, as did other areas of mass communication), the role of cognition in developmental media research closely followed the historical shifts in psychology from cognitive to behaviorist to cognitive emphasis.

Most of the research after the introduction of television, up through the 1972 Surgeon General's Report on Television and Social Behavior, focused on children's modeling of televised behavior and closely followed the notions of social learning theory that were dominant in other areas of psychology. Research in the 1970s and 1980s, however, has been decidedly cognitive, focusing more on what children *do with* media rather than on what a medium does to them (Wartella, 1979; Collins, 1981). Although the research has been cognitively oriented, there have not been distinct lines between social and nonsocial cognition. The cognitive developmental theories of Piaget, for example, are as likely to be applied to children's ability to understand persuasive appeals (Ward et al., 1977) as to the perception of people (Reeves, 1979). We will briefly review studies that are directly related to the social information-processing model described above, as well as research that has focused on similar cognitive proposals about how children process information.

At least one recent study is a direct test of Wyer and Srull's idea about the organization of information in long-term memory (storage bins) and the impact of that information on subsequent judgments that children make about people (Reeves and Garramone, 1980). The storage bin model suggests that children and adults may not make exhaustive searches of all cognitions when making evaluations of other people. Once information is activated or "primed," it is returned to the top of a storage bin and is, therefore, more likely than other information to influence the encoding and organization of incoming stimuli. It was hypothesized that television may suggest to children traits (or trait schemata) that would be used in subsequent person judgments. Past research has found that there are traits that children reliably use to describe television people and that the trait "funny" is the most dominant across the elementary school years (Reeves and Greenberg, 1977; Reeves and Lometti, 1979). A group of children in the second, fourth, and sixth grades watched a 10-minute videotape designed to prime the trait "funny" by showing children representative segments of humorous situation-comedy programs. After viewing, children evaluated a child they had never met on several traits including "funny" and two others taken from past research, "attractive" and "strong." A control group evaluated the new child only.

The television stimulus affected children's evaluations of the new child, although in different directions, depending on age. Second-grade children in the experimental group rated the new child lower on the traits "funny," "attractive," and "strong" in comparison to the control group. Sixth-graders rated the new child higher on the same traits, and fourth-graders showed no differences between the two conditions. The priming effects were different, depending on how funny the children considered the people on television (for example, second-graders thought the television people were the funniest and therefore judged that their peers were less funny in contrast). The major result, however, was that increasing trait accessibility did affect later judgments. Similar questions could be asked about (1) the effects of different television content and whether unique trait schemata exist for people in each content area (for example, situation comedies versus action-adventure programs); (2) implicit relationships between primed and other schemata; (3) the purity of the stimulus needed to activate a trait or schema; (4) the interaction of processing goals with priming effects; and (5) the time delay between stimulus and response necessary to diminish or extinguish a priming effect.

Other research also has relied on elements of cognitive structure to explain how children process media information, although the information of interest has consisted more often of television stories and plots rather than specific television people. Several studies conducted by Collins have suggested that the development of a concept of narrative structure (that is, a schema) will affect children's ability to comprehend television plots and stories (see Collins, 1979, for a review). Collins says that mature comprehension involves at least three tasks: (1) parsing essential information from extraneous detail, (2) ordering information according to some scheme, and (3) making inferences that go beyond explicit presentations. In terms of the model presented, we could think of these functions as preencoding (differentiating relevant from irrelevant information according to processing goals) and encoding/organizing (collating information in terms of existing schemata and placing the result in an appropriate bin). Implicit inferences would be possible, according to Wyer and Srull (1980), because of the implicit association between information items in the same storage bin.

One pertinent result from Collins's research is that younger children are relatively unaffected by jumbling the content of a television program (Collins et al., 1978). Second-grade boys were not reliably worse on recall measures when segments were randomly scrambled than when they were presented in chronological order. Older children and adolescents, however, recalled consistently more when the scenes were in the proper order. It is possible that appropriate schemata are not available to younger children and that they are therefore unable to use a schema as a template for storing complex information that would otherwise be difficult to sort and organize. Several studies about children's comprehension of stories (as read by or to them) suggest that schema development is important in helping children encode, represent, and remember narratives (for a review, see Baker and Stein, 1981). Interestingly, these models are based on early schema theory (Bartlett, 1932), as is more recent schema research in other areas of social cognition. Those studying story narratives talk about schemata as "rewrite rules" that help children organize stories according to the generic structure of narrative. Thus, as children increasingly develop story schemata, they are better able to filter out story-irrelevant information and to organize the most important segments as an aid to later recall of detailed information.

Similar to the story narrative research, Roloff (1981) has used the concept of scripts to review studies on the content of television plots and has suggested that scripts for conflict resolution on television may be generalized to actual interpersonal situations. Scripts may, as children formalize them, aid in recalling appropriate sequences of action. At some point, however, they could become so overlearned as to promote "mindless" application to one's own behavior. Furthermore, Roloff points to several characteristics of television scripts that might signal a greater impact than for scripts learned from real-life experiences: (1) Media scripts are more structured and presented in a discrete fashion with an identifiable beginning and end; (2) there is more certainty about scripts because plot information is more explicit and characters are more familiar; and (3) media scripts are more recoverable and have a higher probability of being presented again in identical or similar ways. The actual use of television scripts will, however, depend on children's ability to acquire scripts, initial participation in a script (subsequent uses would then be more likely), and the realism associated with the television script.

Watkins et al. (1982) have actually tested the relationship between television viewing and children's construction of stories about hypothetical events. Third-, fifth-, and eighth-grade children were asked to write stories about an interpersonal conflict and about a foreign visitor. Two versions of each story were required, one a "television" story and the other a "real-life" story. The stories of high television viewers showed more similarity between the two versions in both structure and content, although their stories were also judged to be richer in detail and imagery.

A related area of mass communication research in which there has been considerable recent activity is the study of children's attention to television during the course of a single program. Most cognitive studies of children and television are concerned with recall and comprehension after the fact rather than the moment-to-moment processing that takes place during viewing. Most of the definitions of attention in this research deal with the time children spend looking at the television screen in relation to various characteristics of the content and form of the stimulus. Unlike selective perception, which is similar to the function of the preencoder, this process of selective exposure is not covered by the model previously discussed. The process is important, however, since the qualities of media that elicit attention—whether characteristics of the form or content of media presentations—will obviously determine the information on which the system will operate. We would extend the notion of "active information processing" to attention patterns as well as perceptual processes.

Anderson et al. (1979) have shown that certain program attributes can attract children's attention to the screen when they are not looking, and others may help maintain or interrupt attention when children are already watching. This research indicates, however, that attention to visual information (such as looking at a television picture) is related to attention to audio information. Even young children seem to have strong expectations about what will follow on the screen after they hear certain comments, musical phrases, or even silence. Television scripts include both audio and visual information, and as scripts develop children may be better able to use the early elements in scripts to predict later ones, especially later elements of interest. Wright et al. (1979) have made a similar suggestion about the development of attention patterns, adding that this knowledge may include expectations about message form as well as content. There is even evidence that the complexity or unpredictability of television may be part of a television script. Krull et al. (1978) have found that cycles of children's attention precede cycles of complexity in television programs and that older children's attention patterns are predictably more selective. This research on attention is particularly important because the variability in children's attention reminds us that cognitive processing of media information is structured by the information that initially enters the system and is not just a function of the information contained in the stimulus.

Several other research areas have combined cognitive and developmental issues. Although their focus has not been on social information or media, the findings are important for mass communication research on cognitive processing. The most popular topic has been memory development in children. Research has been organized around three memory stores—sensory, short-term, and long-term memory—which are similar to the cognitive models in experimental psychology. Research on sensory memory (or iconic storage, lasting less than a second) shows that younger children (less than five years old) take more time to identify visual material than do older children (Hoving et al., 1978). This difference may be important in determining whether children can focus on the functions of media information once structure has been identified. A fast-moving television program, for example, may force a younger child to deal with the question, "What is it?" rather than, "What do I do with this?"

Studies on short- and long-term memory have suggested that children's development of cognitive rehearsal strategies will also explain the persistent finding that older children recall more information than younger ones (Ornstein and Naus, 1978). This would suggest that between-media differences in rehearsal opportunity should be examined, along with different presentation formats within a medium that may encourage or preclude rehearsal. We have suggested that media may influence the format of mental representation. It is also possible that developmental changes in the predominant format may occur and may influence the format in which media information is stored. Kosslyn (1978) has suggested, for example, that memory for children changes from predominantly image-based representations to predominantly verbal-linguistic representations and that ontogenetically later formats are more powerful.

Political Communication

Recent conceptions of political communication also acknowledge that people are active information processors (Chaffee et al., 1977;

Kraus and Davis, 1976). This trend, at least in part, is reflected in the shift in concern from attitudinal and behavioral outcomes to cognitive outcomes mentioned at the outset of this chapter. We are now beginning to find evidence that political communication research has developed sufficient interest in cognition to become seriously concerned with processing mechanisms. For example, Sears and Chaffee (1979: 252) offer an interpretation of findings from political communication research on the 1976 presidential debates largely in terms of cognitive processing mechanisms:

> So voters tended to simplify the cognitive content down to the bare bones, and presumably interpreted it evaluatively in ways that maximize consistency with prior attitudes. Despite their many fascinating specifics, the debates testify to people's ability to assimilate details in simplified evaluative processes that are not likely to disturb their initial judgments much.

Without specifying a formal information-processing model, Sears and Chaffee have addressed the importance of encoding processes and the importance of "prior constructions" to the integration of new information. This concern with the interplay between the information and experience an individual brings to a situation and the cognitive impact of new information represents a meeting ground for political communication research and social cognition research.

Along this line, Fiske and Kinder (1981) have recently proposed what they term a schematic approach to understanding political information processing. They argue that the individual's understanding of political events and actions is determined by the interaction between existing cognitive structures and new information. In their view, a key variable in the availability and use of cognitive structures (or schemata) for political information is involvement. Fiske and Kinder's work in this area has direct implications for political communication research, since many operationalizations of political involvement are based mainly on measures of mass media use (see Chaffee and Dennis, 1979; Nie et al., 1979). The fact that high-involvement subjects are better able to organize political information is generally consistent with recent work suggesting that the patterns of news media use developed during adolescence may have long-term implications for basic political orientations (Chaffee and Tims, forthcoming). Individuals whose patterns of news media use primarily involve the electronic media have less information about event-specific political matters, such as the names of political candidates, and are less likely to hold more abstract political information, such as the identification of party symbols and party issue positions. Beyond the involvement issue, important questions need to be addressed concerning the impact of the mass media on the structure of political schemata and the role of the mass media in the development of political schemata.

Patterson and McClure (1976) have made strong statements about the "myth" of television's influence in election campaigns, concluding that television news coverage of a campaign has no influence on voters' views of the candidates or their understanding of election issues. Yet in our study of the 1980 presidential election we found that a sizable minority (28 percent) of the adults and a majority (55 percent) of the adolescents (10- to 17-year-olds) said they rely almost exclusively on television or radio for political information. Does the fact that television news is more likely to focus on the characteristics of the candidates and the "horserace" nature of an election campaign have implications for the development of political schemata? If so, should we be ready to conclude that television represents a benign influence on political understanding? Meadow (1980) alerts us to the fact that the mass media convey much more than just news and information. Through television in particular, young people learn about the roles of political authorities, political values, and political norms. In other words, the mass media shape the young person's outlook on the political world beyond the simple transmission of political facts. We suspect that in areas such as politics, where direct experience is often minimal, the mass media play a crucial role in the development of schemata. The relationship between schema development, mass media use, and schema use is nonrecursive. That is, patterns of mass media use may serve to develop political schemata that may, in turn, affect attention and the ability to integrate subsequent political information. To illustrate this point, consider the following passage cited by Fiske and Kinder:

> If an informed observer hears a surprising policy statement in the news by the secretary of defense, he may prick up his ears and pay close attention. He relates this information to what he knows of recent policy, what he knows of the secretary's relationship to the president, what he knows of past positions the secretary may have taken, and the like, since he is intensely interested to detect even small reorientations of national policy. In short, he automatically imports enormous amounts of prior information that lends the new statement high interest. The poorly informed person, hearing the same statement, finds it as dull as the rest of the political news. He only dimly understands the role of the secretary of defense and has no vivid image grounded in past information as to the inclinations of the current incumbent. His awareness of current policy is sufficiently gross that he has no expectation of detecting nuances of change. So the whole statement is confronted with next to no past information at all, hence is just more political blather: in five minutes he probably will not remember that he heard such a statement, much less be able to reconstruct what was said [Converse, 1975: 97].

What the individual brings to the situation has tremendous importance for understanding the differences in the impact of the news on the two individuals described above. To the extent that the mass media affect what the individual brings to the situation through the representation of the political world, influence is in turn exerted on subsequent integration of new information. Models of social cognition such as the one described in this chapter provide us with a starting point for raising questions about the role of the mass media in these situations.

Conclusions

Where will theories of social cognition lead mass communication researchers? It is our observation that cognitive theories require that we take seriously the mechanisms people use to think about mass communications. We must concentrate on the process of thinking rather than the results of thinking. This also suggests that new concepts that regulate this process should be considered. Unfortunately, our theories will likely become more complex and initially more speculative as we model unobservable mental processes. Research will also become more detailed as additional concepts are interposed between stimulus and response. Our past emphasis on immediate short-term results of media exposure may have biased us against looking at the complex, but quick, operations that constitute thinking. We seem to have convinced ourselves that since the responses we observe closely follow the stimuli of interest, nothing much of importance—or at least of measurable importance—could be happening in between. In this sense, the computer analogy is helpful. Knowledge of the structure and sequencing of a working computer system is crucial to understanding its operation, yet chronologically, the operations are completed within seconds.

Cognitive theories are not recommended without hesitation, however. We have mentioned that mental models are often merely plausible explanations of how people think rather than sources of falsifiable propositions about cognition. Different models have been shown to mimic one another, making it difficult, if not impossible, to distinguish between radically different proposals. An important example of this is research by John Anderson (1978) that shows that a model proposing a propositional representational code for memory can be perfectly predicted with a model proposing a pictorial memory code. To some, these problems seem fatal, and the results constitute evidence that this approach should be abandoned. Anderson (1978: 275), however, disagrees with this prescription in the following statement:

> I think the implication of this possibility (that models are equivalent) is not that cognitive psychology should be abandoned; rather, it should undergo a slight change. Our goal should be to develop some model

capable of accounting for human intelligence, that is, predicting behavior in a wide variety of situations where human intelligence is manifested. The fact that the model may be indistinguishable scientifically from other quite similar models need not be a source of unhappiness.... The function is to discover what *is* the case, not to prescribe what should be the case. If equivalence and nondeterminancy seem to be the case, we should not be timid about acknowledging that possibility.

Hastie and Carlston (1980) note that similar problems have been raised in other disciplines and appropriately have not led to an abandonment of theory. To conclude this point, we are not applying *answers* from another field to questions about mass communication. We are suggesting an approach, as yet still developing, that will focus attention on a process relevant to mass communication.

Since the beginning of mass communication research, social psychology has been our bridge to other social sciences. Social psychology, defined as the study of the relation between social systems and individuals, accurately describes the major interests of mass communication researchers. It is possible, however, to think of a dimension running from *social* psychology to social *psychology*, depending on whether the social system or individual is emphasized. It is interesting to note that many of the current changes in mass communication research seem to be polarizing research emphases on this dimension. Several people have advocated more system-level analyses of media that take more macroscopic approaches to questions about *social* psychology (Hirsch, 1977; Chaffee, 1975; Blumler, 1982). Clearly, this chapter suggests research that moves mass communication questions in the opposite direction (social *psychology*). Some of the authors we have cited even view their formulations as prephysiological descriptions of what people do with information.

We do not view these different emphases as incongruous or differentially important. Paisley (1972) mentioned that variable fields such as communication research have both the problems and the opportunities associated with framing questions and theory at the level of several traditional disciplines (such as biology, psychology, sociology, and anthropology). In the interest of understanding how individuals interact with the larger social system, we should not be afraid to stray from the "average" discipline to explore mass communication questions at each level of inquiry.

Notes

1. It would, of course, be unreasonable to assert that this conclusion is applicable to mass communication research without exception. The most notable exceptions are cognitive research on consumer behavior and research on media and the socialization of children.

2. Glucksberg (1981) notes that the recent relationships between cognitive and pesonality psychology represent a full circle back to before 1950, when there was much less differentiation between the research areas. He also notes that the two areas have always been part of the same study section with the National Institutes for Health.

3. In the interest of maintaining some consistency within this book, we should point out that Hewes and Planalp (this volume) define six functions as central to a study of social cognition: focusing, storage, integration/inference, retrieval, selection, and implementation. These functions are quite similar to components of the Wyer and Srull (1980) model *infra* and to other models cited in this chapter.

4. The metaphorical nature of this model is important, although it is probably unfamiliar to mass communication researchers. There are four major similarities between machines and human information-processing systems that recommend the analogy (Lachman et al., 1979). The first is generality of purpose. The computer, like humans, can follow any instructions put in proper symbolic order and, in fact, can simulate any other machine. The computer can store information in the form of subroutines and algorithms that can be accessed all at once. Computers can follow conditional instructions. Most important, computers can store programs and data in the same form, which means they can recursively operate on their own programs, according to specified conditions.

5. Researchers in social cognition (for example, Cohen, 1981) and authors in this volume (such as Roloff and Berger) point out that an important issue for research is the clarification of the meaning attached to cognitive terms such as "schema," "prototype," and "script." As the terms are currently defined, they are not conceptually independent. Hewes and Planalp (this volume) point out some of the differences and indicate the commitments researchers make when they use each term.

6. Taxonomies in mass communication research have varied from simple differences between learning and entertainment to lists that detail other specific motivations (such as relaxation, excitement, and behavioral guidance). Social cognition research has mostly been concerned with task learning and impression formation. It may be important for mass communication researchers to determine if there are goal schemata that are unique to media stimuli.

References

Allen, R. L. The reliability and stability of television exposure. *Communication Research* 1981, *8,* 233-256.

Anderson, D. R., Alwitt, L. F., Lorch, E. P., and Levin, S. R. Watching children watch television. In G. A. Hale and M. Lewis (Eds.), *Attention and cognition.* New York: Plenum, 1979.

Anderson, J. R. Arguments concerning representations for mental imagery. *Psychological Review,* 1978, *85,* 249-277.

Appel, V. S., Weinstein, S., and Weinstein, C. Brain activity and recall of TV advertising. *Journal of Advertising Research,* 1979, *19,* 7-15.

Baker, L., and Stein, N. L. The development of prose comprehension skills. In C. Santz and B. Hayes (Eds.), *Children's prose comprehension: Research and practice.* Newark, NJ: International Reading Association, 1981.

Banta, T. J. The Kennedy assassination: early thoughts and emotions. *Public Opinion Quarterly,* 1964, *28,* 216-224.

Bartlett, F. C. *Remembering: A study in experimental and social psychology.* Cambridge: Cambridge University Press, 1932.

Becker, L. B., McCombs, M. E., and McLeod, J. M. The development of political cognitions. In S. H. Chaffee (Ed.), *Political communication: Issues and strategies for research.* Beverly Hills, CA: Sage, 1975.

Becker, L. B., Weaver, D. H., Graber, D. A., and McCombs, M. E. Influence on public agendas. Pp. 418-428. In S. Kraus (Ed.), *The Great Debates: Carter vs. Ford 1976.* Bloomington: Indiana University Press, 1979.

Becker, L. B., and Whitney, C. The effects of media dependencies on audience assessment of government. *Communication Research,* 1980, *7,* 95-121.

Blumler, J. G. Mass communication research in Europe: Some origins and prospects. In M. Burgoon (Ed.), *Communication Yearbook 5.* New Brunswick, NJ: Transaction, 1982.

Blumler, J. G., and Katz, E. *The uses of mass communications: Current perspectives on gratifications research.* Beverly Hills, CA: Sage, 1974.

Boorstin, D. *The image: Or what happened to the American dream?* New York: Atheneum, 1962.

Bower, G. H. Cognitive psychology: An introduction. In W. K. Estes (Ed.), *Handbook of learning and cognitive processes.* Hillsdale, NJ: Erlbaum, 1975.

Bybee, C. R. Fitting information-presentation formats to decision-making: A study in strategies to facilitate decison-making. *Communication Research,* 1981, *8,* 343-370.

Cairns, R. B., and Ornstein, P. A. Developmental psychology. In E. Hearst (Ed.) *The first century of experimental psychology.* Hillsdale, NJ: Erlbaum, 1979.

Cantor, N., and Mischel, W. Traits as prototypes: Effects on recognition memory. *Journal of Personality and Social Psychology,* 1977, *35,* 38-48.

Cantor, N., Smith, E. E., French, R., and Mezzich, J. Psychiatric diagnosis as prototype categorization. *Journal of Abnormal Psychology,* 1980, *89,* 181-193.

Carter, R. F. Communication and affective relations. *Journalism Quarterly,* 1965, *42,* 203-212.

Carter, R. F. *Theoretical development in the use of signaled stopping.* Presented to the Association for Education in Journalism, 1971.

Carter, R. F., Ruggels, W. L., Jackson, K. M., and Heffner, M. B. Application of signaled stopping technique to communication research. In P. Clarke (Ed.), *New models for communcation research.* Beverly Hills, CA: Sage, 1973.

Chaffee, S. H. The diffusion of political information. In S. H. Chaffee (Ed.), *Political communication.* Beverly Hills, CA: Sage, 1975.

Chaffee, S. H. Presidential debates—Are they helpful to voters? *Communication Monographs,* 1978, *49,* 330-346.

Chaffee, S. H., and Dennis, J. Presidential debates: An empirical assessment. In A. Ranney (Ed.), *The past and future of presidential debates.* Washington, DC: American Enterprise Institute, 1979.

Chaffee, S. H., Jackson-Beeck, M., Durall, J., and Wilson, D. Mass communication and political socialization. In S. Renshon (Ed.), *Handbook of political socialization.* New York: Free Press, 1977.

Chaffee, S. H., and McLeod, J. M. Individual vs. social predictors of information-seeking. *Journalism Quarterly,* 1973, *50,* 237-245.

Chaffee, S. H., and Petrick, M. J. *Using the mass media: Communication problems in American society.* New York: McGraw-Hill, 1975.

Chaffee, S. H., Stamm, K. R., Guerrero, J. L., and Tipton, L. P. Experiments on cognitive discrepancies and communication. *Journalism Monogographs, 1969, 14.*

Chaffee, S. H., and Tims, A. R. News media use in adolescence: Implications for political cognitions. In M. Burgoon (Ed.), *Communication Yearbook 6.* Beverly Hills CA: Sage, forthcoming.

Clarke, P., and Kline, F. G. Media effects reconsidered: Some new strategies for communication research. *Communication Research,* 1974, *1,* 224-240.

Cohen, C. E. Goals and schemata in person perception: making sense from the stream of behavior. In N. Cantor and J. F. Kihlstrom (Eds.), *Personality, cognition, and social interaction.* Hillsdale, NJ: Erlbaum, 1981.

Cohen, C. E., and Ebbesen, E. B. Observational goals and schema activation: a theoretical framework for behavior perception. *Journal of Experimental Social Psychology,* 1979, *15,* 305-329.

Collins, A. Children's comprehension of television programs. In E. Wartella (Ed.), *Children communicating: Media and development of thought, speech, understanding.* Beverly Hills, CA: Sage, 1979.

Collins, A. Recent advances in research on cognitive processing television viewing. *Journal of Broadcasting,* 1981, *25,* 327-334.

Collins, A. Cognitive processing in television viewing. In D. Pearl (Ed.), *Television and behavior: Ten years of scientific progress and implications for the 80's.* Washington, DC: National Institute of Mental Health, forthcoming.

Collins, A., Wellman, H., Keniston, A., and Westby, S. Age-related aspects of comprehension and inferences from a televised dramatic narrative. *Child Development,* 1978, *44,* 154-161.

Converse, P. E. Public opinion and voting behavior. In F. I. Greenstein and N. W. Polsby (Eds.), *Handbook of political science* (Vol. 4). Reading. MA: Addison-Wesley, 1975.

Crowder, R. G. *Principles of learning and memory.* Hillsdale, NJ: Erlbaum, 1976.

DeFleur, M. L., and Ball-Rokeach, S. *Theories of mass communication.* New York: David McKay, 1975.

Donohew, L, and Tipton, L. P. A conceptual model of information seeking, avoiding, and processing. In P. Clarke (Ed.), *New models for mass communication research.* Beverly Hills, CA: Sage, 1973.

Douglas, D. F., Westley, B. H., and Chaffee, S. H. An information campaign that changed community attitudes. *Journalism Quarterly,* 1970, *47,* 479-481.

Ebbesen, E. B. Cognitive processes in understanding ongoing behavior. In R. Hastie, T. M. Ostrom, E. B. Ebbesen, R. S. Wyer, D. L. Hamilton, and D. E. Carlston (Eds.), *Person memory: The cognitive basis of social perception.* Hillsdale, NJ: Erlbaum, 1980.

Edelstein, A., and Tefft, D. Media credibility and respondent credibility with respect to Watergate. *Communication Research,* 1974, *1,* 426-439.

Fiske, S., and Kinder, D. R. Involvement, expertise, and schema use: Evidence from political cognition. In N. Cantor and J. F. Kihlstrom (Eds.), *Personality, cognition, and social integration.* Hillsdale: Erlbaum, 1981.

Gantz, W. *Uses and gratifications and the recall of television news.* Presented to the Association for Education in Journalism, 1976.

Gerbner, C., Gross, L., Morgan, M., and Signorielli, N. The "mainstreaming" of America: Violence profile no. 11. *Journal of Communication,* 1980, *30,* 10-29.

Glucksberg, S. General discussion of issues: Relationships between cognitive psychology and the psychology of personality. In N. Cantor and J. F. Kihlstrom (Eds.), *Personality, cognition and social interaction.* Hillsdale, NJ: Erlbaum, 1981.

Greenberg, B. S. Gratifications of television viewing and their correlates for British children. In J. G. Blumler and E. Katz (Eds.), *The uses of mass communications: Current perspectives on gratifications research.* Beverly Hills, CA: Sage, 1974.

Greenberg, S. R. Conversations as units of analysis in the study of personal infuence. *Journalism Quarterly,* 1975, *52,* 128-131.

Grunig, J. E., and Stamm, K. R. Cognitive strategies and the resolution of environmental issues: A second study. *Journalism Quarterly,* 1979, *56,* 715-726.

Hartman, F. R. Single and multiple channel communication: A review of research and a proposed model. *Audiovisual Communication Review,* 1961, *6,* 235-262.

Hastie, R., and Carlston, D. Theoretical issues in person memory. In R. Hastie et al. (Eds.), *Person memory: The cognitive basis of social perception.* Hillsdale, NJ: Erlbaum, 1980.

Hawkins, R. P., and Pingree, S. Uniform messages and habitual viewing: Unnecessary assumptions in social reality effects. *Human Communication Research,* 1981, *7,* 291-301.

Hawkins, R. P., and Pingree, S. Television influence on constructions of social reality. In D. Pearl (Ed.), *Television and behavior: Ten years of scientific progress and implications for the 80's.* Washington, DC: National Institute of Mental Health, forthcoming.

Heffner, M. B. *Inoculation and stopping behavior.* Presented to the Association for Education in Journalism, 1972.

Hewes, D. E., and Haight, L. The cross-situational consistency of communicative behaviors. *Communication Research,* 1979, *6,* 243-270.

Hirsch, P. M. Occupational, organizational, and institutional models in mass media research: toward an integrated framework. In P. M. Hirsch, P. V. Miller, and F. G. Kline (Eds.), *Strategies for Communication Research.* Beverly Hills, CA: Sage, 1977.

Hoving, K. L., Spencer, T., Robb, K. Y., and Schulte, D. Developmental changes in visual information processing. In P. A. Ornstein (Ed.), *Memory development in children.* Hillsdale, NJ: Erlbaum, 1978.

Hovland, C. I., Mandell, W., Campbell, E. H., Brock, T., Luchins, A. S., Cohen, A. R., McGuire, W. J., Janis, I. L., Feierabend, R. L., and Anderson, N. H. *The order of presentation in persuasion.* New Haven, CT: Yale University Press. 1957.

Hyman, H. H., and Sheatsley, P. B. Some reasons why information campaigns fail. *Public Opinion Quarterly,* 1947, *11,* 412-423.

Katz, E., Blumler, J. G., and Gurevitch, M. Uses and gratifications research. *Public Opinion Quarterly,* 1973/1974, *37,* 509-523.

Kline, F. G., Miller, P. V., and Morrison, A. J. Adolescents and family planning information: An exploration of audience needs and media effects. In J. G. Blumler and E. Katz (Eds.), *The uses of mass communications: Current perspectives on gratifications research.* Beverly Hills, CA: Sage, 1974.

Kosslyn, S. M. The representational-development hypothesis. In P. A. Ornstein (Ed.), *Memory development in children.* Hillsdale, NJ: Erlbaum, 1978.

Kosslyn, S. M., and Pomerantz, J. R. Imagery, propositions, and the form of internal representations. *Cognitive Psychology,* 1977, *9,* 52-76.

Kraus, S., and Davis, S. *The effects of mass communication on political behavior.* University Park: Pennsylvania State University Press, 1976.

Krull, R., Husson, W. G., and Paulson, A. S. Cycles in children's attention to the television screen. In B. D. Ruben (Ed.), *Communication Yearbook 2.* New Brunswick: Transaction, 1978.

Kuiper, N. A., and Derry, P. A. The self as a cognitive prototype: An application to person perception and depression. In N. Cantor and J. F. Hihlstrom (Eds.), *Personality, cognition and social interaction.* Hillsdale, NJ: Erlbaum, 1981.

Lachman, R., Lachman, J., and Butterfield, E. *Cognitive psychology and information processing.* Hillsdale, NJ: Erlbaum, 179.

Lasswell, H. D. The structure and function of communication in society. In L. Bryson (Ed.), *The communication of ideas.* New York: Harper & Bros., 1948.

Lazarsfeld, P. F., and Merton, R. K. Mass communication, popular taste, and organized social action. In L. Bryson (Ed.), *The communication of ideas.* New York: Harper & Bros., 1948.

Lerner, D. *The passing of traditional society: Modernizing the Middle East.* New York: Free Press, 1958.

Lippmann W. (1922) *Public opinion.* New York: Harcourt, Brace, 1922.

Lometti, G., Reeves, B., and Bybee, C. R. Investigating the assumptions of uses and gratifications research. *Communication Research,* 1977, *4,* 321-338.

Massad, C. M., Hubbard, M., and Newtson, P. Perceptual selectivity: Contributing process and possible cure for impression perseverance. *Journal of Experimental Social Psychology,* 1979, *15,* 513-532.

McCain, T. A., and Ross, M. G. Cognitive switching: A behavioral trace of human information processing for television newscasts. *Human Communication Research,* 1979, *5,* 121-129.

McCombs, M. E., and Shaw, D. L. The agenda-setting function of mass media. *Public Opinion Quarterly,* 1972, *36,* 176-187.

McLeod, J. M., and Becker, L. B. Testing the validity of gratification measures through political effects analysis. In J. G. Blumler and E. Katz (Eds.), *The uses of mass communications: Current perspectives on gratifications research.* Beverly Hills, CA: Sage, 1974.

McLeod, J., and Becker, L. The uses and gratifications approach to political communication research. In D. Nimmo and K. Sanders (Eds.), *Handbook of political communication.* Beverly Hills, CA: Sage, 1981.

McLeod, J. M., Becker, L. B., and Byrnes, J. E. Another look at the agenda setting function of the press. *Communication Research,* 1974, *1,* 131-166.

McLeod, J. M., and Chaffee, S. H. Interpersonal approaches to communication research. *American Behavioral Scientist,* 1973, *16,* 469-500.

McLeod, J., and Reeves, B. The nature of mass media effects. In S. B. Withey and R. P. Abeles (Eds.), *Television and social behavior: Beyond violence and children.* Hillsdale, NJ: Erlbaum, 1980.

Meadow, R. G. *Politics as communication.* Norwood, NJ: Ablex, 1980.

Mulholland, T. A program for the EEG study of attention in visual communication. In B. S. Randhawa and W. E. Coffman (Eds.), *Visual learning, thinking, and communication.* New York: Academic Press, 1978.

Newell, A., and Simon, H. A. *Human problem solving.* Englewood Cliffs, NJ: Prentice-Hall, 1972.

Newtson, D. A. Attribution and the unit of perception of ongoing behavior. *Journal of Personality and Social Psychology,* 1973, *28,* 28-38.

Newtson, D. A., and Engquist, G. The perceptual organization of ongoing behavior. *Journal of Experimental Social Psychology,* 1976, *12,* 436-450.

Newtson, D., Engquist, G., and Bois, J. The objective basis of behavior units. *Journal of Experimental Social Psychology,* 1977, *12,* 436-450.

Nie, N. H., Verba, S., and Petrocik, J. R. *The changing American voter.* Cambridge, MA: Harvard University Press, 1979.

Nisbett, R., and Ross, L. *Human inference: Strategies and shortcomings of socia judgment.* Englewood Cliffs, NJ: Prentice-Hall, 1980.

Ornstein, P. A., and Naus, M. J. Rehearsal processes in children's memory. In P. A. Ornstein (Ed.), *Memory development in children.* Hillsdale, NJ: Erlbaum, 1978.

Osgood, C. E., Suci, G. J., and Tannenbaum, P. H. *The measurement of meaning.* Urbana: University of Illinois Press, 1957.

Osgood, C. E., and Tannenbaum, P. H. The principle of congruity in the prediction of attitude change. *Psychological Review,* 1955, *62,* 42-55.

Paisley, W. *Communication research as a behavioral discipline.* Stanford, CA: Institute for Communication Research, 1972.

Patterson, T. E., and McClure, R. D. *The unseeing eye: The myth of television power in national elections.* New York: Putnam's, 1976.

Pearce, W. B., and Stamm, K. R. Coorientational states and interpersonal communication. In P. Clarke (Ed.), *New models for mass communication research.* Beverly Hills, CA: Sage, 1973.

Pylyshyn, Z. W. What the mind's eye tells the mind's brain: A critique of mental imagery. *Psychological Bulletin*, 1973, *80*, 1-24.

Reeves, B. Children's understanding of television people. In E. Wartella (Ed.), *Children communicating:* Media and development of thought, speech, understanding. Beverly Hills, CA: Sage, 1979.

Reeves, B., and Garramone, G. *The influence of television portrayals on children's encoding of information about new people.* Unpublished manuscript, Mass Communication Research Center, University of Wisconsin—Madison, 1980.

Reeves, B., Garramone, G., and Meadowcroft, J. *The effects of processing goals on the perceptual unitization of audio-visual information.* Unpublished manuscript, University of Wisconsin—Madison, forthcoming.

Reeves, B., and Greenberg, B. Children's perceptions of television characters. *Human Communication Research*, 1977, *3*, 113-127.

Reeves, B., and Lometti, G. The dimensional structure of children's identification with television characters: A replication. Human Communication Review, 1979, *5*, 247-256.

Rice, R. E., and Paisley, W. J. *Public communication campaigns.* Beverly Hills, CA: Sage, 1981.

Roberts, D. F., and Bachen, C. Mass communication effects. *Annual Review of Psychology*, 1981, *32*, 307-346.

Roberts, D. F., and Maccoby, N. Information processing and persuasion: Counterarguing behavior. In P. Clarke (Ed.), *New models for communication research.* Beverly Hills, CA: Sage, 1973.

Rogers, E. M. *Diffusion of innovations.* New York: Free Press, 1962.

Rogers, E. M. Communication and development: The passing of the dominant paradigm. *Communication Research*, 1976, *3*, 213-240.

Roling, N. G., Ascroft, J., and Wachege, F. The diffusion of innovations and the issue of equity in rural development. *Communication Research*, 1976, *3*, 155-170.

Roloff, M. Interpersonal and mass communication scripts: An interdisciplinary link. In G. C. Wilhoit and H. de Bock (Eds.), *Mass Communication Review Yearbook 2.* Beverly Hills, CA: Sage, 1981.

Rosch, E. Principles of categorization. In E. Rosch and B. B. Lloyd (Eds.), *Cognition and categorization.* Hillsdale, NJ: Erlbaum, 1978.

Rosenberg, M. J., Hovland, C. I., McGuire, W. J., Abelson, R. P., and Brehm, J. W. *Attitude organization and change: An analysis of consistency among attitude components.* New Haven, CT: Yale University Press, 1960.

Rosenberg, S., and Sedlak, S. Structural representations of implicit personality theory. In L. Berkowitz (Ed.), *Advances in experimental social psychology* (Vol. 6). New York: Academic Press, 1972.

Rosenberg, S., and Simon, H. Modeling semantic memory: Effects of presenting semantic information in different modalities. *Cognitive Psychology*, 1977, *9*, 293-295.

Rosenthal, T. L., and Zimmerman, B. J. *Social learning and cognition.* New York: Academic Press, 1978.

Salomon, G. *Interaction of media, cognition, and learning.* San Francisco: Jossey-Bass, 1979.

Schafer, E. Brain responses while viewing television reflect program interest. *International Journal of Neuroscience*, 1978, *8*, 71-77.

Schank, R., and Abelson, R. *Scripts, plans, goals and understanding: An inquiry into human knowledge structures.* Hillsdale, NJ: Erlbaum, 1977.

Schramm, W. How communication works. Pp. 3-26 in W. Schramm (Ed.), *The process and effects of mass communication.* Urbana: University of Illinois Press, 1954.

Schramm, W. *Men, messages, and media.* New York: Harper & Row, 1973.

Seamon, J. G. Coding and retrieval processes and the hemispheres of the brain. In S. J. Dimond and J. G. Beaumont (Eds.), *Hemispheric function in the human brain.* New York: John Wiley, 1974.

Sears, D. O., and Chaffee, S. H. Uses and effects of the 1976 debates: An overview of empirical studies. In S. Kraus (Ed.), *The great debates, 1976: Ford vs. Carter.* Bloomington: Indiana University Press, 1979.

Shiffrin, R. M., and Atkinson, R. C. Storage and retrieval processes in long-term memory. *Psychological Review, 1969, 76,* 179-193.

Singer, J. The power and limitations of television: A cognitive-affective analysis. In P. Tannenbaum (Ed.), *Entertainment functions of television.* New York: Erlbaum, 1980.

Szczepkowski, K. *Cognitive representation and visual media comprehension.* Presented to the International Communication Association, Minneapolis, 1981.

Taylor, S. E., Crocker, J., and D'Agostino, J. Schematic bases of social problem solving. *Personality and Social Psychology Bulletin, 1978, 4,* 447-451.

Tversky, A. Features of similarity. *Psychological Review,* 1977, *84,* 327-352.

Tversky, A., and Kahneman, D. Availability: A heuristic for judging frequency and probability. *Cognitive Psychology,* 1973, *5,* 207-232.

Wackman, D. B., and Wartella, E. A review of cognitive development theory and research and the implications for research on children's responses to television. *Communication Research,* 1977, *4,* 203-224.

Wade, S., and Schramm, W. The mass media as sources of public affairs, science and health knowledge. *Public Opinion Quarterly,* 1969, *33,* 197-209.

Ward, S., Wackman, D. B., and Wartella, E. *How children learn to buy: The development of consumer information processing skills.* Beverly Hills, CA: Sage, 1977.

Wartella, E. The developmental perspective. In E. Wartella (Ed.), *Children communicating: Media and development of thought, speech, understanding.* Beverly Hills, CA: Sage, 1979.

Watkins, B., Cojuc, J., Mills, S., Kwiatek, K. K., and Tan, C. Z. *Children write about TV real life: The relationship of prime-time televiewing to children's schematic representations.* Presented to the International Communication Association, 1982.

Weaver, D. H., Graber, D. A., McCombs, M. E., and Eyal, C. H. *Media agenda-setting in a presidential election: Issues, images, and interest.* New York: Praeger, 1981.

Weinstein, S., Appel, V., and Weinstein, C. Brain activity responses to magazine and television advertising. *Journal of Advertising Research,* 1980, *2,* 57-63.

Weiss, W. Effects of the mass media of communication. In G. Lindzey and E. Aronson (Eds.), *The handbook of social psychology* (Vol. 5). Reading, MA: Addison-Wesley, 1969.

Welch, A. J., and Watt, J. H. Visual complexity and young children's learning from television. *Human Communication Research,* 1982, *8,* 133-145.

Wright, J. C., Watkins, B. A., and Huston-Stein, A. *Active versus passive television viewing: A model of the development of television information processing by children.* Unpublished manuscript, University of Kansas, 1979.

Wyer, R. S., and Carlston, D. E. *Social cognition, inference and attribution.* Hillsdale, NJ: Erlbaum, 1979.

Wyer, R. S., and Srull, T. K. The processing of social stimulus information: A conceptual integration. In R. Hastie et al. (Eds.), *Person memory: The cognitive basis of social perception.* Hillsdale, NJ: Erlbaum, 1980.

Zajonc, R. The process of cognitive tuning in communication. *Journal of Abnormal and Social Psychology,* 1960, *61,* 159-167.

Zimmerman, C., and Bauer, R. A. The effect of an audience upon what is remembered. *Public Opinion Quarterly,* 1956, *20,* 238-248.

The Authors

CHARLES R. BERGER is Professor of Communication Studies and Director of the Communication Research Center at Northwestern University. He received his Ph.D. in communication from Michigan State University. His areas of interest are in the development and disintegration of interpersonal relationships, attribution processes in interpersonal relationships, and social knowledge structures. He has recently co-authored (with James Bradac) *Language and Social Knowledge*.

STEVEN H. CHAFFEE is Director of Communication in the Institute for Communication Research at Stanford University. A Stanford University Ph.D. in communication, he has published research on such diverse topics as interpersonal co-orientation, the role of television in child development, and cognitive models of information processing. He is co-author (with Michael Petrick) of *Using the Mass Media: Communication Problems in American Society* and co-author (with George Comstock and others) of *Television and Human Behavior*. He is a past president of the International Communication Association.

JESSE G. DELIA is Professor and Head of the Department of Speech Communication and a Research Professor in the Institute of Communication Research at the University of Illinois at Urbana-Champaign. He has contributed to the development of the constructivist approach to communication and to its applications to problems in social cognition, communication development, and interaction processes.

HOWARD GILES is a Professor of Psychology at the University of Bristol in Bristol, England. His research interests include motivational, attributional, and situational factors affecting speech and language production in interpersonal and intercultural contexts. He co-authored (with Peter Powesland) *Speech Style and Social Evaluation*.

DEAN E. HEWES received his Ph.D. from Florida State University. He is currently Associate Professor of Speech Communication at the University of Illinois, Urbana-Champaign, while actively pursuing postgraduate work in social cognition at the University of Montana at Billings. His research interests include interrelationships of communicative and cognitive processes, formal models of the impact of message campaigns on behavior, and the analysis of social interaction.

FREDRIC M. JABLIN is Assistant Professor of Speech Communication at the University of Texas, Austin. He received his Ph.D. from Purdue University. His research has been published in communication, psychology, and management journals, and he has served as a consultant/researcher to a number of organizations. His current research interests include communication and organizational assimilation, influence processes in superior-subordinate interaction, and communication correlates of the selection interview.

GERALD R. MILLER, who received his Ph.D. from the University of Iowa, is Professor of Communication at Michigan State University. His major research interests are in the areas of interpersonal communication, persuasion, and communication in legal settings. The author of numerous books and journal articles, he has previously edited two Sage Annual Reviews of Communication Research, *Explorations in Interpersonal Communication*, and (with Michael Roloff) *Persuasion: New Directions in Theory and Research*. He recently co-authored (with Norm Fontes) *Videotape on Trial: A View from the Jury Box*. He is past editor of the journal *Human Communication Research* and is past president of the International Communication Association.

BARBARA J. O'KEEFE is Assistant Professor of Speech Communication at the University of Illinois—Urbana, where she received her Ph.D. in communication. Her research interests are in social cognition and communication and processes of social interaction, and she has contributed to the development of a general constructivist approach to communication.

SALLY PLANALP is Lecturer of Speech Communication at the University of Illinois—Urbana, and is finishing her Ph.D. at the University of Wisconsin—Madison. Her primary research interests include interpretive processes in relational communication, discourse processing, and theoretical issues in social cognition.

BYRON REEVES is Associate Professor of Journalism and Mass Communication and Associate Chairperson of Mass Communication Research at the University of Wisconsin—Madison. He received his Ph.D. in communication from Michigan State University. His research interests are concentrated in the general area of media and children, specifically in children's perceived reality of television, children's perceptions of television characters, children and television news, and television and sex-role development.

MICHAEL E. ROLOFF is Associate Professor of Communication Studies at Northwestern University. He received his Ph.D. in communication from Michigan State University and was Assistant Professor of Human Communication at the University of Kentucky prior to moving to Northwestern. His interests include persuasion, bargaining and negotiation, interpersonal conflict resolution, and the formation of cognitive scripts. He recently co-edited (with Gerald R. Miller) *Persuasion: New Directions in Theory and Research* and authored *Interpersonal Communication: The Social Exchange Approach*.

ALAN L. SILLARS is Assistant Professor of Communication at Ohio State University. He received his B.A. from Humboldt State University and his M.A. and Ph.D. from the University of Wisconsin—Madison. His chief interest is in communication and conflict in close relationships, particularly with respect to the role of social cognitive factors. His general interests are in interpersonal communication.

RICHARD L. STREET, Jr., is Assistant Professor in the Department of Speech Communication at Texas Tech University. His research interests are focused on the factors affecting the production and evaluation of speech style features during social interaction.

ALBERT TIMS is Assistant Professor of Communication at Purdue University. He is working on his Ph.D. at the School of Journalism and Mass Communication at the University of Wisconsin—Madison.